THE WINTER KING

For Stephen and Sandra Pursell, whom I cannot thank enough.

The Winter King

Frederick V of the Palatinate and the Coming of the
Thirty Years' War

BRENNAN C. PURSELL

ASHGATE

© Brennan C. Pursell, 2003

Published by
Ashgate Publishing Limited
Gower House
Croft Road
Aldershot
Hants GU11 3HR
England

Ashgate Publishing Company
Suite 420
101 Cherry Street
Burlington
VT 05401-4405
USA

Ashgate website: http://www.ashgate.com

British Library Cataloguing in Publication Data
Pursell, Brennan C.
  The Winter King : Frederick V of the Palatinate and the coming of the Thirty Years' War
  1. Frederick, V, Elector Palatine 2. Heads of state – Germany – Palatinate – Biography
  3. Thirty Years' War, 1618–1648 4. Palatinate (Germany) – History – Frederick V, 1610–1623
  I. Title
  943.4'35'041'092

Library of Congress Cataloging-in-Publication Data
Pursell, Brennan C., 1967–
  The winter king : Frederick V of the Palatinate and the coming of the Thirty Years' War /Brennan C. Pursell
    p. cm.
  Includes bibliographical references.
  ISBN 0-7546-3401-9 (alk. paper)
    1. Frederick I, King of Bohemia, 1596–1632. 2. Palatinate (Germany)–History. 3. Bohemia (Czech Republic)–Kings and rulers–Biography. 4. Thirty Years' War, 1618–1648–Causes. 5. Thirty Years' War, 1618–1648–Historiography. 6. Europe–History–17th century. 7. Holy Roman Empire–Politics and government. I. Title.

DB2161.F74 P87 2002
943'.435041'092–dc21
[B]
                                                                    2002032986
ISBN 0 7546 3401 9

Typeset by MHL Production Services Ltd, Coventry.
Printed in Great Britain by MPG Books Ltd, Bodmin, Cornwall.

Contents

List of Illustrations

Preface

This study is a contribution to the historiography of the Thirty Years' War, the worst military, economic, and demographic disaster to befall Europe during the early modern period. The basic subject is the nature of the war in its crucial, developmental stages. The work questions whether it is entirely correct to classify this immensely complicated conflict as a 'war of religion'. The ostensible subject of the book, the means to approach the problem of classification, is the life and career of Elector Palatine Frederick V, a prince much neglected by professional historians but nonetheless a figure of central importance during the war's inception, intensification, and internationalization. The twentieth century has seen the publication of a handful of articles about Frederick V, but because his role has been misunderstood, we do not have a monograph of this ruler whose aims and actions were very different from what has been assumed, and very important as well.

The subject matter demands that the work combine the elements of biography and political analysis. In historiography, the greatest significance of Frederick V was his role in the development of the Thirty Years' War, and any satisfactory understanding of the international political crisis that he helped to induce must take his personality into account. His character, values, and beliefs contributed much to the formation of his political policy. Frederick was only known as 'the Winter King' during the latter portion of his short, troubled life. He never considered himself deserving of this derogatory title, but the course of events and his contribution to them determined that his reign as King of Bohemia would never see more than the passing of a single winter.

Focussing on Frederick V allows for a detailed analysis of the war's causes from the perspective of one of its main contributors. The central argument is that the driving force of the war in its early stages was a struggle between competing visions of the constitution of the Holy Roman Empire. Frederick's constitutionalism incorporated both political and religious interests. His political goal was to maintain German liberty in the face of a perceived move by his enemy, the Habsburg dynasty, to transform the Empire into an absolutist monarchy, and his religious interest was to protect the freedom of worship for Protestant princes and estates in the Empire. Frederick's faith and an obsessive concern for his honor cemented his constitutional convictions and guided his actions and decisions. For these same reasons he never relented, though he was soundly defeated at every turn. He resisted negotiations for peace and rejected all peace treaties. His decisions helped to internationalize the war, which began as a local, religious uprising in Bohemia. Frederick's subsequent expulsion from his lands, the deprivation of his titles, and his unrelenting obstructionism created 'the Palatine crisis', which broke the fragile peace between the great powers of Europe and provided foreign princes with a motivation, or an excuse, to invade the Empire. He sought for years to establish an international alliance of Protestant and Catholic powers to achieve his constitutional objectives by force, but these efforts ended in failure. The work ends with his death, though the causes for which he fought and suffered were not to be resolved until the war's conclusion in 1648.

This book could not have been completed with the help of many. The greatest thanks go to my supervisors, Mark Kishlansky and Steven Ozment, whose patient guidance over the years deserves more than commendation can confer. I would also like to thank Geoffrey Parker for his indispensable advice at numerous junctures. My gratitude to Dieter Albrecht for his assistance in this project must unfortunately be paid posthumously. His work on this period of history has been an inspiration for my own. I am grateful for advice and support from Paul Seaver, Patrice Higonnet, Heinz Duchhardt, Walter Ziegler, J.H. Elliott, I.A.A. Thompson, Diego Hidalgo, Michael McClean, Peter Haarpaintner, Abt Wolfgang Hagl, Pater Prior Adalbert Seipolt, and the Benedictine community at Metten. Without the generosity of the *Deutscher Akademischer Austauschdienst* and the *Real Colegio Complutense*, the research never could have been done. Further gratitude must be expressed to the staff members at the archives and libraries where I worked, especially to those at the *Bayerisches Hauptstaatsarchiv* in Munich and the *Archivo General de Simancas*. Sandra Pursell's assistance made research in Spain much more efficient than it otherwise might have been, and Irmgard Pursell receives exceptional thanks for her loving support during the hours of need.

A word about conventions: all proper names in the text have been left in their native language, with the exception of kings, popes, and notable princes such as Frederick V. All titles have been translated into English. For example, instead of *Herzog*, I have used 'Duke'. Where English place names for continental locations are available, I have used them. München is called Munich, and Köln Cologne. In all transcriptions from sources in English, French, German, Spanish, Italian, and Latin there has been no attempt to modernize spelling, punctuation, or diacritics. Abbreviations have been written out where necessary. In quotations from German manuscripts, the flourishes for accusative and dative noun endings have been transcribed according to the given word's modern usage. The obsolete 'e' ending for dative singular nouns has been irregularly observed. For all dates, the year begins on the first of January, and for the numbering of the days I have preferred the Gregorian calendar (New Style) to the Julian (Old Style). In the endnotes, the archival documents that bear an Old Style date will be marked accordingly or will show both the Old and the New day and month.

List of Abbreviations

ADB	*Allgemeine Deutsche Biographie*
AGS	Archivo General de Simancas EI–Estado Inglaterra EA–Estado Alemania
AP	Michael Caspar Londorp, *Acta Publica*
AR	Algemeen Rijksarchief, The Hague
BHStA	Bayerisches Hauptstaatsarchiv, Munich KB–Kasten Blau KS–Kasten Schwarz
BL	British Library, London HMSS–Harleian Manuscripts
BN	Biblioteca Nacional, Madrid MSS–Manuscripts
BR	Biblioteca Real, Madrid MSS–Manuscripts
CSPV	*Calendar of State Papers, Venetian*
fl.	Gulden
HHStA	Haus-, Hof-, Staatsarchiv, Vienna
NF	Neue Folge
PRO	Public Record Office, London SP–State Papers
RT	Reichsthalers
StACK	Statni Oblastni Archiv, or Statni Archiv Trebon (Český Krumlov)
StUAP	Státní Ustrední Archiv u Praze, Prague
SV	*stilo vetero*, Old Style

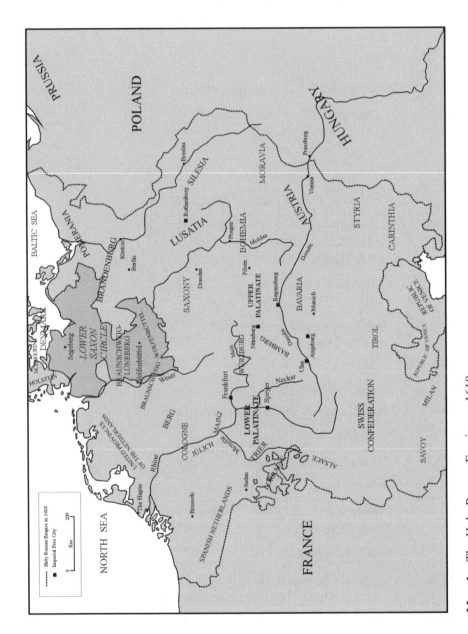

Map 1 The Holy Roman Empire, *c.* 1618

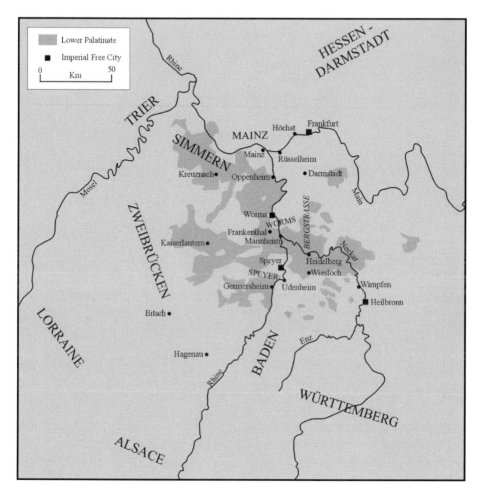

Map 2 The Lower Palatinate and its environs

Introduction:
Frederick V and the Thirty Years' War

Elector Palatine Frederick V would be an insignificant figure in the history of Europe were it not for the tremendous conflagration that he helped to ignite. This was the prince whose conflict with Holy Roman Emperor Ferdinand II over the throne of Bohemia plunged Europe into thirty years of savage violence, fiery devastation, and ruinous deprivation during the first half of the seventeenth century.[1] Frederick's defeat on the battlefield earned him the contemptuous sobriquet, 'the Winter King', because his reign over Bohemia did not withstand more than a single winter. This notable failure, however, was not a sign of powerlessness; even without a kingdom, Frederick could be a potent foe. His persistent refusal to come to terms foiled almost every ensuing attempt to stop the march of death in its tracks. This prince should be recognized as one of the authors of the Thirty Years' War.[2]

The present study is not just a detailed biographical account, but a contribution to the historiography of the war itself. The basic argument is not about the Winter King, but about placing constitutionalism instead of religion at the center of our understanding of the Thirty Years' War, a momentous event in Western history that altered the constitution of the Empire, the nature of religious politics, and the balance of power in Europe for the rest of the early modern era. This is in no way an attempt to take religion out of the Thirty Years' War, as it were, but to put it in its proper place.

For centuries historians have portrayed intra-confessional rivalry as the primary, sufficient cause of the crisis. Magisterial works by Frederick Schiller, Anton Gindely, and Moriz Ritter convey this argument, and current historians still second it.[3] Scholarly opinion in the twentieth century, however, has not been unanimously in favor of depicting the war as a conflict with predominantly religious causes. Some have preferred to explain it as merely an episode in the extended struggle between rival dynasties for hegemony in Europe. The same have also questioned the accuracy of the war's nomenclature and periodization, but these views have been discredited.[4] H.G. Koenigsberger recast the conflict as 'the

European Civil War', and Gunter Barudio has called the war a '*Bürgerkrieg*'.[5] In a more recent work, Johannes Burkhardt argued that the Thirty Years' War was an accumulation of lesser wars conducted by sovereign states and the princes and estates of the Empire that were in the process of establishing their own sovereignty. This model makes the Thirty Years' War primarily a constitutional struggle among emerging modern states.[6] In one of the latest treatises on the war as a whole, Ronald G. Asch identifies the Imperial constitution as the 'one central issue' that gives coherence to the Thirty Years' War.[7]

The Winter King is a further exploration of the war's constitutional causes. This study examines the early stages of the Thirty Years' War from the standpoint of one of its most prominent protagonists, Frederick V, the Elector Palatine. The goal is to reconcile the forces of confession, conscience, and constitutionalism affecting his decision-making at various junctures throughout the crisis. Relying heavily on Frederick's political and personal correspondence, the work presents his choices and alternatives and interprets his words and actions in response to them. Considering the war from Frederick's perspective and experience, I argue that it is best to understand it as an extended constitutional conflict, entailing religious and political factors together, fought within the Holy Roman Empire.

Most historians agree that religion and politics were inextricably linked in late sixteenth- and early seventeenth-century Europe. Matters of the church were almost always of concern to the members of the state, and vice versa. In many territories, churchmen held major political offices, and princes were invested with religious titles and prerogatives. The primary cause of events on earth was normally attributed to God, though people readily acknowledged the influence of numerous secular, secondary causes. Philosophies and belief systems such as empiricism, skepticism, materialism, positivism, and atheism were as yet undeveloped or, at least, still rather unsophisticated. It has even been argued that it was impossible for people not to have believed in the Christian religion to some degree.[8]

Nonetheless, it must be said that affairs of church and state, though inseparable in importance, were certainly not indistinguishable. To insist on any absolute division of the two is of course anachronistic, but historians might still venture to explain the dynamic of their influence on the leaders of early modern Europe during the Thirty Years' War. Naturally such a project has a greater likelihood of success when applied to a specific individual, and Frederick V provides a splendid figure for a case-study, because of both the prominence of his role in the early stages of the war and the wealth of sources relevant to his life and career.

It will be argued here that Frederick V engaged in a battle to protect the Imperial constitution: its electoral character, its guarantees for Protestant worship, and, above all, his own status within it as a prince of the Empire. His papers are suffused with the conviction that the Empire's constitution was in grave danger. In his view the Austrian and Spanish branches of the Habsburg dynasty were conspiring to transform the Kingdom of Bohemia and the Holy Roman Empire from free, elective monarchies into heritable possessions of their dynasty. They were also determined, he believed, to extirpate Protestantism. They had begun the process in their own lands and seemed to be willing to do the same in others, whether they were heritable possessions or not. When Frederick moved to obstruct these designs, the Austrian and Spanish Habsburgs attacked him with all their might. From 1620 till his death in 1632, Frederick was convinced that the Habsburgs sought his total destruction. More often than not he formulated his policy in accordance with his understanding of the dictates of Imperial constitutional law. His vision of the Imperial constitution derived in part from his exalted view of the electoral dignity that belonged to him by right of birth and which, he adamantly believed, could not be removed except by the due process of Imperial law as he understood it.

His conscience supported and cemented his constitutionalism. Frederick's religious faith and his sense of personal honor seem to have made up the greater part of his conscience. Faith in God played a prominent role in Frederick's life, above all on the personal level. It was unshakable, and it enabled him to withstand the trials and tribulations of a disastrous political career. His faith assured him that God was on his side in the war, despite the relentless march of failure. For Frederick, as for many other princes throughout history, God was the God of battles, showing His favor on the field, but He was not necessarily the author of a prince's policy. Sometimes Frederick turned to prayer to make political decisions, and a desire to please God often guided his actions. That his faith worked in tandem with his political convictions did not make him exceptional among his fellow princes, regardless of the Christian confession they espoused. Historians working on Maximilian I, Duke of Bavaria, Emperor Ferdinand II, and Christian IV, King of Denmark have noted the same tendency.[9]

The other guide for Frederick's conscience was his sense of honor. In the early modern period, honor was a kind of measure of one's personal, social, and political worth, an individual's credit among his or her peers. A protective concern for honor suffused all ranks of society, and for a prince, his honor was a measure of his strength, bravery, dignity, nobility, and reliability. Honor enshrined assertive, competitive, and aggressive behavior among princes and justified violence in politics.[10] Abusive words or deeds from a social equal could damage a person's honor, and violence was the normal means to redress such an injury; this applied to

peasants and princes alike.[11] In early modern Europe, honor was a
legitimate cause of war, peace, and revolution.[12] A prince's war-like
nature was publicly glorified as chivalric heroism. In festival processions,
Frederick V appeared dressed as Jason the Argonaut, Scipio, the conqueror
of Carthage, and Arminius, the ancient German hero whose armies
annihilated three Roman legions in 9AD. Such public displays were a
common feature of court culture among German principalities during the
years preceding the Thirty Years' War.[13] During the war, while Frederick
lost all his lands and titles, and his reputation suffered severe degradations,
his concern for his honor rose to extreme heights. It was the last dignity
that he could truly call his own. To protect his princely, royal honor,
Frederick refused to back out of alliances, to break confidences, and to
renege on certain promises. Concern for his honor rendered him nearly
incapable of making peace on anyone's terms but his own. The
conjunction of Frederick's conscience and his constitutionalism helped
to condemn the Holy Roman Empire to thirty years of war.

What of confession? Frederick was the most powerful and prominent
Calvinist prince in the Empire, and from contemporary observers to
historians of the twentieth century, an apparent association between
Calvinism and rebellion has received a certain degree of note.[14] One of the
few studies in English on the Palatinate attributes, rather crudely, the
'aggressiveness' of its leaders in part to their 'Calvinist intolerance'.[15] It
will be argued here, however, that Frederick, in his own mind, considered
himself and his actions neither aggressive nor intolerant, but defensive and
actually in favor of tolerance.[16] Confessionalism, which may be defined as
an individual's strict adherence to the spiritual and secular interests of a
certain church or creed, undeniably played a role in determining
Frederick's personal attitudes about religion, but an exclusively Calvinist
confessionalism seems to have had at best a limited influence in making
his political decisions. Both his words and his actions prove this point. The
evidence strongly indicates that though he remained a devout Calvinist
throughout his entire life, his policy was guided by more than the interests
of his church alone. The confessionalism that informed his constitutionalism was not definitive or restrictive, but inclusive.

Frederick was no fanatic; his sympathies were actually ecumenical,
encompassing all forms of Protestantism. His own court was staffed by
Lutherans, Anglicans, and Philippists, as well as Calvinists. In Bohemia he
even visited a group of the universally vilified Anabaptists and purchased
examples of their handiwork as gifts for his wife. Outside of his own lands
in the Palatinate, he did not play the Calvinist missionary; in general he did
little to advance his confession at the expense of any other. The famous
instance of his reforming St. Vitus' cathedral at the castle Hradschin near

Prague was the exception rather than the rule. It was carried out because it was the royal church under his direct jurisdiction as King of Bohemia. In the other notable instance, when the people of Prague objected to the attempted removal of the statues of the Virgin Mary and St. John from the Charles bridge over the Moldau, Frederick called off the project immediately. He and the Bohemian Estates did order the expulsion of the Jesuits from Bohemia and the incorporated lands (Moravia, Silesia, and Lusatia), but members of that priestly order had been clearly identified as political operatives. Dispossessions of land were only carried out against Catholics if they refused to sign the oath of obedience to Frederick's new regime in Bohemia. He is known to have handed over just one Jesuit church in Brünn to the Calvinists of that town. When he officially condoned Calvinist worship in Breslau, he authorized services to be held in the royal castle. In multiple proclamations he insisted that he was a tolerant king at the head of a regime tolerant of all Christian confessions. His commitment to the Empire's Protestant churches was essentially defensive, and he often bemoaned the mutual mistrust among their members.

In Frederick's official correspondence, emphases on confessional considerations varied over time and according to the audience, as the situation demanded. His allies and sympathizers were a motley crew, including Calvinists, Lutherans, Catholics, and Muslims, and he tailored his message to fit their interests, in so far as it was possible. To the King of France and the Duke of Savoy he understandably did not have much to say about 'das evangelische Wesen' (the Protestant cause), by which he meant a general defense of Protestantism in the Empire. To these and to the Ottoman sultan he complained of the Habsburg oppression of the many princes and estates of the Empire. In letters to Protestant powers he usually added a call for solidarity between all Protestant confessions against the alleged Habsburg design to stamp out their religion. Such appeals varied depending on the political inclinations of the Protestant prince being addressed. King James I, for example, detested the suggestion that he partake in a 'war of religion', but his son and successor, Charles I, did not. Calvinist potentates received calls to save the 'orthodox' or the 'reformed' religion, but Lutherans usually received reminders that the fate of 'Protestantism' was at stake. Despite Frederick's sensitivity to confessional interests, few Calvinists and even fewer Lutherans paid much heed to his tocsins until the later 1620s, when the war came to their doorsteps. In general his diplomatic campaigns for Protestant unity in the face of Habsburg aggression in the Empire failed miserably, even when he was riding on the coat tails of the belligerent kingdoms of England and Denmark.

Constitutional arguments for intervention appear in his diplomatic correspondence with greater consistency. The claim to be fighting for the purity, integrity, and dignity of the Imperial constitution had universal application. Frederick's constitutionalism can lend some sense to what otherwise looks like years of relentless, reckless belligerence. In his own mind he was waging a battle over the fate of the Imperial constitution, and that contest involved both the electoral nature of the Imperial and Bohemian crowns and the status of Protestant confessions throughout the Empire. Frederick's conscience told him that God was on his side, and that his personal honor was invested in the matter. His absolute conviction of the justice of his cause and of the righteousness of his position helped the war to persist through the 1620s and beyond.

His constitutional struggle against Emperor Ferdinand II intensified and internationalized the Thirty Years' War in its early stages. It transformed an uprising in Bohemia into a civil war within the Holy Roman Empire that embroiled much of the rest of Europe. Frederick made every effort to bring foreign powers of various religious orientations into this conflict, and despite repeated failures and disastrous defeats, he refused to capitulate. His interventionist diplomacy, obstructive Imperial politics, and relentless militarism perpetuated and expanded the war despite international, multi-confessional efforts to re-establish the peace.

Finally, this book calls for a revision of the prevailing view of Frederick as an early modern prototype of princely incompetence. The traditional depiction of this prince as an insipid character totally lacking in abilities derives from unreliable but influential works of nineteenth-century scholarship. This is not to suggest that Frederick had no limitations, and let it be said that this book is in no way an attempt to make a hero out of this narrow-minded, obstinate man. But instead of attributing his disastrous career to the effects of personal weakness, I seek to explain the thought behind his fateful decisions and the apparent reasoning behind his perversity. If we are to understand the princely belligerents in the Thirty Years' War, we need to do justice to the method behind their seeming madness. For this end Frederick V certainly makes a worthy case-study.

The book has a narrative structure that conveys the arguments outlined above. The first chapter presents the Holy Roman Empire and its constitution, the Palatinate and its prince, Frederick V, and his neighbors, allies, and enemies. It will be suggested that the Empire was not on the verge of either collapse or catastrophe in 1618, though there were significant problems within that polity. The narrative begins with the outbreak of the Bohemian rebellion, which at first was a local quarrel over the constitutional religious rights of Protestants under the Habsburg Bohemian monarchy. Later, however, with Palatine involvement, the rebellion escalated despite resistance from several European courts. It developed into a crisis for the whole Empire in 1619 at the election of

Frederick V to the Bohemian throne and when the deposed King of Bohemia, Ferdinand of Styria, became Holy Roman Emperor.

An examination of Frederick's brief reign as King of Bohemia demonstrates that he did not act primarily out of interest for his own Calvinist confession, but for the defense of the constitutional rights and privileges for all Protestants in Bohemia. After his defeat and flight from his newly acquired kingdom, Frederick spent the next few years trying to enlist the support of other potentates for the defense of the Palatinate and for his restoration to the Bohemian throne. His promulgation of 'the Protestant cause', which called for a war of religion on behalf of Protestantism in the Empire, was a resounding failure. The princes of the Empire and other European leaders felt more reluctance than enthusiasm to partake in Frederick's wars. While he lost all his lands and was stripped of his princely dignities, his promulgation of 'the common cause', a war to procure his restitution, received more notice than 'the Protestant cause', but obtained few advantageous results. After Frederick personally took to the battlefield in 1622 and met with still more defeats, he consigned himself to a period of passive resistance and active obstruction of the international diplomatic efforts, led by pacific father-in-law, James I, King of Great Britain, to solve the conflict by means of a peaceful compromise.[17]

His personal faith and an obsessive protection of his honor enabled him to withstand the enormous pressure to capitulate, and so 'the Palatine crisis', the problem of what to do with the dispossessed, recalcitrant Elector Palatine and his devastated lands, remained unresolved. Frederick was completely convinced that his opponents were bound and determined to corrupt the Imperial constitution, to transform that polity into an hereditary, absolutist monarchy, and to remove the rights and privileges for Protestants from the fundamental law of the constitution. All his decisions, he believed, were made in the interest of protecting the Imperial constitution, maintaining its electoral structure and its guarantees of traditional freedoms for its members and for the Protestants especially, be they Lutherans or Calvinists.

Frederick's tactics reaped some reward when the Palatine crisis brought an end to the roughly twenty-year period of peace between England and Spain in 1624. Thereafter England led the charge for a return to arms on behalf of the 'common' and 'Protestant' causes, but the international alliance that formed on Frederick's behalf was sown with more seeds for dissolution than for success. While the Palatine crisis remained unresolved, the wars in the Empire left it behind with the passage of time. Frederick became more of a pawn than a player in the continuing struggle between belligerents in the Thirty Years' War. When at last the

King of Sweden invaded Germany and successfully rolled back the prior gains of the emperor's party, Frederick saw that his chance for restitution had come, but even then he refused to mollify his demands when they did not coincide with those of the Swedish conqueror. Frederick's life came to a sudden end just when it appeared that he could retake possession of part of his patrimony. The Palatine crisis did not find its final resolution until the war came to an end in 1648.

The story of Frederick V is, above all, one of bitter frustration, and there can be no doubt that he was to a great extent the author of his own misery. Without the necessary economic and military resources, this prince inserted himself between the great powers of Europe and tried to turn them against each other in order to further his political and religious agenda. Comprehending Frederick's behavior on its own terms will increase our understanding of the individual motives of the war's main combatants, and perhaps generate a small degree of sympathy for them as well, though they caused so much suffering for so very many.

Notes

1. The account of the war with the broadest range of international perspectives is Geoffrey Parker, ed., *The Thirty Years' War* (2nd edn, London, 1997).
2. Though the last two centuries have seen the production of thousands of treatises on the war, no monograph has made an intensive, critical examination of the Winter King's contribution to the war. For a very informative, reliable biography of Frederick V, see Peter Bilhöfer, 'Nicht gegen Ehre und Gewissen: Friedrich V., Kurfürst von der Pfalz – der "Winterkönig" von Böhmen (1596–1632)', Inauguraldissertation zur Erlangung des akademischen Grades eines Doktors der Philosophie der Universität Mannheim (2000). John Gustav Weiß's biography was never published – the typescript is in the *Generallandesarchiv* in Karlsruhe – and his published works, though valuable, are incomplete. See idem, 'Die Vorgeschichte des böhmischen Abenteuers Friedrichs V. von der Pfalz', *Zeitschrift für die Geschichte des Oberrheins*, 53, NF (1940), pp. 383–492; and 'Beiträge zur Beurteilung des Kurfürsten Friedrich V. von der Pfalz', *Zeitschrift für die Geschichte des Oberrheins*, 46, NF (1933), pp. 385–422. The nineteenth century's foremost historians of the Thirty Years' War had little to say about Frederick V beyond cursory observations. See Anton Gindely, *Friedrich V von der Pfalz, der ehemalige Winterkönig von Böhmen seit dem Regensburger Deputationstag vom Jahre 1622 bis zu seinem Tode* (Prague, 1885) and Moriz Ritter, 'Friedrich V., Kurfürst von der Pfalz', ADB, vii, pp. 621–7.
3. Friedrich Schiller, *Geschichte des dreißigjährigen Kriegs* (4 vols, Leipzig, 1802–9), also published as *Der Dreißigjährige Krieg* (München, 1975). Anton Gindely, *Geschichte des Dreißigjährigen Krieges* (3 vols, Prague, 1882). Moriz Ritter, *Deutsche Geschichte im Zeitalter der Gegenreformation und des dreissigjährigen Krieges (1555–1648)* (3 vols., Stuttgart, 1889; reprinted Darmstadt, 1974). Claus-Peter Clasen, 'The Empire before 1618', in *The Golden Age of Europe*, Hugh

Trevor-Roper, ed, (London, 1987). Robert Bireley, 'The Thirty Years' War as Germany's Religious War', in Konrad Repgen, ed., *Krieg und Politik 1618–1648* (München, 1988), pp. 85–106. Heinz Schilling, *Aufbruch und Krise: Deutschland 1517–1648* (Berlin, 1988), pp. 397–401 and passim.

4. S.H. Steinberg, *The Thirty Years War and the Conflict for European Hegemony* (New York, 1966), and N.M. Sutherland, 'The Origins of the Thirty Years War and the Structure of European Politics', *English Historical Review*, 107 (1992), pp. 587–625. For criticism of these, see Konrad Repgen, 'Zum Begriff Dreißigjähriger Krieg', in *Von der Reformation zur Gegenwart* (Paderborn, 1988), pp. 25–9.

5. H.G. Koenigsberger, 'The European Civil War', in Hugh Trevor-Roper, ed., *The Golden Age of Europe* (New York, 1968) pp. 133–46, and Gunter Barudio, *Der Teutsche Krieg, 1618–1648* (Frankfurt am Main, 1985), p. 24.

6. Johannes Burkhardt, *Der Dreißigjährige Krieg* (Frankfurt am Main, 1992).

7. Ronald G. Asch, *The Thirty Years War: the Holy Roman Empire and Europe, 1618–1648* (New York, 1997), p. 3.

8. Lucien Febvre, *The Problem of Unbelief in the Sixteenth Century: the Religion of Rabelais*, trans. Beatrice Gottlieb (Cambridge, 1982).

9. In Maximilian, Frederick's Catholic cousin and arch-rival, the interests of religion and politics worked together 'hand in hand'. See Dieter Albrecht, *Die Auswärtige Politik Maximilians von Bayern, 1618–1635* (Göttingen, 1962), and idem, *Maximilian I. von Bayern, 1573–1651* (München, 1998). Frederick's other great rival, Ferdinand II, was regularly guided in matters of state by his Jesuit confessors. See Robert Bireley, *Religion and Politics in the Age of the Counterreformation: Emperor Ferdinand II, William Lamoraini, S.J., and the Formation of Imperial Policy* (Chapel Hill, 1981). Confessional interest profoundly influenced the military policy of Frederick's uncle, the Lutheran King of Denmark. See Paul Douglas Lockhart, *Denmark in the Thirty Years' War, 1618–1648: King Christian IV and the Decline of the Oldenburg State* (Selinsgrove, 1996).

10. Mervyn James, *English Politics and the Concept of Honour, 1485–1642 Past & Present*, Supplement 3 (1978).

11. Michael Frank, 'Ehre und Gewalt im Dorf der Frühen Neuzeit: Das Beispiel Heiden (Grafschaft Lippe) im 17. und 18. Jahrhundert', in Klaus Schreiner and Gerd Schwerhoff, *Verletzte Ehre* (Köln, 1995), pp. 320–338. James Kelly, *'That Damn'd Thing Called Honour', Duelling in Ireland, 1570–1860* (Cork, 1995), p. 12.

12. See Donald Kagan, *On the Origins of War and the Preservation of Peace* (New York, 1995), and M. A. Kishlansky, *The Rise of the New Model Army* (Cambridge, 1979).

13. See Helen Watanabe-O'Kelley, *Triumphal Shews: Tournaments at German-speaking Courts in their European Context, 1560–1730* (Berlin, 1992), pp. 37–63 and Hiram Morgan, 'Festive Irishmen: an "Irish" Procession in Stuttgart 1617', *History Ireland*, v, 3 (1997), pp. 14–20.

14. Aart A. van Schelven, 'Der Generalstab des politischen Calvinismus in Zentraleuropa zu Beginn des Dreißigjährigen Krieges', *Archiv für Reformationsgeschichte*, 36 (1939), pp. 117–141. Michael Walzer, *The Revolution of the Saints: a study in the origins of radical politics* (Cambridge, MA, 1965).

15. Claus-Peter Clasen, *The Palatinate in European History, 1559–1660* (Oxford, 1963), pp. 1–9.

16. Policies of toleration had more than adequate intellectual support in the later sixteenth and early seventeenth centuries. See John Christian Laursen and Cary J.

Nederman, eds, *Beyond the Persecuting Society: Religious Toleration Before the Enlightenment* (Philadelphia, 1998) and idem, *Difference and Dissent: Theories of Toleration in Medieval and Early Modern Europe* (Lanham, 1996).

17.   In Steve Murdoch, ed., *Scotland and the Thirty Years' War, 1618–1648* (Leiden, 2001), a strong argument is made for preferring 'Britain' and 'British' over 'England' and 'English' where non-English denizens of the British Isles were involved in diplomatic and military actions. In this work, however, James I will be called King of England and King of Great Britain almost interchangeably, because contemporary political figures around Europe did so. The same applies to 'English' troops as opposed to 'British'. Scots served in 'English' forces, but in most armies during the Thirty Years' War, people from numerous national, linguistic, and religious groups served together. See Geoffrey Parker, 'The Soldiers of the Thirty Years' War', in Konrad Repgen, *Krieg und Politik, 1618–1648* (Munich, 1988), pp. 303–15.

Chapter 1

Signs of Impending Disaster?

Before beginning an analysis of Frederick V and his contribution to the Thirty Years' War, it is necessary to present the main field of battle: the Holy Roman Empire and its constitution. It will be argued here that the structure of the Empire, despite the diversity of its constituent parts and the tensions between them, was not inviting an inevitable catastrophe to begin in 1618. At that time there were very few who could have predicted the dimensions of the crisis to come. In 1618 the Holy Roman Empire was one of the largest realms in Europe, encompassing all of Germany, the Kingdom of Bohemia and its incorporated lands (Moravia, Silesia, and Lusatia), the Austrian territories, the Netherlands, and parts of northern Italy. The Empire spanned from the North Sea and the Baltic over the Alpine lands to the Mediterranean and the Adriatic. Although the main language of the Imperial government, administration, and justice was High German, the Empire's populace included speakers of most major European languages: Dutch, French, Italian, German, Polish, and Czech, not to mention the vast array of dialects and regional variations of each.

The Imperial Constitution

This sprawling, diverse polity was at once united in a single constitutional system and yet fissured with myriad rifts.[1] The Empire contained some 2500 separate 'estates'.[2] An Imperial estate was 'either a person or a community that occupied a land or territory, and, because of this, held a seat and vote in a general assembly'.[3] There were hundreds of municipalities and secular and ecclesiastical principalities, each with its own local rights and privileges, possessing varying degrees of independence. Individual estates could take many different forms: abbeys, bishoprics, archbishoprics, free cities, villages, castellanies, principalities, counties, manors, duchies, archduchies, landgraviates, margraviates, electorates, and a kingdom. The 2000 odd Imperial knights were 'estates' in their own right. A few foreign potentates, such as the Kings of Spain and Denmark, held estates of the Empire by right of inheritance and were therefore considered Imperial princes. By 1618, a couple of regions, namely the Swiss Confederation and the United Provinces of the Netherlands, had developed polities that were wholly separated from the Imperial constitution except in name. The overwhelming majority of other estates, however, showed no inclination toward secession or a general dissolution.

The Imperial constitution is almost impossible to classify. Early modern theorists found little agreement, arguing variously in favor of pure aristocracy, monarchy with indivisible sovereignty, a mixed constitution, and a federal state. Some praised its uniqueness, and others declared it monstrous and degenerate.[4] At the head of the Imperial constitution was as an elective monarchy that was meant to balance the authority of the emperor with that of seven electors and the other estates. The core of this constitution was the Golden Bull of 1356, which had established the procedure for the election of the emperor and the constitution of the Electoral College.[5] The emperor-elect had to be an orthodox Christian and supposedly the man best suited for the position. At the time of his election, each emperor-elect had to consent to a set of electoral concessions, or *Wahlcapitulation*, a kind of contract that guaranteed the electors' independence from the emperor and their pre-eminence in the Empire. The concessions invariably included promises not to try to change the Empire into a heritable monarchy and to let the right of free election stay with the electors forever, and other articles guaranteed various rights and privileges of other estates of the Empire. Furthermore, the emperor was dependent on the electors' support for his power, because 'their consent was necessary to all public acts of consequence'.[6] He had to consult with the electors and other Imperial estates on questions of war and peace, foreign policy, alliances, domestic peace, and taxation. Without the electors' consent, the emperor could not call an Imperial diet, make use of an escheated fief, or apply the Imperial ban to an estate of the Empire.[7]

The Imperial ban was the one of the most powerful weapons that the highest jurisdiction of the Empire had at its disposal, and it figures prominently in the story of Frederick V. It was used against those who violated the public peace, committed the crimes of lèse-majesté, organized counterfeit, and so on. Those subjected to the ban lost all protection under the law for their persons and their property. All legal contracts were dissolved, and all fiefs held reverted to the liege lord. All assistance for this person or community was forbidden. Traditionally the right to declare the Imperial ban belonged to the emperor alone, but the electors, using the electoral concessions, limited this power by making it contingent on the consent of a majority of the electoral college.[8] Despite this restriction, the emperor's prestige and legal authority were separate and superior.

In the seventeenth century the emperor maintained his medieval prestige as the protector of Christendom – although he lacked the resources to act as such – and as the *Reichslehnsherr*, or feudal overlord of the Empire. He had the power to bestow the status of Imperial prince, count, knight, and free lord, to give out an array of legal privileges and dispensations, to declare children to be in their legal majority, and to grant legitimacy to bastard offspring. He could also name notaries, judges, and members of the *Reichskammergericht*, the Imperial Supreme Court. This court was the central legal authority that functioned according to Roman law, based on Justinian's *Corpus Iuris*, and bolstered the emperor's prerogative, effectively elevating him, it has been argued, above the law.[9] In addition the emperor dominated the *Reichshofrat*, the Aulic Council, which served as a central institution of governmental and judicial authority, and was considered the second highest legal authority in the Empire.[10] With thirty members at most, the Aulic Council was located at the emperor's court in Vienna and served to defend his interests against those of the estates of the Empire.

The seven electors were members of the Electoral College, the highest order of the Empire under the emperor. The Golden Bull named them – the Archbishops of Mainz, Cologne, and Trier, the Count Palatine on the Rhine, the Duke of Saxony, the Margrave of Brandenburg, and the King of Bohemia – and elevated them above other princes and estates of the Empire. They were, according to the Golden Bull, the 'foundations and fixed pillars of the Empire'; their duty was to protect its constitution and insure its peace and stability.[11] The Golden Bull stipulated that they should convene periodically to guarantee their rights and regulate their relationship.[12] They exercised full sovereignty over their estates, which were not to be subdivided. They enjoyed regalian rights to tax, mine, and issue coinage in their own lands. Their subjects were wholly under their legal jurisdiction; cases could be tried and appealed only in the elector's law courts, unless justice had been blatantly denied, in which case, it was possible to appeal to the emperor. The electors' persons were declared inviolable, and they commanded much of the prestige, popularity, and power that would have belonged to the emperor, had the Empire been more a monarchy and less a federation.[13]

The other estates of the Empire, the princes, prelates, free cities, *et al.*, could participate in the Imperial polity through three representative institutions of the Imperial constitution: the Imperial circles, the Imperial Supreme Court, and the Imperial diet. The Empire was subdivided, more or less according to geographic region, into ten Imperial circles, each with their own officials and representative assembly elected by the estates within them.[14] The purpose of the circles was to help maintain the peace on a local level and provide for a speedy defense of their region of the Empire in case of foreign invasion. The Imperial Supreme Court had been established in 1495 to help enforce the proclamation of a permanent, domestic peace within the Empire as an effort to repress endemic feuding. The Court normally met in Speyer, far from the emperor's main residences in Vienna and Prague, and the emperors, despite their efforts, exercised less control over it than did the Imperial estates.[15] The estates paid a tax to cover their expenses, and, with the Imperial circles, selected the majority of the court's membership, a mix of lawyers and nobles of lesser and greater status. The Court made an indispensable contribution to the process of legal standardization in the areas of trial and civil law in the Empire.[16] Unlike the circles and the Court, the Imperial diet was a temporary institution, an assembly that met seldom and, in times of need, somewhat more often.[17] It included the emperor and the three colleges: those of the electors, the princes and prelates, and the Imperial Free Cities.[18] The diet presented an opportunity to make provisions for various issues affecting the Empire as a whole, such as the maintenance of domestic peace, inter-confessional strife, declaration of war, general taxation, and the administration of justice.[19] Although the diet was meant to build consensus between the emperor and the estates, in the later sixteenth and early seventeenth century agreement among the emperor, the colleges, and their individual members had been a rare phenomenon. The Diets of 1608 and 1613 had failed to make any resolutions at all because of intensive inter-confessional bickering.

The exercise of religion in the Empire lay under the jurisdiction of Imperial constitutional law, which applied to both church and state. The Peace of Augsburg in 1555 had resolved the Schmalkaldic War between Catholics and Protestants by enshrining the principle of *cuius regio eius religio* in Imperial law. This principle guaranteed that it was the right of the ruler of an Imperial estate to determine which Christian confession, either Roman Catholic or Lutheran, the populace would practice. Official toleration of Lutheranism, therefore, became a part of the Imperial constitution. The Peace, however, also had an 'ecclesiastical reservation' that dictated that Catholic prelates who converted to Protestantism had to relinquish control of their lands and titles, a provision meant to limit the spread of the new confession. The Peace was an ad hoc compromise and, unfortunately, rife with inherent contradictions and impracticalities.[20] For example, although Calvinism and sectarian confessions were not named in the Peace, the principle of *cuius regio, euis religio* appeared to allow Calvinist rulers to institute official toleration of Calvinism in their principalities, if they did not expressly reject the tenets of the Augsburg Confession of 1530, which served as a litmus test for legitimate Protestantism in the Peace. There is no reason why Calvinism should have been incorporated in the Peace; in 1555 Calvinism was a regional sect particular to some of the Swiss Cantons. No major princes of the Empire had converted, and Calvin had only just begun his campaign to evangelize in France. But by 1618 Calvinism had become a prominent component of the Empire's religious diversity. Generally speaking there tended to be a fundamental disagreement on how to interpret and execute the Peace.[21] Catholics were ready to rely on the judgments of Imperial institutions and on the will of the majority in the electoral and Imperial diets, where the benefit of greater numbers usually guaranteed results favorable to their interests. Protestants, however, preferred an unstructured approach that favored voluntary action, persuasion, and consensus over the will of the majority.[22] They wanted representational parity in the organs of the Imperial government, but the Catholic majority consistently confounded their efforts, not least because unity among Protestant confessions was seldom to be had.

These tensions produced no small amount of mutual antagonism, but it did not lead inevitably to the relentless bloodshed from 1618 to 1648. The Peace of Augsburg had placated warring confessions in 1555, but it had not prearranged the series of crises that incited and escalated the Thirty Years' War. Rather than guaranteeing constitutional paralysis and extensive international interference, the Peace of Augsburg had provided grounds for at least fifty years of what has been called 'unusual constitutional liveliness and openness'.[23] During this time, institutions like the Imperial circles and Supreme Court had attained a maturity that had allowed the Imperial estates as a whole to pass legislation to address various socio-economic and political problems. Furthermore, feuding counts and knights had rarely resorted to open warfare after 1555, preferring litigation in the Supreme Court and Aulic Council instead of military conflict. In the cases where they did resort to violence, its scale was limited.[24]

The flexibility of the Imperial constitution prevented confessional rivalry from tearing the Empire apart. The high degree of local autonomy of the individual estates had admittedly allowed for a century of private war and pandemic local struggles, and the Protestant Reformation had brought new grounds for conflict. The complexity of the Imperial polity, however, also provided the Empire with a means for survival. The strength of local authorities in their own territories, the regional structure provided by Imperial circles, and the accessibility of justice from the Imperial Supreme Court and Aulic Council, had enabled the Empire to function without regular Imperial diets. The boundaries between the institutions and jurisdictions of Imperial government had not always been clear; they overlapped, clashed, and allowed important issues to fall through the gaps. They were also slow, inefficient, and vulnerable to corruption, but not wholly ineffective.

It is common to speak of a collapse or a breakdown of the Imperial constitution by 1618, and this description may apply to some of the central institutions, such as the Imperial Supreme Court and the Imperial diet, but not to the Empire as a whole. By the 1590s the Imperial Supreme Court had lost its reputation of neutral justice among many Protestant estates because of some controversial decisions against the secularization of some monastic institutions. For the Protestants, the emperor's Aulic Council was no place to turn for confessionally neutral rulings, and so they had wanted to prevent Catholic domination of the Supreme Court. When the Catholic majority of the Imperial diet had tried to transfer visitation rights of the Court to the *Deputationstag*, or diet of deputies, the Protestants had refused and dissolved the diet.[25] After 1601 the Court could no longer effectively settle conflicts with great confessional or political implications, but it had continued to handle cases of lesser importance with success.[26] Only an Imperial diet could have reformed the Court, but two acrid confessional disputes (described below) had paralyzed the Diets of 1608 and 1613. This breakdown of the Imperial Supreme Court and diet, however, did not threaten the Empire with imminent, internal self-destruction, though it did sometimes force emperors and princes to settle their disputes by taking matters into their own hands.

A powerful spirit of constitutional conservatism kept the centrifugal forces of monarchical centralization and federalism in check. The fact that consensus had been a rare commodity in the Imperial diets in the late sixteenth and early seventeenth century had only increased its worth. Though the instruments of Imperial justice had lost their reputation for partiality since the 1590s, 'the rule of law still seemed to offer the best opportunity to overcome the political impasse in the Empire'.[27] During the series of horrors that would befall the Empire during the Thirty Years' War, there would be no significant movements to dissolve the Imperial constitution and polity. The Golden Bull would remain at the heart of the constitution, and it would be a commonly held view that the difficulties in the Empire came from the misapplication of its tenets and the corruption of its justice. Not even Frederick V, the Elector Palatine, whom the emperor would declare an outlaw, subject to the Imperial ban, and deprive of his lands and titles, would consider scrapping the Imperial constitution in favor of an alternative. Indeed, he would consistently refuse to countenance any alterations to its dictates. This study will demonstrate that what primarily motivated Frederick V to engage in a series of wars in and around the Empire was an intense desire to protect the Imperial constitution from what he considered to have been specific, willful, malignant abuses by enemies within and abroad.

The Protagonist: Frederick V[28]

In 1618 Elector Palatine Frederick V was twenty-two years old, a vigorous young prince who had been in full control of his principality since he had reached his majority four years before. He was a member of the Wittelsbach dynasty, and the wealth of his lands was considerable in comparison to other Imperial princes and estates.[29] As Elector Palatine, Frederick V had the highest ceremonial prestige in the Holy Roman Empire after the emperor himself.[30] The Elector Palatine was the only Imperial prince who could claim the prerogative to sit in judgment of an emperor.[31] According to the Golden Bull, an emperor accused of a legal violation must answer to the Elector Palatine, who would exercise this jurisdiction at an Imperial diet with the emperor in attendance.[32] Frederick was also one of the two Imperial vicars – the other was the Elector of Saxony – who were to share control of the Emperor's jurisdiction and the conduct of his affairs during an interregnum, the period after the death of an emperor and before the election of the next.[33] To say the least, Frederick was a young man in a position of great authority.

Perhaps because of his inglorious fate, historiography has depicted him as a weakling in more ways than one. According to J.V. Polišenský, 'Frederick was not a strong character'; to S.H. Steinberg, a 'pleasure-loving nonentity'; to C.V. Wedgwood, 'He was strong neither in body nor in spirit'; to Julius Krebs, 'a wavering, indecisive character – not an oak, but a reed incessantly trembling in the wind'; to S.R. Gardiner, 'weak and shallow'; to Schiller, 'like the usual kind of weak souls'; and so on.[34] Although scholars have repeated this notion for at least two centuries, it is in many ways erroneous.[35] Judgments about Frederick's qualities have not been based on reliable primary sources. C.V. Wedgwood, for instance, the author of one of the most popular narratives of the Thirty Years' War, it appears, based her eloquent and unflattering description of Frederick more on imagination than evidence.[36] An enduring myth, articulated by Moriz Ritter and repeated ever since, is that Frederick's policy was determined by his wife, Elizabeth Stuart, the only daughter of James I, King of England.[37] Several historians have argued that she drove him to accept the crown of Bohemia in 1619, the decision that marked the beginning of the end of his political fortune. Two memorable but fictitious quips are normally cited as evidence. The first is that Elizabeth told her husband that she would 'rather eat sauerkraut with a king than roast meat with an elector', and, according to the second, she said that if Frederick had been bold enough to marry a king's daughter, then he should have the courage to take a crown.[38] Both lines are creations of Palatine enemies, lack primary documentary evidence, have been refuted in secondary historical literature, and should be permanently dismissed.[39]

The sources show that Frederick was not an effete creature of the court but a vigorous, affable young man, possessing many of the qualities that were conventionally admired in a seventeenth-century prince. He was convivial and good-natured, and, despite the dismal misfortune in his own affairs, usually wished others well, almost as a matter of principle. 'I', he stated unequivocally, 'do not like to keep anyone from his happiness and well-being'.[40] Nature had given him a well-proportioned body, a dark complexion, and a pleasant facial expression and character.[41] During his youth he had spent some years in Sedan, at the court of his uncle, Henri de la Tour, the Duke of Bouillon, where he learned Latin, practiced his French, and honed his riding, fencing, dancing and other courtly necessities. When Frederick came to England to wed Elizabeth, he impressed the Jacobean court with his 'well-becoming confidence'.[42] Some found that his face bore the mark of 'witt, courage, and judgement', and on the day after the wedding, a display of his equestrian skills won particular praise.[43] Throughout his life he was an avid huntsman, and he enjoyed the chase in the Palatinate and the various parts of Europe that he visited throughout his life: England, the Netherlands, Bohemia, Brandenburg, and the Lorraine, to name a few. In 1619 a visiting English nobleman judged him 'muche beyond his yeirs, religious, wise, active, and valiant, ... estemed and redowbted in all Germany, ... loved and honored by all his owne people'.[44]

Frederick was neither weak-minded nor weak-willed. He has even been described as 'an intellectual and a mystic', though the classification is somewhat exaggerated.[45] His education had certainly been sufficient. While at his uncle's court, his main tutor had been Tilenus, a Calvinist theologian at the famous Academy in Sedan, whose views about the constitution of the Holy Roman Empire may well have had a lasting influence on his pupil. In 1606–8 he had studied in Heidelberg before to returning to Sedan until his father's death in 1610.[46] Frederick V's court at Heidelberg was a notable center of culture, which welcomed artists, alchemists, and intellectuals.[47] The garden at the castle, the 'Hortus Palatinatus', with its elaborate geometric design, grottoes, fountains and statuary, was regarded as a wonder of the world.[48] Heidelberg itself was an important center of learning, with its famous university, founded in 1386, the third oldest in the Holy Roman Empire, known especially for its Protestant scholarship and magnificent library.[49] Frederick liked men of learning and appointed them to prominent positions in his court, but he was not a scholar himself. In his religion he had an active prayer life, but he exhibited no real interest in theological enigmas or esoteric rites. Based on his writings, he may be called a 'mystic', if by that term one means that he believed it possible to have direct knowledge of God and His will through insight, intuition, prayer, or some other form of subjective experience. He was, more simply, a straightforward, devout Calvinist.

Frederick lived his faith. His court exhibited a sober piety, and he avidly attended sermons by Calvinist preachers.[50] His religion was a guiding influence; the belief that all would occur according to God's will suffuses his personal and political correspondence. His motto was 'Rule me, Lord, according to your word'.[51] The sincerity of his faith, however, did not prevent him from tolerating other Protestant churches. He accepted his wife's English Protestantism without objection, though in the Palatinate the Church of England seems not to have been regarded as a true Calvinist church, probably because of its episcopal structure and the remnants of Roman Catholic ceremonies in the Prayer Book.[52] During Easter 1613, he had even taken the sacrament of the Lord's Supper with her in England.[53] In the realm of Imperial and European politics, his interests among Protestants were ecumenical. Throughout his correspondence, he almost never referred to himself or his religion as 'Calvinist' and seldom as 'reformed'; 'Protestant' was the term of choice. He was the head of the Protestant Union, an international alliance with both Calvinist and Lutheran members, not to mention England as well. The lion's share of Frederick's most important advisers were Calvinists, but some, including Ludwig Camerarius, shared their prince's ecumenism in Imperial politics.[54] Even his court preacher, Abraham Scultetus, a zealous Calvinist preacher with a style reminiscent of Old Testament prophets, spoke frequently in favor of peace between the churches of the Reformation.[55] Although Frederick was well aware of the antagonism between Lutherans and Calvinists, he thought the threat of Counter-Reformation Catholicism could bring Protestants into cooperation in spite of their jealousy and suspicion. His anti-Catholicism was more specific than general. He and his advisers were convinced that the pope and the Jesuits, backed by the forces of the King of Spain, were set against almost every other power in Europe, Catholic and Protestant. One of the goals of Palatine policy during the first stages of the Thirty Years' War was to bring together Protestant powers and Catholic enemies of Spain for common defense.[56] Frederick was able to separate his religion from his politics, though he did not always do so. His Calvinism was never so doctrinaire as to preclude a useful political or military alliance with Catholics and even Muslims.

The bulk of the evidence indicates that Frederick was usually in control of his affairs and determined the formation of his policy. He worked hard on affairs of state when the situation demanded. During one period of crisis, it was observed that 'the Elector, because of the many important affairs of the time, was in meetings every day from 6 to 11am and, after eating, from 1 to 6pm'.[57] After he had reached his majority in 1614, he ruled his principality in a sovereign capacity. The Palatine Council (*Oberrat*) handled much of the business of domestic government, but the advanced age of several of the members limited the extent of its productivity. The documentary evidence shows that the Palatine council's political activity actually decreased between 1614 and the outbreak of the Thirty Years' War. Volker Press entertains the most reasonable explanation, namely that Frederick V increasingly took personal charge of his own affairs during that time, something for which his education had prepared him.[58]

Frederick was no cipher, no mere mouthpiece for his advisers. It is true that his views often reflected those of his advisers, but it is equally true that those of his advisers reflected his own. They were trusted men who administered Frederick's principalities and served in his foreign embassies. They performed services according to the will of their prince. Some had more responsibility and independence than others, but all were dependent on the prince's favor for their influence. Among the foremost servants of the Palatine regime were the Grand Chamberlain, Count Johann Albrecht von Solms, the Chancellor, Johann Christoph von der Grün, and the leading advisor on foreign affairs, Volrad von Plessen.[59] Other men who served in an advisory capacity included Count Johann VII of Nassau, Dietrich von Schönberg, Georg Friedrich Pastoir, Johann Friedrich Schloer, Karl and Andreas Pawel, Achaz and Christoph von Dohna, Joachim Rusdorf, the court preacher, Abraham Scultetus, and, most notably, Ludwig Camerarius and the Governor of the Upper Palatinate, Prince Christian von Anhalt-Bernburg.

Historiography has long held that Anhalt single-handedly dominated Frederick and determined Palatine foreign policy.[60] This view is only partially accurate. Anhalt had a long history of service for the Palatinate. He led the Palatine army that aided Henry IV, King of France, in 1591, and four years later, Frederick's father, Elector Frederick IV, made Anhalt the Governor of the Upper Palatinate. As Frederick IV's bibulousness destroyed his health, Anhalt gained control over Palatine foreign affairs.[61] In 1607–9 he corresponded busily with members of the Bohemian Protestants Estates and negotiated on their behalf during an uprising against Emperor Rudolf II.[62] He was instrumental in 1608 in the formation of the Protestant Union, also known as the Auhausen Alliance, a defensive arrangement of mainly German Protestant princes and estates, and in the conduct of Palatine foreign policy in the years thereafter.[63] He did not, however, dominate the administration of the Palatinate completely. After the death of Frederick IV, the control of the Palatinate passed to the designated regent, Duke Johann II of Zweibrücken, who held authority over the region and led the Protestant Union until Frederick reached his majority in 1614.[64]

It is unlikely that Anhalt was in command of young Frederick's person and will. If a servant was to dominate his prince, he needed constant access to his ear, and Anhalt did not always have a place at Frederick's side. Anhalt was often in Amberg, executing his duties as Governor of the Upper Palatinate, and Frederick visited this eastern part of his patrimony only on a rare occasion.[65] When Frederick reached his majority, it seems that he immediately embraced the obligations of regency. He immediately began to attend meetings of the Palatine council and assemblies of the Protestant Union, and he would continue to attend these and other conferences and to consult with other great Imperial princes directly as long as he remained in central Europe. Though Frederick diligently consulted with his advisers on almost every important issue of state, he still seems to have been the master of his own house. No official document was allowed to leave Anhalt's hand without Frederick's approval.[66]

Apart from Christian von Anhalt, Ludwig Camerarius is generally recognized as next most influential figure in Palatine politics, especially in the years following 1620. This view derives from an exhaustive biography by F.H. Schubert, which tells much about Camerarius' personal view of Palatine foreign affairs, but little about his actual role in their formation and execution.[67] Schubert was chiefly interested in Camerarius as an intellectual, his ideology, religion, and latinity above all. Schubert repeats throughout the book that Camerarius was a pedantic, bookish man who lacked a strong sense of reality and therefore made a hopeless ambassador. Camerarius' political career provides more evidence against his supposed leadership of the Palatine regime-in-exile than for it.[68] He was away from his prince more often than not; his recommendations were often not followed; and sometimes even his reports during his embassies abroad were not fully deciphered, implying that they were not always judged necessary to read. There are numerous references in Camerarius' letters that indicate that he held Frederick in high regard and followed his orders whether he approved of them or not.[69] Camerarius was dedicated and respectful toward his prince, but he would have been happier with less work, more pay, more authority, and more time off.[70] There is no doubt that Camerarius was the main Latin secretary, a copious correspondent, and a talented publicist of pro-Palatine polemic.[71]

There is little evidence that Frederick's wife informed or influenced his political decisions significantly, though certainly he loved her with a passion that was seldom seen in princely couples of the seventeenth century. Numerous longing letters, several eye witness accounts, and thirteen children indicate that theirs was a uxorious marriage. In his letters to her, he often included brief descriptions of the development of their political affairs, but he never asked her advice nor made any recognition of having considered, carried out, or even received any from her. During the times when they were separated, Frederick's work took precedence over corresponding with his wife. He often thanked her for writing so often and once added, 'I would like to be able to write to you as often, but I have so many other letters to write and so little spare time that it is impossible for me. Believe that I do not love you the less for that'.[72] Elizabeth was a persistent lobbyist for his interests (and later for her sons') in England, even if she rarely received much for her pains. Like a good seventeenth-century royal spouse, she seems to have tried to serve her husband's political objectives without demanding a role in shaping them.

Frederick was involved in the composition and conduct of his own correspondence while at home and on campaign. He did not often take up the pen himself, but he sometimes composed the first drafts of letters to his father-in-law, King James I. Usually they were drafted by one of the Palatine French secretaries.[73] On some of the documents generated at his court, marginalia describe the procedure that led to the decision contained therein. An example from 1621, a document endorsing one of King James' several suggestions for a peace treaty between Frederick and his enemies, displays the following:

> NB: What was crossed out with red ink has been done by the English ambassador with the advice of the English agent. But the King of Bohemia [that is Frederick] did not want all those words to be left out, but that some (those he wrote in with his own hand) should remain.[74]

He usually had drafts of documents read to him. He solicited advice from those most knowledgeable about the situation at hand and then made his own decisions on how to proceed. Sometimes he gave specific instructions about what his emissaries should say and not say in a given situation. When he was not satisfied with the suggestions provided by his advisers, he asked for more until he was.[75] He worked this way throughout his life. At times he rejected all advice and set policy agenda in his own terms. Memos from 1630 show the same degree of participation as those from the previous decade.[76]

In 1618 Frederick had reason to consider himself a lucky prince. He was happily married to a king's daughter, and in the first five years of marriage, she had given birth to two potential heirs. The first, Friedrich Heinrich, had been born just before midnight on New Year's Day, 1614.[77] The next, Karl Ludwig, had come just before Christmas 1617, and at the end of 1618 Elizabeth would give birth to their first daughter, also named Elizabeth. Frederick was ecstatic at the safe delivery of his first daughter.[78] In 1619 an observer said that Elizabeth was 'so dearly loving and beloved of the Prince her husband, that it [was] a joy to all that [beheld] them'.[79]

The Palatinate in a European Context

In 1618 the Palatinate was a prosperous estate of the Holy Roman Empire.[80] In its situation, structure, and leadership, there was little indication of the calamity that would befall this principality in the years to come. The territories of the Electoral Palatinate lay in two halves on opposite sides of central Germany, supporting a population of roughly 600,000.[81] The larger, richer, and more populous of the two was the Lower Palatinate, whose center was situated at the confluence of the Rhine and the Neckar. This area was known as 'the garden of Germany', because of its fertile lands and exceptionally warm climate.[82] The Lower Palatinate produced wine, corn, fruit, and nuts, sustained sheep farming, produced timber for export, and boasted rich game preserves and some mineral deposits as well. Heidelberg, Mannheim, and Frankenthal were the three largest cities. Heidelberg, situated on the Neckar, was the capital and the seat of the university; Mannheim was the great fortress-city that protected the confluence of the Rhine and the Neckar; and Frankenthal, which lies a few miles northwest of Mannheim, protected the fertile plain on the left bank of the Rhine. The Upper Palatinate was the poorer of the two territories. It lacked the fertile plains and large towns of the Lower Palatinate, though it had greater mineral resources. A higher altitude, a generally hilly and mountainous landscape, and a severe climate contributed to its relative poverty. Even today some refer to the Upper Palatinate – a part of the state of Bavaria – as 'German Siberia'. The governments of the Upper and Lower Palatinate operated separately from each other. The Elector Palatine, the ruler of this divided principality, usually maintained his residence in Heidelberg, but he visited the Upper Palatinate on occasion.

The Elector Palatine was the sovereign of his territories. By the end of the fifteenth century, the Electors Palatine had acquired a degree of control over their territory that was more comparable to the powers of the kings in France, Spain, and England than to that of the Holy Roman Emperor. The Elector Palatine's courts were almost totally independent from the emperor's jurisdiction; his local officers kept the towns under his thumb; and the representative assemblies were not necessary to his administration of the electorate.[83] He maintained a force of 15,000 men for the defense of the land and was commander-in-chief.[84] The churches were also wholly under the elector's control.

The Palatinate was known as a Calvinist state, but it may well have been more Calvinist in reputation than in fact. Since 1562 the Electors Palatine had been Calvinists, apart from an eight-year Lutheran interval (1576–84) under Elector Ludwig, and by 1618 their university in Heidelberg had been a factory of Calvinist theologians for nearly a half-century.[85] Nonetheless, the electors' success in reforming their territory had been at best limited, though their efforts had been hardly desultory. A visitation in the mid-1590s that had examined Heidelberg's heads of households on their command of five points of Calvinist Christian doctrine ('the Ten Commandments, the Apostles' Creed, the Lord's Prayer, and the nature of baptism and the eucharist') had found that barely one third passed the test without error and that many could not recite the Lord's Prayer, account for salvation, or define 'faith'.[86] The situation beyond the capital can scarcely have been better; only a small minority were fully aware, accepting, and supportive of Protestant theology.[87] Frederick IV had tried to eliminate the general ignorance by providing instruction and explanation of the Heidelberg Catechism.[88] Nevertheless, there remained in the Lower Palatinate a small number of Lutherans despite the fact that they did not have an official freedom of worship, and in places such as the town of Oppenheim, the majority of the inhabitants was Lutheran. In other towns, such as Kreuznach, the burghers were divided between Lutheran and Calvinist confession, and the county of Sponheim was fully Lutheran. The Catholic minority in the Lower Palatinate was quite small, but they were allowed to reside there even if they had no right to worship publicly.[89] In general members of the Palatine rural populace tolerated their neighbors' confession.[90]

Although Frederick V continued his father's efforts to convert the country to Calvinism, he and his government did not favor religious extremism. Palatine theologians favored irenicism, and the Palatine Church Council took measures to quell polemicists. David Pareus, a Silesian theologian in Heidelberg, argued in favor of Protestant unity in his *Irenicum*, of 1614.[91] Catechismal writings tended to ignore points of controversy with the Lutherans, and Frederick V's court preacher, Abraham Scultetus met with prominent Lutheran divines in an effort to advance Calvinist-Lutheran understanding.[92] The Palatine Privy Council issued declarations of toleration in the country for Lutherans, Catholics, and even sectarians, as long as they were orderly and practiced their religion quietly.[93] There were, however, limits to this toleration. The population of the Upper Palatinate was largely Lutheran and incorporated some Catholics, and all had resisted their princes' efforts to reform the region. In 1615 Frederick V was still trying to bring the churches and schools of the province into conformity with those of the Lower Palatinate.[94] Continued efforts reveal as much a lack of conformity in the Upper Palatinate as the government's desire to alter the confessional balance in that region in favor of Calvinism.

Some of the Palatinate's immediate neighbors were Calvinist estates, ruled by princes of the Wittelsbach dynasty, some of whom were also

Counts Palatine, not to be confused with the one Elector Count Palatine. Frederick V's brother, Count Palatine Ludwig Philipp, held the principalities of Simmern and Lautern on the northwestern edge of the Lower Palatinate and some towns and offices: Kaiserslautern, Kirchberg, Kreuznach, Stromberg, *et al.*[95] Other members and relations of the Palatine house occupied the principalities of Neumarkt, Mosbach, Sulzbach, and Veldenz, and the duchies of Zweibrücken and Neuburg.

Adjacent to the Lower Palatinate were many neighboring territories that espoused various confessions, belonged to different dynasties, and showed varying degrees of friendliness. This was not an unusual situation for estates in the early modern Holy Roman Empire. Bordering the northern side of the Lower Palatinate were the archbishoprics of Trier and Mainz, two of Frederick's electoral colleagues. The Elector of Mainz, Johann Schweikard von Kronberg, was by far the richer and more powerful of the two, the Arch-Chancellor of the Empire and the first in prestige among the ecclesiastical electors. The little bishopric of Worms, though almost entirely encircled by the Palatinate, gave Frederick cause for complaint because of the activity of its Jesuit community.[96] The Landgraviate of Hessen-Darmstadt, a Lutheran estate, lay across the Rhine on the northern edge of the Palatinate. To the south lay the lands of two Protestant Union members, Georg Friedrich, the Margrave of Baden-Durlach, a Calvinist and a steady ally, and Johann Friedrich, the Lutheran Duke of Württemberg.[97]

The Upper Palatinate had a similarly motley array of neighbors. The Elector of Saxony, Duke Johann Georg, whose lands bordered the Upper Palatinate on the northern side, was the most powerful Lutheran prince in the Empire. Johann Georg was neither a member of the Union nor an ally of the Palatinate, not only because of his antagonism toward Calvinists, but also because of his allegiance to the emperor. To the north and west resided two Lutheran princes who were union members, Joachim Ernst, the Margrave of Ansbach, and his brother, Christian, Margrave of Kulmbach (Bayreuth).[98] The Imperial free city of Nürnberg sent emissaries to Union meetings and helped to bankroll some of the Elector Palatine's military projects. To the south lay the bishoprics of Eichstätt and Regensburg as well as some territory belonging to Wolfgang Wilhelm, the Duke of Neuburg, a close relative of the Palatine house.[99] Despite his Lutheran upbringing, Wolfgang Wilhelm had converted to Catholicism in 1613 and in the following year had acquired the Rhineland territories of Jülich and Berg as well as his father's inheritance. The Duke of Bavaria, Maximilian I, was a staunch Catholic, a competent, disciplined, rich prince, and a relative of Frederick V. They were both members of the Wittelsbach dynasty, and the two branches had a checkered history of war and peace. The Upper Palatinate shared a long eastern border with Bohemia, whose king in 1618 was also the Holy Roman Emperor, Matthias, a member of the Habsburg dynasty, also known as 'the House of Austria'.

Though the Palatinate shared no border with Brandenburg, the two ruling houses had established a strong connection. Margrave Johann Sigismund von Hohenzollern, the Elector of Brandenburg, had joined the Union in 1610 and converted to Calvinism three years later, but his attempts to induce the Lutheran populace to follow his cue failed.[100] Although his conversion alienated him from his own populace, it brought him closer to the Palatinate. In 1616 he married his son, Georg Wilhelm, to Frederick V's sister, Elisabeth, and the pair took over the margraviate after Johann Sigismund's death at the end of 1619. Brandenburg was to be a friendly and supportive, if fairly inactive, ally to Frederick V during the first decade of the Thirty Years' War.

The Palatine desire to increase the security of all Protestants in the Empire inspired the establishment of alliances with foreign Protestant powers. The Palatinate enjoyed its strongest foreign connection with the United Provinces of the Netherlands, the seven northern provinces of the Spanish Netherlands that had rebelled in the 1570s against their Habsburg overlords, the King of Spain and the Archdukes of Netherlands.[101] This little country occupied one of the most heavily populated, most urbanized, and richest areas of Europe; it had become the greatest entrepôt of European overseas trade. Survival had been their victory, and their wealth had only grown greater, especially after 1590, despite the enormous expenditures of money and men for defense.[102] Their connection to the Palatinate was manifold. The dominant confession of both states was Calvinism, although the populations of both states were religiously diverse.[103] Frederick V's mother, Louisa Juliana, was a daughter of William of Orange, and a half-sister of Maurits of Nassau. Members of the house of Nassau had been leaders of the Netherlands and were advisers at the Palatine court and commanders in the Palatine army, and the Palatinate had supplied men and money to the Dutch army during the rebellion. Because the Rhine ran through both territories, they shared a common strategic and commercial interest in its defense. Since May 1613 the Dutch Republic had been an ally of the Protestant Union.

England was the other major foreign ally of the Palatinate by virtue of a marriage alliance between Frederick V and Elizabeth, not to mention the commonality of Protestant confession. In a diplomatic triumph, he had won her hand over many royal and noble suitors, including Prince Gustavus Adolphus of Sweden, and Philip III, the King of Spain.[104] The marriage had established a diplomatic bond between England and the

Palatinate, and in April 1612 England had joined the Union in a treaty of mutual defense. King James I had been pleased with his new son-in-law and had honored him with the Knighthood of the Order of the Garter, but Queen Anne, a Danish princess and a Catholic convert, had not at first approved of the match. She had preferred to see her daughter as the Queen of Spain or maybe the Holy Roman Empress, but Elizabeth's refusal to sacrifice her Protestantism had limited her choice to Protestant suitors. After a short time, however, Queen Anne had softened and even grown somewhat affectionate towards her new son-in-law.[105] The Archbishop of Canterbury had officiated the public ceremony in the King's Chapel at Whitehall on Shrove Sunday, 14 February 1613, and Frederick had taken his marriage vow in the English language, according to the Book of Common Prayer of the Church of England.[106] After the marriage, members of the regime in Heidelberg had established friendly relationships with English gentlemen, in which gifts and information were exchanged regularly.[107]

The royal houses of Sweden and Denmark had familial connections with the Palatinate. Frederick V's aunt, Anna Maria, had been the first wife of Gustavus Adolphus' father, King Charles IX. Gustavus Adolphus' half-sister, Catherine, was married to Johann Kasimir of Pfalz-Zweibrücken-Kleeburg.[108] Frederick's marriage to Elizabeth made him a nephew to King Christian IV of Denmark, whose sister was Elizabeth's mother, Queen Anne. Neither Denmark nor Sweden were members of the Union, and they shared no common economic or strategic interests with the Palatinate. Their Lutheran confession did not prevent them from maintaining friendly relations with the Calvinist Palatinate.

In 1618 the Palatinate's relations with France were ambiguous. The Palatine court was francophone, despite the fact that the first language of the majority of its members was German. The French language enabled the English, Dutch, French, and German members of the court to communicate with one another. In the latter half of the sixteenth century, the Palatinate had been a most active supporter of Henry of Navarre, later King Henry IV, and the Huguenots during the Wars of Religion. In 1568 the Palatinate had sent a force of 10,000 soldiers to France, in 1576 20,000, and in 1587 25,000.[109] In 1591 Christian von Anhalt personally had led another force that had cost him over one million RT.[110] Three years later, with the contributions of other German Protestant princes, the Palatinate had loaned Henry 400,000 fl.[111] By 1600, the debts that the French King owed the Palatinate had taken on massive proportions. After Henry IV had converted to Catholicism in 1593, and after the Wars of Religion had come to an end, he had distanced himself from the Palatinate in order to maintain the precarious peace in France.[112] It had not helped

Franco-Palatine relations that the Duke of Bouillon, a prominent Huguenot who was married to Frederick V's aunt, Elizabeth of Nassau, had fled to Heidelberg after he had been implicated in a conspiracy against Henry IV in 1602. After the accession of the young Louis XIII, his mother and regent till 1617, Marie de Médicis, and his chief adviser as of late 1616, Armand-Jean du Plessis, later Cardinal Richelieu, had renewed France's commitment to peace in the Empire, in Italy, and with Spain for the sake of peace in France.[113]

The Palatinate had no formal diplomatic relations with Spain in 1618. The two states held no interests in common and shared no ground for mutual understanding. They would soon become enemies, though they were most unequal. If Spain were the Goliath of the early seventeenth century, then the Palatinate was, at worst, a gadfly. The Spanish monarchy commanded the largest empire the world had yet seen; its territorial possessions outside the Iberian peninsula were located in northern and southern Italy, Mexico, central and southern America, the Caribbean, the Philippines, and the coasts of Africa and South and West Asia. The flow of wealth from the empire to Spain contributed to the maintenance of the most feared military machine in Europe, though it had been unable to crush the upstart Dutch republic in the Low Countries.

The Spanish Netherlands, in the southern part of the Low Countries, was a sovereign, Catholic, 'satellite state' under the rule of Archduke Albert and his wife, Isabella, Philip III's sister, but Spain controlled its defense and foreign policy.[114] In 1618 the Spanish were considering a renewal of the Twelve Years' Truce with the Dutch republic or a new land campaign from the Spanish Netherlands. During the peace, the Spanish Army of Flanders had atrophied, and Spanish and Portuguese shipping had suffered at the hands of the Dutch throughout the Spanish Empire. Although the Spanish regime generally recognized the impossibility of conquering the Dutch, peace had not been beneficial to Spanish trade or morale.[115] The costs of maintaining the Army of Flanders had risen, and the Spanish monarchy's finances were not strong enough to afford a war that they knew they could not win. Next to the troubles in the Netherlands, Spain had to defend its holdings in northern Italy from France, Savoy, and Venice. The Spanish monarchy was in no position to fight with all of them at once. Though, as said above, the Palatinate posed no threat to Spain, the Palatine Electors were able to prevent the passage along the Rhine of the Spanish troops heading north to fight in the Low Countries, but this posed only a mild inconvenience. The main arteries of the 'Spanish road' passed to the west of the Palatinate through the Duchy of Lorraine, and the Spanish regime did not seriously entertain any plans of conquering the Rhineland for the sake of the transport of its troops.[116] With regard to

Spanish interests in the Holy Roman Empire, however, the Palatinate would prove to be worse than a gadfly.

Ever since the first half of the sixteenth century, from the reign of Charles V of Habsburg, King of Spain and Holy Roman Emperor, the interests of the Spanish monarchy had been linked to those of the Empire. The Kings of Spain had been obligated to take into consideration their relationship with the Holy Roman Emperor and the situation in Germany, and both had often been confusing. Because the King of Spain held the Netherlands and the Duchy of Milan as fiefs of the Empire, he owed homage to the emperor. This may seem paradoxical, because it is difficult to exaggerate the extent to which the King of Spain's wealth, military might, and influence exceeded the emperor's. Nevertheless, the emperor, who had monetary and military resources of his own, held the loftier dignity and greater ceremonial prestige than the Spanish king. The king could not order the emperor to obey him, and it was more often the case that the former took pains to help the latter than vice versa. Nevertheless the connection to the Empire was not entirely useless to the Spanish king. He could claim to be fighting for his sovereignty in the Netherlands, not as the King of Spain, but as the Duke of Burgundy, and in Italy, as the Duke of Milan. Despite this claim, France, England, and other European states commonly accused Spain of trying to establish a *monarchia universalis* in Europe. With regards to the Empire, however, this accusation was false. Spain's first priority was the maintenance of her sovereignty in the heritable territories of the Spanish monarchy. Because this commitment often entailed war in the Netherlands and in Italy, and because the English and French often threatened to intervene against Spanish interests, there was a compelling need to keep the peace in the Empire, especially in the Habsburg dominions.[117]

The Habsburg dynasty, also called the House of Austria, dominated much of the eastern edge of the Holy Roman Empire. The core of the Habsburg patrimony was the Archduchy of Austria, divided into an Upper and a Lower region, the Duchy of Styria to the south, the Alpine Duchy of Carinthia and the County of Tyrol, and, south of the Alps, the County of Gorizia and the Duchy of Carniola, both of which had ports on the Adriatic Sea. In addition, there were pieces of the Austrian patrimony on either side the upper Rhine, in and near the Black Forest, and in Alsace. Since 1526 Habsburg princes had been elected Kings of Bohemia and of Hungary, which was adjacent to the Empire on its southeastern border. The Habsburg claim to Hungary was restricted to the area that they controlled. In the early seventeenth century the north and west perimeter of the kingdom was free from the domination of the Turks, and the Prince of Transylvania, a 'Christian vassal' of the Turkish sultan, dominated the eastern extremity.[118] Although there had been no major campaigns against the Turks since 1606, arguments over religious privileges in the Hungarian and Bohemian constitutions had denied the Habsburg rulers an extended period of peace.

The Austrian Habsburgs were a Catholic dynasty, but the populations of their lands in central Europe, nobles and commoners alike, were by and large Protestant. In the latter half of the sixteenth century Protestants in each Habsburg duchy, county, and kingdom had formed representative assemblies called 'Estates'. They had taken full advantage of their rulers' need to fight against the Turks in Hungary, but the concessions that they had extracted had a dubious constitutionality in the lands of the Habsburg patrimony, because they violated the principle of *cuius regio eius religio.* Habsburg princes had embraced the Counter-Reformation and had enlisted the Jesuits in returning Habsburg territories to the Catholic fold, to the great vexation of their Protestant subjects. In the 1590s the tide had begun to turn with the conversion of many prominent noble families.[119] The populations of the Kingdoms of Bohemia and Hungary were still more Protestant than those of the Habsburg patrimonial lands, and the constitutions of these kingdoms increased the security of their religious privileges. Because the two monarchies were exempt from the principle of *cuius regio eius religio*, the Habsburg rulers could not use this constitutional argument to enforce Catholic conformity. Furthermore, both monarchies were electoral, and each new king had to agree to a new set of concessions on his election. As a result, resistance to the Counter-Reformation in these lands had been stubborn and efficacious.

Since the later sixteenth century, the Bohemian and Hungarian Estates had learned that armed resistance was an effective means of guaranteeing their constitutional religious privileges against the contrary inclinations of their Habsburg rulers. In 1575 the Lutherans, Hussites (Utraquists), and Bohemian Brethren (a radical Hussite sect) had agreed to subscribe to a common confession, the *Confessio Bohemica,* and they had forced their king, Rudolf, to grant them official toleration as a concession for his election. In turn, Rudolf, who had become Emperor in 1576, had not made good his promise; in 1602 he had managed to expel the Bohemian Brethren from the Kingdom. He had proven to be equally unreliable in Hungary. During an extended period of war against the Turks, 1593–1606, Emperor Rudolf II, also King of Hungary, had taken advantage of the presence of his armed forces to push through measures against the Hungarian and Transylvanian Protestants (Calvinists, Lutherans, and other sects alike) in favor of the tiny Catholic minority there. The policy had incited open rebellion. Even Rudolf's Habsburg relatives had then abandoned him and had appointed his brother, Archduke Matthias, to take over affairs. In 1606, to end the uprising,

Matthias had granted religious freedom to the Protestant nobles and burghers in Hungary, but Rudolf had not become more cooperative. His resistance to the implementation of the treaty had driven Matthias to make an alliance with the Hungarian, Austrian, and Moravian Estates that had named him King of Hungary in return for constitutional recognition of their religious freedom.[120] In 1608 a Habsburg-led army had marched on Prague, and Rudolf had acquiesced. In the next year, the Estates of Bohemia, Silesia, and Lusatia had followed suit, mobilizing an army in order to force Rudolf to sign the Letter of Majesty, which had allowed Bohemians of all ranks in society to practice either Catholicism or a creed of the Bohemian Confession and had given nobles, knights, and towns the right to build their own churches even on royal lands. But Rudolf had once again proved to be recalcitrant. In 1611 his cousin, Archduke Leopold, had invaded Bohemia with the Emperor's permission, but the Bohemian Estates had repelled the attack and then, disgusted with Rudolf's behavior, had deposed him and crowned Matthias King of Bohemia, after he had signed the Letter of Majesty. Rudolf had died in 1612, Matthias succeeding him as Emperor, but during the years that followed the strife did not dissipate. The successful uprising in 1611 showed the Bohemian Estates that armed resistance was a viable option. The Bohemian rebellion of 1618 was to be the third in ten years.

An Inevitable Religious War?

These localized conflicts, however, gave no indication of the extent of the catastrophe that would beset the Empire from 1618 to 1648. The forces that marched on Prague in the early years of the seventeenth century were not harbingers of the massive armies that would bring misery, destruction, dearth and death wherever they went, ultimately reducing the population of Germany by as much as one third.

The second half of the sixteenth century had seen an appalling amount of violence throughout Europe between the rival confessions of the Christian religion. The Wars of Religion, a vicious Catholic-Calvinist conflict of tragic dimensions, had crippled France from 1562 to 1598, and a rebellion in the Netherlands against the Spanish Habsburg overlords had been raging with comparable savagery since the 1560s. England had also engaged in a lengthy war against Spain, but the Empire had been comparatively quiet. Its one major Catholic-Protestant war, the Schmalkaldic War, had been settled in 1555 with the Peace of Augsburg, and thereafter the Empire had only been disturbed by smaller internal conflicts, usually of a confessional, dynastic, and/or territorial nature. Relations between confessions had been still better to the east of the Empire in the politically diffuse Kingdom of Poland, a

Catholic country with places where Lutherans, Calvinists, Anabaptists, and Antitrinitarians could exercise their religion unmolested.

By the early seventeenth century, it appeared that the majority of Europe's leaders had learned to despise wars of religion, for their impracticability if for nothing else. The Wars of Religion in France had ended in 1598 with the Edict of Nantes, which had recognized French Protestants' rights to public worship, assembly, university education, public office, et al. The Edict had brought an end to more than thirty years of intermittent civil war between religious parties; in the early seventeenth century, France lived in relative peace and could enjoy a period of recovery. King James I had restored the peace between England and Spain and would remain committed to peace between Christians till the end of his days. In 1609 the Dutch and the Spanish had signed a truce for twelve years. Despite the fact that it was widely expected that the Spanish would resume the conflict on the treaty's expiration in 1621, there was peace in the Low Countries during the second decade of the seventeenth century. This does not mean, however, that there was perfect repose.

The threat of armed conflict between members of rival confessions was ever-present.[121] Though the Schmalkaldic War was scarcely within the scope of living-memory, the Wars of Religion in France and the more recent conflict in the Netherlands contributed to the general fear of a major war in Central Europe. In the early years of the seventeenth century, there were some regional conflicts that threatened to draw in other powers and expand into another religious war, but they did not.[122] A Catholic-Protestant squabble over processions in the Imperial free city of Donauwörth, where both Catholicism and Protestantism were supposed to be officially tolerated, had resulted in the Emperor's placing the city under the Imperial ban. Maximilian I, the Duke of Bavaria, had executed the ban and, with dubious legality, had taken the city as a reimbursement for his services. He had then reinstituted Catholicism and repressed Protestants with impunity and alacrity. This situation had ruined the Imperial Diet of 1608, several Protestant estates walking out in disgust and desperation, but no grand conflagration had ensued.

In the next year a quarrel had erupted over the inheritance of the Imperial provinces of Jülich and Kleves, which bordered the Low Countries. Although it had appeared that Spain, France, and England would send armies into the fray and turn the affair into a general war of religion, they had not. During the early stages of the Jülich-Kleve crisis, Henry IV had shown no inclination to interfere, but, despite his distaste for religious war, in 1610 he had offered to send an army to Jülich on behalf of the Protestants, and he had threatened to attack the Spanish in the Netherlands and in Italy to prevent their intervention on behalf of the

Catholics. With Henry's assassination, however, these bellicose plans had dissolved. The brief episode of fighting that had taken place in 1610 had not engulfed the whole of Europe. When violence had broken out once again in the region in 1614, Spanish and Dutch troops had mobilized, but, both desirous of peace, they had studiously avoided engaging each other in battle, quickly settled a truce, and then signed a treaty with English and French mediation in a matter of months.[123]

A general war had been avoided, but tension in the Empire had not diminished as a result. In the early seventeenth century, many Imperial princes had increased their expenditures on fortifications in their towns and cities.[124] Sometimes these defense works, instead of promoting security, provoked neighboring princes to acts of aggression. On 25 June 1618, while the Bishop of Speyer was building a large fortress on the Rhine at Udenheim, just a few miles from Palatine territory, 4,000 Palatine troops marched in and reduced it to rubble. Frederick V insisted that it was his right as Elector and Count Palatine to defend himself from apparently aggressive acts, which the construction of this fortress had entailed.[125]

The threat of confessional violence in the Empire had inspired the formation of Protestant and Catholic defensive alliances. The Electors Palatine had tried to use their influence, wealth, and authority to guarantee the protection of all Protestants in the Empire against potential aggression by Catholics.[126] After the failed Diet of 1608, a defensive, military alliance had been sealed in Auhausen, the Protestant Union, and the Elector Palatine, at first Frederick IV and later Frederick V, had stood at its head. By 1610 the members of the Union had included the Electoral Palatinate, Württemberg, Baden-Durlach, Ansbach, Kulmbach, Neuburg, Hessen-Kassel, Zweibrücken, Electoral Brandenburg, and a number of southern German Imperial cities. Similarly, Maximilian I, Duke of Bavaria, had formed the Catholic League in response to the Jülich-Kleve crisis. The first members had been Bavaria and some of the neighboring bishoprics and principalities, but as the crisis had developed, the three ecclesiastical electors and other bishops on the Rhine had joined the organization.[127] The Union and the League were provisional military arrangements; they sought to counterbalance the potential threat of the other. They neither provided nor proposed a challenge or an alternative to the Imperial constitution.[128] Internal bickering had plagued both alliances and prevented them from becoming organizations that reflected the interests of the members of their confession as a whole. The division of the League into geographically-based directorates led by rival princes had rendered it largely ineffective. When Emperor Matthias had demanded in 1617 that both the League and the Union disband, the League had complied, but the Union had not.

The Union was meant to be a defensive alliance against attacks by aggressors within the Empire and by foreign powers. The articles of the alliance described the Union as a supplementary organization that was to bolster and strengthen the ever-weakening Imperial constitution. The Union lacked common political objectives and a single leader behind whom all Protestants could rally despite their differences. The goals of the Union were less than clear; among the members there were two opposite poles of intentions. One side preferred to restrict the Union's activities and membership to the Empire alone, strengthen the emperor as a neutral judge, and avoid a war. The other wanted to draw in foreign Protestant powers, weaken the emperor as the head of an opposing party, and arm in expectation of a war that was considered unavoidable. The majority of the Union members tended towards the latter pole, and those Protestant princes, like the Elector Saxony, who were firmly committed to the former had stayed out. The Union had actually begun its process of collapse just two years after its formation.[129] Differences in opinion over Heidelberg's international and domestic politics, especially during the Jülich-Kleve crisis, had prevented the Union from becoming the institution for the defense of all Protestants that the Electors Palatine had wanted. While the Union's membership in the Empire had weakened, the Heidelberg leadership had turned its attentions abroad. In April 1612, England, and in May 1613, the Estates General of the United Provinces had joined the alliance.

It has been said that Lutheran and Calvinist Princes who managed to form the Union 'detested each other cordially [and] had not been capable of uniting'.[130] The Union's lack of political direction reflected the confessional differences among the members and among Protestants within the Empire, but confessional differences alone neither induced nor drove the process of the Union's demise. It is undeniable that the many broadside attacks or pithy deprecations published by Lutheran polemicists against Calvinists testified to intra-confessional antagonism.[131] Pugnacious Calvinist and Catholic publicists readily engaged in the same sort of activity.[132] Despite this passionate and at times petulant wrangling, it remained possible for some princes to make political decisions without giving great weight to their clergymen's enmities. Frederick V was such a prince. The Union was a creation of the Palatine leadership, and it was not a religious institution. It had a defensive, militaristic *raison d'être*; its intention was to protect a conception of the Imperial constitution; its sphere of activity was primarily political and diplomatic; and its leadership was predominantly Palatine.

* * *

In 1618 the appearance of a comet in the night sky evinced the usual dire warnings of inevitable cataclysm, but this time astrologers were not far off the mark.[133] Nonetheless, the conflagration that was to follow in the wake of the renewal of violence in Prague only began to develop gradually at first. As the Thirty Years' War unfolded, the overwhelming majority of Imperial princes and estates showed their resistance to the conflict instead of a belligerent lust to join the fray, but their peaceable intentions were insufficient to contain the spreading flames of war. Not all Germany ignited at the first lightning strike, and few expected it to do so. There was to be no great explosion of pent-up confessional hatred. As the war developed, some areas were to be only lightly singed, while others would be scorched to the ground. While the Empire certainly had a plentiful supply of combustibles (men, money, and enmity), it took the winds of willful princes to carry the flames from one region to the next. The driving forces behind these winds were competing visions of the Imperial constitution.

Notes

1. The best short treatise on the Empire in English is Peter H. Wilson, *The Holy Roman Empire, 1495–1806* (New York, 1999).
2. There were 136 ecclesiastical lords, 173 secular lords, 85 Imperial Free Cities, and 2000 roughly Imperial knights. John Gagliardo, *Germany Under the Old Regime, 1600–1790* (London, 1991), p. 2.
3. Helmut Neuhaus, *Das Reich in der Frühen Neuzeit* (München, 1997), p. 19. I use 'estate' to refer to an Imperial *Stand*. The context should make clear which definition of the word is being used.
4. Alois Riklin, Gemischte oder monströse Verfassung?, *Beiträge und Berichte*, Institut für Politikwissenschaft Hochschule St Gallen, 190 (1992), pp. 1–36. For a brief description of the early modern Imperial constitution, see Hermann Weber, 'Empereur, Électeurs et Diète de 1500 à 1650', *Revue d'Histoire Diplomatique*, vol. 89 (1975), pp. 281–297; and James A. Vann and Steven W. Rowan, eds, *The Old Reich: Essays on German Political Institutions, 1495–1806* (Bruxelles, 1974).
5. For a published edition of the Golden Bull, see Konrad Müller, ed., *Die Goldene Bülle Kaiser Karls IV. 1356* (Bern, 1957).
6. James Bryce, *The Holy Roman Empire* (New York, 1961), p. 249.
7. Neuhaus, *Das Reich*, p. 19.
8. All emperors claimed as their prerogative the power to ban members of the Empire who broke the public peace. The Imperial Supreme Court held a similar power to inflict the ban in the name of the reigning emperor. Christoph Kampmann, *Reichsrebellion und kaiserliche Acht: Politische Strafjustiz im Dreißigjährigen Krieg und das Verfahren gegen Wallenstein 1634, Schriftenreihe der Vereinigung zur Erforschung der Neueren Geschichte* (Münster, 1992), pp. 32–5.
9. Bryce, *The Holy Roman Empire*, p. 366, note i.
10. Neuhaus, *Das Reich*, pp. 51–2.

11. 'die Grundfesten und unverrückbaren Säulen des Reiches (solide bases imperii et columpne immobiles)', Arno Buschmann, *Kaiser und Reich* (München, 1984), p. 133.
12. The King of Bohemia was not to take part in these diets. This elector had only the right to vote in an Imperial election and in every Imperial diet, but not to participate in the governing capacity of the electoral college or the Empire unless of course he were the emperor himself, as was often the case.
13. Neuhaus, *Das Reich*, p. 250.
14. The Kingdom of Bohemia and its incorporated lands (Moravia, Lusatia, and Silesia), Switzerland, the Italian lands of the Empire, all the Imperial knights, and a few Imperial counts and barons were not included in the Imperial circles.
15. In the first half of the sixteenth century, Emperor Charles V failed to subject the Court to his will, which led to the development of the Aulic Council as a rival legal institution. H. Duchhardt, *Deutsche Verfassungsgeschichte 1495–1806* (Stuttgart, 1991), pp. 96–8.
16. Ibid., p. 99.
17. Only six diets met between 1555 and 1603. Parker, *The Thirty Years' War*, p. 14. Three of these met in the ten years from 1594 to 1603 to provide for a defense against the Turkish invasions.
18. Imperial Free Cities were answerable to no lord other than the emperor. Imperial knights and lesser nobles did not officially comprise an order or college of the Empire and had no representation at the Imperial diet.
19. It was also possible to call an *Ordentlicher Reichsdeputationstag*, an assembly that was meant to help restore the peace in times of strife. Members included representatives from all orders of the Empire.
20. Duchhardt, *Deutsche Verfassungsgeschichte*, p. 143.
21. For an explanations of the opposing confessional interpretations of the Peace of 1555 and the Imperial constitution, see Martin Heckel, 'Die Krise der Religionsverfassung des Reiches und die Anfänge des Dreißigjährigen Krieges', in Konrad Repgen, ed., *Krieg und Politik 1618–1648* (München, 1988), pp. 107–31.
22. Axel Gotthard, 'Protestantisch "Union" und Katholische "Liga"-Subsidiäre Strukturelemente oder Alternativentwürfe?' in Volker Press, *Alternativen zur Reichsverfassung in der Frühen Neuzeit?* (München, 1995), p. 88.
23. Duchhardt, *Deutsche Verfassungsgeschichte*, p. 145.
24. Asch, *The Thirty Years War*, p. 11.
25. Duchhardt, *Deutsche Verfassungsgeschichte*, p. 149. Also see Rudolf Smend, *Das Reichskammergericht* (Weimar, 1911), pp. 193–4.
26. Asch, *The Thirty Years War*, p. 27.
27. Ibid., p. 20.
28. For an expanded version of this section, see Brennan C. Pursell, 'Elector Palatine Friedrich V and the Question of Influence Revisited', *The Court Historian*, 6, no. 2 (2001), pp. 123–39.
29. Clasen, *The Palatinate*, p. 6. The principality also had high debts, about 1,800,000 fl. at the time when Frederick V reached his majority. Volker Press, *Calvinismus und Territorialstaat: Regierung und Zentralbehörden der Kurpfalz, 1559–1619* (Stuttgart, 1970), p. 504.
30. Clasen, *The Palatinate*, p. 6. This statement only applied when the King of Bohemia was also emperor, which was more often than not the case during the sixteenth and seventeenth centuries. The Golden Bull of 1356 dictated that the King of Bohemia

was to have the first place of honor at Imperial diets and other meetings. He was to sit at the emperor's immediate right, and then, next to the king, sat the Elector Palatine. When the king was also emperor, the Elector Palatine occupied the first place of honor to his right. Buschmann, *Kaiser und Reich*, p. 123.

31. Duchhardt, *Deutsche Verfassungsgeschichte*, p. 35.

32. Buschmann, *Kaiser und Reich*, p. 125.

33. For a description of the Imperial vicars and their role in the Empire, see Wolfgang Hermkes, *Das Reichsvikariat in Deutschland* (Karlsruhe, 1968).

34. J.V. Polišenský, *The Thirty Years War* (Berkeley, 1971), p. 163; Steinberg, *The Thirty Years War*, p. 38; C.V. Wedgwood, *The Thirty Years' War* (London, 1938, New York, 1961), p. 56; 'ein schwankender, unentschlossener Charakter, – keine Eiche, sondern ein unablässig im Winde zitterndes Rohr', Julius Krebs, *Christian von Anhalt* (Leipzig, 1872), p. 106; S.R. Gardiner, ed., *Letters and Other Documents Illustrating the Relations Between England and Germany at the Commencement of the Thirty Years' War*, 2 vols, *Camden Society, Second Series*, 1865–8, vol. i, p. v; 'Nach der gewöhnlichen Art schwacher Seelen…', Friedrich von Schiller, *Geschichte des dreißigjährigen Kriegs* (Stuttgart, 1850), p. 105. This last work was written 1791–93. It must be said that Schiller also makes an accurate, positive observation about Frederick's character. 'Friedrich der Fünfte war von einem freien und aufgeweckten Geiste, vieler Herzensgüte, einer königlichen Freigiebigkeit'. p. 104.

35. For one of the few sympathetic accounts, see Karl Bayer, 'Churfürst Friedrich V', in *Programm der Königlichen Studienanstalt zu Schweinfurt* (1873), pp. 2–21.

36. Wedgwood writes of Frederick: 'Gentle, trustful, equally incapable of anger, hatred, or resolution, he strove conscientiously to fulfill his responsibilities although the pleasures of hunting, playing tennis, swimming and even lying in bed were very tempting to him', *The Thirty Years' War*, pp. 55–56. She cites Friedrich Spanheim, *Mémoires sur la vie et la mort de Loyse Julian, Électrice Palatine* (Leiden, 1645), p. 315, but there is no such information on the page. In fact the passage that extends from pp. 310–20 is apologetic, if not laudatory, in tone. It acknowledges that Frederick's education lacked hard military training, but it praises the nobility of his character in the face of catastrophe. His election as King of Bohemia was indicative in part of the high esteem that he had acquired until that point. After his defeat on the battlefield, many of his would-be supporters turned their backs on him, but, says Spanheim, he behaved nobly and never stooped to desiring vengeance. From this account Wedgwood concludes, 'Ironic fate had given him no vices, and all the virtues most useless to a ruling prince'.

37. Ritter, *Deutsche Geschichte*, p. 49.

38. For the first, see Wedgwood, p. 97. Also quoted in M.A.E. Green, *Elizabeth: Electress Palatine and Queen of Bohemia* (London, 1909), pp. 129–30, and Weiß, 'Die Vorgeschichte', p. 471. For the second, see ibid., p. 471, and Green, *Elizabeth*, p. 130.

39. Weiß, 'Die Vorgeschichte', p. 471. S.C. Lomas, in the introduction to the 1909 edition of M.A.E. Green's *Elizabeth*, checked the citation for the sauerkraut quip in Friedrich Spanheim, *Mémoires*. Lomas says that 'the copy at the British Museum does not contain the remark, or anything at all like it'. The courage quip derives from a contemporary letter from one who had little or no direct contact with the Palatine court. See James Howell, *Epistolæ Ho-Elianæ: Familiar Letters* (London, 1726), p. 83.

40. 'dan Ich nicht gern Jemandt an seinen gluck undt wohlfahrt verhindere'. Joseph Fiedler, 'Correspondenz des Pfalzgrafen Friedrich V. und seiner Gemahlin Elisabeth mit Heinrich Mathias von Thurn', in *Archiv für Kunde österreichischer Geschichts-Quellen*, vol. 31 (1864), p. 388.

41. Green, *Elizabeth*, p. 40. John Nichols, *The Progresses of King James the First*, vol. ii, (London, 1828), p. 464.

42. Nichols, *The Progresses*, p. 464.

43. Ibid. Green, *Elizabeth*, p. 55.

44. Gardiner, *Letters and Other Documents*, vol. i, p. 118: 18/28 June 1619, Viscount Doncaster to James I.

45. Frances B. Yates, *The Rosicrucian Enlightenment* (Boston, 1972), p. 14.

46. Harmut Kretzer, *Calvinismus und französische Monarchie im 17. Jahrhundert: die politische Lehre der Akademien Sedan und Saumur, mit besonderer Berücksichtigung von Pierre Du Moulin, Moyse Amyraut und Pierre Jurieu* (Berlin, 1975), pp. 69 (n. 24), 106–7, 126–7. V. Press, *Calvinismus*, p. 488.

47. Yates, *Rosicrucian*, pp. 28ff. Yates argues that the Palatine court was a center of Rosicrucianism, an intellectual movement which is purported to have linked the spirit of the waning Renaissance to that of the Enlightenment.

48. Ibid., p. 12. For a thorough analysis of these gardens, see Richard Patterson, 'The "Hortus Palatinatus" at Heidelberg and the Reformation of the World. Part I: The Iconography of the Garden', *Journal of Garden History*, i (1), 1981, pp. 67–104 and 'The 'Hortus Palatinatus' at Heidelberg and the Reformation of the World. Part II: Culture as Science', *Journal of Garden History*, i (2), 1981, pp. 179–202.

49. This university was a leading institution in the development and spread of Calvinism from the mid sixteenth century. Members of its faculty produced the Heidelberg Catechism.

50. For Scultetus' estimation of the Palatine court, see Gustav Adolf Benrath, 'Abraham Scultetus (1566–1624)', in Kurt Baumann, ed., *Pfälzer Lebensbilder* (Speyer, 1970), ii, p. 105. The main source for this text is Scultetus' autobiography. See Gustav Adolf Benrath, ed., *Die Selbstbiographie des Heidelberger Theologen und Hofpredigers Abraham Scultetus (1566–1624)*, Veröffentlichungen des Vereins für Kirchengeschichte in der evang. Landeskirche in Baden, (Karlsruhe, 1966).

51. 'Rege me domine secundum verbum tuum'. This motto appears on an etching by Delphius after a portrait by Mierevelt, published as an unnumbered plate in Kurt Pfister, *Kurfürst Maximilian I von Bayern* (München, 1980).

52. Elizabeth brought a chaplain with her to the Palatinate so that she could worship 'according to the rites and liturgies of the Church of England'. Green, *Elizabeth*, p. 33. Only sometimes in Heidelberg and in Prague did Elizabeth take the eucharist publicly with her husband in order to show that their religions were not incompatible. From Prague she wrote to her father to ask his permission to continue this practice. She felt she had to because people in Prague considered her a Lutheran. Green, *Elizabeth*, p. 147.

53. Green, *Elizabeth*, p. 62.

54. F.H. Schubert, *Ludwig Camerarius, 1573–1651, Eine Biographie* (Kallmünz, 1955), pp. 33–34. The Palatinate had a legacy of a confessionally neutral Imperial policy that was devoted to the maintenance of peace and the support of the organs of Imperial government. See Albrecht Pius Luttenberger, *Glaubenseinheit und Reichsfriede: Konzeptionen und Wege Konfessionsneutraler Reichspolitik (1530–1552) (Kurpfalz, Jülich, Kurbrandenburg)* (Göttingen, 1982).

55. Press, *Calvinismus*, pp. 511–12.

56. Weiß, 'Beiträge zur Beurteilung', pp. 391–8.

57. '...der Kurfürst wegen vieler wichtiger Geschäfte derzeit alle Tage des Morgens von 6–11 und nach dem Essen von 1–6 Rat hielte...', quoted in Georg Tumbült, 'Die kaiserliche Sendung des Grafen Jakob Ludwig zu Fürstenberg an den Kurfürsten Friedrich V. von der Pfalz i. J. 1619', *Zeitschrift für die Geschichte des Oberrheins*, NF, 19 (1904), p. 13.

58. Press, however, dismisses this possibility based on Frederick's youthful age and out of respect for the traditional historiographical assessment of his laziness and weakness of character. See Volker Press, *Calvinismus*, pp. 486–9.

59. Press, *Calvinismus*, p. 487.

60. This view derives from Krebs, *Christian von Anhalt*, and Julius Krebs, 'Zur Geschichte der kurpfälzischen Politik am Beginn des dreißigjährigen Krieges, 1618–1619', *Städtisches Gymnasium zu Ohlau* (Ohlau, 1875). Historians have tended to repeat Krebs' views; a modern study of this prince is long overdue.

61. Parker, *The Thirty Years' War*, pp. 23–4.

62. Hans Georg Uflacker, 'Christian I. von Anhalt und Peter Wok von Rosenberg: eine Untersuchung zur Vorgeschichte des pfälzischen Königtums in Böhmen', Inaugural-Dissertation zur Erlangung der Doktorwürde der hohen philosophischen Fakultät Sektion I der Ludwig-Maximilian-Universität München (1926). For this author, who follows Krebs and attacks Anton Gindely, Anhalt was more than the single most important political figure in the Palatinate. 'Der Fürst ist der wichtigste Faktor in den Beziehungen der Pfalz zu Böhmen, ja darüber hinaus eine der treibenden Kräfte in der inneren Geschichte des Reiches', p. 17.

63. Parker, *The Thirty Years' War*, pp. 24–5.

64. Ritter, 'Friedrich V', vii, pp. 621–2. Also see Press, *Calvinismus*, pp. 479–81.

65. Amberg was the seat of Anhalt's administration of the Upper Palatinate, from which he conducted most of his correspondence regarding Palatine foreign affairs. See Press, *Calvinismus*, p. 489–90. Discounting Frederick's birth in the Upper Palatinate, he was there on only two occasions prior to 1619: in 1602, at the age of six, for a ceremonial recognition of his lordship, and in 1615 with Elizabeth. J.B. Götz, *Die religiösen Wirren in der Oberpfalz von 1576 bis 1620, Reformations-geschichtliche Studien und Texte*, (Münster, 1937), lxvi, pp. 282–5.

66. 'Es durfte kein offizielles Dokument aus [Anhalts] Hand gehen, das Friedrich nicht gebilligt hatte oder das ihm nicht wenigstens nachträglich zur Billigung vorgelegt werden konnte'. Weiß, 'Beiträge', p. 401.

67. F.H. Schubert, *Ludwig Camerarius, 1573–1651*.

68. Also see F.H. Schubert, 'Die pfälzische Exilregierung im Dreißigjährigen Krieg: ein Beitrag zur Geschichte des politischen Protestantismus', *Zeitschrift für die Geschichte des Oberrheins*, vol. 102, NF, 63, 1954, pp. 575–680.

69. See Pursell, 'Elector Palatine', pp. 130–132.

70. For example, see Michael Caspar Londorp, *Acta Publica* (17 vols, Frankfurt am Main, 1668–1719), i, pp. 696–700.

71. BHStA, KB, 122/3a, fols. 52, 94, and Fiedler, 'Correspondenz', p. 384. The Bayerische Staatsbibliothek, München, Handschriftenabteilung, Collectio Camerariana, is the greatest collection of Camerarius' papers. Titles of his polemic works include 'AchtsSpiegel', 'Bericht und Antwort...', 'Beharrlicher General Rath der Stände...', 'Prodromus oder Vortrab', 'Ein Denkwürdig Modell...', 'Literae Interceptae...', 'Hispanica Cancellaria', 'Der Römisch

Spannischen Cantzley Appendix', 'Der Römisch-Spanischen Cantzley Nachtrab', 'Mysterium Iniquitatis'.

72. 'Je voudrois vous pouvoir ecrire si souvent, mais j'ay tant d'autres lettres à ecrire et si peu de loisir qu'il m'est impossible. Croyés que je ne vous ayme pas moins pour cela'. Johann Christoph Freiherr von Aretin, ed., 'Sammlung noch ungedruckter Briefe des Churfürsten Friderich V. von der Pfalz, nachherigen Königs von Böhmen; von den Jahren 1612–1632', in *Beyträge zur Geschichte und Literatur*, (9 vols, München, 1806), vii, p. 178.

73. Mr. Hugnes, Bouchel, and Bringel. For the identification of these men, see BHStA, KB122/3b, fol. 418, and KS 9254/2.

74. 'Nota, was mitt rotter dinte durchgestrichen, das hatt der Englische Gesandte, sampt und mit Rhat des Englischen Agenten gethan, Es hatt aber der könig in Böheme nicht haben wollen daß solche wortt alle, außen gelassen werden, sondern das diese (deren er dan etliche mitt eigner handt eingeruckt) bleiben solten'. BHStA, KS, 9254/2, fol. 113: 25 November/5 December 1621.

75. For example, see BHStA, KB, 121/3g, fol. 1.

76. See BHStA, KB, 122/2I, fols. 70–3: 1/11 April 1630, Memo from Plessen, Rusdorf and Camerarius. For an example of his participation in 1627, see fol. 213.

77. BHStA, Fürstensachen, 1030: 2 January 1614, Frederick V to Joachim Ernst, Margrave of Brandenburg.

78. BHStA, Fürstensachen, 1030, 26 November 1618, Frederick V to Christian von Anhalt.

79. Gardiner, *Letters and Other Documents*, i, p. 118: 18/28 June 1619, Viscount Doncaster to James I.

80. With 'Palatinate' I refer to the territories of the Electoral Palatinate (*Kurpfalz*). 'Palatinate' (*Pfalz*) actually designated the lands on the west bank of the Rhine.

81. Parker, *The Thirty Years' War*, p. 14.

82. H. J. Cohn, *The Government of the Rhine Palatinate in the Fifteenth Century* (Oxford, 1965), p. 3.

83. Cohn, *The Government*, pp. 247–8. For an exhaustive study of Palatine government and administration from the sixteenth century to 1619, see Press, *Calvinismus*.

84. Winfried Dotzauer, *Der historische Raum des Bundeslandes Rheinland-Pfalz von 1500–1815: der fürstliche Politik für Reich und Land, ihre Krisen und Zusammenbruche* (Frankfurt am Main, 1993), p. 93.

85. Ibid., p. 85.

86. Henry J. Cohn, 'The Territorial Princes of Germany's Second Reformation, 1559–1622', in Menna Prestwich, ed., *International Calvinism, 1541–1715* (Oxford, 1985), p. 161.

87. Bernard Vogler, 'Die Entstehung der Protestantischen Volksfrömmigkeit in der Rheinischen Pfalz zwischen 1555 und 1619', *Archiv für Reformationsgeschichte*, 72 (1981), pp. 158–96.

88. Ibid., pp. 161–2.

89. Anna Egler, *Die Spanier in der Linkrheinischen Pfalz, 1620–1632* (Mainz, 1971), pp. 114–15.

90. Marc R. Forster, *The Counter-Reformation in the Villages: Religion and Reform in the Bishopric of Speyer, 1560–1720* (Ithaca, 1992), p. 135.

91. R.J.W. Evans, 'Calvinism in East Central Europe: Hungary and Her Neighbours', in Prestwich, *International Calvinism*, p. 180. Pareus' irenicism applied to Protestants alone; he was virulently anti-Catholic. For a commentary on Pareus and his views,

see Günter Brinkmann, *Die Irenik des David Pareus: Frieden und Einheit in ihrer Relevanz zur Wahrheitsfrage* (Hildesheim, 1972).

92. The conference in Stuttgart had mixed results. Scultetus wrote, 'Sie hätten uns allezeit in die politische und weltliche Gesellschaft aufgenommen, wollten es auch hinfort tun, aber in die theologische Brüderschaft nimmermehr'. Quoted in Benrath, 'Abraham Scultetus', p. 106.

93. Press, *Calvinismus*, pp. 514–15.

94. He instituted a general visitation and personally took part in Neumarkt. Götz, *Die religiösen Wirren*, pp. 285–90.

95. Dotzauer, *Der historische Raum*, p. 93. Ludwig Philipp's estates were estimated to have a value of 100,000 fl. Green, *Elizabeth*, pp. 30–1.

96. Frederick issued a caustic complaint to the Bishop of Worms in July 1618 about the increasing number of the Jesuits in or near Palatine lands. BHStA, Fürstensachen, 1032, fol. 5. 18 July 1618, Frederick V to Bishop of Worms.

97. For a study of Johann Friedrich's politics during this time, see Axel Gotthard, *Konfession und Staatsräson: Die Außenpolitik Württembergs unter Herzog Johann Friedrich, (1608–1628)* (Stuttgart, 1992).

98. Joachim Ernst exhibited cryptocalvinist tendencies. Hans-Jörg Herold, *Markgraf Joachim Ernst von Brandenburg-Ansbach als Reichsfürst* (Göttingen, 1973), p. 4.

99. His father had been Philipp Ludwig, the Lutheran prince who made his failed claim to take charge of Frederick's wardship in 1610.

100. For an analysis of these moves, see Bodo Nischan, 'Confessionalism and Absolutism: the case of Brandenburg', in Andrew Pettegree, ed., *Calvinism in Europe, 1540–1620* (Cambridge, 1994), p. 183.

101. It is not exactly correct to call the northern provinces of the Netherlands a 'foreign' power, because they were still officially part of the Holy Roman Empire, if only in name. For an account of the rebellion, see Geoffrey Parker, *The Dutch Revolt* (2nd edn, London, 1990).

102. Jonathan I. Israel, *The Dutch Republic and the Hispanic World, 1606–1661* (Oxford, 1982). For an explanation of the development of the entrepôt, see idem, *Dutch Primacy in World Trade, 1585–1740* (Oxford, 1989).

103. The majority of the population was Catholic, and the proportion of Calvinists varied greatly from town to town. See Alastair Duke, 'The Ambivalent Face of Calvinism in the Netherlands, 1561–1618', in Prestwich, *International Calvinism*, pp. 109–112.

104. She also received offers from Friedrich Ulrich, Duke of Braunschweig-Wolfenbüttel, Prince Maurice of Nassau, Otho, Hereditary Prince of Hesse, Henry Howard, Earl of Northampton, and Theophilus, Lord Howard of Walden. The Queen, Anne of Denmark, herself a Catholic, preferred the King of Spain, but because Elizabeth would have had to convert to Catholicism, the match was impracticable. Green, *Elizabeth*, pp. 25–9.

105. Nichols, *The Progresses*, pp. 467, 512–5, 524.

106. BHStA, Fürstensachen, 1030. Nichols, *The Progresses*, p. 547.

107. BHStA, KS, 16301: Letters from Damberon, Murray, *et al.* to Secretary Veyras, 1618–9. BHStA, Fürstensachen, 1031: Letters to Secretary Dathenus, 1613.

108. Michael Roberts, *Gustavus Adolphus* (New York, 1973), p. 42.

109. Clasen, *The Palatinate*, p. 31. According to Häusser, in 1587 the Palatinate and Hessen sent a force of 15,000. Ludwig Häusser, *Geschichte der Rheinischen Pfalz nach ihren politischen, kirchlichen und literarischen Verhältnissen* (2 vols, Pirmasens, 1856), ii, p. 169.

110. Parker, *The Thirty Years' War*, p. 24.
111. Häusser, *Geschichte*, p. 194.
112. Parker, *The Thirty Years' War*, p. 24.
113. Victor-L. Tapié, *La Politique Étrangère de la France et le Début de la Guerre de Trente Ans (1616–1621)* (Paris, 1934), pp. 2, 5–7, 13–50.
114. Parker, *The Thirty Years' War*, p. 2; idem, *Spain and the Netherlands, 1559–1659* (London, 1990), ch. 9.
115. Peter Brightwell, 'The Spanish system and the twelve years' Truce', *English Historical Review*, 89, (1974), pp. 270–292.
116. Eberhard Straub, *Pax et Imperium: Spaniens Kampf um seine Friedensordnung in Europa zwischen 1617 und 1635* (Paderborn, 1980), p. 121. For description of the 'Spanish road', see Geoffrey Parker, *The Army of Flanders and the Spanish Road, 1567–1659* (Cambridge, 1972).
117. Straub, *Pax*, pp. 109–121.
118. Parker, *The Thirty Years' War*, p. 4.
119. Ibid., p. 6.
120. The settlement in 1606 granted religious freedom to the Hungarian Estates and 'without prejudice to the Catholic religion'. Matthias's next pact with the Hungarian Estates was arranged at the diet in Pressburg in 1608 and included 'self-determination for village communities' and 'even – ostensibly – for peasants on the lands of a Catholic lord'. Evans, 'Calvinism', in Prestwich, *International Calvinism*, p. 177 and note #26.
121. 'There was rioting or rebellion in some twenty cities of the Empire between 1595 and 1618'. Parker, *The Thirty Years' War*, p. 20.
122. Besides the conflicts described here, there were many instances of urban uproar in the Empire during the first two decades of the seventeenth century, in Schwäbisch Hall, Worms, Frankfurt am Main, Wetzlar, Paderborn, Höxter, Lemgo, Braunschweig, Emden, Lübeck, Wismar, Stralsund, Greifswald, Stettin, and Berlin. None, however, threatened to incite a general war of religion.
123. A.D. Anderson, 'The Jülich-Kleve Succession Crisis (1609–1620): a Study in International Relations', Ph.D. thesis, University of Illinois at Urbana-Champaign (1992), p. 277. Parker, *The Thirty Years' War*, p. 32.
124. Parker, *The Thirty Years' War*, pp. 11–12.
125. Gotthard, *Konfession*, p. 239. Also see Johannes Philipp Abelin, *Theatrum Europaeum* (21 vols., Frankfurt am Main, 1643–1738), i, pp. 28–9.
126. It has been suggested that fear of a papal plan to extirpate Protestantism in Europe guided Palatine politics, but this is overstated. Weiß, 'Vorgeschichte', pp. 383–492.
127. Parker, *The Thirty Years' War*, pp. 27–8. For an authoritative study of the Catholic League, see Franziska Neuer-Landfried, *Die Katholische Liga: Gründung, Neugründung und Organisation eines Sonderbundes, 1608–1620* (München, 1968).
128. Gotthard, 'Protestantische "Union"', pp. 81–112.
129. Ibid., pp. 82–90.
130. '... qui se détestaient cordialement, n'avaient pas été capables de s'unir'. Jean Bérenger, *Histoire de l'Empire des Habsbourg, 1273–1918* (Paris, 1990), p. 291.
131. Parker, *The Thirty Years' War*, pp. 19–20.
132. For examples see Nischan, 'Confessionalism' in Pettegree, *Calvinism*, pp. 181–204.
133. For some predictions, see BN, MSS 2349, Sucesos del año 1618, nos 15–18, fols 257–83, and Abelin, *Theatrum Europaeum*, i, pp. 100–1.

Chapter 2

Rebellion in Bohemia: a Local Crisis

The fateful lightning bolt fell in Bohemia. On 23 May 1618 members of the Estates went to the royal castle in Prague, declared Emperor Matthias's two regents public enemies, and ejected them, along with a secretary, from the window of the council chamber. During the brutal scuffle, the perpetrators were said to have shouted, 'Now we will deal honestly with our religious enemies!'[1] The would-be executioners, however, did not use a fail-safe method. The three victims plummeted a distance of eighty feet into the castle ditch, but all somehow managed to survive, two completely unharmed. They later swore that the Virgin Mary had broken their fall, but the story that a rubbish pile had served the same purpose has greater currency among modern readers.[2] The three escaped into the chancellor's house nearby, while the men up in the castle pelted them with shots in vain. The secretary fled the city immediately and headed for Vienna to inform the Emperor of these events. The lady of the house then single-handedly barred entry to the men who came to finish off the two regents. On the next day one left Prague for Bavaria, but injuries and illness forced the other to stay behind. This initial failure did not provide the rebels with a prognostication of future success.

The Defenestration of Prague marked the third rebellion to have beset Bohemia in the preceding ten years.[3] This one began as a quarrel over the interpretation of Bohemian constitutional religious rights, and for a short time it appeared that it might remain a matter of merely regional concern. But the Bohemian rebellion would grow to a more serious magnitude than other previous local struggles in the Empire, because it conjoined with uprisings in the other lands under Ferdinand Habsburg, Archduke of Styria and King of Bohemia. Habsburg efforts to quell the rebellion and Palatine moves to nurture it transformed the uprising into a matter of international significance, though it met resistance on all sides. As the occasion with which the Thirty Years' War began, the rebellion was a necessary cause, but alone it was insufficient to consign the Holy Roman Empire to the flames of war.[4] The Bohemian rebellion was yet another fire ignited by a few men's unwieldy passions in a time and place that needed more patient discretion than brazen valor.

Traditionally the tendency has been to interpret the Bohemian rebellion as a war inspired primarily by religion.[5] Hans Sturmberger, however, argues that the three main causes were as follows: 'above all' the ambivalent relationship between the Austrian Habsburg rulers and the Bohemian populace which fluctuated between neighborliness and hostility, the social and political tensions between princes, estates, and the monarch, and, finally, 'in no way less important', confessional difficulties, which bonded the other problems together and added to them the heat of spiritual zeal.[6] Sturmberger suggests that revolutionary ideas and resistance theories in favor of rebellion and tyrannicide originating in France and the Low Countries gave the Bohemian and Austrian Estates a kind of Calvinist 'élan' and 'a spiritual basis' to resist their sovereign princes' Counter-Reformation measures. The goals of the leaders of the rebel Protestant estates were, Sturmberger states, 'to preserve the old corporative state and the new religion of the gospel'.[7] Though Calvinism had only made significant headway in Hungary, Sturmberger argues that Calvinist thought exercised influence in Bohemia and Austria, especially among the Bohemian Brethren, though this group was not strictly Calvinist.

Josef Polišenský also does not share the view that religion was the primary cause of the Bohemian rebellion. His extensive writings reflect the conviction, unchanged since the late 1940s, that diplomatic and political history does not make sense if the historian does not analyze the social structure of the countries in question.[8] He sees the causes of the Bohemian rebellion, and indeed, of the whole Thirty Years' War, as a conflict between two rival socio-economic structures, two ways of life, best exemplified by the Dutch and the Spanish.[9] He has argued strenuously to demonstrate the connection between Bohemia and these and other distant countries during the early stages of the Thirty Years' War.[10] His work, however, has been criticized for 'deal[ing] with one aspect of the conflict at the expense of the rest'.[11] The Bohemian Estates fought, Polišenský claims,

> not for the ideals of religious, social and national radicalism, but for the order of Estates against that of a revived feudalism, for the idea of a Bohemian state against that of the all-embracing monarchy, for religious tolerance against dogmatic bigotry.[12]

It is argued here, however, that the Bohemian rebels did not so much want to change their monarchy as their monarch's religious policy. The uprising was an attempt to put an end to what they perceived as abuses of their constitutional religious rights.

Ferdinand of Styria, King of Bohemia

The revolt began shortly after the designation of Archduke Ferdinand of Styria as the successor to the throne of Bohemia. The process had closely resembled that of an actual royal election, but since it had been held during the lifetime of the reigning King of Bohemia, Emperor Matthias, Ferdinand had become King-elect without fully taking over the reigns of government. The election had proceeded more or less smoothly. The Estates of Bohemia had requested that Ferdinand confirm all their rights and privileges, including the Letter of Majesty. He had complied and had been crowned on 19 June 1617. Protestants had qualms about Ferdinand's reputation as a fanatical Catholic with an insalubrious partiality for the Jesuit Order, but as long as they were assured that the King-elect would abide by the Letter of Majesty and respect their religious privileges, there had been no pressing need to contest the continuity of the elected Habsburg monarchy in Bohemia.

By all accounts Ferdinand was a likeable man with a generous nature, but his tendency to give bounteous gifts kept him in relative poverty. His adherence to Catholicism was more than worthy of a Habsburg prince, but his alleged dependence on the Jesuits did not win him respect among the members of his dynasty.[13] At the archducal court in Brussels, Ferdinand was deemed 'a silly Jesuited soule'.[14] He had received his education at the Jesuit university in Ingolstadt and maintained Jesuit confessors at his court. Ferdinand was a zealous participant in the Counter-Reformation. His desire to benefit the Catholic church seems to have surpassed all other personal wishes. He often sought theological advice before he made political decisions, and his declarations to his confessor demonstrate that confessional interest may well have lain closer to his heart than the interests of state.[15] With predictable regularity, he had directed the re-Catholicization of his own patrimonial lands. As Archduke of Styria, Ferdinand had ordered the exile of Protestant clergymen and the repression of the recalcitrant. He would identify the Protestant religion as the cause of the rebellions during his reign as King of Bohemia and later as Holy Roman Emperor.[16] Nevertheless his readiness to interpret laws to the advantage of the Catholic faith helped to cause the Bohemian rebellion and would contribute to the perpetuation of the Thirty Years' War.

A religious conflict wrecked the peace between the Bohemian Protestants and their Habsburg monarchy. Emperor Matthias had previously demonstrated his inclination to work against the Letter of Majesty. In the towns of Broumov (Braunau) and Hroby (Klostergrab) and on other royal domains, he had been able to close Protestant churches and impose the Catholic confession on the Protestant inhabitants by transferring the land, and the oversight of those churches, to the Archbishop of Prague.[17] Conveniently the Letter of Majesty neither applied to ecclesiastical lands explicitly nor restricted the activities of Catholic prelates. Shortly after Ferdinand's election, this pro-Catholic policy had expanded; the new King had empowered the royal judges to review the charters of Prague's parishes, regulate their finances, and, when deemed appropriate, restore the property to Catholics. This commission had thrown the Protestant parishes of Prague into turmoil. Furthermore, Prague's printing presses had been ordered not to produce any polemics or criticisms of the government, and non-Catholics had been banned from taking civil office.[18] After issuing these commands, Matthias and Ferdinand had departed for Vienna, having appointed ten regents to administer the government in their absence. It appeared to Bohemian Protestants that their Habsburg Emperor and King-elect were moving them slowly into a situation where the very existence of Protestantism could be endangered.[19]

The Uprising Begins

In early March 1618 the Bohemian Protestant Estates convened and communicated their grave misgivings to the Bohemian diet and the ten regents. The diet then appealed to the Emperor and invited the Estates of the incorporated lands and their other neighbors to join them in their protest. Matthias rejected the appeal outright and demanded that the Protestant Estates not meet again. He then called the main proponents of the appeal to trial.[20] When the Estates dispersed but then defiantly planned a meeting for late May, Matthias softened his tone and declared that he did not intend to infringe on the rights of the Estates. He requested once again that they break off their meetings and instead send their leaders to see the regents in the castle Hradschin in Prague. Count Thurn informed the Estates about rumors of a possible plot by the regents, and he demanded permission from the ten that the Estates' leaders could come to the castle armed.[21] Ironically the request was granted with the intent to ease the escalating tension; it procured the opposite result. On 22 May, the day before the audience, Thurn, Wenzel Vilém Ruppa, Colonna von Fels, and others decided that an act of violence was necessary to demonstrate the level of their exasperation.

The Defenestration of Prague did little more than just that. As has been related, the members of the Estates went to the castle Hradschin on 23 May and pushed two of the regents, Jaroslas Martinic and Vilém Slavata, and a secretary, Philipus Fabricius, out the window of the council chamber adjacent to the medieval great hall.[22] Dismayed at their survival, Thurn and his armed men went to the chancellor's house, presumably to finish the job, but the chancellor's wife, Polyxena Lobkovic, blocked their path and managed to dissuade them from further violence. On the next day Martinic fled to Bavaria, but injuries and illness forced Slavata to stay.[23]

The Habsburg reaction to the defenestration was mixed. The news came to Emperor Matthias in Vienna and to Ferdinand in Pressburg, where he was working to secure his accession to the Hungarian throne.[24] While Matthias preferred to negotiate for peace and avoid a war, Ferdinand wanted to fight fire with fire, especially with Spanish fuel.[25] He and Count Oñate, the Spanish ambassador at the Imperial court, had made a bargain in the preceding year that had saved Ferdinand in a war against the Venetians.[26] The 'Oñate treaty' said that the Spanish King would abandon his own claims to the Emperor's throne, recognize Ferdinand as Matthias' heir, and give him one million RT, if Ferdinand would cede Alsace and two Imperial territories in Italy to Spain.[27] With this unconstitutional arrangement, Ferdinand had established a relationship with Madrid that permitted him to pursue his will in Bohemia. The treaty was also symptomatic of Ferdinand's tendency to give away what was not his own, a variation of his generosity that would contribute to the disastrous course of events in the years to come.

Ferdinand's next step was to prevent Matthias from negotiating an unfavorable peace with the Bohemians. Ferdinand and Archduke Maximilian of Tyrol believed that Cardinal Khlesl, Matthias' chief adviser, was the author of the Emperor's reluctance to engage the rebels in combat, so they had him kidnapped and removed from Vienna to a castle near Innsbruck in Tyrol, and later handed over to the pope in Rome. With Khlesl out of the way, Ferdinand and Maximilian then persuaded Matthias to take the bellicose step of taking up arms and forcing his will on the Bohemians. Matthias gave in, but his ensuing requests for aid from other lands had limited returns. The Hungarian Estates remained neutral and urged the Bohemians to make a peaceful resolution.[28] Upper and Lower Austria refused to offer Matthias any assistance, and the Duke of Bavaria and the Catholic bishops of Germany declined as well. Matthias, using his own limited resources and with some financial assistance from the city of Vienna, sent an army under General Bucquoy to attack Prague.

The Protestant Estates meanwhile devoted themselves to the survival and expansion of the rebellion. In their correspondence and publications, they unabashedly proclaimed that the cause of the conflict was the abuse of their religious privileges, and they denied that they intended any constitutional adjustments to the disadvantage of their King and Emperor.[29] Their rebellion was against their monarch, not against the monarchy. Nonetheless, having thrown a couple of the royal regents from the window and having seized power from the rest, the Estates had to establish a provisional regime to oversee the maintainence of the rebellion. They appointed thirty-six directors to function as a governing body, named Ruppa its president, appointed Count sThurn and Fels to the direction of the army, and granted it financial resources.[30] They banished the Jesuits from the kingdom and ordered the confiscation of the property of Catholic enemies.[31] They then sought assistance from the incorporated lands, neighboring states in the Empire and beyond, and their co-religionists throughout Europe.

As on the Emperor's side, initial efforts brought little concrete assistance. It appeared the latest Bohemian rebellion would remain a local conflict in the Habsburg dominions. Lusatia joined the rebellion in the summer of 1618, but Moravia remained aloof.[32] The Moravians' first response actually appeared pro-Habsburg. Karel Žerotín, a member of the Bohemian Brethren who had assisted Matthias against Rudolf II in 1608 and had governed Moravia until 1615, convinced the Estates not to join the rebellion. Žerotín made a journey to Vienna in June of 1618 to advise Matthias to use peaceful measures to quell the rebellion, and he then returned to Moravia and persuaded the Estates to grant passage to the Emperor's troops on their way to fight in Bohemia. The Estates in Silesia sent the Duke of Brieg to Vienna both to criticize the Emperor for his policy in Bohemia and to dissuade him from war. Under the influence of Margrave Johann Georg of Jägerndorf, however, they enlisted an army of 6,000, ostensibly for their own protection.[33] The Margrave of Jägerndorf later led a well-outfitted force of 2,000 infantry and 1,000 cavalry from Silesia to join with the Bohemian forces in October 1618.[34] The Estates of Upper Austria, led by Georg Erasmus Tschernembl, denied passage along the Danube to military traffic in an attempt to protect their land. They also tried to lure Emperor Matthias to Linz, away from Ferdinand, but this failed. Eventually they obtained security for their lands from campaigning armies in return for a grant of 20,000 florins to the Emperor.[35] Lower Austria, dominated by Vienna, did not lend a hand to the rebels. No help seemed likely to come from abroad. In early June 1618 the Bohemians had dispatched earnest appeals for assistance to the Union, the United Provinces, England, and France, but no favorable answer came immediately in return.[36]

Palatine Involvement

While almost every prominent Protestant prince or state did not move to help the rebels, Frederick V provided them with immediate recognition and speedy assistance. The Palatine regime had been paying particular interest to Bohemian affairs for some time. Christoph von Dohna, a Palatine ambassador, had been in Bohemia and Austria since 1617 and had reported that the House of Austria was on the edge of disaster because of the widespread expectation of rebellion.[37] After the outbreak of the rebellion, Frederick sent an agent to assess its extent and potential. After the report had been received, Frederick sent his Grand Chamberlain, Count Albrecht of Solms, to dissuade the rebels from making a peaceful settlement with the Emperor. He was to guarantee that the Union would inhibit any assistance on behalf of the Emperor, and he offered them Palatine diplomatic and financial support, contingent upon the aims of their resistance.[38] By September 1618, Frederick sent the Bohemian Estates a force of 4,000 men, the costs shared equally between himself and the Duke of Savoy, under the command of a mercenary general, Count Ernst von Mansfeld, who laid siege to Pilsen, a city loyal to the Emperor.[39] Because the Bohemian directors did not know about the subsidies from Savoy, they believed that the Elector Palatine alone had supplied Mansfeld's army.

With the immediate support from Frederick V, the Bohemian directors strengthened their resolve and achieved a measure of success that raised their hopes for an impending victory. Furthermore, after they learned in early October 1618 that the Silesian Estates voted to contribute a force of 3,000 to aid the Bohemian cause, the directors no longer entertained the possibility of a making a quick armistice with the Emperor.[40] With Palatine and Silesian reinforcements, the Bohemian and Habsburg forces amounted to roughly the same size.[41] The Bohemians were able to repel the army that had approached Prague, driving it into southern Bohemia by mid November. Count Thurn then led the rebel forces to Vienna, in hopes that a quick and successful siege would end the contest. On 25 November Count Heinrich Schlick and a vanguard of 4,000 troops entered Austrian territory, and just four days before, Mansfeld had taken Pilsen.[42] By December the Bohemians had driven most of their enemy's forces into Moravia and confined the rest to two towns in the south of Bohemia, Budweis (Budějovice) and Krumlov.[43] While Bohemian arms were prospering against the Habsburg forces, the directors decided to explore the possibility of deposing King-elect Ferdinand and replacing him with another, one more amenable to their confessional dispositions. Wenzel Vilém Ruppa, the president of the directors, asked Achaz von Dohna, another Palatine ambassador, to find out if Frederick V would accept the crown of Bohemia if it was offered to him. The question should not have come as a complete surprise to the young prince.

There had been a history of rumors and designs whereby an Elector Palatine would relieve the Bohemian throne of its Habsburg occupant.

Both John Casimir and Frederick IV had entertained similar aspirations, but not very seriously.[44] The repeated rebellions in Bohemia in the first years of the seventeenth century had raised the level of these aspirations for Frederick V, which, for some, were becoming expectations by the time of his marriage in 1613. Hans Meinrad von Schönberg had supposedly boasted at the wedding that his master was 'a better man than the King of Denmark, and that he is to take place of him in the Empire, at leastwise of a greater King than he, the King of Bohemia'.[45] But bragging of this nature is not to be taken as evidence for a policy under serious consideration. Nonetheless, sources show that the Spanish monarchy, the papacy, the Venetians, the Imperial court, and perhaps the Ottoman Turks as well had heard rumors of an intended usurpation of Bohemia by Frederick V, which would have made the election of a Protestant Holy Roman Emperor a distinct possibility.[46] In 1617 the Palatines had indeed made a token effort to prevent Ferdinand's election to the Bohemian throne, but Frederick's candidacy had not been pursued.[47]

The remote possibility of an Elector Palatine occupying the Bohemian throne first became a tentative option after the outbreak of the rebellion in the summer of 1618. Thereafter both Heidelberg and Prague flirted with the other's intentions of union, yet both resisted a hasty consummation. Ruppa's inquiry did not come uninvited; Solms had broached the subject with him in secret during a visit to Prague in July.[48] But because Solms had presented this business as a private opinion and not as a part of his official ambassadorial assignment, the regime in Heidelberg was able to remain silent on the issue until the Bohemians officially asked Dohna to learn of his master's intentions.

The documents produced by the Palatine court show that Frederick wanted nothing more than for peace to return to Bohemia, but the peace had to be on terms favorable to the Protestant Estates and in accordance with the Letter of Majesty. To attain this peace, Frederick was willing to use diplomacy, resort to military means, and submit to no small amount of dynastic opportunism. His later actions show that he may well have regarded the Bohemian rebellion as a chance to advance the current and future fortunes of the Palatine Wittelsbachs. Set against his desire for peace, and matching it in intensity, was his total distrust for the members of the House of Austria. For Frederick, the Habsburgs' intentions were malicious, their promises worthless, and their behavior reprehensible; they were among the reprobate. The Jülich-Kleve crisis had convinced the Palatine regime that Habsburg monarchs were determined to corrupt the Imperial constitution. Moreover, they had demonstrated their willingness to bring Spanish troops into the Empire to execute their designs. In 1618 Emperor Matthias was old, childless, and not in good health. The Palatines wanted the King of Bohemia and the next Holy Roman Emperor to be a non-Habsburg.

But in such a momentous matter Frederick did not make a decision in haste. On 25 November 1618 in Crailsheim, he met with Anhalt, the Margrave of Ansbach, Solms, and Camerarius to consider Dohna's report. Ruppa had wanted a clear, immediate answer, and the general opinion among these advisers was that Frederick should give the Bohemians what they wanted. But he did not satisfy them. He waited until December before he put his response into writing. There was no reason to have hurried. The election of a new King of Bohemia was contingent upon the death of Emperor Matthias, which, although expected relatively soon, was an event that lacked a definite date. Furthermore, Frederick knew that he was not the only candidate under consideration. To expose the rebels' perfidy, the Habsburgs had published intercepted letters revealing that the Bohemians had intimated the possibility of election to the Elector of Saxony, the Duke of Savoy, and Bethlen Gábor in addition to the Elector Palatine.[49] Frederick took the option seriously nonetheless, investigated it with due consideration, but refused to give the Bohemians premature promises.

Frederick's response to the Bohemian directors and his actions through December 1618 indicate his belief in the justice of the uprising.[50] In extending his greetings to the directors, he first insisted that he was not seeking to elevate his dignity or status. He then recognized the righteousness of the Bohemian cause and the responsibility bestowed on him by God. Frederick articulated his intentions in ambiguous terms: 'while it [was] then pleasing to God that [Frederick] should be an instrument to achieve something good for the glory of God, the fatherland and republic, on the other hand he should recognize his guilt if he evaded His will and providence'.[51] Palatine assistance for the Bohemian directors was then, for Frederick, nearly obligatory, but in what capacity he would continue to assist was tactfully left unsaid. This does not necessarily mean that Frederick was merely being careful about revealing a wholehearted willingness to accept the crown. It could well be that a general cautiousness prevailed. A letter to Anhalt, written during this time, demonstrates that Frederick was fully aware of the potential danger in the business.[52]

Despite his faith in the Bohemian cause, Frederick was dubious about the legality and feasibility of the rebellion. In keeping with his status as the foremost secular elector of the Empire, 'Imperial law was the guiding principle of his politics'.[53] He asked the directors for precise information about the Bohemian Estates' legal right to elect a king and how the proposed election might proceed.[54] He inquired about the nature of the Habsburgs' abuses of Bohemian constitutional privileges. Revealing the extent of his dynastic ambition, he said that the main problem with his interest in the crown was that the Bohemian Estates had not yet guaranteed that it would be securely passed on to his posterity. Taking on such a great risk for a dignity that would only benefit Frederick for his lifetime was, he said, 'much too expensive to be purchased'.[55]

He knew that accepting the crown would definitely bring on only more war and suffering. The new king would have to assume leadership of the war against the Habsburgs, a move which would certainly place Frederick's patrimonial lands under threat of invasion. He knew that the Palatinate could not withstand attacks from Spain, the House of Austria, the Catholic League, the papacy, Poland, Florence, and other potential enemies. Receiving assistance from other Protestant powers was unlikely. The Dutch and the French Protestants, he noted, were too occupied with the interests of their own security to render significant help. Frederick was worried about the potential jealousy of the Elector of Saxony, and the inevitable controversy at the next Imperial election if the new King of Bohemia were to occupy two electorates and, thereby, be entitled to two votes. He asked the directors to explain how the Bohemian army would be maintained and managed if a new king were to be elected. He wanted the Estates to send him information about the size of the Bohemian infantry and cavalry, their pay, supplies, munitions, lists of officers, and the state of the passes from Bohemia to Passau and to Austria. He asked the Estates to keep his councillors fully informed of all particulars, and that they correspond with the Protestant Union, the United Provinces, and the King of Great Britain.

Based on Palatine actions until the end of 1618, it is clear that Frederick V's concern for the survival and success of the Bohemian rebellion against the Habsburgs was greater, at that time, than his interest in obtaining the crown. Since the beginning of the rebellion, he had endeavored to win over foreign powers of various confessional persuasions to the Bohemian cause. In these negotiations he was more inclined to support the election of another prince instead of himself, namely Carlo Emanuele, the Duke of Savoy, a Catholic prince and an ardent enemy of the Habsburgs.[56] Frederick was more anti-Habsburg than anti-Catholic, more political than doctrinaire.

Savoy had readily joined the Palatinate in giving military assistance to the Bohemian rebels, and the Duke's first concern was to win a crown. Carlo Emanuele had little interest in the religious content of the rebels' complaints against their Habsburg overlords.[57] He had provided payment for 2,000 troops ostensibly without conditions, but he had commissioned Mansfeld to persuade Frederick to support Savoy's candidacy for the Imperial throne.[58] Frederick agreed. He then sent Christoph von Dohna to

Turin to request more troops and deliver a promise that Frederick would win over a majority of the electoral college for Savoy with the help of English and Dutch influence. Though the claims made by both sides were fundamentally unrealistic, they were submitted in all seriousness. The Palatines desperately wanted Savoy's troops and were willing to make extraordinary promises in order to get them. Although Carlo Emanuele at first wanted to be the next Emperor, his ambitions grew to match Frederick's increasing requests for aid. In January 1619 the Duke offered to send an army of 6–7,000 men and 1.5 million ducats in subsidies and to allocate Hungary, Alsace, and parts of Austria to Frederick, in exchange for both the Imperial and the Bohemian crowns. To make this offer more compelling, the Duke stopped paying for Mansfeld's troops in March 1619. On the last day of that month, Frederick and his advisers decided to accept Savoy's offer and to send Anhalt to Bohemia in April to obtain the consent of the directors' as well.[59] Anhalt then traveled on to Rivoli in May and signed a formal treaty on the plan, but the promised subsidies did not materialize.[60] Palatine negotiations with Savoy continued nonetheless.[61]

For some time, however, Carlo Emanuele joined Frederick in an effort to muster an international group of the Habsburgs' traditional enemies: the United Provinces, the Venetian republic, France, and England. While the Duke worked on Venice and France – he had engaged his son, Victor-Amadeus, to Louis XIII's sister, Christina – Frederick tried to move Maurits, Prince of Orange, and the King of Great Britain to action. In January 1619, however, Maurits would only recommend the Bohemians' cause to James.[62]

The Anglo-Spanish Nexus

Immediately after the Defenestration of Prague, both the Bohemian Protestant Estates and Frederick V had portrayed the uprising to King James I as a defense of Bohemian constitutional religious privileges, not as a rebellion against their monarchy. They had sought to cast their actions in the light of constitutional legitimacy and religious sympathy. The Jesuits, they had claimed, were the authors of the attacks on Bohemian religious freedom and of the perversion of Bohemian government.[63] In the autumn of 1618, Frederick had reiterated this claim, adding that the Bohemians intended to make no offense against their king but to defend their 'lives, liberty, and the exercise of their religion in conformity with the Imperial concession'.[64] Frederick had invited James, with an indirect plea, to take an active, military, defensive stance; Frederick had declared that if the

House of Austria persisted in spreading violence throughout the Empire, he was sure that the King 'would not abandon him in a time of need'.[65] He had described the danger menacing all Protestant churches in Germany and had appealed to James' zeal for 'the true religion' to intercede for the re-establishment of peace and for the rescue of the Bohemian Estates, by whatever means necessary.[66] The papists, Frederick had claimed, 'only thirst[ed] for the extirpation of Protestantism'.[67]

Despite these arguments, however, King James was fundamentally opposed to military intervention in Bohemia. Three months after the rebels had called for his help, he had still not responded to them.[68] In early 1619 he acknowledged that he was 'engaged in case of necessity to help to maintain the Bohemian cause', but he only offered to act as a mediator in peace negotiations with the Emperor.[69] He told the Duke of Savoy, who had sought his support for the uprising, that the military prospects of the conflict were hopeless. James doubted whether Savoy and his allies had the power to remove two crowns from the House of Austria, 'who are and will infallibly be supported with all the forces of Spayne'.[70] James declared that he would not engage in a military effort until 'there was not onely possibility, but some probability also in the designe'.[71]

In response to Frederick's plea, however, the English monarch did make some provisions to defend the Palatinate and the Union. In January 1619 he asked the Dutch to assist in paying for a force of 2,000 men for the Palatinate's defense until the conflict in Bohemia was resolved.[72] Shortly afterwards James renewed his defensive alliance with the Union for another six years. At the audience where Christoph von Dohna received this news, the King asked him if the Bohemian Estates intended, after the death of Emperor Matthias, to elect a Protestant prince, namely Frederick, as their new king. James expressed his displeasure at the idea, saying that such an election would lead to a war of which he wanted no part. He added that Frederick, as a young prince, should follow the advice of his father-in-law.[73] But fundamental scruples about wars and rebellions were not the only factors to prevent James from assisting the Bohemians. Peace in Europe, especially with the Habsburgs, was more important to him than the Bohemians' religious rights.

James wanted an alliance, not a war, with Spain. Shortly after his accession to the throne he had formally ended the long Elizabethan war against Spain with the treaty of London in 1604. The available grounds for conflict had retracted further in 1609 when the Dutch, allied to England, had signed the Twelve Years Truce with Spain. Soon after the Treaty of London, discussions had begun over a possible Anglo-Spanish marriage, between Prince Henry and a Spanish princess, which, it was hoped, would bring the two crowns still closer together and reduce the confessional antagonism between them and within the British Isles.[74] The negotiations had not been intense and had run quickly into difficulty when the Spanish had requested tolerance and freedom of worship for Catholics in Britain. James had declined to satisfy them. The ensuing alliance with the Protestant Union, Prince Henry's death, and Princess Elizabeth's marriage to the Elector Palatine had not put an end to the negotiations for an Anglo-Spanish match; they had given the project more urgency, especially for the Spanish, who did not want to see England drift into the camp of pro-French, anti-Habsburg Protestants. In 1613 the Spanish ambassador, Don Diego Sarmiento de Acuña, later Count Gondomar, had come to England to develop a positive Anglo-Spanish relationship and to discuss a Spanish match for James' second son, Prince Charles. After a short time, James had established a friendly rapport with Gondomar, and the two had worked together on the developing Anglo-Spanish alliance.

James displayed this desire for an Anglo-Spanish alliance through word and deed. To please the King of Spain, he had executed Sir Walter Ralegh, who had attacked Spanish territories on multiple occasions, on a charge of treason. After the Defenestration of Prague, James had informed Madrid that his honor and conscience urged him to prevent a massacre of his fellow Protestants, and so he wanted to act as a mediator along with the King of Spain. This statement had pleased Philip III, and his Secretary of State, Juan de Ciriza, had replied that no massacre had been intended against the Bohemians though they were rebels and traitors.[75] Moreover James had assured the Spanish that he would actively work against the Bohemian cause. He had made it known that if the Bohemians proved refractory during his mediation, he would 'order his son-in-law and the other princes of the Union in Germany not to give them aid nor any assistance'.[76] These measures achieved their desired effect. In January 1619 Gondomar advised the Spanish Council of State that although James' connections apparently lay with Frederick V, the Union, and German Protestants, the King's commitment to peace with the House of Austria was sincere.[77] On Gondomar's advice, Philip III asked James to send an ambassador to the Emperor and promised that Count Oñate would assist the embassy.[78] The Spanish needed England to be neutral, if not completely on their side, if they were to safeguard the Habsburg patrimony in central Europe.

The Spanish regime, it must be said, had not come easily to a decision to intervene in Bohemia.[79] The Spanish Habsburgs could not ignore the plight of their Austrian brethren because of their common commitment to maintain and protect the patrimonial lands and Catholicism in those lands. It was in Spanish interests to defend the Habsburg patrimony from aggressors, and the prestige of the Imperial dignity in Europe was worth a fight when push came to shove. This does not mean, however, that the Spanish regime was eager to commit itself to a war in central Europe on the Emperor's behalf. In the summer of 1618, the Council of State, the most powerful advisory body to the Spanish King in foreign affairs, had been sharply divided over their response to the Bohemian rebellion, and Philip III had had to decide the matter himself. On 15 July Franz Christoph von Khevenhüller, the Imperial ambassador, had informed Emperor Matthias that Philip would give money and men 'as far as possible' to secure a victory over the rebellion.[80] Count Oñate, the Spanish ambassador at the Imperial court, was strongly in favor of armed intervention. He had hoped to separate the revolt's religious issues from the political, so that the Protestant Union would not aid the Bohemians. Oñate had recommended that Matthias offer to hear the rebels' grievances and then appeal for assistance to the Elector of Saxony, the Duke of Bavaria, and the Archbishop of Salzburg, but not the Catholic League. Don Balthasar de Zúñiga, the ascendant advisor in the Spanish monarchy, had worked on Philip III with arguments based on Catholic piety, Austrian chauvinism, and a rudimentary reason of state. On the other hand Zúñiga's rival, the Duke of Lerma, had advocated that Spain withdraw from German affairs completely and direct her might against the corsairs in the Mediterranean.

During the next months Zúñiga's arguments appear to have prevailed, despite diplomatic and military difficulties. Although Philip III had wanted to make his intervention in favor of the Emperor contingent upon support from the French King and the pope, he had relented when the latter two withheld. Philip had preferred that the Emperor compromise with the rebels, but he had come to the conclusion that Matthias was unable to make a favorable peace unarmed. The grave danger that the rebellion posed to the dynastic and religious interests of the House of Austria could not be ignored. Accordingly, provisions had been made in August for money and men to be sent to central Europe. In October 1618 Philip had declared that he looked on the Bohemian rebellion 'as his owne quarell ... both in respect of his alliance in blood unto the King of Bohemia, as also in regard of the Emperour when the cause of religion did nothing move him'.[81] He had been pleased with James' offer to mediate, but the Spanish regime had heard that Frederick was acting against his father-in-law's plan for peace. Philip was sure that the Elector Palatine 'observed not the orders given him by [James]'.[82]

The poor performance of Habsburg forces against the Bohemian rebel army further raised the pressure on Madrid to shore up their Austrian relatives. By January 1619 Oñate communicated to Philip III the desperateness of the situation as follows: 'It seems to be necessary for Your Majesty to consider which will be of greater service to you, ... the loss of these provinces or the dispatch of an army of fifteen to twenty thousand men to settle the matter'.[83] On 3 February Philip authorized forces from the Netherlands and Italy to join the Emperor's army. This measure decidedly swung the balance in the war toward the Habsburgs' favor.[84]

The Rebellion Wavers

The winter of 1618 to 1619 had taken its toll on both the Habsburg and the Bohemian armies, but the latter, sitting outside the city walls of Budějovice and Vienna, had suffered worse losses from disease and exposure. The Emperor's army, on the other hand, received reinforcements of 2,000 Walloons and a division under Dampierre, and soon Bucquoy was able to break out of Budějovice and took control of the pass from Passau into Bohemia. The weakened condition of the Bohemian army increased the insubordination among the ranks, but this was not enough to break the will of the rebels. The Bohemian directors refused to accept a truce, and they called for the mobilization of the general militia.[85]

Foreign assistance to the Bohemians remained minimal; the Dutch continued to promise support and express sympathy but provided no concrete assistance. Only after news of Spanish intervention was confirmed, the Estates General resolved to send monthly subsidies of 50,000 guilders, but only from May through August.[86] The Dutch wanted to make their contributions contingent upon assistance from England and the Union, and both had proven reluctant to do anything in that regard.[87]

Like James I, the princes of the Protestant Union had resolved not to fight for Bohemia, because they wanted no part in a religious or civil war that threatened none of them directly. In the autumn of 1618 at a meeting in Rothenburg, the Union had agreed that interference in the Bohemian war would lead to a war with the House of Austria, or a 'civil war in the Empire whose outcome is doubtful and whose results would be far-reaching'.[88] The Union had decided to recognize and observe the Bohemian rebellion as a cause of general concern to religion and liberty, and they had resolved to allow the Bohemians to solicit recruits and contributions in Union lands, a gesture that amounted to little value.[89]

Since the beginning of the rebellion, various electors, princes, and estates of the Holy Roman Empire and a few foreign potentates had offered to mediate a settlement of the conflict, and these negotiations had actually shown some progress. The results of the war in the autumn of 1618 had convinced Matthias and Ferdinand that they could not simply call for peace and expect the Bohemians to throw down their arms while

Habsburg forces remained deployed against them. Matthias had agreed to a mediation by the Duke of Bavaria and the Electors of Mainz, Saxony, and the Palatinate, set to begin on 20 January 1619. Efforts to bring the Bohemian Estates to the negotiating table had been modestly successful. Although no conditions for an armistice had been determined, delegates from both sides were scheduled to meet in mid April at Eger and to discuss their differences in the presence of the mediators.[90]

It looked as if this meeting was going to take place. The Bohemian diet met in mid March and heard sobering reports about the sorry state of its army and the ever-increasing need for a new one. It ordered new taxes and confiscations of the property of noblemen whom they considered hostile. It called for another general levy to fill the ranks and made provisions for a better sustenance of the army. It selected emissaries for the negotiations at Eger and drew up terms for peace. The Estates refused to allow the Eger negotiations to bind them on matters of religion and church lands; they wanted royal permission to maintain an alliance with the Estates of the Austrian territories for the preservation of their religious and political privileges; and they wanted royal recognition of their confiscations.[91] It would have been impossible for Matthias and Ferdinand to accept such conditions without significant adjustment of their governing policies. Nonetheless, though the chances for success at Eger were not particularly high, the conference would have been a venue for talks that might have led to some kind of compromise.

During the course of these preparations, Emperor Matthias died on 20 March 1619. He had suffered constantly from gout, and his death had been expected since 1617. Exhaustion and dejection had finally brought his life to an end.[92] His death left Ferdinand alone to wage the struggle – Archduke Maximilian had died on 20 November 1618 – and his first reaction was less than bellicose. One week after Matthias' passing, Ferdinand made the Bohemians a generous offer of oblivion, indemnity, and a reconfirmation of their constitutional privileges if they relinquished their arms and sued for his mercy.[93] They did not accept, and the plans for the Eger negotiations were scrapped. Ferdinand then suggested another round of negotiations under the mediation of Bavaria and Saxony, but the Bohemians rejected that as well.[94] Ferdinand had no choice but to press on with the war or accept total defeat.

After the Emperor's death, the rebellion's opposing parties turned to military escalation and increased political extremity. Ferdinand threw his military hopes on Spain, and Spanish assistance for the King continued through 1619.[95] In the spring, the Bohemian army went on the attack. In mid April Count Thurn invaded Moravia with 8,000 men, put an end to Moravian neutrality, and established a regime like the Bohemian.[96] He then invaded Austria again, with Vienna as his target. The Bohemians appealed to the Dutch to induce the Swiss and the Venetians to close their passes to Spanish troops and to give money to the rebellion.[97] The Estates also tried to build a confederation with Upper and Lower Austria and Hungary. They continued their negotiations with other princes about the possibility of replacing Ferdinand with a monarch more amenable to their interests.

As the Estates prepared to depose their King and elect a new one, the rebellion took on a more overtly constitutional character than it had displayed earlier. The rebels' demands had previously indicated that the war might have come to an end if Ferdinand and Matthias had agreed to adhere to the Bohemian Estates' interpretation of the Letter of Majesty. But when representatives from Bohemia, the incorporated lands, and the Austrian Estates gathered for a general diet (*Generallandtag*) in the summer of 1619, they agreed to make fundamental changes in their leadership and constitution, while still maintaining their form of elective monarchy. They resolved to restrict the power of the monarch significantly. They insisted on a supervisory power over the highest offices and an absolute right to elect and depose the king. They forbade his designating an heir and reserved the right to adjust his prerogative taxation. No king was allowed to reduce the Estates' privileges, and he had to accept the diet's vote on all propositions as final. A group of 'Defensors', elected by the various Protestant Estates, were to defend the constitution and the state, and address grievances along with the king. Protestants were to receive the preferential treatment in government and law that Catholics had previously enjoyed. Catholics had to swear an oath of loyalty, and Jesuits were expelled. Members of all confessions, however, received equal rights to do business and conduct trade. The Estates planned to depart from the dualism that had characterized the constitutional relationship between monarch and estates to that point.[98] What had begun as a revolt in the name of religious rights had developed into a movement for thorough reform of the kingdom's government.

Regarding Ferdinand, the diet's representatives voted in favor of his deposition due to his infringement of the Letter of Majesty, his kidnapping of Cardinal Khlesl, the invasion of Moravia, his reliance on the Jesuits, and his alleged vow to destroy all Protestants with the help of Spanish military might. These crimes, they argued, dissolved their vows of loyalty, homage, and obedience.[99] By deposing Ferdinand, the Estates brought a sudden end to nearly a century of uninterrupted Habsburg dominance over Bohemia and the incorporated lands.[100] Their next task was to find a new king.

Notes

1. 'Jetzt werden wir uns gegen diesen unsern Religionsfeinden rechtschaffen verhalten', Miroslav Toegel, ed., *Documenta Bohemica Bellum Tricennale Illustrantia* (Prague, 1972), ii, p. 48.
2. Schilling, *Aufbruch*, p. 414.
3. Defenestration was a Bohemian practice from the time of the Hussite movement in the early years of the fifteenth century. Hans Sturmberger, *Aufstand in Böhmen: Der Beginn des Dreißigjährigen Krieges* (München, 1959), pp. 8–9.
4. Hans Sturmberger, *Land ob der Enns und Österreich: Aufsätze und Vorträge* (Linz, 1979), pp. 76–7.
5. Gindely, *Geschichte*, i, pp. 1–2.
6. Sturmberger, *Aufstand*, p. 15.
7. Ibid., pp. 22–4.
8. J.V. Polišenský, *Anglie a Bílá Hora: The Bohemian War and British Policy, 1618–1620* (Prague, 1949). This reference comes from Polišenský's bibliographical introduction to idem, *Tragic Triangle: the Netherlands, Spain and Bohemia, 1617–1621* (Prague, 1991), p. 12.
9. J.V. Polišenský, *The Thirty Years War* (Berkeley, 1971); and idem, *War and Society in Europe, 1618–1648* (Cambridge, 1978).
10. Polišenský, *Tragic Triangle*; idem, 'El Centro de Europa y el Siglo de Oro de España', *Ibero-Americana Pragensia*, iii (1969), pp. 151–62; idem, 'La Política de España y la Europa Central en los Años 1621–1625', *Ibero-Americana Pragensia*, viii (1974), pp. 69–84; idem, 'Denmark-Norway and the Bohemian Cause in the Early Part of the Thirty Years War', in *Festgabe für L.L. Hammerich*, (Copenhagen, 1962), pp. 215–227.
11. Parker, *The Thirty Years' War*, p. 248.
12. Polišenský, *Anglie*, p. 205.
13. Parker, *The Thirty Years' War*, p. 35. For a good character sketch of Ferdinand II, see Hans Sturmberger, *Kaiser Ferdinand II. und das Problem des Absolutismus* (München, 1957). For an accessible biography, see Johann Franzl, *Ferdinand II. Kaiser im Zwiespalt der Zeit* (Graz, 1978).
14. Gardiner, *Letters*, i, p. 107: 30 May/9 June 1619, Doncaster to Naunton.
15. G. Franz, 'Glaube und Recht im politischen Denken Kaiser Ferdinands II.', *Archiv für Reformationsgeschichte*, 49 (1958), pp. 258–69. Also see Bireley, *Religion and Politics*; and ADB, vi, pp. 644–64.
16. R.J.W. Evans, *The Making of the Habsburg Monarchy, 1550–1700* (Oxford, 1979), p. 68.
17. Gindely, *Geschichte*, i, pp. 24–7.
18. Parker, *The Thirty Years' War*, p. 39.
19. Sturmberger, *Aufstand*, p. 10.
20. Gindely, *Geschichte*, i, p. 31.
21. Gindely suggests that Thurn resorted to rumor mongering in order to execute a premeditated coup by assassinating the regents. Gindely, *Geschichte*, i, pp. 35–7.
22. Martinic and Slawata had refused to sign the amnesty for the Bohemian rebels who had forced Emperor Rudolf to sign the Letter of Majesty in 1609. Their refusal had led to their imputation as enemies of the Letter of Majesty and as the authors of its violations. Sturmberger, *Aufstand*, pp. 11–13.
23. Gindely, *Geschichte*, i, pp. 41–3.

24. The conflict between the Hungarians' right to elect their king and the Habsburgs' claims to the crown by hereditary right was as ambiguous and acrid as it had been in Bohemia. Nonetheless, after protracted negotiations from March to June of 1618, and Ferdinand was 'elected' unanimously and crowned on 1 July 1618. Gindely, *Geschichte*, i, pp. 46–53.

25. Gindely, *Geschichte*, i, pp. 53–4.

26. This was the uzkok war, compounded by another war over the succession in Montferrat. See Parker, *The Thirty Years' War*, pp. 35–7.

27. Parker, *The Thirty Years' War*, p. 37. Spain would not take possession of Alsace.

28. Gindely, *Geschichte*, i, p. 58.

29. Sturmberger, *Aufstand*, p. 35.

30. Gindely says that there were only thirty Directors, in *Geschichte*, i, p. 43. The number thirty-six comes from Parker, *The Thirty Years' War*, p. 43.

31. Sturmberger, *Aufstand*, p. 36.

32. Parker, *The Thirty Years' War*, p. 46.

33. Gindely, *Geschichte*, i, pp. 59–63.

34. Their arrival coincided with the Bohemians' disbandment of a militia force of 8,000 infantry and 2,500 cavalry, a sign that the rebels did not feel the need to use all their resources at once. Polišenský, *Tragic Triangle*, p. 100.

35. Sturmberger, *Aufstand*, p. 37.

36. Polišenský, *Tragic Triangle*, p. 93.

37. Gindely, *Geschichte*, i, p. 10.

38. Ibid., pp. 63–5.

39. Ibid., p. 68. Mansfeld had recruited his troops for the Duke of Savoy in the Palatinate, and he had a 'longstanding acquaintance' with Anhalt and the Margrave of Ansbach. Ruth Kleinman, 'Charles-Emmanuel I of Savoy and the Bohemian Election of 1619', *European Studies Review*, v, no. 1 (January, 1975), p. 9.

40. Gindely, *Geschichte*, i, p. 73.

41. Polišenský, *Tragic Triangle*, p. 105.

42. Gindely, *Geschichte*, i, pp. 74–5. According to Geoffrey Parker, Mansfeld took Pilsen in September 1618. Parker, *The Thirty Years' War*, p. 46.

43. Polišenský, *Tragic Triangle*, p. 103.

44. Heinz Duchhardt, *Protestantisches Kaisertum und Altes Reich: Die Diskussion über die Konfession des Kaisers in Politik, Publizistik und Staatsrecht* (Wiesbaden, 1977), p. 131.

45. Nichols, *The Progresses*, p. 515. In Nichols the man's name was 'Schomberg'.

46. Duchhardt, *Protestantisches Kaisertum*, pp. 133–4.

47. Camerarius had been in Prague for Ferdinand's election and had tried to prevent members of the Bohemian Diet from voting for him. Gindely, *Geschichte*, i, p. 10.

48. Ritter, *Deutsch Geschichte*, iii, p. 14. Also see M. Ritter, 'Die pfälzische Politik', pp. 241–2.

49. Ibid., pp. 45–6.

50. His reply to Ruppa's inquiry lies in instructions to Achaz von Dohna for negotiations with Ruppa and those members of the Bohemian Directors who knew of his inquiry. Ritter, 'Die pfälzische Politik', p. 242.

51. '...da es nun Gott dem Herren gefällig, daß Sie ein instrumentum sein sollten, pro gloria Dei, patria et Repub: etwas gutes außzurichten, so erkenneten Sie sich schuldig, Seinem willen undt schickungen Sich nit zu entziehen'. BHStA, KS,

16738, fol. 162: 8 December 1618, Frederick V to Achatius von Dohna. 'Sie' refers to 'seine churfürstliche Gnade'.

52. 'Sie werden eine so wichtige große Sach der gestallt sich trewlich anbevohlen sein laßen, damitt dadurch weder dem gemeinen Wesen, noch auch unß, oder den Böhmischen Ständen einige gefahr nit zugezogen werde'. BHStA, KS, 16738, fol. 160: 8 December 1618, Frederick V to Christian of Anhalt. Anhalt knew exactly what Frederick was referring to. Anhalt had wanted Frederick to become King of Bohemia for some time. Herold, *Markgraf*, p. 222.

53. '... das Reichsrecht war ihm Richtschnur seiner Politik'. Helmut Weigel, *Franken, Kurpfalz und der Böhmische Aufstand, 1618–1620. Erster Teil: Die Politik der Kurpfalz und der evangelischen Stände Frankens, Mai 1618 bis März 1619* (Erlangen, 1932), p. 144.

54. Ritter, 'Die pfälzische Politik', p. 243.

55. '...so möchte er das gewieß für ein ungewißes zu periclitiren, billich bedencken haben, In dem eine solche dignitet nur für seine person, undt auff sein Lebetag, viel zu thewer gekauffet seyn würde'. BHStA, KS, 16738, fol. 165: 8 December 1618, Frederick V to Achatius von Dohna.

56. It is not strictly correct to call Savoy a 'foreign' power, because this region of northwestern Italy was a member state of the Empire, and its prince was an Imperial vicar. Kleinman, 'Charles-Emmanuel I', p. 8.

57. Kleinman, 'Charles-Emmanuel I', p. 7. 'The Duke had posed too long as a champion of orthodoxy to appear credible as a friend of toleration if anyone cared to look closely'. p. 17.

58. For full description of Palatine relations with Savoy during this period, see Ritter, 'Die pfälzische Politik', pp. 245–78.

59. Gindely, *Geschichte*, i, pp. 80–1.

60. Kleinman, 'Charles-Emmanuel I', pp. 10–14.

61. BHStA, KS, 3733, fol. 364: 19/29 August 1619, notes from a meeting between Ambassador de Bausse from Savoy and Christian von Anhalt. Savoy's commands continued to be quite unrealistic. In this conversation, the ambassador demanded the Palatine regime impede the King James I's plan for a marriage between his son and a Spanish princess, delay Ferdinand's Imperial coronation – his recent election notwithstanding – make no peace treaties without consulting the Duke of Savoy, get the Dutch to break their peace treaty with Spain, and arrange that Savoy be ranked and styled 'Perpetual Vicar of the Empire in Italy'.

62. Polišenský, *Tragic Triangle*, p. 103.

63. Gardiner, *Letters*, i, pp. 1–2, 17–21: 6/16 June 1618 and 24 October/3 November 1618 Estates of Bohemia sub utraque to James I.

64. '...leurs vies, liberté et exercice de leur religion conformement audit octroy imperial...'. Gardiner, *Letters*, i, p. 7: 10/20 September 1618, Frederick V to James I.

65. '...ne m'abandonneroit pas en un cas de besoing...'. Gardiner, *Letters*, i, p. 8: 10/20 September 1618, Frederick V to James I.

66. Gardiner, *Letters*, i, p. 15: 8/18 October 1618, Frederick V to James I.

67. '... ne respirent que l'extirpation de la religion Evangelicque'. Gardiner, *Letters*, i, p. 35: 22 January/1 February 1619, Frederick V to James I.

68. Gardiner, *Letters*, i, pp. 22, 24: ? November 1618, Buckingham to Cottington.

69. Gardiner, *Letters*, i, p. 38: 23 January/2 February 1619, Dutch commissioners in England to the Estates General.

70. Gardiner, *Letters*, i, pp. 109–10: 5/15 June 1619, Isaac Wake to Buckingham.
71. Gardiner, *Letters*, i, p. 110: 5/15 June 1619, Isaac Wake to Buckingham.
72. Polišenský, *Tragic Triangle*, p. 111. Gardiner, *Letters*, i, p. 33: 21/31 January 1619, Naunton to Carleton.
73. Gardiner, *Letters*, i, pp. 33–5, note 'a'. Frederick had sent Christoph von Dohna to The Hague and London to arrange for British and Dutch contributions to the Union's defense.
74. Roger Lockyer, *The Early Stuarts* (London, 1999), p. 154.
75. Gardiner, *Letters*, i, pp. 10–1: 17/27 September 1618, Francis Cottington to Robert Naunton.
76. '...pedira a su hierno y a los demas Principes de la Union en Alemaña que no les den ayuda ni assistencia ninguna'. Gardiner, *Letters*, i, p. 13: 30 September/10 October 1618, Buckingham to Gondomar.
77. Gardiner, *Letters*, i, pp. 27–8, 29–30 (English translation): 4/14 January 1619, Consulta by Gondomar. Gondomar, however, believed that this commitment was more due to James' vanity and the threat of a war against a Catholic alliance than to his friendship with the King of Spain. The two men never came to trust one another fully.
78. Gardiner, *Letters*, i, pp. 36–7: 22 January/1 February 1619, Juan de Ciriza to Cottington.
79. See Peter Brightwell, 'The Spanish Origins of the Thirty Years' War', *European Studies Review*, 9, 4 (October, 1979), pp. 409–31.
80. Polišenský, *Tragic Triangle*, p. 95.
81. Gardiner, *Letters*, i, p. 16: 8/18 October 1618, Cottington to Carleton.
82. Gardiner, *Letters*, i, p. 26: 3/13 December 1618, Cottington to Naunton.
83. Quoted in Parker, *The Thirty Years' War*, p. 44.
84. Polišenský, *Tragic Triangle*, p. 113.
85. Ibid., pp. 110–12.
86. Ibid., pp. 109–17. The subsidies were contingent on the Bohemians not negotiating with the enemy without the consent of Estates General. They actually paid the first three subsidies in a lump sum of 150,000 guilders but did not pay the August subsidy at all.
87. Polišenský, *Tragic Triangle*, p. 116.
88. This was the opinion the Palatine adviser Volrad von Plessen gave to the English ambassador Dudley Carleton. Quoted in Polišenský, *Tragic Triangle*, p. 99.
89. Sturmberger, *Aufstand*, p. 37. For a detailed account of this Union meeting, see Weigel, *Franken, Kurpfalz*, pp. 103–27.
90. Gindely, *Geschichte*, i, pp. 81–3.
91. Ibid., pp. 84–5
92. Ibid., pp. 85–6.
93. Wedgwood, *The Thirty Years War*, p. 91.
94. Gindely, *Geschichte*, i, pp. 87–8.
95. For a detailed account of the Spanish military assistance to Ferdinand in 1619, see Peter Brightwell, 'Spain and Bohemia: The Decision to Intervene, 1619', *European Studies Review*, 12, 2 (April, 1982), pp. 117–41.
96. Sturmberger, *Aufstand*, p. 42.
97. Polišenský, *Tragic Triangle*, p. 115.
98. Winfried Becker, 'Ständestaat und Konfessionsbildung am Beispiel der böhmischen Konföderationsakte von 1619', in Dieter Albrecht, ed., *Politik und Konfession:*

Festschrift für Konrad Repgen zum 60. Geburtstag (Berlin, 1983), pp. 77–99. Also see Rudolf Stanka, *Die böhmischen Conföderationsakte von 1619* (Berlin, 1932). For the relevant document, see *Documenta Bohemica*, ii, pp. 151–65.

99. Becker, 'Ständestaat', pp. 85–8.
100. The Habsburgs had occupied the Bohemian throne without an interlude since 1526, when the reigning king, Ludwig II, a member of the Polish dynasty of Jagiellonen and also King of Hungary, had fallen in battle against the Turks at Mohács. The crowns of Bohemia and Hungary had then passed to Ferdinand I.

Chapter 3

The Elections of 1619:
an Imperial Crisis

While the Bohemian Estates were maneuvering to deprive Ferdinand of his royal crown, the Palatines were endeavoring to prevent him from obtaining the Imperial diadem. Not one, but two momentous elections would take place in the Holy Roman Empire during the summer of 1619: the Bohemian and the Imperial. The Estates of Bohemia and the Imperial electors would conduct their elections independently, but the outcome of each would have grave consequences for the future of the Holy Roman Empire. Frederick V played crucial roles in both; in the former he was the protagonist, and in the latter, the antagonist. Against his preferences, he would eventually vote for Ferdinand Habsburg as Emperor but then accept his Bohemian royal crown from the rebel Estates one month later. Frederick's constitutionalism and religious faith explain these apparently paradoxical actions. A genuine desire to defend the political and religious freedoms of the Imperial and Bohemian constitutions from Habsburg encroachment would guide Frederick's actions in the two elections of 1619. He took the crown for three reasons: he thought that the Bohemians had the right to elect him as their king; he figured that the odds were worth the risk; and he believed that God had called him to do it.

Interregnum

After the death of Emperor Matthias in March 1619, according to the Imperial constitution, Frederick V and Johann Georg, the Elector of Saxony, had automatically become the Imperial vicars, who assumed power comparable to the Emperor's jurisdiction over the regions subject to Saxon and Frankish law, which had placed Frederick in charge of the Rhineland, Swabia and Franconia, and Johann Georg over greater Saxony. Frederick had hoped to use his vicarial powers to bring an end to the conflict in Bohemia by constitutional means. In his published commission as Imperial vicar, he pointed to the impending danger of war in the Empire and his desire to use the office to re-establish order.[1]

His vicariate, however, lacked direct legal jurisdiction in Bohemia, but he could strongly influence the Imperial Supreme Court's administration of justice. Through the vicarial dominance of the Court, he might conceivably have secured a favorable ruling for the Bohemian rebels in their struggle against Ferdinand Habsburg. Frederick had suggested that the Elector of Saxony authorize him to use both their vicarial powers to bring the Court more quickly under their jurisdiction. Johann Georg had refused, saying that there was no emergency on account of the Court, but he had consented to sharing a common vicarial seal.[2] Despite Frederick's efforts, the Court delayed using the seal, which produced aggravation in the commission that he had established in Heidelberg for the vicarial arbitration of disputes. The achievements of the Palatine vicariat of 1619 would amount to little more than some authorizations of heraldic arms and publishing privileges.[3]

Another way to aid the Bohemian rebels would have been to prolong the interregnum, delay the Imperial election, and, thereby, temporarily prevent the accession of another Habsburg Emperor. In 1619 Ferdinand Habsburg, King of Bohemia, was the favored candidate, and denying him the status, prerogatives, and resources of the Empire's highest dignity was in the interest of the rebellion's success, if not its very survival. Frederick V's effort to persuade the Archbishop-Elector of Mainz, the Imperial arch-chancellor, to postpone the election shows the seriousness of his concerns for the future of the Empire. He looked on the Imperial election as a chance to halt Habsburg ambitions against the Imperial constitution.

After hearing of the death of Emperor Matthias, Johann Schweikard von Kronberg, Elector of Mainz, had called the Imperial electors to meet in Frankfurt am Main on 20 July 1619 in order to select the next emperor. In general Mainz was dedicated to the Imperial constitution and to peaceful measures of resolving conflicts between its princes through its authority. As a stalwart Catholic and a neighbor of the Palatinate, he was nervous about Palatine militancy, particularly, one may suppose, in support of the Protestant rebels in Bohemia.[4] Nonetheless he consented to meeting privately with Frederick V in late June to discuss the forthcoming election.[5] While the two electors agreed that it directly concerned the liberty of the Empire, Mainz was confident that a strict set of Imperial concessions would guarantee the freedom and authority of the electoral college. Frederick, however, was not so sanguine.

He pressured Mainz to postpone the election, principally because it was dangerous, Frederick said, to let one dynasty take possession of the succession to the Imperial throne as a heritable right. He insisted that he sought nothing in accordance with private interests and held no personal grudge against the House of Austria or Ferdinand, but Frederick took the opportunity to criticize Ferdinand's Jesuit education and the Jesuits' influence over him.[6] What made him so dangerous to peace in the Empire was the combination of his alleged Habsburg desire for dominion and his ardent, aggressive confessionalism. Frederick reminded the Archbishop that the most important thing to consider at the time of an election was the constitution and fundamental law of the Empire. He probably determined that any arguments on behalf of the privileges of the Empire's Protestants would not persuade Mainz in the least. As it was, the Archbishop's replies to the constitutional arguments were rather terse, but Frederick persisted nonetheless.[7]

He wanted to use the electoral college, as it sat in its moment of greatest power, as a venue where he could voice complaints and discuss Habsburg infringements against the Bohemian and Imperial constitutions. He wanted the electors to have the time to give adequate consideration to the qualities, especially the integrity, of the individual candidates for the throne. He referred to the electors' oath, stipulated by the Golden Bull, which required them to elect 'an honest ruler'.[8] The duty of the electors, he insisted, was too important for them to gather and merely say, '"I give my vote to this man or that man", in the same way that one elects a village mayor among peasants'.[9] Regardless of when the election actually took place, he recommended that the electors thoroughly discuss various aspects of the Imperial constitution before they cast their votes. These arguments, however, did not achieve their desired ends. Mainz remained intractable and would not postpone the election, but in theory his was not the final word. If the majority of the electors had agreed to postpone the election, Mainz would have had to comply.

Procuring this majority, however, was politically impossible. The Archbishop-Elector of Cologne argued that a postponement would only make the rebellion in Bohemia grow worse over time. According to the Golden Bull, he noted, an interregnum should be restricted to the shortest amount of time possible, and he exhorted the electoral college to uphold legal justice in the Empire.[10] The Archbishop-Elector of Trier expressed a similar point of view.[11] With the three spiritual electors in firm opposition, this left the four secular electors, including Frederick. The Elector of Brandenburg usually followed the Palatine cue in Imperial matters, but the Elector of Saxony had refused to agree to a postponement. In April 1619 Frederick had sent Camerarius on a special mission to Dresden, but Johann Georg would only provide vague expressions of his goodwill.[12] He was loyal to the Habsburg emperors and fully supported their resistance to the Bohemian rebels.[13] Lastly, it goes without saying that Ferdinand, as King of Bohemia, would never have agreed to postpone the forthcoming Imperial election, especially when he was the favored candidate. But the fact that delay was out of the question did not deter Frederick and his advisers from making plans for a last-minute obstruction.

The Palatine Vote

Frederick V had no interest in making a futile bid for the Imperial crown himself.[14] Instead he wanted to bestow that dignity on a prince who was not a Habsburg. Members of that dynasty made unacceptable candidates, he believed, not because of their Catholicism, but because of their apparent readiness to trample on constitutional privileges. The conduct of Emperors Rudolf II and Matthias during the Jülich-Kleve crisis and Ferdinand's deeds in the Bohemian rebellion had convinced Frederick and his regime that the Habsburgs posed a serious threat to the Imperial constitution and to the safety that it guaranteed the Protestant religion in the Empire. Habsburg rulers had demonstrated that they would bring Spanish troops into the Empire to execute their wishes, and Frederick feared that they would do so again in order to render the Emperor's throne a heritable possession.

By July 1619 Frederick had decided not to attend the election in Frankfurt in person, because, as he claimed, the precarious state of affairs made the journey too dangerous. A more likely explanation is that, fearing the worst, he had already decided to spend the next month in the Upper Palatinate, positioning himself more or less equally between Frankfurt and Prague, ostensibly to oversee the forces of the Protestant Union. In July he selected the emissaries for his own delegation to Frankfurt and had their instructions prepared.[15] He was considering four princes as alternative candidates to Ferdinand Habsburg: Christian IV, King of Denmark, Johann Georg, Elector of Saxony, Carlo Emanuele, Duke of Savoy, and Maximilian I, Duke of Bavaria.[16] Frederick's favorite candidate was his Wittelsbach cousin, Maximilian I.

If purely confessional interests had guided Frederick's choice, the Bavarian Duke would not have been his first preference. Maximilian had attended the same Jesuit school as Ferdinand Habsburg, like him maintained Jesuit confessors, and had suffused Bavaria with the spirit of the Counter-Reformation. His enthusiastic adherence to the Catholic faith was certainly comparable to Ferdinand's.[17] Maximilian's treatment of Donauwörth roughly a dozen years before should have been especially worrying to any leading figure among the Empire's Protestants. Furthermore, he was the leader of the Catholic League, the nemesis of the Protestant Union.

It is also unlikely that dynastic pride was the primary determining factor in Frederick's preference for Maximilian. Since 1300, only two

Wittelsbachs had been Holy Roman Emperor, Ludwig IV (1314–1347) and Ruprecht (1400–1410), as opposed to four from Luxemburg and ten Habsburgs.[18] Though Frederick must have been well aware of this imbalance, there is no explicit discussion of the interests of the Wittelsbach dynasty as a whole in the documentation from his consultations with his advisers. Frederick did not need a sense of dynastic jingoism in order to find the Habsburg dominance of the Imperial and Bohemian thrones repugnant and dangerous.

Of utmost importance in the choice was that Maximilian actually had a chance to be elected. His brother was the Elector of Cologne. If Frederick could convince Brandenburg and either Saxony or Mainz to vote for Maximilian – Trier was too attached to the House of Austria to be a possibility – and if the Duke's brother voted for him out of familial duty, then the requisite majority would have been procured. The project lay within the realm of possibility, that is, if Maximilian would stand for election.

The Palatines had wanted to place the Duke on the Imperial throne since 1616.[19] Volrad von Plessen had discussed the idea with the resident French emissaries in Düsseldorf as early as September 1617 in hopes of winning French backing against the Habsburgs, but the French response had been resoundingly negative.[20] In the same year Frederick had discussed the project with the Duke of Bouillon in Sedan, accompanied by an English agent, Sir Thomas Edmondes, who participated without appropriate orders. When King James had heard about the meeting, he had demanded that Edmondes return to England, had subjected him to censure, and had dispatched Albert Morton to dissuade Frederick from such plans.[21] Other attempts to include the English in the scheme had also failed.[22] Frederick and his regime, however, remained undaunted, and he had even traveled to Munich with Camerarius in the first months of 1618 to discuss the issue with Maximilian in private. The Duke, believing that the unlikely venture did not warrant the risks, had refused to stand as a candidate, because, he had said, he could not win the necessary votes. But he had also indicated some interest in an interruption of the Habsburg occupation of the Imperial throne, if it could be procured without significant danger. Frederick had left the interview with the conviction that his cousin might stand if the opportunity presented itself. 'It is clear', he had written, 'that [the Duke] may not refuse it at all if he would see some possibility; they are very envious of the House of Austria'.[23] Frederick had also come to believe that Catholics and Protestants in the Empire were not on a collision course. He and Maximilian had agreed to correspond regularly as a precautionary measure against confessional conflicts.[24]

Frederick and Maximilian had had this conversation in light of an electoral diet scheduled for May 1618, at which Emperor Matthias was to have requested that the electors name Ferdinand 'King of the Romans', the Emperor's designated successor. The Defenestration of Prague, however, had postponed that diet indefinitely. Matthias' death had made an electoral diet inevitable, but in the summer of 1619, the electors were to elect a Holy Roman Emperor directly. Ferdinand's position was much more precarious than it had been a year before, and the Palatines now hoped more than ever that Maximilian could be persuaded to declare his candidacy. In April 1619 Frederick had planned to go to Munich again, but an illness kept him at home. By letter he had reminded Maximilian of their meeting in 1618. Frederick referred to the recent, significant changes in the Empire – presumably Emperor Matthias' death – and declared himself fully ready to do what was necessary in order to maintain what little liberty remained in the Empire. He asked Maximilian 'to take good care and not to allow this liberty to be totally suppressed by force of arms and violence or other inappropriate means'.[25] Frederick asked for his advice, guaranteed his affection for him, and informed him that the Elector of Mainz had scheduled the Imperial election for 20 July. This letter reveals that Frederick feared and perhaps expected that the violence in Bohemia would spill into Germany, and that he did not want to have to face his cousin on the opposing side. Because he still did not know what Maximilian would do until the Imperial election actually took place, it appears that the Duke may well have given the Elector more than a little cause to hope for his candidacy.[26]

In July 1619 Frederick, Solms, Plessen, Camerarius, and other advisers composed the Palatine delegation's instructions, which testify to Frederick's conviction that the electors would lose their right to a free election if the Imperial dignity were allowed to remain the property a single dynasty any longer.[27] The instructions explained that Frederick's goal was not to exclude the House of Austria from the Imperial throne forever but to prevent it from establishing a hereditary succession, and they named the King of Denmark, the Duke of Bavaria, the Elector of Saxony, and the Duke of Savoy as Frederick's candidates, though none of these princes had publicly declared their candidacy.[28] Neither Denmark, Saxony, nor Savoy stood a chance of receiving a majority. Maximilian had not announced his candidacy, but he would have been able to do so in the last moment. Frederick said that he preferred Maximilian above the others because his lands were in good order and he was not involved in a war.[29] Frederick solemnly allotted his vote to the Duke of Bavaria, fully expecting, however, that the majority of votes would go to King Ferdinand, or possibly to Archduke Albert, the Habsburg ruler of the Spanish Netherlands.[30] Frederick insisted pointedly that he did not have any private quarrel or grudge against either Ferdinand or Albert, as long as the electors maintained their right to conduct a free election.[31]

Frederick was prepared not to get his way in the Imperial election of 1619, but he did not want to let the electoral assembly in Frankfurt completely go to waste. His goal was to convert the electoral deliberations into a discussion of the precarious state of the Imperial constitution.[32] The instructions ordered the Palatine emissaries to seek the support of Saxony and Brandenburg for a last-minute effort to procure a postponement until after the electoral college settled peace in Bohemia.[33] If this effort failed, then they were to procure an audience for the emissaries from the Bohemian Estates, who, armed with copies of the Golden Bull, would formally protest the validity of Ferdinand's title and electoral vote as King of Bohemia.[34] It was not expected, however, that the Elector of Mainz and the other spiritual electors would permit any audiences until the election was concluded. When it was the turn in the election proceedings for the Palatine deliberation, Frederick's emissaries were to declare, rather untruthfully, that they had no intention to delay the election, prolong the interregnum, or prevent a given candidate's election. Frederick, they were to say, did not want to prejudice the Golden Bull, nor did he want 'to begrudge anyone on whom God and a free, unforced election granted the Imperial crown'.[35] A free election was necessary to keep the Empire at peace, but the large number of Spanish troops in the Empire appeared to put that freedom, and that peace, in jeopardy. William Trumbull, the English agent at Brussels, had informed Heidelberg of this matter before the election. Spanish troops were already fighting in Bohemia, and it was possible to assume that they would fight in Germany to keep the Imperial crown a Habsburg possession.[36]

The Palatine delegation was to try to persuade the Electors of Trier, Cologne, Saxony, and Brandenburg that the greatest threat to the electoral college would be if a single princely house established a right of inheritance over the Imperial throne. One precedent had already been set, whereby the throne of Bohemia was the stepping stone to the Imperial. Indeed, it was said that Archduke Maximilian had intended and Emperor Matthias had actually resolved 'that the foundation be rightly set and held whereby the Roman crown be accessed through the Bohemian, and one would, as it were, lead to the other', which was diametrically opposed to the liberty of electors and elections.[37] The instructions noted that the Electors of Saxony and Brandenburg already espoused this same concern. Frederick wanted to engage the Elector of Mainz in a negotiation over peace in Bohemia instead of hurrying on with the election. He also wanted Mainz to allay the Protestant electors' suspicions and mistrust and thereby avoid a division in the electoral college along confessional lines. The instructions acknowledged that the electoral college had to be exemplary for all other Catholic and Protestant princes and estates, and it was highly undesirable for members of different confessions to attack one another.[38] The Bohemian rebellion was a conflict that threatened to engender a general confessional conflict, and the electoral college should help to procure a peaceful settlement. Despite these good intentions, however, none of these directives would achieve any of their goals.

These discursive instructions attest to the degree of Frederick's concern for the electoral character of the Imperial constitution and for the Habsburgs' designs against it. His choice of candidates shows that his constitutional scruples were not a mere mask for purely confessional interest. It is true that he was chiefly worried about the safety of Protestants under an emperor like Ferdinand Habsburg, and Frederick wanted the Electors of Saxony and Brandenburg to join him in protecting the Bohemian rebels and Protestantism in the Empire in general. Because the Palatine delegates expected immediate cooperation from Brandenburg, they were to pressure the Elector of Saxony in particular. Though the Duke had held himself aloof from the Union, he was still a Protestant. In addition to the constitutional arguments, Frederick tried to make use of Johann Georg's Protestant sensitivities to prevent him from supporting the Habsburgs. The Palatine delegates were to warn him how dreadful it would be for all Protestants in the Empire, Lutherans and Calvinists alike, if Ferdinand became Emperor, 'and how irresponsible it would be against God, the other Protestant Estates, and worthy posterity, when, at this election, one had set and given himself and all Protestantism wholly into the opponent's will and power, so to speak'.[39]

The Bohemian and Imperial Elections

By the summer of 1619 the rebel Bohemian Estates had crossed the point of no return. They had established a federal union with the incorporated lands and had sealed an alliance with the rebels in Upper and Lower Austria. On 22 August 1619 they would formally depose King Ferdinand and four days later elect a prince to take his place. The men casting their votes in Prague would not know what the outcome of the Imperial election in Frankfurt was to be, although they knew that Ferdinand was the favored candidate. The Estates deliberated their election in secrecy, but they would make the results known immediately.

Throughout most of August, during the proceedings of both elections, Frederick was in the Upper Palatinate. For a couple of weeks he was in Amberg, with the Margrave of Ansbach and Christian of Anhalt, overseeing the organization of the Union's army and watching events unfold. The Palatine delegation in Frankfurt kept him informed with frequent, lengthy reports about the negotiations, legal discussions and arguments, official audiences, and other political news. His ambassadors and informers in Prague kept him abreast of the progress of the Bohemian rebellion.[40] He knew that the Bohemian Estates were preparing to topple their king and elect a new one from four possible candidates: the Elector of Saxony, Prince Bethlen Gábor of Transylvania, the Duke of Savoy, and Frederick himself, the Elector Palatine.[41]

Since the beginning of August, the events in Prague and Frankfurt were imposing an increasing amount of pressure on Frederick, and he met it with the same faithful resignation that would carry him through the worst travails of the next thirteen years. When he wrote to his wife of his longing to see her again, he added, 'it is necessary to submit oneself to the will of God'.[42] With evident satisfaction he told her about the alliance between the rebel Estates in Bohemia, Moravia, Silesia, and Upper and Lower Lusatia on terms 'that will not please Ferdinand at all'.[43] He would have informed her of the state of his own affairs but for the danger that the letter might have been intercepted.

At this time Frederick also manifested a character trait that would contribute much to the development of the Thirty Years' War: his tendency to believe what he wished and to expect what he hoped for, in other words, an inability to distinguish the probable from the possible. This tendency was to lead to tragically frequent political miscalculations. When he wrote to his wife on 13 August, for example, he reported that although Ferdinand was expected to win the crown in Frankfurt, it seemed to Frederick that instead Ferdinand 'could well lose two'.[44] Frederick then wished God's blessing on Ferdinand and noted sarcastically that he was 'a very happy prince, because he has the good fortune to be hated by everyone'.[45] The Elector Palatine was probably quite certain that the Duke of Bavaria would proclaim his candidacy at the last minute, then garner the necessary votes, and become the next emperor. But the Habsburgs had more staying power than he thought.

On 23 or 24 August Frederick received news in Amberg that the Bohemian directors had officially revoked Ferdinand's permission to rule and had declared their intention to elect a new king. Frederick learned that his election was the expected outcome.[46] We do not know whether he panicked or rejoiced at the news. His initial reactions, however, indicate an awareness that it would be impossible to hold on to the Bohemian crown securely without support from his allies. He quickly decided to send Christoph von Dohna to England to ask for the advice of James I. Dohna first traveled by way of Heidelberg, picking up special letters from Elizabeth to her father, his favorite, George Villiers, the Marquis of Buckingham, and George Abbot, the Archbishop of Canterbury. In

Elizabeth's letter to Buckingham, she asked him to tell James that Frederick would not make a decision until he received the King's advice. She wanted Buckingham to entreat James 'to manifest to the world the love he hath ever professed to the Prince heere' and to be 'a true loving father to us both'.[47] After dispatching Christoph von Dohna to London, Frederick's next move was to call the members of the Protestant Union to a meeting in Rothenburg, and he informed Achaz von Dohna in Prague that there would be no final decision before word arrived from England.

On 26 August, Frederick's twenty-third birthday, the Estates of Bohemia elected him as their king by an overwhelming majority. The election was conducted under the distressing assumption that, according to one leader in the diet, 'the kingdom of Bohemia and its crown lands cannot long endure without a lord and head', a statement endorsed by the Bohemian diet.[48] The Bohemians elected Frederick in recognition of his best qualities: his pre-eminence in the Empire, his youthful age, his wise counsel, his leadership of the Union, and his connections with the King of Great Britain and the Prince of Orange.[49] His influence with the Duke of Bouillon, the King of France, and the Duke of Bavaria was also mentioned.[50] His personal religious tolerance and the level of official tolerance at his court and in his own lands won praise as well.[51] On the following day an assembly of the deputies of the Estates of Moravia, Silesia, and Upper and Lower Lusatia unanimously followed suit. Although Achaz von Dohna urged the Estates to keep the election results secret until Frederick knew about them, they celebrated boistrously with bonfires and rounds of cannon fire.

In Frankfurt, meanwhile, the emissaries from the Bohemian Estates had not been granted an audience before the electors, because they lacked the necessary commission from Ferdinand, whom they refused to acknowledge as their King and Elector. The majority of the Electors considered Ferdinand to be rightfully one of their rank. There was no sign of foreign infiltration; in accordance with the Golden Bull both the English and Spanish ambassadors, Viscount Doncaster and Count Oñate, had to remain outside the city.[52] Ferdinand and the Electors of Mainz, Cologne, and Trier had come to Frankfurt in person, and they had proposed that the electoral college first perform the election and then address the Bohemian question. The Palatine and the Brandenburg delegations had rejected this proposal, and the Saxon delegation had not been instructed to contribute to the decision. The decision to proceed had therefore been passed, but the election had had to be delayed, because the delegations of the three Protestant temporal electors did not have the correct letters of authorization. When these letters arrived, all delegations but the Palatine were in favor of carrying on with the election. The majority ruled again.

On 28 August a group of four electors and three chief delegates withdrew to the Election Chapel, where the Elector of Cologne promptly announced that his brother, Duke Maximilian, refused to stand as a candidate. Until that moment, the Palatines had hoped that Maximilian could be a contender for the Imperial throne. The Electors of Cologne and Trier then voted for Ferdinand Habsburg. The Palatine chief delegate, Count Solms, probably flustered by Cologne's announcement, read out Frederick's preference, but not his vote, for Maximilian nonetheless. The Brandenburg delegate then voted with the Electors of Cologne and Trier, because, he said, Maximilian had declined. The Saxon vote was next. The Elector of Saxony had only made up his mind seven days before the election, when he had received assurance from Brussels that Spanish troops would come to his aid if the Bohemians molested him.[53] His delegate duly voted for Ferdinand. The Elector of Mainz voted for him as well, and Ferdinand voted for himself. Mainz then turned to Solms and asked if he would estrange himself from the majority. Having expressed his master's preference and facing a truly hopeless situation, Solms gave the Palatine vote to Ferdinand.[54] To have voted against him when he had all the other votes would have been pointless, gravely offensive to Ferdinand, and dishonorable to Frederick. It would have made a mockery of his insistence that he had no private quarrel with the Habsburgs and that he would not begrudge the candidate who received a majority of the votes. Ferdinand's election was, therefore, unanimous.

The Palatine delegation was prepared for failure; hopes had been high, but expectations had not been totally unrealistic. Frederick did not want to give the House of Austria any chance to use its victory to make constitutional gains against the electoral college. After the election, the next task was to extract the most stringent concessions possible from the Emperor-elect. In the Capitulation, the Emperor-elect should not to be permitted, at the very least, 'to interpret the Golden Bull and other Imperial constitutions by himself alone, but with the will and consent of the electors and estates of the Empire'.[55] The Palatine delegation was to demand that the administration of the Empire during an interregnum remain under the Imperial vicars and not be transferred to the Imperial Supreme Court. In addition, the delegation was to complain to the other electors about the presence of foreign soldiers in the Empire and about a general shortage of currency. Because it was expected that Ferdinand would bring a group of Jesuits with him as he acceded the throne, Solms and his company were ordered to press for equal representation of confessions in the membership of the Aulic Council.[56] The Palatines desired that 'the Elect be fettered in the Capitulation', and they were successful.[57] When Ferdinand II signed his Capitulation, almost all the

Palatine demands were met. In general he agreed to uphold the Golden Bull, the Peace of Augsburg, and Imperial liberties and privileges, especially those of the electors. He also promised to make no foreign alliances nor to bring any foreign troops into the Empire without consulting the other six electors.[58] These promises were to have an interesting fate.

The Final Decision

On the day after the Imperial election Frederick received word that he had been unanimously elected King of Bohemia, which was not exactly the case. Either the message did not mention few dissenting voices, or he did not take note of this detail. He learned that his wish to keep the election a secret had not been fulfilled, and he expected Bohemian ambassadors to arrive very soon. He immediately wrote to his wife and asked her to inform his mother of the event. To Elizabeth he could confess his anxiety: 'Believe that I am very troubled about what to decide'.[59] At that point he wanted two things: advice and allies.[60]

In the first days of September Frederick left Amberg for Rothenburg, where he failed to procure the full endorsement from the members of the Union. They congratulated him on his election, wished him well, and exhorted him to care for the well-being of the Empire, liberty, and religious freedom. He should consider no private interests when he made his decision and instead should acknowledge that God was behind it all.[61] Nonetheless, they withheld their advice on the matter for a couple of days. The Margraves of Ansbach and Baden and Christian of Anhalt were in favor of Frederick's taking the crown, but Duke Johann Friedrich of Württemberg, Landgrave Moritz of Hessen, and the Margrave of Kulmbach's emissary spoke against the move. Representatives from the cities of Ulm, Strasburg, and Nürnberg did not give their opinion either way. Frederick declared himself undecided, even when Johann Müller, the Bohemian directors' emissary, begged him to accept the crown. Müller complained about the miserable state of Bohemia and then declared that Frederick's unanimous election, 'through God's special Providence', had been the result of the orderly exercise of the Bohemian constitutional right to elect their king, which was at best an exaggeration if not a complete falsehood.[62] Frederick said that he needed to consider his options carefully and to consult his advisers.[63] When Camerarius spoke, he blamed the Bohemians' opponents for having pushed them to such an extremity, and he insisted on Frederick's innocence in the affair. Camerarius averred that his young master had never dealt with the Estates directly about the business, which was probably true. Camerarius reminded the assembly that God's providence was at work in such situations.[64] The Union meeting ended inconclusively, and Frederick was not entirely dissatisfied. Some had urged him to take the crown, and those who had tried to dissuade him had at least promised to defend the Palatinate even if he did become King of Bohemia, something which he would not forget in the years to come.[65] Frederick and Müller headed for Heidelberg.

The Elector Palatine did not submit his answer to the Bohemians until the end of September. He knew that this was the most momentous decision of his political career to date. Thorough discussion was obviously a necessary step. From Rothenburg Frederick had ordered his chancellor in Heidelberg, Christoph von der Grün, to prepare for a consultation on the several points regarding the potential acceptance of the Bohemian crown: the status of Bohemia's electoral monarchy, mobilization of the soldiery, the condition of the Palatinate and her sister states, the financial resources that Frederick could expect to have at his disposal, the defense of the Palatinate in the event of attack, the Emperor's potential response to Frederick's new title, and expected reactions from France, Denmark, Sweden, Brunswick, Savoy, Lorraine, Electoral Saxony, Bavaria, and the spiritual Electors. Frederick even asked for a list of the advisers and servants that might accompany him if he were to travel to Bohemia.[66] Unfortunately the extant sources do not reveal whether Frederick had decided at this point to accept the crown and was merely going through the motions, or if he had not decided and was making use of his time. Whatever his inclinations may have been, the above request for information indicates that his main consideration was the constitutional, diplomatic, and military feasibility of the project. He recognized that there was little sense in taking on a kingdom that could not be legitimately defended.

When Frederick reached Heidelberg, his wife greeted him with a promise of English support. George Abbot, the Archbishop of Canterbury, had answered their request for advice, while James I had not. Abbot had recommended that Frederick take the crown no matter what, and that he should not tell James of his decision until a later date. The Archbishop believed that the King would provide assistance to his children at any rate, if not in support of their claim to Bohemia, then certainly in defense of the Palatinate in a time of need.[67] In addition to Abbot's message, Frederick had hitherto received other unofficial assurances of English support, and it is probable that Elizabeth persuaded him that her father would not fail to protect them in an emergency.[68] Earnestly wishing that he could rely on England to defend them in the event of attack, Frederick came to believe it.

He assembled his councillors in mid September – Count Johann of Nassau, Solms, Grün, Plessen, Camerarius, Achaz von Dohna, and Schönberg were present – and they discussed the pros and cons of the Bohemian offer.[69] The main advisers, Solms, Plessen, and Camerarius, did not push their prince; they left the decision to Frederick.[70] Those against the project warned Frederick that if he took the crown, the new Emperor could charge him with an Imperial crime. Furthermore, Frederick's occupation of the Palatine and Bohemian electorates together would present a problematic constitutional novelty. There were no precedents, but the Golden Bull neither prohibited nor allowed it. Those opposed feared that taking the crown would infuriate the Empire's Catholics, and the Protestant princes and estates in the Empire would be more jealous than supportive. The Union might tire of their current defensive obligations, and it was doubtful whether the Palatinate had the resources to withstand an attack by outraged Catholic powers. Substantive help, it was claimed, from France, Savoy, and Venice was unlikely to come. Moreover, there was as yet no formal guarantee that the Bohemian throne would be passed to Frederick's son, but to have insisted on a right of succession would have conflicted with the Bohemian constitutional right of free election. The hypocrisy would have been patent to all. The last reason against taking the crown was the most fearsome: Frederick 'would be in for a general war of religion'.[71] A war of religion was Europe's most compelling nightmare, a war between Christian confessions that neither side could win, and that would never end.

Perhaps sensing that reason was not on their side, those in favor of an acceptance argued against an immediate rejection by appealing to the young prince's dynastic ambitions. If Frederick refused outright, they said, he would rob himself and his posterity of an extraordinary opportunity. The counselors in favor of the project extolled the advantages of the acquisition and advocated delaying the decision until they received feedback from Palatine allies. They figured that if England, the United Provinces, Denmark, and Brandenburg sent assistance, then Bohemia could be safely held. If Frederick refused, they said, the religion and liberty of the Bohemian Estates, indeed, of all Protestants in the Empire, could come to great harm. The abandoned Bohemians might, in their desperation, be forced to turn to the Turks for help. The assembly finally resolved that there should be no decision until the Bohemians clarified the conditions on which they elected Frederick and until word came from England and the United Provinces.[72]

This response to the Bohemian offer was only in part procrastination. By late September Frederick had arrived at a typically, but not exclusively, Calvinist explanation for the extraordinary sign of favor that the election bestowed upon him: God had preordained it. It seems that private prayer might have taken precedence over reasoned argument in the course of his decision-making process. Outside spiritual influence had been limited; his court preacher, Abraham Scultetus, though in favor of an acceptance, never broached the subject with his prince until the final decision was already official.[73] However he managed to come to a resolution, Frederick sent the Bohemian Estates a letter in which he stated that he was 'willing to accept', because he was convinced that his election had been the will of God.[74] He told the Estates,

> So from this we must notice along with you the special providence and predestination of God, who gives and confers down from above the kings, princes, and lords, into the hearts of those, who have to elect them.[75]

He insisted that he had never aspired to greater dignities than those it had pleased God to bestow on him. He emphasized that his election was not what he expected and that he had done nothing to influence the outcome, let alone to achieve the unanimous returns, which was not quite the truth. Frederick had in fact made no personal attempt to sway the Bohemian election in his favor, but Achaz von Dohna certainly had on his behalf. The ambassador had been in Prague since 2 August campaigning for Frederick and the Duke of Savoy at the same time.[76] Frederick concluded the letter by recommending that the Bohemian Estates pray to God to bring an orderly outcome to this election that would honor His name, the Kingdom of Bohemia, and all Protestantism. He also urged them to appeal to their friends as well to God for help in this time of great need. He added that he was waiting for advice to come from James I, which he expected almost hourly. As soon as it came, he wrote, he would send his final resolution to the Estates.

To give the Bohemians greater assurance, a letter from Elizabeth accompanied Frederick's in which she thanked the Estates heartily for the affection that they had demonstrated toward the Palatine house. She too noted that God's power had been at work in the unanimous election. She assured them that when God Almighty would grant Frederick the grace to make a final decision, they should not regret the good affection that they had shown him. She promised that she would represent them and their cause as well as she could to her father, the King of Great Britain, and she promised to be 'a good promoter' of their cause in the Palatinate.[77]

The last vestiges of uncertainty vanished soon after the pair's letters were dispatched to the Bohemians. Frederick managed to wait a total of four days for his father-in-law's advice, which still did not arrive. On 25 September Anhalt advised Frederick to put an end to all doubt and just take the crown.[78] Three days later Achaz von Dohna made for Prague with Frederick's formal acceptance. In it he stated that he was willing to accept the inevitable dangers to himself and his lands so that he might, only for the sake of the honor of God, Protestantism, and for the well-being of the Bohemians' lands, 'not to oppose, but much more to follow the will of the Almighty'.[79] Because Frederick believed that God had directed the course of events and expected him to follow His call, according to his faith he effectively had little choice in the matter. If his decision appears impetuous, callow, or foolhardy, one must recall his age as well. One English gentleman attributed Frederick's decision to the fact that he was 'a brave prince, whose yeares may rather moove him to high and worthie thoughtes then to refuse an offred crowne'.[80] Frederick was moved by a desire to rescue and protect the suffering Protestants of Bohemia according to God's will.[81]

The available sources do not reveal to what degree Elizabeth contributed to her husband's decision. In general when Frederick wrote to his wife, he discussed politics only on a superficial level.[82] Elizabeth's correspondence demonstrates that she had only vague ideas about the proceedings at the Imperial election at Frankfurt.[83] Her assessment of Ferdinand's election, for example, was more frivolous than serious: 'they have chosen hear a blinde Emperour, for he hath but one eye, and that not verie good. I am afrayed he will be lowsie, for he hath not monie to buy himself cloths'.[84] It has been argued that Elizabeth, by her own admission, must have done something to encourage Frederick to take the crown – what it was we do not know – and that genuine religious conviction, and not political or social ambition, motivated her action.[85] The extant correspondence between herself, Frederick, the Marquis of Buckingham, and the Archbishop of Canterbury, demonstrates that she only tried to be of assistance to her husband throughout this process.[86] Let there be no doubts: Elizabeth was a princess of great charm, with a rich personality and an even greater intelligence. Her correspondence, however, indicates that she started to become more active in the conduct of Palatine affairs after she became Queen of Bohemia.[87]

Frederick I, King of Bohemia

The news evoked little praise in most European courts. The typical reaction was horror or condemnation, and declarations of an impending, interminable war of religion. Trumbull could not believe that Frederick 'would want to be so badly advised as to accept this dignity, which will bring him a cruel, and an almost eternal war'.[88] When the news reached

James I, it is said that he 'was most afflicted', and he did not understand how it could be doubted that 'this war had become a war of religion'.[89] Pope Paul V said that Frederick had entered 'a filthy labyrinth', in which he would certainly meet his ruin.[90] The other Imperial electors composed a lengthy, passionate plea to their colleague, explaining that his acceptance would result in 'certainly nothing other than a great bloodshed, where only a thorough desolation and ruin of the Holy Roman Empire can follow'.[91] The Duke of Bavaria issued similar warnings in his attempt to persuade Frederick to abandon his folly before it was too late.[92] Even the Duke of Bouillon, who was fully in favor of Palatine support for the Bohemian rebels, recommended that Frederick proclaim himself protector of Bohemia, but he should definitely reject the crown. Even at the Palatine court, the decision produced more anxiety than jubilation.[93]

Given the military and political situation in the summer of 1619, however, the Bohemians did have a possibility of winning or, at least, of bringing Ferdinand to terms. It was common knowledge that the new Emperor had little money of his own, and he was facing thriving rebellions in Bohemia, Moravia, Silesia, Upper and Lower Lusatia, and Upper and Lower Austria. To make matters worse, Hungary had revolted as well. Bethlen Gábor, a Calvininst prince from Transylvania, and his armed forces had guaranteed that no aid would come to Ferdinand from either Hungary or Transylvania, both territories subject to Habsburg claims of sovereignty. In August 1619 Gábor had formally allied himself to the Bohemian cause, overran almost all of Hungary, captured Bratislava, and made plans to invade Austria. In Germany the three spiritual electors and the Catholic League under the Duke of Bavaria had held themselves aloof from the troubles in Bohemia. Ferdinand's cause was kept alive by subsidies from Pope Paul V and the King of Spain and 7,000 veteran troops from the Spanish Netherlands at the core of his army.[94]

The Bohemians' military prospects at that time were reasonably good in comparison with Ferdinand's. The Bohemian army had held its own against Ferdinand's, with its Spanish reinforcements, for a full year. Count Thurn had successfully invaded Moravia in the spring of 1619, set off a rebellion against Ferdinand, and secured the rebels' alliance with Bohemia. In the summer Thurn renewed the siege of Vienna with 5,000 Moravian reinforcements. More alliances had been made with the leaders of the uprisings in Lusatia, Silesia, and Upper and Lower Austria. Bethlen Gábor and his large army were as well-inclined to the Bohemian cause as they were antagonistic to the Austrian Habsburgs. Although the Palatines expected a continuance, if not an increase, of Spanish assistance for Ferdinand, they hoped that their allies who had held themselves aloof would be able and willing to check an expected onslaught by the Spanish behemoth.

In the summer of 1619 the United Provinces had decided partially to fulfill their prior protestations of sympathy and promises of support. They had sent the Bohemians monthly subsidies, and in late July a force of 1,500 Dutchmen had joined the Bohemian army.[95] But Dutch generosity had ended there. They declined to let one Colonel van Mario recruit an infantry guard of 200 for Frederick V.[96] Apparently the Estates General had largely ignored the proceedings in Prague that led to Frederick's election, and they certainly had not encouraged them.[97] Their inclinations after the election, however, were more favorable than not. The majority accepted the fact that their present peace with Spain could not last forever, and they thought it more prudent to act to their advantage than to let inactivity become harmful. A thriving war in Bohemia and the Palatinate would certainly draw Spanish forces away from the United Provinces. Nevertheless the Dutch were not keen to commit themselves to a military campaign without approval and assistance from England.[98] Herein lay the uncertainty.

The English ambassador to the United Provinces, Dudley Carleton, opined that if James I approved of his son-in-law's accession to the Bohemian throne, then he might 'promise himself a joinct concurrence in these United Provinces, and all the assistance they can possibly yeald'.[99] But despite assurances from Archbishop Abbot and presumably Elizabeth, there was reason to doubt that James I would offer any military assistance at all. When Christoph von Dohna had returned from a mission to England in February 1619, he had brought James' unconditional refusal to support the Bohemian rebellion in any way. In July 1619 the King had informed Frederick that the English treasury was in such a diminished state that it was impossible to pay for any military ventures in Bohemia whatsoever.

For James the Bohemian cause had nothing to recommend it; he did not feel obligated to defend the rebels from 'the just resentment and vengeance' that they brought upon themselves because of their 'gaiety of heart'.[100] James' alliance with the Union was only 'defensive and for the maintenance of rights and liberties of the Empire'.[101] Because James was a king, he added, 'it would not be expedient or suitable for us to animate, by such an example, the courage of subjects to a revolt against their princes nor to other extravagant and illegitimate outrages'.[102] James had only been willing, as he had promised the King of Spain, to send an ambassador to mediate between the Bohemians and Ferdinand.

The other main purpose of this embassy had been to demonstrate the genuineness of James' desire for peace. Viscount Doncaster, James Hay, a man known for his politeness, tact, and inordinate profligacy, had been the figure chosen to represent the English King abroad.[103] Doncaster's instructions had given him an impossible commission. He was to restore the *status quo ante bellum* by persuading the Jesuits not to interfere in matters of state, by convincing Ferdinand to abide by his own promises, and by inducing the Protestants to live quietly after they made amends for their war-time confiscations and restored the former government.[104] The result of his audiences with Ferdinand had been unrewarding, and in Prague the Bohemian Estates had given Doncaster a 'hostile' reception, because they had come to believe that James favored Ferdinand's cause over theirs.[105]

The ambassador's assignment had changed after the news of Frederick's election had reached London: it was to defend James' honor as well. The King had ordered Doncaster to make for Vienna, congratulate Emperor Ferdinand on his election, declare James' ignorance and innocence in the Bohemians' election of his son-in-law, and repeat his offer to mediate the conflict. Because the Bohemians, by electing Frederick, had 'made themselves traytors in the highest degree, if theire cause be unjust', James said, the affair had become even more complicated than before.[106] He therefore had requested some time to study the Imperial constitution and legal corpus to inform his mediation. In so doing he had effectively invited a polite refusal of his intercession from Ferdinand. Nonetheless, England was a member of the Protestant Union and was obligated to defend other member states, including the Palatinate, if they were attacked.

The Republic of Venice had likewise been less than receptive to invitations to assist the Bohemians, but her leaders were usually ready to make life difficult for the Habsburgs. Most recently the Republic had attacked Ferdinand's Adriatic territories during the 'uzkok war' from 1615 to 1618.[107] In early 1619 a commission of ambassadors from the Union leaders (England, Palatinate, Anhalt, Ansbach, Brandenburg, Mansfeld), the Bohemian directors, and the Duke of Savoy had appealed for Venetian support. Despite the Venetian expression of good will and their guarantee not to let foreign troops pass through their territory, they did not grant funds for the rebellion.[108]

No one quite knew what to expect from France. Antipathy for the Habsburgs was one of the few commonalities the French monarchy shared with the Palatine regime. The Palatinate had provided military assistance to Henry IV, and some members of the Palatine regime entertained the hope that France would return the favor in their time of need. France had favored Ferdinand in the Bohemian rebellion but had not taken any military action.[109] She had done nothing to influence the Imperial election. Like James I the French King had made polite offers of mediation that accomplished nothing apart from making a convincing demonstration of French neutrality.

Palatine diplomacy sought to create a situation in which France, the United Provinces, Hungary, Savoy, and Venice would all be willing to stand against their various Habsburg neighbors, and, in the event of a strike against the Palatinate, England and the Protestant Union would defend Frederick's patrimonial lands.[110] Such a situation would have severely limited the Spanish ability to provide military and financial support for Ferdinand, and he probably would have been forced to come to terms. And if the rebels of Bohemia, Moravia, Silesia, Lusatia, and Austria could not manage to win their war outright, an extended stalemate could have coerced Ferdinand into accepting a favorable settlement. This was the goal of the Palatine regime that took up the reigns of the Bohemian government.

The journey to Prague began in early October. The Elector Palatine, the King-elect of Bohemia, handed the government of the Lower Palatinate over to Count Palatine Johann of Zweibrücken and the command of the Palatine military to Count Johann of Nassau. Frederick had considered leaving Elizabeth in Heidelberg or sending her back to England till the situation became more secure, but she had insisted that he not deprive her of 'her greatest happiness, to expresse her love to him, and her desire to participate all his fortunes'.[111] They had decided to bring along their five year-old son, Friedrich Heinrich, and to leave their two younger children, Karl Ludwig and Elizabeth, under the care of Frederick's mother in Heidelberg. Frederick spent the morning of their departure listening to a sermon by Abraham Scultetus, and Elizabeth attended an English service by her court clergyman, Dr. Chapman, in her private chapel.[112] With an escort of 800 cavalry and a train of 153 baggage wagons, they left Heidelberg accompanied by Frederick's younger brother, Ludwig Philipp. It was a procession worthy of a king and queen, but for unknown reasons Elizabeth, who had not wept when she had left England and who would not cry when she was to leave Prague one year later, burst into tears.[113]

The massive party traveled to the Upper Palatinate, and in Ansbach Ferdinand's emissary, Count Jakob Ludwig of Fürstenberg, tried to persuade Frederick to partake in an Imperial diet and not to usurp the Bohemian throne. The efforts were in vain.[114] Frederick had a formal explanation of his actions sent to Venice, Savoy, the Elector of Saxony, the King of Poland, and other potentates within and beyond the Empire. The letter sought to shift the blame for the current state of affairs onto Jesuit extremism. If there were to be a general war of religion, Frederick did not want the courts of Europe to blame him for it. In the letter he explained how the Bohemian Protestant Estates were forced to take arms to defend the Letter of Majesty and their other constitutional freedoms and privileges. The Jesuits, he claimed, were endeavoring to bring Bohemia and the incorporated lands 'totally once again under the Papist yoke and an absolute dominion'.[115] He wanted all to know that he only wanted peace and not a war of any sort. Frederick also sent Maximilian a similar letter, asking specifically for his neutrality in the ensuing months.[116] Frederick may have indeed wanted peace above all, but that peace had to be on favorable terms, and he was willing to resort to arms to obtain either. Preparations for war had become essential. While in Amberg he mustered a number of companies, perhaps comprising 1,000 cavalry and 3,000 infantry, and took them with him to Prague.[117]

When the Palatines reached Prague on the last day of October, they made a splendid entrance in the company of many Bohemian and German nobles, and the exuberant throngs led them through the city and up to the castle Hradschin.[118] Before they arrived, the Palatine coat of arms had replaced the Austrian two-headed eagle in the castle's heraldry. The new king's coronation on 4 November adhered to the traditional ceremonial forms except for a change in the entrance processional and the expected absence of a Catholic eucharistic service.[119] Thirty-eight Bohemian Protestant clergymen performed the coronation, and Frederick accepted the blessing and even the unction without objection. Coins were thrown to the crowds, and wine flowed in the streets as tradition demanded. Elizabeth had her coronation three days later, which was equally sumptuous though not quite as expensive, because the public received bread and wine instead of coins.[120] The new king and queen made a positive impression on the populace, although some of the ladies of Prague found Elizabeth's décolletage mildly shocking, and her tardiness to meals and church services caused some irritation.[121] It has been said that Frederick and Elizabeth even won over some of Prague's Catholics with their 'amiable grace'.[122] A good omen blessed the Palatines' arrival – during these days no one in the capital passed away or was buried – but it was to prove a most unworthy supersition.[123]

Up to this point it is better to attribute Frederick V's behavior more to his constitutional considerations and his personal religious faith than to Calvinist confessional interests. He had accepted the Bohemian crown in order to protect the rights of the Protestants in that kingdom, and because it offered a potentially dazzling future for his dynasty. He had tried to frustrate Ferdinand's hopes in the Imperial election, because Frederick was absolutely sure that the Habsburgs were out to destroy the Empire's elective constitution. If one still insists that his goals were confessional, they were so only broadly and defensively. He wanted to preserve Protestantism in general against an allegedly aggressive, unscrupulous, intolerant Catholic prince and his Jesuit flatterers.[124] Of foremost importance to Frederick's cause was his interpretation of the law and the constitutional freedom to worship true Christianity. A contemporary anonymous apology for the Bohemian rebellion states:

It is apparant out of holy and humane Histories, and the examples of all Kingdomes and Provinces: That the safety and prosperitie of all Empires and States doth consist especially in two things. The first is, when the Lawes, covenants, priviledges, and immunities of the Kingdome are religiously observed and kept. And secondly, when the free exercise of true Religion is allowed and maintained, and all persecution and cruelty utterly abrogated. On the other side, whensoever the priviledges of a State are unjustly undermined, and weakened, & the Orthodoxe Religion sharply persecuted or banished; It cannot chuse, but such a Government must needes degenerate into a most outragious tyrannie, and that all bonds of faith, love, and obedience, which doe tye the Magistrate and Subjects to one another, must needes be dissolved.[125]

This statement does not need to have been necessarily true for Frederick to have believed it with all his heart and mind.

Frederick's Calvinism did not have very much to do with the formation of his policy. His conviction of his divine appointment for the opportunity that presented itself to him was commonplace among Catholics, Lutherans, Calvinists, and other Protestants. Frederick's politics were only confessional insofar as they supported Protestantism against encroachment. The Catholic Duke of Savoy, after all, had made strong indications that he would have accepted the Bohemian crown had the rebel Protestant Estates offered it to him. Frederick's taking the crown had entailed the more compelling considerations of legality and military practicability. He and some of the members of his government had calculated the risks and determined that the prize and the circumstances made them worth the taking.

By becoming King of Bohemia, Frederick assumed the leadership of the rebellion and turned it into an Imperial affair. It was no longer a matter of local concern, and in order to succeed he wanted it to become a European affair. Although Frederick insisted that the business in Bohemia concerned Ferdinand Habsburg only in his capacity as an Archduke of Austria, after 28 August 1619, he was also Holy Roman Emperor and, in his own mind, the one rightful King of Bohemia. Frederick knew that in accepting the crown from the Bohemian Estates he would embroil himself in a war against the mighty Habsburg dynasty. Had his hopes for divine and temporal support been realized, he might have held onto his new acquisition.

Notes

1. For a copy of the patent, see AP, i, p. 573.
2. Hermkes, *Das Reichsvikariat*, pp. 53–4.

3. Press, *Calvinismus*, p. 500.

4. Dotzauer, *Der historische Raum*, p. 71.

5. BHStA, KS, 3733, fol. 26: 23 June 1619, Palatine colloquium with Mainz. Notes of a Wednesday meeting. 'P. undt Meintz in privato colloquio in der newen Rahts stuber allein'. Mainz had written to Frederick in April to suggest a meeting. Georg Franz, ed., Die Politik Maximilians I. von Bayern und seiner Verbündeten, 1618–1651, in *Briefe und Akten zur Geschichte des Dreißigjährigen Krieges* (München, 1966), NF, I, i, #87.

6. BHStA, KS, 3733, fols 27–8: 23 June 1619.

7. Frederick's reasons were 'von M[ainz] aber gar schlechtlich beantwort worden'. BHStA, KS, 3733, fols 28–9.

8. Du Boulay, *Germany*, p. 40.

9. 'd[aß] man nicht so blos in dem collegio einer so wichtigen deliberation sagen wolte, ich gebe meine stimme diesem oder ienem, gleich wie wan man nur einen schulteissen under den Bawern erwehlte'. BHStA, KS, 3733, fol. 29.

10. BHStA, KS, 3733, fol. 31: 23 June 1619, Elector of Cologne to Frederick V. Ferdinand Wittelsbach, the Elector of Cologne, was a brother of Duke Maximilian of Bavaria and also a cousin of Frederick V. For an overview of Ferdinand's politics, see Edith Ennen, 'Die Städtepolitik des Kölner Kurfürsten Ferdinand von Wittelsbach: Landesherrliche und gegenreformatorische Bestrebungen', in Albrecht, *Politik und Konfession*, pp. 61–76.

11. BHStA, KS, 3733, fol. 50: 30 June 1619, Elector of Trier to Frederick V. Lothar von Metternich, a student and later a patron of the Jesuits, was Elector of Trier from 1599 to 1623. Dotzauer, *Der historische Raum*, p. 77.

12. Frank Müller, *Kursachsen und der Böhmische Aufstand, 1618–1622*, pp. 237–40. In June 1619 Frederick sent Johann Georg another plea to postpone the election in the interest of peace in the Empire. AP, i, pp. 657–8.

13. Axel Gotthard, '"Politice seint wir bäpstisch," Kursachsen und der deutsche Protestantismus im frühen 17. Jahrhundert', *Zeitschrift für Historische Forschung*, 20, Heft 3 (1993), pp. 293–7. For a narrative of Saxony's initial response to the Bohemian rebellion, see Müller, *Kursachsen*, pp. 148–224.

14. Gardiner, *Letters*, i, p. 63: 11/21 April 1619, Sir John Finnett to Sir George Calvert.

15. Franz, *Die Politik*, I, i, #111.

16. BHStA, KB, 146/3, fol. 69: 7 July 1619, Frederick V to Christian of Anhalt.

17. Albrecht, *Maximilian*, pp. 285–93.

18. This count does not include rivals. Bryce, *The Holy Roman Empire*, pp. xxvii–xxviii.

19. Herold, *Joachim Ernst*, pp. 217–18, 221–2.

20. Victor-L. Tapié, *La Politique Étrangère de la France et le Début de la Guerre de Trente Ans* (Paris, 1934), pp. 163, note 2.

21. Simon Adams, 'The Protestant Cause: Religious Alliance with the West European Calvinist Communities as a Political Issue in England, 1585–1630', D.Phil. thesis, Oxford University (1973), pp. 274–5.

22. Parker, *The Thirty Years' War*, p. 33, and n. 30.

23. 'On voit bien, qu'il ne le refuseroit point, si il y voyoit de possibilité; ils sont en grande jalousie avec la maison d'Austriche'. Franz, *Die Politik*, I, i, #8, n. 2.

24. Albrecht, *Die Auswärtige Politik*, p. 35; idem, *Maximilian*, pp. 484–6. For a series of letters between Frederick and Maximilian, see AP, i, pp. 503–8.

25. 'an Ihrem vornemen ort in guter obacht zuhaben und nitt zuzulassen das etwan durch die waffen undt gewalt oder andere unzimliche mittel und weg solche libertet

gantz undt gar under getrucket werde'. BHStA, KS, 3730, fols 18–19: 13 April 1619, Frederick V to Maximilian. This letter is one of the few extant German letters in Frederick's hand.

26. Schubert, *Camerarius*, pp. 82–3.

27. BHStA, KS, 3733, fols 77–92: 8 July 1619. The document says that these men specifically prepared it, and it bears Frederick's signature. Six of Frederick's councillors were to represent the Elector Palatine in Frankfurt: Johann Albrecht Count of Solms, Johann Christoph von der Grün, Volrad von Plessen, Ludwig Camerarius, Johann Frederick Schloer, and Georg Friedrich Pastoir. BHStA, KS, 3733, fol. 71: 7 July 1619, Frederick to all Imperial Electors and to Archduke Ferdinand. For notes on the meetings concerning Palatine strategy for the election, see AP, iii, pp. 664–7.

28. BHStA, KS, 3733, fol. 87.

29. BHStA, KS, 3733, fol. 255: Undated paper from Frederick V.

30. Archduke Albert, in favor of Ferdinand, refused to stand for the Imperial election.

31. BHStA, KS, 3733, fol. 256. Undated paper from Frederick V.

32. Traditionally the first stage of the election procedure was a period of deliberation and discussion of the candidates to be considered. Bryce, *The Holy Roman Empire*, p. 237.

33. They were confident that Saxony was willing to discuss both the postponement and the restoration of peace in Bohemia. BHStA, KS, 3733, fol. 80.

34. The directors of the Bohemian Estates had written to the Elector of Mainz on 23 July 1619 and, insisting that they were in possession of the government of Bohemia, demanded either a postponement of the election or a concession to them of the Bohemian electoral dignity. Ritter, *Deutsche Geschichte*, iii, p. 36.

35. 'auch unsers theils diese dignitet der Röm. Cron niemandem mißgünnen, deme sie Gott und eine freie ungezwungene Wahl gönnen thete'. BHStA, KS, 3733, fol. 82.

36. During the election proceedings in Frankfurt, Camerarius confirmed the report that Ferdinand was going to receive a large sum of Spanish money to finance his campaign against Bohemia. BHStA, KS, 3733, fol. 211: 26 July 1619, Camerarius to Christian of Anhalt.

37. 'd[as] fundament für richtig gesetzt und gehalten wird, daß die Römische Cron durch die Behmische facilitirt würde, und eine die andere gleichsamb nach sich zöge'. BHStA, KS, 3733, fol. 83.

38. BHStA, KS, 3733, fol. 84.

39. 'und wie unverantwortlich es gegen Gott, den andern Evangelischen Stenden, und der wehrten posteritet sein würde, wan man bei diesem Wahltag sich und daß ganze Evangelische wesen in des gegentheils willen und gewalt gleichsamb ganz und gar gestelt und gegeben hette'. BHStA, KS, 3733, fol. 87.

40. This collection of documents is to be found in BHStA, KS, 3733.

41. Parker, *The Thirty Years' War*, pp. 45–6.

42. 'il se faut soumettre à la volonté de Dieu'. Aretin, 'Sammlung', p. 147.

43. 'qui ne plairont guère à Ferdinand'. Aretin, 'Sammlung', p. 148.

44. 'il y'a apparence, qu'en la place que Ferdinand acquerra une couronne à Francfort, il en pourroit bien perdre deux', G. Bromley, *A Collection of Original Royal Letters* (London, 1787), Letter 1: 13 August 1619, Frederick V to Elizabeth, from Amberg.

45. 'Dieu lui en fasse la grace! C'est un prince fort heureux, car il a le bonheur d'estre haï de tout le monde'. Bromley, *A Collection*, Letter 1: 13 August 1619, Frederick V to Elizabeth, from Amberg.

46. Weiß, 'Die Vorgeschichte', p. 463. I have adjusted his dates to the New Style.
47. Gardiner, *Letters*, ii, p. 2: 22 August/1 September 1619, Elizabeth to Buckingham.
48. Quoted in Polišenský, *Tragic Triangle*, p. 129.
49. Polišenský, *Tragic Triangle*, p. 130.
50. Abelin, *Theatrum Europaeum*, p. 201.
51. 'Es wäre kein Exempel vorhanden, daß jemand von diesem Herrn wäre angefochten worden'. Abelin, *Theatrum Europeum*, p. 201. 'Ob er wol der reformirten Religi: zugethan/bleibet es doch in seinem Lande in gewisser Religions Exercitio unbetrübt/und ganz unendgolten/als daß jeder/der sich nur sonsten Ehrlich verhelt/in seinen Landen sicher und rühig leben/und seiner gelegenhenheit abwarten kan'. This source was admittedly produced after his election. 'Artickel und Motiven warumb Konig Ferdinand von den Stenden in Boheim rejicirt und zum Regiment nicht admittiert, Chur Pfaltz aber vor anderen Potentaten zu einem Konig daselbst erwehlt und angenommen worden', (Prague?, 1619), Houghton Library, Harvard University, Accessions *51–1453.
52. The Golden Bull stipulated that no one was to be admitted to the city of Frankfurt during the election period except for the electors, their ambassadors, their retinues, and the city's inhabitants. See Buschmann, *Kaiser und Reich*, pp. 118–19.
53. Parker, *The Thirty Years' War*, p. 50.
54. Gindely, *Geschichte*, i, pp. 109–14.
55. 'die güldene Bull und andere Reichs Constitutiones vor sich allein, sondern mit willen und consens der Churfürsten und Stendt des Reichs zu declariren', BHStA, KS, 3733, fols 90–1.
56. BHStA, KS, 3733, fol. 92.
57. 'der Electus in der Capitulation auch vinculirt werde', BHStA, KS, 3733, fol. 92.
58. AP, i, pp. 700–5.
59. 'Croyées que je suis bien en peine à quoy me résoudre'. Aretin, 'Sammlung', p. 148. 19/29 August 1619, Frederick V to Elizabeth.
60. On 28 August he wrote to his delegates in Frankfurt to ask their advice. Franz, *Die Politik*, I, i, #120.
61. Weiß, 'Die Vorgeschichte', p. 464.
62. 'durch sonderbare Vorsehung Gottes', StUAP, ACK, 2345: 14/24 September 1619, Frederick V to the Protestant Estates of Bohemia.
63. Weiß, 'Die Vorgeschichte', pp. 464–5.
64. Ritter, 'Die pfälzische Politik', p. 283.
65. In April of 1621, after the Union abandoned their defense of the Palatinate, Frederick said, 'Je trouve bien estonne d'estre abandonne de ceux qui m'a voÿent tant promis de deffendre le palatinat sans la quelle promesse je ne fusse jamais entre en la Boheme'. PRO, SP, 81/20, fol. 331: 12/22 April 1621, Frederick V to James I.
66. BHStA, KS, 3733, fols 397–8: 6 September 1619, Frederick V to Johan Christof von der Grün.
67. G. Goodman, *The Court of James I* (London, 1839), i, pp. 238–40. Cited in Weiß, 'Die Vorgeschichte', p. 465.
68. According to Achaz von Dohna, James had told Baron Christof von Dohna that the Bohemian Estates, in the event of Emperor Matthias' death, would receive English favor and assistance against Ferdinand if they published their complaints and continued to show their favor for Frederick. PRO, SP, 81/20, fol. 355: January 1621, Remonstrance of Achaz von Dohna to James I.
69. Weiß, 'Die Vorgeschichte', pp. 466–7, and C. van Eickels, *Schlesien im böhmischen Ständestaat* (Böhlau, 1994), pp. 230–1.

70. Ritter, *Deutsche Geschichte*, pp. 49, 51. Johann Michael Söltl, *Der Religionskrieg in Deutschland* (3 vols, Hamburg, 1840–2), iii, p. 144.

71. Weiß, 'Die Vorgeschichte', p. 467.

72. Ibid.

73. Benrath, 'Abraham Scultetus', pp. 109–10.

74. 'willig zu acceptiren'. StUAP, ACK, 2345: 14/24 September 1619, Frederick V to the Protestant Estates of Bohemia, p. 2.

75. 'So müssen wir mit und neben E. L. und euch daraus die sonderbare providentz und versehung Gottes, der die könige, Fürsten undt herren von oben herab in die herzen deren, welche sie zuerkiesen haben, gibt und verleihet, spüren'. StUAP, ACK, 2345: 14/24 September 1619, Frederick V to the Protestant Estates of Bohemia, p. 3.

76. Ritter, *Deutsche Geschichte*, iii, pp. 36, 48–9. Konrad Pawel had also served in Prague for the Palatine regime in 1619. Press, *Calvinismus*, p. 487, note #23.

77. 'eine gute beförderin sein', StUAP, ACK, 2346: 14/24 September 1619, Elizabeth to the Directors of the Bohemian Protestant Estates.

78. Ritter, *Deutsche Geschichte*, iii, pp. 51–2. Gindely, *Geschichte*, i, p. 127.

79. 'solchem Willen des Allmächtigen nicht zu widerstreben, sondern vielmehr demselben zu folgen'. Cited in Weiß, 'Die Vorgeschichte', p. 468.

80. Gardiner, *Letters*, ii, p. 61: Lord Digby to Francis Cottington, September, 1619.

81. Bayer, 'Churfürst Friedrich V', p. 12.

82. See Aretin, 'Sammlung', pp. 141–209 and 261–78, and Bromley, *A Collection.*

83. Weiß, 'Die Vorgeschichte', pp. 458–9.

84. Gardiner, *Letters*, ii, p. 1.

85. Weiß, 'Die Vorgeschichte', pp. 480–3. Also see Bayer, 'Churfürst Friedrich V', p. 12.

86. S. C. Lomas seconds this opinion in the 'Introduction' in Green, *Elizabeth*, p. xviii.

87. For a collection of her letters, see L.M. Baker, *The Letters of Elizabeth, Queen of Bohemia* (London, 1953).

88. 'voudroit estre si mal advisé que de acceptier cette dignité la qui lauy apportera sur les bras une guerre cruelle, & casi immortelle'. BHStA, KS, 3733, fol. 410: 4/14 September 1619, Trumbull to 'Medessema'.

89. 'se congojo muchissimo', Gardiner, *Letters*, ii, p. 22: 17/27 September 1619, Julian Sanchez de Ulloa to Philip III; 'questa guerra si facesse per guerra di religione', Ibid., p. 24: 17/27 September 1619, Pietro Antonio Marioni to the Doge.

90. 'in ein schmutziges Labyrinth', Gindely, *Geschichte*, i, p. 136.

91. 'nichts anders und gewissers, als ein groß Blutvergiessung, wo nicht ein gründliche Desolation unnd Ruin deß Heiligen Römischen Reichs erfolgen kan'. AP, i, p. 718.

92. Abelin, *Theatrum Europeum*, pp. 205–7.

93. Ritter, *Deutsche Geschichte*, iii, p. 52.

94. Parker, *The Thirty Years' War*, p. 46.

95. This force not does appear to have been very helpful. Rather than engaging the enemy, they seem to have fomented discord in the ranks and abused the local populace more than the local soldiery was want to do. Polišenský, *Tragic Triangle*, p. 128.

96. Frederick had asked the Estates General to give him 'two of the best soldiers from each company'. Polišenský, *Tragic Triangle*, p. 125.

97. Polišenský, *Tragic Triangle*, p. 130.

98. Ibid., p. 109.

99. Gardiner, *Letters*, ii, pp. 7–8: 3/13 September 1619, Dudley Carleton to Robert Naunton.

100. 'le iuste resentiment et vengence', 'gayeté de coeur', BHStA, KS, 16739, fol. 116: 4/14 July 1619, James I to Frederick V.

101. 'pour la defensive, et pour la manutention des droits et libertez de l'Empire', Ibid.

102. 'il ne nous seroit pas expedient ny convenable d'animer par un tel exemple les courages des sujects a la revolte contre leurs Princes ni à des attentats extravagants & illegitimes', Ibid. For a full discussion of the English reaction to the Bohemian crisis, see Adams, 'Protestant Cause', pp. 270–308.

103. Gardiner, *Letters*, i, p. xxxi. The embassy was expected to cost at least £30,000, and two ships were necessary to carry roughly 150 gentlemen, secretaries, couriers, and other servants to the Continent. Edward McCabe, 'England's Foreign Policy in 1619: Lord Doncaster's Embassy to the Princes of Germany', *Mitteilungen des Instituts für Österreichische Geschichtsforschung*, 58 (Graz, 1950), pp. 473.

104. Gardiner, *Letters*, i, pp. 68 (Spanish), 73–4 (English translation): 14/24 April 1619, Instructions to Doncaster.

105. McCabe, 'England's Foreign Policy', p. 476.

106. Gardiner, *Letters*, ii, p. 58: Instructions to Viscount Doncaster.

107. Parker, *The Thirty Years' War*, pp. 35–8.

108. Hans von Zwiedineck-Südenhorst, *Die Politik der Republik Venedig während des Dreissigjährigen Krieges* (2 vols., Stuttgart, 1882–5), i, pp. 60–6.

109. Tapié, *La Politique Étrangère*, livre ii, ch. ii.

110. See Adams, 'Protestant Cause', p. 279.

111. Gardiner, *Letters*, ii, p. 47: 27 September/7 October 1619, Doncaster to Naunton.

112. John Harrison, *A short relation of the departure of the high and mightie Prince Frederick King Elect of Bohemia* (Dort, 1619).

113. Ritter, 'Friedrich V', p. 626.

114. Georg Tumbült, 'Die kaiserliche Sendung', pp. 15–16.

115. 'gantz und gar widerumb unter das Bäpstliche Joch und einen absolutum dominatum', AP, ii, p. 22.

116. BHStA, KS, 3730, fol. 137: 7/17 October 1619, Frederick V to Maximilian.

117. These estimates are from the report from the visiting Imperial ambassador. Tumbült, 'Die kaiserliche Sendung', p. 14.

118. For a description of the entry, see AP, i, pp. 725–6.

119. For a full text of the coronation in English, see Harrison, *A short relation*. Also see AP, i, pp. 727–9.

120. Green, *Elizabeth*, p. 141.

121. AP, i, p. 861.

122. Green, *Elizabeth*, p. 142.

123. AP, i, p. 727.

124. AP, i, pp. 730–3.

125. 'A cleare demonstration, that Ferdinand is by his owne demerits fallen from the kingdome of Bohemia, and the incorporate prouinces. Written by a noble-man of Polonia. And translated out of the second edition enlarged. at Dort. Printed by George Waters'. (1619?) Houghton Library, Harvard University, STC 10811.

Chapter 4

The New King, 1619–1620

A single anecdote says much about Frederick's approach to his new kingship. While on a royal progress to Brünn (Brno) in Moravia, he paid a visit to a small community of Anabaptists, one of the Christian sects most reviled by both other Protestants and Roman Catholics in the early seventeenth century. This particular group was situated between Brünn and the mansion where Frederick was staying; they were most likely not welcome within the town walls. They gave him as presents an iron bedstead, a few knives, and fur gloves, and for the Queen, some vases. When Frederick wrote to his wife, he made no comment about their religion, but praised the fine quality of their wares and added that if the Anabaptists were in the vicinity of Prague, then he 'would visit them quite often'.[1] Evidently he had found their company tolerable, if not pleasant. He did not seem to care about their beliefs and religious practices. He said nothing about anyone else's reaction to his visit. This event shows the level of his confessional tolerance, which he wanted to extend to everyone in his new kingdom, even to the most marginal groups.

In the annals of history the most memorable event in Frederick's reign as King of Bohemia was the military débâcle that brought down his government after one year, the Battle of White Mountain on 8 November 1620, but it is a mistake to assume that utter defeat was the inevitable result of Frederick's coronation. C.V. Wedgwood imbues the events of this period with a sense of impending doom, describing the utter futility of the venture and the awesome stupidity of Frederick and his adherents.[2] If later generations, however, are to do justice to the motives, aspirations, and desires of historical protagonists, then they should abstain from the self-gratifying practice of declaring in absolute terms the future of the distant past. Frederick's new regime had a certain chance of survival, and its behavior shows that it had a measure of confidence in its own success. In one sense precedent was in their favor. Recent rebellions in Bohemia had extracted favorable resolutions from the Habsburg emperors. Furthermore, the military advantage usually lay with the defenders of strongholds rather than with the attackers in the field.

The regime failed nonetheless, but not through the King's fault alone. Frederick appears to have done all that he could to erect a solid, stable, tolerant government and to defend it from its enemies. The main cause of the downfall lay in two fundamental weaknesses: the new government's inability to force the Estates to make the necessary financial contributions and its ineffective diplomatic relations. The rebellion's cause did not significantly excite the broad confessional sympathies of Protestants in and beyond the Empire who were not already engaged in the struggle. As a result there was no unified Protestant effort to guarantee the new regime's survival. To the contrary, the interest of peace in the Empire managed to unify enough members of all Christian confessions against the regime so that the rebels were ultimately forced to face alone the powerful array of the Habsburgs and their allies. Ferdinand's success was due to the strength of his bond with Spain and his willingness to entice the intervention of the Duke of Bavaria with a bouquet of seductive though constitutionally dubious prizes.

The Palatine-Bohemian Regime

For the short amount of time that he ruled as King of Bohemia, Frederick proved to be a fairly competent, passably intelligent, and seemingly committed monarch. After arriving in Prague, Frederick did not try to take more power than was already allotted to him; he allowed high offices to remain in the hands of those who had offered him the crown. Shortly before his coronation, the Bohemian general assembly (*Generallandtag*) transferred the reigns of government from the directors to the King, including full command of the military and the receipt of half of all tolls, taxes, and government income, leaving a quarter for the Queen.[3] Frederick did not attempt to replace the Bohemian regime with the Palatine. The Estates maintained their advisory capacity and participated in the selection of government officials. All the premier offices were assigned to leaders of the rebellion and the former directors, and none of Frederick's privy councilors received a Bohemian office.[4] Only Christian of Anhalt was able to take command of the military leadership, which had been previously shared by Counts Hohenlohe and Thurn, because the directors favored the idea, having actually offered it to him in the preceding August. Although there appears to have been competition in the allocation of the highest Bohemian offices and among the organs of the royal government, the greatest problem in the new monarchy was a lack of money and allies, not a misdirected sense of its mission.[5]

A contemporary caricature accused Frederick of having had the absurd ambition to 'teach the world, and to reform all schools, churches, and law courts, and to bring everything to the state in which Adam found it'.[6] One prominent historian has argued that this source reveals 'the vast scope of the "Palatine's politics" as a religious movement for reforming church and empire, ... the Frederickian movement'.[7] If Frederick had entertained any intention to accomplish such a wildly unrealistic project, he did almost nothing for it during his year in Bohemia. In any case the caricature is a piece of libel literature intended as an attack, not as an analysis. Its author exaggerated Frederick's intentions to make him appear outrageous or repugnant to the reader, but his actions exonerate him of the charge.

During his admittedly short reign, the new King of Bohemia personally ordered the reformation of a single Roman Catholic church, the cathedral at the Hradschin, the royal place of worship, as was his prerogative.[8] On 21 December 1619 Frederick converted the St. Vitus' Cathedral into a Calvinist church. The paraphernalia of Catholic worship – images, altars, crucifixes, relics, memorial slabs, and so on. – were removed, and Calvinist services were instituted. The high magistrates in the Bohemian government who encouraged the renovation were supposedly seen carrying images of saints out of the church. When Count Thurn warned the King about a potentially negative reaction among the populace toward the deed, Frederick supposedly answered, 'I myself neither did it nor bid it; your people have done it themselves and wanted it so; I let it happen'.[9] Whether these words were spoken truthfully or not, the decision to reform the royal church belonged to King Frederick, and members of his government supported it. His court preacher, Abraham Scultetus, had also requested that the job be done, but a stated request is not evidence of direct influence.[10] Scultetus, who had been unable to alter the form of Frederick's coronation rite, was probably not the driving force behind a standard Calvinist reformation of a hitherto Catholic cathedral.[11]

The deed was not universally popular. Naturally the reformation of the cathedral and then the spectacle of King Frederick breaking the bread at the Christmas service horrified those people whose confessional orientation did not match his own.[12] One can hardly expect a Catholic to have been pleased with either event, but on the other hand, a Calvinist king could not have reasonably been expected to tolerate forms of Catholic or even Lutheran worship in his own church. Frederick did not make an example of St. Vitus as a general warning for the future of all non-Calvinist Bohemian churches. His orders for the reformation of St. Vitus were consistent with the requirements for a Calvinist house of worship.[13] On one notable occasion Frederick made an attempt to impose his reformed religion on Prague's public space. Soon after the reformation of St. Vitus', he ordered the removal of the crucifix and the figures of the Virgin Mary and St. John from the bridge over the Moldau, but when a crowd of people immediately and threateningly manifested their displeasure, he rescinded the order.[14] The Jesuit church in Prague was also a target of official iconoclasm, but there seems to have been little or no public outcry concerning it.

As far as the sources indicate, Frederick may not have tried to impose Calvinism on any of the parish churches in Prague or throughout Bohemia and the incorporated lands, let alone in the Holy Roman Empire, during his short reign, with the exception of the Jesuit church in Brünn that he granted to the Calvinist *Brüderunität*.[15] Had he attempted to do so, the outrage probably would have been similar to that over the figures on the Moldau bridge, except on a national scale. It is safe to say that a concerted effort at reformation and conversion would have been foolhardy in the extreme.

The new King and Queen of Bohemia tried to stand for religious tolerance. Their actions were supposed to promote intra-confessional understanding, particularly between Protestants. Elizabeth sometimes took the eucharist with her husband according to his Calvinist rite and sometimes from her private English clergyman. The confessional dividing lines between Protestants may not have been as clear then as they are to historians now. After six months in Prague, Elizabeth was still surprised that 'all the people firmly believed that [she] was a Lutheran'.[16] Shortly after his coronation, Frederick had proclaimed his tolerance of all religions and his commitment to obey the dictates of the Letter of Majesty. In an address to the people of his new country and to all princes in the Empire, he had promised

> that we, also by such government, have been strongly moved to molest and oppress no one on account of their religion (if they show themselves peaceful and irreproachable first to the constitutions of the Kingdom and of the [Incorporated] Lands, and more importantly, in compliance with the Letter of Majesty, granted on account of religion), or also to have no one prevented in their customary religious practice.[17]

Even if these words were for form's sake, his actions followed suit, though some of his advisers made recommendations of an opposite nature. In August 1620 Scultetus argued that the King had the right to replace Catholic priests with reformed preachers wherever he wished and recommended that he do so.[18] The suggestion was never followed up. Frederick was too busy with the war effort at any rate.

Recognizing that a war could not be won without money, Frederick worked on his allies to gather funds to the Bohemian military campaign. It was a difficult task, considering the confused and impecunious state of the Bohemian governmental offices and the dubious international reaction to his taking the crown.[19] His first step was to commit the Union and as many Protestant princes of the Empire as possible to the Bohemian cause. Immediately after his coronation, Frederick hurried off to Nürnberg with Volrad von Plessen for a meeting to which the King of Denmark and all Protestant princes and states of the Empire had been invited.

The actual attendance was not so grandiose. In addition to Frederick, the Union members, the Count Palatine of Neuburg, and the three Dukes of Sachsen-Weimar were present, and the Dukes of Lünenburg and Braunschweig sent representatives. Count Johann Georg von Hohenzollern also came, uninvited, on orders from Ferdinand to inform the assembly that the Emperor had resolved to observe the religious privileges of Bohemia, because nothing was more important to him than the restoration of peace. Needless to say, this announcement had a dampening effect on whatever enthusiasm there might have been for Frederick's cause.

Despite the Union's previous hesitance, he hoped for an alliance between it and Bohemia. But this hope was a pipe dream. At Nürnberg the Union only distanced itself from the Bohemian conflict still further. The members complained that Frederick had not consulted them when, on his way to Prague, he had taken the Union troops in Amberg with him, and they attacked him for diverting English subsidies for the Union to Prague. These deeds had undermined the Union's solidarity and their already limited readiness to take part in a war.[20] Furthermore, the Union requested that their troops be sent back, and that Frederick give up his monthly salary of 6,000 fl. as Commander-in-Chief of the Union military forces, because, it was said, he was no longer in a position to perform his duties.[21] In the end, against his wishes, the Union members granted neither troops nor financial assistance to the Bohemians but promised to defend the Palatinate in the event of an invasion.[22] The meeting at Nürnberg had been a total failure. Frederick returned to Prague, but could only stay for a few weeks before he departed on his royal progress to receive the homage from his subjects in the incorporated lands.

The Progress

The young King made his first and only progress in order to bolster the war effort, not to prepare Bohemia and the incorporated lands for a Calvinist reformation.[23] He withstood the vicissitudes of winter travel to journey through Moravia, Silesia, and Upper and Lower Lusatia to rally political, financial, and military support before the campaign season fully resumed in the spring. It was vital for the political consolidation of his reign that the Estates of the incorporated lands have an opportunity to pay homage to the new King of Bohemia. Without it, his government was not fully authorized to take up power in the incorporated lands. The progress was a resplendent, extravagant, and extremely expensive affair – a retinue of 300 attendants accompanied Frederick – as was necessary in order to persuade the populace that the majesty and authority of the Bohemia's first Protestant king was equal or superior to that of the Habsburgs. The semblance of parsimony would have been politically damaging.[24] It was also crucial to disprove any malicious rumors against the new King, procure a widespread acceptance of his regime's legitimacy, and thereby garner popular support for the war effort. If those who swore their allegiance to Frederick devoted themselves to the war against Ferdinand, the rebellion would have had a better chance of survival. Frederick's relentless gift giving was a form of investment, not of profligacy.

The progress was also a chance for Frederick and his supporters to determine and adjust the inclinations of the leaders of the incorporated lands and to root out leaders of the opposition. When the company reached Brünn in Moravia in early February, they sensed a warm affection for the new King.[25] As expected Frederick confirmed Moravian freedoms, and the assembled Moravian nobility made their oath of vassalage to him. A couple of notable members, however, did not, namely Karel Žerotín and Prince Karl von Liechtenstein, and Frederick warned that if Žerotín did not change his mind, he would lose his property.[26] Frederick asked the Moravian Estates to double the size of their troop contribution and mobilize every twentieth man in two weeks. He also made a request for the traditional gift due to the King at his accession.[27] The Estates gave him 15,000 Moravian Gulden in addition to some confiscated properties, but they refused to grant him troops and resolved to mobilize 1,500 infantry and 500 cavalry to defend Moravia for six months only.[28] That gesture showed the limit of their affection. Despite this disappointment, Frederick was pleased with the present of two manors to himself and his queen which returned a significant sum in rents.[29]

The war was not a distant danger for the Moravians, and the proximity of the violence made the apparent passivity in Moravia all the more alarming. Frederick's stay in Brünn was prolonged by news of an invasion of 8,000 Cossacks from Poland into Upper Silesia and the principality of Teschen, called in by Archduke Karl, Bishop of Breslau and Neisse, and brother of Emperor Ferdinand II, who had fled to Poland in September 1619. The Cossacks were on their way to join the Emperor's forces in Vienna, and they passed within a few miles of where Frederick was staying. During the night of 7 February 1620, one could see from Brünn the glow of the villages that a band of these Cossacks had put to flames.[30] Frederick tried to coordinate a counter-attack, calling on the Duke of Brieg in Breslau to dispatch companies to cut them off. He also wrote to the King of Poland to demand their withdrawal.[31] After pausing for a couple of days, Frederick decided to continue his progress despite the danger. He tried to remain in good spirits throughout.[32]

He did not see any strong signs of Lutheran-Calvinist tensions at this or the next stage of the progress. On 14 February the party left Brünn for northern Moravia, quickly reaching Jägerndorf. One week later he was welcomed in the episcopal town of Neisse by an enthusiastic reception from the Lutheran populace, who were overjoyed to be rid of their exacting and oppressive bishop, Archduke Karl. Frederick promised the townsmen peace and protection, guaranteed their freedom of worship, and allowed them to reform the Catholic church of Maria in Rosis for their Lutheran services.[33] At the next destination, however, the relations between the confessions were more brittle. For much of the rest of the progress Frederick tried to relieve tensions among the members of the various Christian confessions in Silesia, especially in Breslau, its capital.

Breslau's predominately Lutheran populace treated their Calvinist king to a sumptuous reception. On 23 February, Frederick entered the town through a triumphal arch which alone cost nearly 3,000 RT, and beheld an array of festivities of unparalleled splendor and magnificence for Breslau.[34] Frederick found it the most beautiful town in the whole kingdom, after Prague.[35] The Silesian Estates made their homage to Frederick, who in return, but not as a condition, guaranteed their rights and privileges, heard their grievances, and promised to rectify them as soon as possible.[36] He left the Estates the right to select their own local government officials, but he rejected their proposal to expel Jews from Silesia.[37] He confirmed the Calvinist Duke of Brieg, as the head of the provincial government.

Frederick also tried to relieve the fears of Breslau's Catholics. The Protestant Estates in Silesia had imposed an oath of allegiance to the Confederation articles of 1619 on all the Silesian clergy. The Estates claimed that the oath was meant to guarantee the peace between Catholics and Protestants. It was a political measure in support of Frederick's new regime, not an attempt to reform the church.[38] Catholics who did not take the oath of allegiance were in danger of being subject to confiscations, not because of their religion per se, but because of their politics. Some Catholic prelates had signed, and some had not. Frederick publicly denied that he entertained any design to eradicate the Catholic confession; he said that he wanted to find a way to let both the Catholic and the Protestant confessions co-exist in peace, each maintaining their privileges.[39] On behalf of the small Calvinist community in Breslau, he issued a Letter of Majesty that granted them freedom of worship, and he offered them the use of the great hall in the royal castle for their religious services. During his stay, it seemed to him that Calvinists and Lutherans shared a kind of mutual understanding, but after he issued the new Letter of Majesty, some members of the Lutheran majority could not contain their resentment. Frederick then ordered the city's soldiery to protect the Calvinists in case of the outbreak of violence.[40] In the following month, on 12 April, Palm Sunday, some Lutherans insulted the Calvinist minister and disrupted the Calvinist service at the castle, where some twenty-six people were assembled. This minor event demonstrates that not all of Frederick's subjects shared his level of tolerance.

The events of the war brought a premature end to the progress. After leaving Breslau on 6 March, worrying news about the military situation led him to order the Duke of Brieg to send a detachment to search out Habsburg troops in Moravia and to guard the Silesian border from further incursions by the Cossacks.[41] He continued westwards to Görlitz in Upper Lusatia and there enjoyed yet another joyful reception. He wanted to visit Spremberg in Lower Lusatia and then meet with the Elector of Saxony in order to allay Johann Georg's apparent antagonism and extract a promise of neutrality from him, but another piece of bad news from the war front cut the progress short. After Frederick heard that Ferdinand's army had taken the town of Wittingau (Třeboň), near Budějovice, he named Count Solms his representative to receive the homage of the Lower Lusatians, and then hurried back to Prague, where he arrived on 14 March.[42]

The truncated progress was not necessarily an indication of a complete failure. Everywhere the populace showed its excitement to receive a visit from their new, Protestant king. Frederick's affability had won him affection from many of the people who had met him. An observer reported that Frederick had behaved so graciously toward everyone, that 'the common man gained a particular affection toward his Majesty, and wish[ed] him luck and victory against [the enemy], that they might be for a long time with this lord in peace and tranquility'.[43] Those who had hosted and served him had received presents of gilded drinking vessels and money, and even some of those who had merely congratulated him had enjoyed a similar generosity. The Estates of the incorporated lands had shown their willingness to render him homage and gifts, but not more. The Estates' desire to confirm and increase their local privileges was greater than their willingness to sacrifice to their king the requested amounts of financial and military assistance. This resistance has been attributed to the political immaturity of the Estates, whose members believed that they could endorse their new monarch's regime and side-step the war in its defense without suffering dire consequences. Their lack of insight ranks their politics 'no higher than that of the masses'.[44]

The young King of Bohemia felt that the progress had been a part of his divine calling. Soon after the journey had begun, he had written to his wife, 'it is necessary to entrust oneself in everything to the will of God, that is my entire consolation amid the many setbacks that one encounters'.[45] He confirmed this view one month later: 'I must follow whither my calling brings me'.[46] One of the most trying aspects of the progress for Frederick had been the separation from Elizabeth. The constant exchange of letters and gifts reveals the intensity of the emotional bond between the pair. Many of his letters contain apologies for having been too preoccupied to write more often, and they usually end with a protestation of eternal love, the declaration that she was never out of his thoughts, an expression of his annoyance at sleeping alone, the promise to be true unto the grave, or the hope that God would grant them the grace of being together for many years.[47] In his first letter from Brünn, he promised that he would return as soon as possible, and he asked her to keep her promise not to be too melancholy during his absence.[48] Once he admonished her, 'I beg you not to let go of yourself, because you do yourself harm and offend God to grieve without reason. In the end one must resolve to want what God wants, and each must follow what he is called to do'.[49]

Despite the rigors of the journey, the periods of terrible cold, and the political and military disappointments that Frederick had encountered along the way, the journey had not been without its pleasures and diversions. The countryside in Moravia had pleased him more than the Bohemian. He had stayed at the homes of many Bohemian, Moravian, and Silesian nobility, and had received their finest hospitality. The festivities in Breslau, and especially the ladies, their gowns, and their jewelry had evoked his praise.[50] Placing his faith in God and relying on Him to make difficult things turn out for the best, Frederick was able to enjoy the splendid pleasures of the royal existence. Only in this sense should one interpret Camerarius' complaint that Frederick 'takes the matter lightly and leaves everything to God and good hope'.[51] Neither lazy nor weak, the young King of Bohemia's faith would offer him periods of light-hearted resiliency during the most difficult of times.

A Birth and a Ban

When Frederick returned to Prague, there was another series of festivities waiting for him, besides his anxiously awaited reunion with his queen. On the last day of March 1620 the royal pair celebrated the baptism of their fourth child and third son, and the King took advantage of the occasion to request a donative from the Estates of Bohemia and the incorporated lands. Ruprecht had been born on 17 December 1619, another sign of God's blessing on the reign of Frederick and Elizabeth.[52] Ruprecht was the name of the last Wittelsbach Elector Palatine to have been Holy Roman Emperor, from 1400–1410, and the christening was a ringing statement of intention, which did not apply to Ruprecht necessarily, but to Frederick's posterity in general. He had wanted security for his family in the Bohemian succession, and in April the Bohemian Estates designated Frederick's first son, Friedrich Heinrich, successor to the throne.[53] Nonetheless, Frederick made no move towards the Imperial throne, but, given the preponderance of Bohemian kings who had also worn the Imperial crown, he most likely entertained similar aspirations for his first son.

While the Bohemian Estates guaranteed the rule of Frederick's dynasty, the most powerful princes of the Empire exhorted him to abdicate. In March 1620, a meeting of Catholic and Protestant Imperial princes in Mühlhausen, including the Electors of Mainz, Cologne, Trier, and Saxony, the Duke of Bavaria, and Landgrave Ludwig of Hessen, condemned the Bohemian election and resolved to back the Emperor's efforts to undo it.[54] Emperor Ferdinand openly threatened Frederick: if he did not relinquish the Bohemian crown by 1 June 1620, he would be declared a rebel against the Empire and be subjected to the appropriate punishment according to the Imperial constitution, the Imperial ban.[55] The Imperial ban was the severest punishment that the Emperor could inflict on a prince or estate in the Empire. It rendered the recipient an outlaw, deprived of any protection under the law and forbidden to hold titles or property or receive assistance of any kind. There was no price on his head per se, but he made a tempting target for predatory, vengeful neighbors and rivals. Normally the declaration of a ban required a summons, hearing, and trial, and, if it were against a person of high rank, the consultation of the electoral college. Earlier Ferdinand had also issued an edict to nullify the Bohemian election of 1619. Frederick's response to both moves was indignant recalcitrance.

Frederick's regime defended its legitimacy in predominantly secular terms. This tactic was fully in keeping with his constitutionalism, and it was the best form of argumentation to mollify the confessional qualms of potential anti-Habsburg supporters who did not espouse Frederick's own religious orientation. In response to the edict, he issued a declaration which argued that Ferdinand's prior actions had amounted to an abdication. It affirmed the validity of his deposition, the Bohemian privilege of a free election, and the legality of the ensuing election.[56] Frederick stated bluntly that the new Emperor had no jurisdiction in

Bohemia 'beyond what concerns the law of patronage of the Holy Roman Empire'.[57] Furthermore, the declaration claimed that neither the Aulic Council nor the Imperial Supreme Court had authority in Bohemia. The fundamental laws and privileges of Bohemia alone were pre-eminent. Frederick's declaration interpreted the war essentially as a private matter, a conflict over the inheritance of the Bohemian throne, which Ferdinand could wage either as an Archduke of Austria or as Emperor. But the declaration warned that according to the Golden Bull the Elector Palatine was to sit in judgment of the Emperor when he is accused of violating the law, and not vice versa.[58] While Ferdinand charged the rebels and their new king with usurping his crown and breaking the peace of Bohemia, Frederick and the Bohemian Protestant Estates charged Ferdinand with disobeying the Letter of Majesty, spreading murder and mayhem, and inviting foreign soldiers to invade Bohemia. The charges of both sides were quite defensible.

With regards to the threat of the Imperial ban, Frederick condemned it as yet another Habsburg corruption of Imperial law, but he could not dismiss it entirely. Emperor Charles V had set a dangerous precedent during the Schmalkaldic war in the mid sixteenth century, when he had banned Duke Johann Frederick I, Elector of Saxony, and transferred his electorate to Duke Moritz, a member of a rival line of the Wettiner dynasty, in return for his assistance in the ban's execution. Under normal circumstances an emperor needed the consent of the electoral college, if not an Imperial diet, to issue the ban, and by 1620 it was possible that the Electors of Mainz, Trier, Cologne, and Saxony would support the ban against Frederick. If it were ratified, then the case against the Emperor's right to bestow the electorate on another prince would be much weakened. Frederick's brother, Count Palatine Ludwig Philipp, had heard rumors from the Imperial court that Ferdinand intended to remove the electoral dignity from the Palatine house because of the quarrel over Bohemia. Invoking the Golden Bull and the fundamental law of the Empire, Ludwig Philipp asked the Elector of Mainz for support in defense of the Imperial constitution.[59] Unfortunately the Palatine electorate had already been promised in secret to Maximilian, Duke of Bavaria.

The Tide Turns

Emperor Ferdinand, on his way home from his election and coronation in Frankfurt, had stopped in Munich at the beginning of October 1619, accompanied by Count Oñate, the Spanish ambassador, to pay a visit to Duke Maximilian. There Ferdinand had proposed a treaty, seconded by the spiritual electors, that gave Maximilian supreme command of the Catholic League if he raised an army to assist the Emperor. Ferdinand had offered Upper Austria as a pledge for the expenses if the Duke quashed the rebellion there and in other Habsburg lands. Moreover, the Emperor issued a vague, oral promise that if Maximilian successfully executed an Imperial ban against the Elector Palatine, he could take the electoral dignity and keep the Palatine lands that he would conquer during the course of the war.[60] Oñate had added that the King of Spain would support the army of the League and direct the army of Flanders to attack the Lower Palatinate.[61]

The offer had been too delectable for Maximilian to refuse. Although he had held himself aloof at the outset of the rebellion, the twin interests of expanding his estate and of protecting the Catholic Church led him to intervene militarily on the Emperor's behalf. The outbreak of the third rebellion in ten years by Protestants in Habsburg lands had not been sufficiently compelling, but the Palatine's taking the Bohemian crown had spurred him to action. If Frederick managed to remain both King of Bohemia and Elector Palatine, then the age-old Catholic majority in the electoral college would be overturned, which could conceivably have led to the election of a Protestant Emperor, to the almost certain detriment of the Roman Catholic Church in the Holy Roman Empire. Wishing to maintain the religious *status quo ante bellum* and fearing for the future safety of Catholicism in the Empire, Maximilian, who was unimpressed by Frederick's promises to rule Bohemia as a tolerant monarch, had signed the Emperor's treaty on 8 October 1619.[62] In the month before, he had tried to dissuade Frederick by using mainly constitutional arguments, urging him instead to uphold peace between the Empire's members. Like Frederick, Maximilian was moved by a powerful sense of duty to the well-being of the Empire and to the safety of Christians on his side of the confessional divide, yet he was well aware of the secular advantages that successful intervention in the Bohemian rebellion could provide. Both he and Frederick were willing to risk a general war of religion to uphold their vision of the political and religious order dictated by the Imperial constitution.[63]

At about the same time Frederick had sent Maximilian a plea to maintain his neutrality during the future course of the conflict, but this warmly-worded request had made a poor showing against the Emperor's offer of new lands and titles. Maximilian had answered Frederick's letter with a simple statement of fact: a decision to accept the Bohemian crown would escalate the war.[64] On 5 December Maximilian had held a meeting of the members of the Catholic League in Würzburg and had declared himself the head of a force of 25,000 to go the Emperor's aid. Plessen,

Solms, and two emissaries from Nürnberg had come to Munich shortly afterwards, in hopes of persuading Maximilian to remain neutral towards Bohemia and the Union. Maximilian had said that he was mustering his troops for defensive purposes, but he declined to articulate his precise intentions.[65] In mid summer 1620 the Bavarian army, commanded by Count Jean 't Serclaes of Tilly, invaded Austria and quickly quashed the rebellious Protestant Estates.[66] Frederick could do nothing to help them, apart from making passionate declarations in their favor to the Bohemian general assembly.[67] To make matters still worse for Frederick, the Spanish, who had supported Ferdinand's cause with consistent reluctance, finally resolved to invade the Lower Palatinate in the summer of 1620.

The Spanish invasion almost did not take place.[68] On 10 December 1619, the Spanish Council of State had discussed Archduke Albert's request for funds to invade the Lower Palatinate. About one million ducats had been spent throughout the year on the war in central Europe, and a much larger sum would be needed for the troops already mobilized in the Empire and for the new invasion. The general situation in Europe had given the councilors cause for great worry. They had not been aware of any forthcoming support from the three Imperial spiritual electors, the pope, or the French King. Moreover, the Venetians and the Dutch had recently sealed a defensive alliance against Spain, not expecting a renewal of the Twelve Years' Truce. Don Balthasar de Zúñiga believed that the Dutch, the German Protestants, Bethlen Gábor, Savoy, and Venice were conspiring against the House of Austria, and he even feared that if the Dutch were to ally with the English, they could invade Portugal and set up a rival regime of Portuguese pretenders. Only Zúñiga and Cardinal Zapata had been in favor of the invasion of the Palatinate. The rest of the council had been against it, because the regime had no way to pay for it. Philip III had accepted this view and requested that contributions for the Emperor's forces in Bohemia continue.

Zúñiga, however, had not given up. He had enlisted the services of Ferdinand's ambassador, Khevenhüller, who had browbeaten Padre Aliaga, the King's confessor and a main opponent to the invasion of the Palatinate, with sarcasm, insults, and extraordinary threats. Then, two days before Christmas, a dire report had arrived from Count Oñate about Bethlen Gábor's attack on Vienna. The need to alleviate the pressure on the Emperor had suddenly become critical. Shortly after Christmas the Council of State had had another meeting about the situation in Germany. It had been observed that a swift, massive attack on the Palatinate would serve three purposes: to intimidate the Dutch and perhaps win Spain more favorable terms than those in the truce of 1609, to ease the pressure on the Emperor's army and divert the attention of Frederick V, and to protect

Habsburg Alsace from potential Protestant aggression. Zúñiga and other councilors had griped about papal parsimony and the reputedly massive size of Paul V's treasure in the fortress of Sant' Angelo, while they had observed that their own financial situation had gone from bad to worse. It had been estimated that in the next year Oñate would spend over one and half million ducats for Ferdinand's forces, and Archduke Albert would need over three and half million to invade the Palatinate with a force of 35,000 men. These were staggering sums of money, and the treasury did not have such revenue at its disposal. But Zúñiga, convinced that extraordinary sums could be always found in times of extraordinary need, had pressed for the invasion in order to save the Habsburg position in the Empire. Apparently because of Oñate's desperate report about the siege of Vienna, council members Don Messía, the Marquis of Villafranca, and the Duke of Infantado had changed their minds. Even Aliaga had consented in the end, not without objection, to Archduke Albert's invasion of the Palatinate, probably because the council had resolved to reduce the monthly subsidy for the campaign from 300,000 to 100,000 ducats.[69]

The Spanish invasion was to be a campaign of diversion, not of acquisition.[70] According to the Council of State, the attack against the Palatinate was meant to protect the patrimony of the House of Austria against the advances of Frederick V. The expected declaration of the Imperial ban against Frederick bestowed legitimacy on the campaign, because Archduke Albert could claim to be merely helping its execution.[71] The detachment of 20,000 veteran troops from the Army of Flanders that would enter the Lower Palatinate in August 1620 under the command of Ambrosio Spínola was intended to make a crippling attack, reducing the strongholds, and then return to the Spanish Netherlands when the Bavarian and Austrian Habsburg armies would put an end to the rebellion in Bohemia. Spínola's army was not supposed to be an army of occupation.

The first concern of the Spanish was the maintenance and defense of the Habsburg patrimony, and the expiration of the Twelve Years' Truce and the expected resumption of war with the United Provinces were the greatest threats, after the Bohemian rebellion. Adding the Palatinate to the Spanish dominions was not their goal. The Council of State rejected Oñate's suggestion of inviting the French to join in their campaign and then dividing the Palatinate between them. Instead they resolved that Frederick's restitution, after order was restored to Germany, could not be precluded.[72] Furthermore, Madrid dreaded a general war between the Catholic and Protestant confessions, and they wanted to maintain peace with Protestant powers, particularly with the Union and England. In fact they would invade the Palatinate with the assurance that James I would make no move to stop them.

The Defense Falters

Throughout the 1620 campaigning season Frederick and his regime devoted themselves to meeting the new threats from Bavaria and Spain. Reports streaming into Heidelberg and Prague from Venice, Rome, Milan, Vienna, and many cities in Germany kept them abreast of war preparations, war news, and Spanish troop movements.[73] Prague regularly provided Heidelberg with intelligence about the movements of the Habsburgs and their allies. Frederick had repeatedly proclaimed during his progress that he would spare no personal expense and reserve none of his own energy to defend the lands under the Bohemian Crown and their religious freedoms.[74] He had asked the princes and estates of the kingdom and incorporated lands to redirect the taxes meant for the maintenance of his court to the funds meant to defray defense costs, and he had encouraged them to pay their other arrears to the same fund. In August 1620 he published a general plea for all subjects to resist the enemy, but he was unable to force the various Estates to make extraordinary sacrifices to pay for the war, though they had endorsed his regime.[75] The nagging financial troubles seriously marred the Bohemians' performance in the war, but their allies' unreliability ultimately proved fatal to their cause.

Both problems had prevented the Bohemians from making an effective strike against Vienna in late 1619. In the autumn, while the Emperor's army had been in retreat, the Bohemian troops had mutinied, because they had not received their pay for months. The mutiny had momentarily destroyed the opportunity for an effective counterattack. The directors had then resorted to monetary fines, confiscations of property, seizure of gold and silver plate in Prague's monasteries, and a debasement of the coinage to raise the necessary cash.[76] After discipline had been recovered, the Bohemian army had crossed the Danube and, joined with a Hungarian contingent, made a force of 50,000 which reached Vienna by the end of November.[77] This army might have been able to execute an effective siege, but Bethlen Gábor had had to call his men back to Pressburg. The Silesians and Moravians had then pulled back in early December.[78] The opportunity was never to arise again.

Frederick and his regime were then forced to place their greatest hopes in their allies. The financial weakness of the new constitutional monarchy made an effective, coordinated coalition of military forces all the more necessary for its survival. The Palatine leaders of Bohemia conducted an active, open diplomacy that invited and offered alliances on attractive terms with other powers within and beyond the Empire to the east and the west.[79] Unfortunately domestic distractions or alternative interests diverted the attentions of both western and eastern European powers, the incorporated lands, and the Austrian Estates allied to the Bohemians. Confessional sympathy, where it was to be found, could not overcome these barriers, leaving the Palatine-Bohemian regime to fend for itself.

One of the most prominent allies was Bethlen Gábor, the Prince of Transylvania, whom Frederick held to be a 'most honest man'.[80] Despite Gábor's humble origins he had acquired a princely title through military prowess and political intrigue.[81] Throughout 1620 Gábor's actions demonstrated that he was more devoted to consolidating his own rebellion against the Habsburgs in Hungary than to sacrificing it for the uprising in Bohemia. In mid October 1619 Bethlen Gábor had taken Pressburg and completed his conquest of northern Hungary. He had then made known his intention to send troops into Moravia. News of his victory had sent Emperor Ferdinand fleeing from his residence in Vienna, roughly thirty miles west of Pressburg, to Graz in Styria. But an uprising against Gábor by the Emperor's Hungarian adherents south of the Danube had forced him to recall his troops from the siege of Vienna. After the Estates of Hungary in Pressburg had proclaimed him a Prince of Hungary, he had indulged in concurrent negotiations with the Bohemians and the Emperor. On 15 January 1620 the allied Estates of Hungary, Bohemia, Moravia, and Upper and Lower Austria had agreed to Gábor's proposed defensive alliance, but he had shocked the emissaries on the following day with the announcement that he had signed a cease-fire with the Emperor to last till 29 September 1620. Nonetheless Frederick had accepted Gábor's offer to mediate a cease-fire with Ferdinand, but nothing came of it.[82] Gábor had proceeded to bargain with Ferdinand over the possibility of the former giving up his control over Hungary in return for an annual pension of 300,000 fl., but soon Gábor took the crown of Hungary for himself.[83] He did not contribute to the Bohemian campaign till the latter half of 1620, and, when he finally did, his relief forces would come too late.

As with Bethlen Gábor, Frederick's allies gave greater weight to their own concerns than to protecting the new regime in Bohemia and the constitutional religious freedoms of the kingdom. The Union preferred peace with the Catholic League in Germany over a war throughout the Empire for the sake of Frederick's novelties. In January 1620 the Union members had agreed to allow Ferdinand's troops to pass through their territories, and the amount of unpaid Union dues had been increasing.[84] Still they had armed themselves in expectation of an attack by the League. By May they had assembled a force of 13,000 in Ulm, and Maximilian's 24,000 soldiers were camped nearby down the Danube. In July the Union and the Catholic League ended their face-off with a neutrality pact under French mediation. Each side agreed not to attack the territories of the other, but both were free to go to fight in Bohemia. The Union forces then went to defend the Lower Palatinate from the Spanish.[85] Neither the Union nor the League wanted to ignite a war of religion in the Empire for the sake of the Bohemian rebellion.

England proved to be nearly as disappointing. James' objections to the Bohemian rebellion had been common knowledge, and he never addressed his son-in-law with Bohemian royal titles. In November 1619 he had even appeared disinclined to defend the Palatinate from attack.[86] But these messages were mixed with occasional signs of favor. In January 1620 James asked the Dutch to send 1,200 cavalry to Bohemia in expectation of Archduke Albert's supposed plans to deploy Spanish forces there. The Union, James had said, could not sustain itself in the Empire without assistance, but because he held 'nothing in the world as precious as his honor', he was obligated to declare his innocence in his son-in-law's acceptance of the throne.[87] When this news had reached Frederick, he had been much annoyed. He had written to Elizabeth, 'the King is still amusing himself by disputing the justice of the cause, and it seems that he would like well to be rid of [Dohna (Frederick's ambassador)] and let him return empty-handed'.[88] According to Elizabeth, certain pro-Spanish members of the English court had been responsible for her father's unsympathetic policy toward Bohemia: 'I think I can easilie guess who it is that doth chieflie hinder the King in resolving, but I am sure that though they have English bodies they have Spanish hartes'.[89] In March 1620 James had refused to grant the Union's request for troops and money. He had denied that he was obligated to do so and had sent away their emissary in disgrace.[90]

But at the same time James offered a token of support for his children, especially in the defense of the Palatinate. He let Colonel John Gray recruit a regiment of 2,500 volunteers in England for service in Bohemia.[91] James also permitted the Palatine ambassador to hold public collections for the war effort, which may have gathered as much as £80–90,000.[92] He could hardly have refused, however, having granted similar permission to the King of Spain.[93] For the Palatinate James ordered the mustering of a force 4,000 volunteers to defend it in his name and in his pay. Sir Horace Vere assumed command of the force, which comprised only 2,250 men, and led them to the Palatinate in the early autumn.[94] Yet even this measure did not improve Anglo-Palatine relations. In recommending Vere, Dohna quarreled with the King's favorite, the Marquis of Buckingham, who preferred another candidate. Buckingham said 'that if it had not been for [Dohna's] privileged status, he would have thrown him out of the window'.[95]

Fundamentally James refused to abet the Bohemian rebellion, because he did not want to further a war of religion in Europe. To have done so would have compromised his honor as the self-proclaimed *rex pacificus*. Although his religious and familial bonds obligated him to defend the Palatines, James said, 'we will not contradict ourself by our own actions and not open a breach in the reputation of our integrity'.[96] To Frederick's claim that he had accepted the Bohemian crown in order to help his dynasty and the common cause of his religion, James observed that Frederick could have aided both without taking on such a hazardous acquisition. James would not join the war for the sake of religion because, he claimed, he did not want other princes to do the same. 'That would certainly have drawn this quarrel of state into a general war of religion, to the great scandal and evident peril of all Christendom'.[97] Frederick continued to plead for help nonetheless, because he hoped that James would honor his previously stated intention to defend the Palatinate from attack. In August Frederick sent Achaz von Dohna to England to inform the court about the Spanish designs on Frederick's crown and all his lands, to describe the dreadful desolation of the land and misery of the people, and to ask James for £20,000.[98] Dohna's success was limited at best. Though he received nothing from James, at the end of October the Earl of Huntingdon gave him £1,020 that he had collected and guaranteed the delivery of another £600 after Michaelmas.[99] This generosity would come too late to help the Bohemians.

King James provided diplomatic support in the interest of peace instead of money, men, and arms for the pursuit of a war of which he did not approve. Two more ambassadors, Sir Edward Conway and Sir Richard Weston, were dispatched in July to display their prince's desire for peace in Bohemia. They had no success in arranging an end to the war. They first stopped in Brussels and tried in vain to extract a promise from Archduke Albert not to invade the Lower Palatinate. Just after they left, the Archduke informed the Union that Spínola would indeed attack. In Dresden they would fail to win over the Elector of Saxony, who would promptly invade Upper Lusatia in support of the Emperor. Their commission directed them to bring Frederick into negotiations with the Emperor, but this too would prove a hopeless task.[100]

Though the Estates General of the United Provinces and the House of Orange could have devoted themselves to the new King of Bohemia out of dynastic, political, and religious interest, the first concern for the Dutch was their own security. They had quickly acknowledged Frederick as King of Bohemia, but during the peace with Spain, the Estates General had been hesitant to give him much financial support. Under pressure from Maurits, Prince of Orange, they had increased somewhat their limited contributions to the new Bohemian regime.[101] Nonetheless the Dutch were reluctant to send their valuable troops so far because there was too much danger immediately threatening their own borders. The Estates General did not see themselves as the sole power to uphold the situation in Bohemia. The Union, they felt, above all, needed to be convinced of the threat of 'absolute domination of Spain, the total desolation of both the reformed religion and the liberty of the same Princes of the Union in the Empire'.[102] To James I's offers of mediation, the Estates General countered that the Habsburgs were inherently untrustworthy, neglecting the duties of conscience, failing to observe treaties, holding nothing more important than their ambition. The House of Austria, they asserted, was trying to form a coalition in the whole of Europe for the purpose of subduing the Empire and extirpating the reformed religion. The Dutch complimented James for caring about Frederick and his cause, but they would only join in the conflict if many other princes were already assisting, and if Frederick's enemy showed some lack of resolution. At the time of the invasion of the Palatinate, the Estates General would authorize a monthly payment of 50,000 fl. to Frederick V's forces, but they would suspend it in October upon receiving bad news about the war in Bohemia. When the Bohemian agents in the Netherlands accused each other of embezzlement, the Estates General instituted a commission of inquiry and decided to apply the money for their own defense.[103]

From the other powers that had quickly recognized Frederick as King of Bohemia little or no assistance was forthcoming. Gustavus Adolphus, King of Sweden, had at first welcomed the overtures for an alliance with Bohemia and the Protestant Union. The King had some interest in the fortunes of the Palatine dynasty, but it was not strong.[104] Throughout the summer of 1620 Gustavus Adolphus was actually in Germany, but otherwise unavailable, committed to winning as his bride Maria Eleonora, the sister of the Elector Georg Wilhelm of Brandenburg. During the negotiations Gustavus Adolphus took the opportunity to travel across Germany incognito, visiting Heidelberg and other towns, and making contact with leading Protestant princes like Johann of Nassau. He did not go to Bohemia to meet Frederick. The journey gave him first-hand experience with the fractiousness of German Protestants and the limitations of their military capabilities.[105] For the time being a greater concern for his wars against Poland prevented Gustavus Adolphus from developing much enthusiasm for the Bohemian cause. Nevertheless, he provided Frederick with eight guns and a supply of ammunition.[106]

Though more was expected from Denmark, less assistance came when it was most needed. King Christian IV, Elizabeth's uncle, had been willing to provide an army of 4,000 men, but the resistance of his council had prevented him from doing so.[107] He had sent an ambassador, Detlev von Rantzau, who had met Frederick on his progress to deliver Christian's congratulations and assurances of support. Frederick had showered Rantzau with hospitality, covered his expenses, given him a diamond-studded portrait of himself, and sent him on his way.[108] Though after the Mühlhausen conference Christian had urged his nephew to re-establish peace with the Emperor, he still loaned him 100,000 RT for the defense of his regime.[109] But the famous military disaster at White Mountain intervened to render these efforts ineffectual.

All requests for aid from the Venetians received expressions of goodwill but no money. They promised, however, to prevent foreign troops from passing through their territory. The Venetians and the Dutch had joined in an alliance at the end of 1619 against Spanish aggression, and the Dutch ambassador had tried to get Venice to help Frederick without success. The Venetian Republic remained committed to its neutrality in affairs within the Empire. The Doge congratulated and sent the same warm, friendly greetings to Frederick, Ferdinand, and the Union leaders alike. In the end, not a single ducat was provided for the Bohemians.[110]

Both contending sides in the Bohemian war negotiated with the Turkish Sultan, but the reigning peace between him and the Emperor would turn the diplomatic contest to Ferdinand's favor.[111] Emperor Ferdinand's ambassador in Istanbul, Baron Ludwig von Mollard, had encouraged the Ottoman regime to remain neutral or even to take some action against Bethlen Gábor. Frederick, meanwhile, had sent an ambassador, Heinrich Bitter, to Istanbul in January 1620, accompanied by an emissary of the Hungarian Estates, to counter the Imperial negotiations. During his royal progress, Frederick had invited the Estates in Moravia to advise him about making a gift to the Sultan in order to win his sympathy for a confederation of the Bohemians with Hungarians and Transylvanians.[112] This plan had not been negotiated in secrecy. In Silesia Frederick had asked the princes and Estates to follow the Moravians in supporting an embassy bringing gifts to the Sultan Osman II to cajole his help against Ferdinand and his allies.[113] In April Bitter had a successful audience with the Sultan, who sent the ambassador back to Bohemia with an ambassador of his own, Mehmed Aga. When Aga reached Prague in July, he was received in state. He informed Frederick that the Sultan was prepared to grant him a force of 60,000 cavalry, and that there were plans to invade Poland with 400,000 men as a punishment for the Cossacks' invasion of Bohemia. Letters from the Sultan and the Grand Vizier, Ali Pasha, endorsed the actions of the Estates against Ferdinand and requested that Frederick maintain formal diplomatic relations with the Ottomans.[114] Given the prospect of such enormous military assistance, Frederick of course complied. While Aga was in Prague, he supposedly continued to negotiate with the leaders of the Bohemia about an annual tribute of 700,000 RT for the Sultan. The Bohemians put up 200,000 RT for Bethlen Gábor, requested further military assistance against Bavaria and Saxony, and suggested an invasion of Styria and Carinthia. At the embassy's conclusion Frederick sent one of his own to Istanbul to express his gracious thanks, his hope for perpetual peace, good correspondence, friendship, and a guarantee of future deliveries of tribute.[115] But Frederick would never reap any advantage from these warm beginnings, and instead it would harm his reputation and his cause in the years to come.

The End of the Regime

Bereft of effective assistance, the Palatine-Bohemian regime could not protect itself against the combined powers of the Spanish and Austrian Habsburgs, Electoral Saxony, Bavaria, and the Catholic League. Attacked on all sides by Catholics and Protestants and left to their fate by their many allies and sympathizers, the new monarchy would suffer a mortal military defeat in the autumn of 1620. With the fall of Prague the rebellion would effectively come to an end.

The major blow was the invasion of the Lower Palatinate. In August 1620 Spínola and 25,000 soldiers from the Army of the Netherlands, bearing a commission from the Emperor, began their march from Brussels, and in early September they entered the Lower Palatinate, taking Kreuznach, Oppenheim, and the Bergstrasse district. The Union forces that had come to defend the Palatinate failed to attack the Spanish forces and simply withdrew from the stronghold at Oppenheim to Worms.[116] Neither the English nor the Union forces would engage Spínola's troops in a serious battle during the autumn of 1620.[117] By the end of November Vere would quarter his volunteers in the three main fortress-towns of Mannheim, Heidelberg, and Frankenthal, and the Spanish would also go into winter quarters.[118]

In the east Tilly's army, having subdued Austria, joined with Ferdinand's army in September and entered Bohemia, and a matter of days later the forces of Johann Georg, Elector of Saxony, invaded Upper Lusatia. Palatine efforts to secure Saxony's neutrality had totally failed. In keeping with the traditional Saxon political adherence to the Emperor, Johann Georg favored Ferdinand's side, though his position had been neutral during the early stages of the Bohemian rebellion.[119] Johann Georg had offered the Emperor assistance in exchange for a confirmation of religious rights for Lutherans in Bohemia and a guarantee for secularized church lands in the Upper and Lower Saxon circles. By March 1620 he had decided against neutrality and had arranged to receive a commission from the Emperor to invade Lusatia and Silesia.[120] Ferdinand had offered Lusatia to the Duke as a pledge for Saxon military services, and though Johann Georg disapproved of the idea of an Imperial ban upon the Elector Palatine, his territorial interests had prevented him from standing against it.[121]

The attack on Upper Silesia incensed Frederick. He quickly issued a proclamation that revoked the fiefs that the Elector of Saxony held in Bohemia. Frederick angrily, and correctly, accused the Elector of acting in conjunction with the Catholic League and the Spanish.[122] The gesture, however, did nothing to help the Bohemian cause. Apart from some resistance at Bautzen, Saxon forces took the region without great difficulty. The combination of the Saxon invasion of Upper Lusatia and the Bavarian and Habsburg invasion of Bohemia opened the war on two fronts, which quickly proved to be too much for the Bohemian army.[123]

In late September 1620 Frederick joined his forces in the field to take part in the campaign. He received constant reports about the diplomatic and military situation in Bohemia, the incorporated lands, Austria, Hungary, and the Palatinate, and Anhalt sent him regular updates about the campaign in general. Frederick expected daily reports from Anhalt, and when a day or two was skipped, he expressed surprise and probably some annoyance as well.[124] The young King of Bohemia could not have contributed much to the war effort besides his presence to boost the troops' morale. He had had no experience in the field as a general and could offer no professional military advice, and an awareness of his own impotence sometimes bothered him. He once complained to his wife, 'the time weighs extremely heavily upon me, not knowing how to pass the hours'.[125] Frederick's faith bolstered him against the steady flow of bad news from the front. 'I recommend everything to God, and am resolved to take everything in patience from His paternal hand. He has given it, he has deprived me of it, he can reward me, his name be glorified'.[126] No matter what his expectations for the future were, the King of Bohemia remained in the field, once riding as far west as the outskirts of Pilsen to view the position of the enemy forces.[127] In October he tried to persuade Duke Maximilian to consent to a cease-fire and a personal meeting, but to no avail. The Duke refused, citing the Mühlhausen resolution to carry out the Emperor's orders against the rebels.[128]

Elizabeth did not share her husband's sanguinity during the enemy's inexorable approach to Prague. In the last days of October she wrote to him of her growing fear, perhaps for their own lives. Frederick bade her never to send him such letters again, adding 'if it pleases God, we will see each other still for many years'.[129] He ordered her to make a Christian resolution to submit herself to God's will. In his next letter, however, he asked her to make preparations to leave, though she should not if there were no need.[130] He assured her that nothing would hurt him more than if she were to receive the slightest harm. During that time Frederick was very close to the enemy, and he prayed that God would not abandon him and his men. He visited the wounded, including a steward who had lost a leg in cannon fire and then died minutes after Frederick left him.[131] Though he did not fear for himself, he wanted his wife to leave Prague for a safer place. When he discussed it with the Duke of Weimar, the Duke disagreed, saying that Prague was well fortified, and that the people wanted her to stay. This remark angered Frederick, because he was not satisfied with the measures taken to provide for her security.[132] But time would not allow for any improvements to be made. On 5 November both opposing armies turned and made for Prague, and three days later they clashed on the large, broad topped hill to the northwest of the city.

The Battle of White Mountain marks the closure of Frederick's rule in Bohemia. Professor Polišenský described it as a 'skirmish' that was 'entirely futile'.[133] It was all over in about two hours. Frederick's force of 33,000 exhausted, diseased, mostly unpaid and mutinous men faced 55,000 enemy soldiers in the same awful condition but for the fact that they had been paid more regularly.[134] The Emperor's side also benefited from the exertions of a Carmelite friar whose ecstatic exhortations may have significantly bolstered morale.[135] The number killed was not catastrophically high – both sides may have lost a few hundred each – but it did not take long for the Bohemian side to break into flight.[136] Frederick did not have a chance to take part. The evening before he had returned to the Hradschin to meet with the English ambassadors on the following day. After they had finished their meal together, Frederick had ridden toward the battleground. The flight of his troops in the opposite direction quickly conveyed the outcome.

The Bohemian army quickly melted away, because its highest leaders abandoned the capital. Immediately after the battle Frederick appealed to Duke Maximilian to negotiate. Because no answer returned, on the following morning Frederick, Elizabeth, their children, and their followers fled the Hradschin in desperation. There was no time to make an orderly departure. In the chaos they left behind the crown, scepter, and royal orb of Bohemia, Frederick's jewel-encrusted collar of the Order of the Garter, and, still worse, his chancery documents, including the secret Palatine-Bohemian correspondence with the Habsburgs' various enemies. These and other treasures fell into Duke Maximilian's hands.[137] For a short time the leaders of the Palatine-Bohemian regime considered making a stand in the city of Prague. Tschernembl and the younger Count Thurn were convinced that Prague's resources, manpower, and defenses could withstand a siege, but others, including the elder Count Thurn and Anhalt, were not convinced that the soldiers and the citizenry would cooperate. Fear quickly resolved the debate. Frederick was not eager to become a martyr, and, probably above all considerations, he wanted to bring his wife and children into safety. On the following day he and his family, accompanied by some of the high officials of the Bohemian government, fled toward Silesia, where they hoped to make a stand and to revive the campaign. Frederick's flight marked the defeat of his regime. The Bohemian Estates would sue for mercy less than two weeks after the battle.[138]

Duke Maximilian and Emperor Ferdinand regarded the victory as an act of God's grace and celebrated it lavishly, but indulging in the triumph over the rebels did not prove beneficial to all participants. During the commemorative victory procession in Rome, Pope Paul V would suffer a first stroke, and a second one would kill him shortly afterwards.[139]

Notes

1. 'Je les irois fort souvent visiter'. Aretin, 'Sammlung', p. 151: 27 January/6 February 1620, Frederick to Elizabeth.
2. Wedgwood, *The Thirty Years' War*, chs 2–3.
3. The brief period of Frederick's reign in Bohemia is best described in van Eickels, *Schlesien*, chs 5–6.
4. van Eickels, *Schlesien*, pp. 261–3.
5. See van Eickels, *Schlesien*, p. 264, for Camerarius' dire estimation of the situation. This document is also printed in AP, i, p. 861.
6. A.E. Beller, *Caricatures of the 'Winter King' of Bohemia* (London, 1928), pp. 60–64.
7. Yates, *Rosicrucian*, p. 58.
8. The title of Frederick's order to reform the church is 'Verzeichnuß der fürnehmsten Articuln, so der Chur Pfalz *in seiner Kirchen* verordnet und getroffen'. The italics are mine. van Eickels, *Schlesien*, p. 267, note 144.
9. 'ich habs vor mich selbst weder gethan noch geheissen/die eurigen selbst habens gethan und also haben wöllen/habs geschehen lassen'. AP, i, p. 925.
10. Benrath, 'Abraham Scultetus', p. 110. Scultetus was fully convinced of the righteousness of the act and later claimed some responsibility for its occurence. p. 111.
11. van Eickels, *Schlesien*, p. 244.
12. Gottfried Ferdinand von Buckisch und Löwenfels, *Observationes Historico-Politicæ in Instrumentum Pacis Osnabrugo-Westphaliscum* (Frankfurt and Leipzig, 1722), pp. 588–93. Also see AP, i, pp. 923–6.
13. Buckisch und Löwenfels, *Observationes Historico-Politicæ*, pp. 595–6.
14. Green, *Elizabeth*, p. 144.
15. van Eickels, *Schlesien*, p. 282, and K. Bruchmann, *Die Huldigungsfahrt König Friedrichs I. von Böhmen nach Mähren und Schlesien* (Breslau, 1909), p. 11.

16. Baker, *The Letters of Elizabeth*, p. 51.
17. 'daß wir auch bey solchem Regiment uns festiglich vorgesetzet, der Religion halber niemand (wann sie sich nur den Verfassungen des Königreichs und der Länder, und zuförderst denen wegen der Religion ertheilten Majestätsbriefen gemäß, friedlich und unsträflich erzeigen) belästigen und unterdrücken, oder auch an ihrem hergebrachten Religions-Exercitio verhindern lassen'. Quoted in van Eickels, *Schlesien*, p. 244. The document is printed in its entirety in Franz Christoph von Khevenhiller, *Annales Ferdinandei* (12 vols, Leipzig, 1716–26), ix, pp. 614–26.
18. Benrath, 'Abraham Scultetus', p. 112.
19. AP, i, pp. 861–2.
20. Gotthard, 'Protestantische "Union",' p. 91.
21. van Eickels, *Schlesien*, p. 246.
22. Ibid.
23. A thorough, up-to-date description of this progress is in van Eickels, *Schlesien*, pp. 281–314. Her account is heavily based on Bruchmann, *Die Huldigungsfahrt*.
24. Bruchmann, *Die Huldigungsfahrt*, pp. 1–2.
25. AP, i, p. 986–7.
26. Aretin, 'Sammlung', pp. 150–1: 27 January/6 February 1620, Frederick to Elizabeth. In the same letter Frederick says that he expected to receive a share of the spoils from the confiscations.
27. van Eickels, *Schlesien*, p. 283.
28. Bruchmann, *Die Huldigungsfahrt*, p. 14.
29. He estimated that 'if God only wanted to provide a good peace', that the manors would be worth 10,000 livres in rent. 'si Dieu vouloit seulement donner une bonne paix', Aretin, 'Sammlung', p. 154: 4/14 February 1620, Frederick to Elizabeth.
30. Bruchmann, *Die Huldigungsfahrt*, pp. 15–16.
31. Toegel, *Documenta Bohemica*, ii, #539.
32. AP, i, p. 987.
33. Bruchmann, *Die Huldigungsfahrt*, p. 23.
34. For an exhaustive description of the arch and the festivities, see Bruchmann, *Die Huldigungsfahrt*, pp. 24–60.
35. Aretin, 'Sammlung', p. 157: 15/25 February 1620, Frederick to Elizabeth.
36. van Eickels, *Schlesien*, pp. 291–2.
37. Ibid., pp. 302–3.
38. Ibid., pp. 273–80.
39. Bruchmann, *Die Huldigungsfahrt*, p. 78.
40. Ibid., p. 87. van Eickels, *Schlesien*, pp. 304–5.
41. van Eickels, *Schlesien*, p. 305.
42. Bruchmann, *Die Huldigungsfahrt*, pp. 96–7.
43. 'der König habe sich gegen "Jedermenniglichen" so gnädig erzeigt, "also das der gemeine Man eine sonderliche affection zur deroselben [nämlich: Majestät] gewonnen, und wünschen ihr glück und Sieg wider alle drei feinde, das sie lange Zeit bey diesem herren in friedt und ruehe sein mögen."Quoted in Bruchmann, *Die Huldigungsfahrt*, p. 89.
44. 'nicht höher als die der Massen', Bruchmann, *Die Huldigungsfahrt*, p. 98. It took the coming of war 'to rouse them from their philistine indifference, political immaturity, pharisaic intolerance, and immoderate hedonism'. 'aus philisterhafter Gleichgültigkeit, politischer Unreife, pharisäischer Unduldsamkeit und unmäßiger Genußsucht aufzurütteln'.

45. 'il se faut remettre du tout à la volonté de Dieu, c'est toute ma consolation parmis beaucoup de traverses qui se rencontrent'. Aretin, 'Sammlung', p. 152: 29 January/8 February 1620, Frederick to Elizabeth.

46. 'il faut que je suive là, où ma vocation m'appelle', Aretin, 'Sammlung', p. 158: 2 March 1620, Frederick to Elizabeth. Frederick used 'vocation' in a religious and judicial sense. On his way to Prague, he had spoken of his taking the crown as 'als eine ordentliche rechtmässige Vocation im Nahmen Gottes'. AP, i, p. 725. Also see pp. 732, 918, for other examples.

47. Aretin, 'Sammlung', p. 153 *passim*.

48. Ibid., p. 151: 27 January/6 February 1620, Frederick to Elizabeth.

49. 'Je vous prie de ne vous y laisser aller, car vous vous faites mal avec et offencés Dieu de vous affliger sans raison. Au bout de tout il se faut resoudre à vouloir ce que Dieu veut, et suivre un chacun sa vocation'. Aretin, 'Sammlung', p. 155: 6/16 February 1620, Frederick to Elizabeth.

50. Aretin, 'Sammlung', p. 159: 4 March 1620, Frederick to Elizabeth.

51. 'machen sich die sach selbst leicht und setzet alles auf Gott und gute Hoffnung'. AP, i, p. 860. Paraphrased in Ritter, *Deutsche Geschichte*, iii, p. 65. In AP, 'die sach' that Camerarius referred to was the bad appearance and disorderliness of the train accompanying Frederick and Elizabeth to Prague. The entry into the city turned out to be a success, and even Camerarius was pleased. AP, i, pp. 860–1.

52. The ADB says that Ruprecht was born on the 18th, but an undated manuscript (BHStA, Kasten Blau, 89/3c, 'Liberi Frederici IV C. P. E, Liberi Friderici V C. P. E.') says that he was born 'abends um halb 10 uhr den 17 Dec 1619'.

53. van Eickels, *Schlesien*, p. 323. The prince was named after his godfather, Frederik Hendrik, later the Prince of Orange. Polišenský, *Tragic Triangle*, p. 175.

54. AP, ii, pp. 12–14. Abelin, *Theatrum Europeum*, p. 308. Of these princes, all were present in person except for Bavaria and Trier, who sent emissaries. On 29 January 1620 Ferdinand had declared the election illegal by Imperial edict. AP, ii, pp. 1–5.

55. Abelin, *Theatrum Europeum*, pp. 318–9. AP, ii, pp. 27–8.

56. Khevenhiller, *Annales*, ix, pp. 1020–2.

57. 'ausserhalb was die von dem h. Röm. Reich ruhende Lehnschaft belanget', Khevenhiller, *Annales*, ix, p. 1026.

58. Khevenhiller, *Annales*, ix, p. 1027. Also see Abelin, *Theatrum Europeum*, pp. 321–5. AP, ii, pp. 41–3. For the relevant passage in the Golden Bull, see Buschmann, *Kaiser und Reich*, p. 125.

59. BHStA, Fürstensachen, 1032, fols 11–12: 7/17 October 1620, Ludwig Philipp to Elector of Mainz, copy.

60. There was some precedent for this guarantee in a similar promise by Emperor Charles V to Duke Wilhelm IV in 1546. Albrecht, *Maximilian I.*, p. 506.

61. For an account of Oñate's diplomacy during this period, see Peter Brightwell, 'Spain, Bohemia and Europe, 1619–1621', *European Studies Review*, 12 (1982), pp. 371–99.

62. At his insistence, Maximilian would receive secret written confirmation of Ferdinand's oral promises in May 1620. Albrecht, *Maximilian I.*, p. 507.

63. Ibid., pp. 503–9.

64. BHStA, KS, 3730, fol. 147: 26 October 1619, Maximilian to Frederick V. For letters exchanged between the two after the Bohemian election, see AP, i, pp. 912–22, and ii, pp. 20–5.

65. van Eickels, *Schlesien*, pp. 247–8.

66. Tilly has been described as 'a Fleming whose monkish character, according to his enemies, was marred only by an inordinate love of sweetmeats'. A.E. Beller, 'The Thirty Years War', in J.P. Cooper, ed., *The New Cambridge Modern History* (Cambridge, 1970), iv, p. 314.

67. StUAP, Staré Militare, K. 31: 25 August 1620, Frederick to *Generallandtag*.

68. The following narrative derives from Brightwell, 'Spain, Bohemia and Europe'.

69. By May 1620 the Council of State had become persuaded that the attack on the Palatinate was 'muy conveniente' for preventing Ferdinand's loss of Bohemia and Hungary. Franz, *Die Politik*, I, i, #182.

70. Brightwell mistakely believes that Spain had territorial designs on the Lower Palatinate. Brightwell, 'Spain, Bohemia and Europe', p. 392.

71. Gardiner, *Letters*, ii, p. 155: Phillip III to Archduke Albert, 3 February 1620.

72. Straub, *Pax et Imperium*, pp. 160–1.

73. See BHStA, KS, 16742. These reports were endorsed to Frederick, Grün, Anhalt, and other Counts Palatine. During the war effort in 1620, a much repeated goal was to shift the war onto the lands of Frederick's enemies. See BHStA, KS, Protestantische Correspondence, 16740: 1619–1626, fols 1–412. The vast majority of these papers are from the year 1620.

74. van Eickels, *Schlesien*, p. 308.

75. StUA Praha, Staré Militare, K. 31, 18 August 1620, 'Ad Mandatum Sacræ Regiæ Majestatis proprium'.

76. van Eickels, *Schlesien*, p. 254.

77. Polišenský, *Tragic Triangle*, p. 149.

78. Ibid., p. 150.

79. Joachim Bahlcke, '"Falcko – české království" (Motivy a púsobení zahraničněpolitické orientace Falce od české kralovské volby po ulmskou smlouvu 1619–1620)', *Časopis Matice Moravské*, 2 (1992), pp. 227–51.

80. 'fort honnete homme', Aretin, 'Sammlung', p. 151: 27 January/6 February 1620, Frederick to Elizabeth.

81. David Angyal, 'Gabriel Bethlen', *Revue Historique*, clviii, 1 (1928), pp. 19, 22, 26.

82. Toegel, *Documenta Bohemica*, ii, #562, 586.

83. van Eickels, *Schlesien*, pp. 256–9.

84. Ibid., p. 249.

85. Gindely, *Geschichte*, i, pp. 195–6. For the text of the treaty at Ulm, see AP, ii, p. 48.

86. Gardiner, *Letters*, ii, p. 89: Pietro Antonio Marioni to the Doge, 5/15 November 1619.

87. 'Sa Ma.te n'a rien au monde si cher que son honneur', BHStA, KB, 22/9: January 1620, 'des Englischen Gesandtens proposition, so er an die general Staaten und der vereinigten Niederlanden so wol mund- und schriftlich gethan'.

88. 'Le roy s'amuse toujours à disputer de la justice de la cause, et semble qu'il voudroit bien être quitte de luy et le laisser retourner a mains vuides'. Aretin, 'Sammlung', p. 158: 15/25 February 1620, Frederick to Elizabeth.

89. Quoted in Carola Oman, *Elizabeth of Bohemia* (London, 1938), p. 205.

90. 'Correspondencia Oficial de Don Diego Sarmiento de Acuña, Conde de Gondomar', ed. Antonio Ballesteros Beretta, *Documentos Inéditos para la Historia de España* (4 vols, Madrid, 1943), ii, pp. 282–4.

91. Polišenský, *Tragic Triangle*, p. 180.

92. Thomas Cogswell, 'Phaeton's chariot: The Parliament-men and the continental crisis in 1621', in J.F. Merritt, ed., *The Political World of Thomas Wentworth, Earl of Strafford, 1621–1641* (Cambridge, 1996), p. 28.

93. Gindely, *Geschichte*, i, pp. 178.
94. Elmar Weiß, *Die Unterstützung Friedrichs V. von der Pfalz durch Jakob I. und Karl I. von England im Dreißigjährigen Krieg* (Stuttgart, 1966), pp. 24–5.
95. Roger Lockyer, *Buckingham* (London, 1981), p. 84.
96. 'pour ne nous dementir nous mesmes par nos propres actions, & n'ouvrir une bresche à la reputation de nostre integrité'. BHStA, KS, 16741, fol. 225: 29 June 1620, James I to Frederick V.
97. 'ce qui eust infailliblement tiré ceste querelle d'Estat en guerre generalle de Religion, au grand scandale & peril evident de toute la Chrestienté'. BHStA, KS, 16741, fol. 225: 29 June 1620, James I to Frederick V.
98. BHStA, KB, 121/1/II, fol. 2: 4/14 August 1620, Frederick V to Achaz von Dohna.
99. Huntingdon also gave Dohna a list of the various knights and esquires from Leicester and Rutland counties who were 'most forward' to help. BHStA, KS, 16742, fol. 561: 31 October 1620, Huntingdon to Baron Dohna.
100. Gindely, *Geschichte*, i, p. 199.
101. Nicolette Mout, 'Der Winterkönig im Exil: Frederick V von der Pfalz und die niederländischen Generalstaaten, 1621–1632', *Zeitschrift für Historische Forschung*, 15, 3 (1988), pp. 258–9. Johann Ernst, Duke of Saxe-Weimar, managed to extract a subsidy from the Estates General for the regiment that he recruited in the Netherlands for Frederick's service. Polišenský, *Tragic Triangle*, p. 169.
102. 'absolute domination d'Espagne, a la totale desolation et de la religion reformee et de la liberte des dits Princes de l'Union dans l'Empire'. BHStA, KB, 22/9: 2 Jan 1620, 'Responce donne par Messieurs des Estats sur la proposition faicte par l'ambassadeur d'Angleterre'.
103. Mout, 'Der Winterkönig', pp. 259–60.
104. Michael Roberts, *Gustavus Adolphus: A History of Sweden, 1611–1632* (2 vols, London, 1953), i, p. 188.
105. Ibid., pp. 178–9.
106. Ibid., p. 193.
107. Lockhart, *Denmark*, p. 87.
108. Bruchmann, *Die Huldigungsfahrt*, p. 74.
109. Lockhart, *Denmark*, p. 88.
110. Zwiedineck-Südenhorst, *Die Politik*, i, pp. 100–5.
111. In 1606 Emperor Matthias and the Ottomans had concluded the armistice of Zsitvatorok, which had guaranteed peace for twenty years. For a thorough account of the negotiations during the Bohemian rebellion, see R.R. Heinisch, 'Habsburg, die Pforte und der Böhmische Aufstand (1618–1620)', *Südostforschungen*, 33 (1974), pp. 125–65, and, 'Habsburg, die Pforte und der Böhmische Aufstand (1618–1620), II. Teil', *Südostforschungen*, 34 (1975), 79–124.
112. van Eickels, *Schlesien*, p. 283.
113. Ibid., p. 308.
114. H. Forst, 'Der türkische Gesandte in Prag 1620 und der Briefwechsel des Winterkönigs mit Sultan Osman II.', *Mittheilungen des Instituts für Oesterreichische Geschichtsforschung*, 16 (1895), pp. 568–9.
115. Forst, 'Der türkische Gesandte', pp. 570, 580.
116. Abelin, *Theatrum Europaeum*, pp. 381–4.
117. Egler, *Die Spanier*, p. 48.
118. Green, *Elizabeth*, p. 33.
119. Gotthard, 'Politice seint wir bäptisch', pp. 297–8.

120. For a full account of these negotiations, see Frank Müller, *Kursachsen und der Böhmische Aufstand, 1618–1622* (Münster, 1997), pp. 283–396.

121. Parker, *The Thirty Years' War*, p. 54. Gotthard, 'Politice seint wir bäpstisch', pp. 298–9.

122. Khevenhiller, *Annales*, ix, pp. 101719.

123. Polišenský, *Tragic Triangle*, p. 121.

124. Aretin, 'Sammlung', pp. 160–71.

125. 'le tems me dure extremement icy ne sachant à quoy passer le tems', Aretin, 'Sammlung',p. 161: 20/30 September 1620, Frederick to Elizabeth.

126. 'Je recommande tout à Dieu, et suis resolu de prendre tout en patience de sa main paternelle. Il l'a donné, il me l'a oté, il me peut rendre, son nom soit glorifié'. Aretin, 'Sammlung',   p. 162: 30 September/10 October 1620, Frederick to Elizabeth. Also see p. 164.

127. Aretin, 'Sammlung', p. 164: 8/18 October 1620, Frederick to Elizabeth.

128. Abelin, *Theatrum Europaeum*, pp. 404–5.

129. 's'il plait à Dieu nous nous verrons encore force années'. Aretin, 'Sammlung', p. 169: 21/31 October 1620, Frederick to Elizabeth.

130. They had recently sent their eldest son to safety in Holland. Abelin, *Theatrum Europaeum*, p. 403.

131. Aretin, 'Sammlung', pp. 169–70: 1 November 1620, Frederick to Elizabeth.

132. Ibid., pp. 170–1: 4 November 1620, Frederick to Elizabeth.

133. J.V. Polišenský, 'Scottish Soldiers in the Bohemian War', in Murdoch, *Scotland and the Thirty Years' War*, p. 113.

134. The troop numbers derive from J.V. Polišenský, 'Scottish Soldiers in the Bohemian War', in Murdoch, *Scotland and the Thirty Years' War*, p. 113. Regarding payment of troops, see Polišenský, *Tragic Triangle*, p. 225, and Dieter Albrecht, 'Zur Finanzierung des Dreißigjährigen Krieges: Die Subsidien der Kurie für Kaiser und Liga, 1618–1635', *Zeitschrift für bayerische Landesgeschichte*, 19, 3 (1956), pp. 538–9.

135. The most thorough and thrilling account of the battle is Olivier Chaline, *La Bataille de la Montagne Blanche (8 November 1620)* (Paris, 1999).

136. Of Frederick's army 500–700 were killed, while 400–500 fell on the Emperor's side. Chaline, *La Bataille*, p. 181.

137. Some of these treasures now lie in the *Schatzkammer Museum* in the *Residenz* in Munich. See Hubert Glaser, *Um Glauben und Reich: Kurfürst Maximilian I., Wittelsbach und Bayern* (München, 1980). Duke Maximilian had Christian of Anhalt's correspondence sent to Bavaria, and Emperor Ferdinand had two of his councilors work through Frederick's. Forst, 'Der türkishe Gesandte', p. 572. The most secret documents of Palatine diplomacy were to be published in the *Anhaltische Kanzlei* in 1621, and newer editions of this text appeared during the course of the same year.

138. AP, ii, p. 237.

139. J.N.D. Kelly, *The Oxford Dictionary of Popes* (Oxford, 1986), p. 278.

Chapter 5

The Palatine Crisis, 1620–1621

During the year after the defeat at White Mountain, the main theater of war would transfer from Bohemia to the Palatinate, while Frederick's greatest concern would shift from trying to maintain Bohemia to defending his Palatine territories and dignities. The Emperor's declaration of the Imperial ban against Frederick in January 1621 marks the beginning of 'the Palatine crisis', which refers to his extended struggle for the possession of his electoral lands and titles against the rising tide of his enemies, despite the general ebb of his allies. From all sides he would seek support for 'the common cause', by which he meant the defense of the Palatinate and his restoration as Elector Palatine, and to Protestant powers specifically, he would propagate 'the Protestant cause', a war to protect the supposedly endangered existence of Protestantism in the Empire. Depending on his audience, during this period he would usually depict his constitutional quarrel with Ferdinand II as a fundamentally religious conflict. But while the Protestant cause touched the sympathies of some of his prospective supporters, it could not inspire them to contribute to that which they most wanted to avoid: a war of religion in the Empire. Almost every one of Frederick's allies and enemies, Protestants and Catholics alike, had compelling individual reasons for wanting to end the war as soon as possible, but his obstinacy, based on his personal religious faith and sense of princely honor, confounded all efforts to stop the bloodshed and re-establish peace. His righteous insistence on the correctness of his interpretation of the Imperial constitution was a major contributor to the perpetuation of the Thirty Years' War.

The Rebellion Collapses

Even after fleeing Prague, Frederick had no intention of ending the war against the enemies of the uprising. After all, despite the disintegration of his main army, Count Mansfeld still occupied Pilsen, and the towns of Tábor, Třeboň, and Zvíkov (Klingenberg) remained loyal to Frederick. Johann Georg, the Margrave of Jägerndorf, was armed and in the field, and Dukes Johann Ernst and Wilhelm of Saxe-Weimar maintained their command over some divisions of the Bohemian military forces. Bethlen Gábor was in full strength. Above all Frederick needed a base where he could regroup his forces and provide them with money and supplies. In Silesia he hoped to find such a place and continue the war with the allegiance of Moravia and Hungary. Immediately after leaving Prague he and his companions traveled first to the fortress-town of Glatz, in the mountain range along the Bohemian-Silesian border, where they could rest in safety until 15 November 1620. They reached Silesia's capital two days later, and there Frederick made his intentions known.

Unfortunately in Breslau Frederick encountered political resistance and confessional resentment. The head of the Silesian government, Duke Johann Christian of Brieg, had asked Frederick to remain in Glatz, because Breslau was unwilling to take on the costs of supporting his court and opening a new theater of war. Despite the fact that neither the Emperor nor the Elector of Saxony had yet invaded Silesia, there were threats from roving bands of Cossacks and from the proximity of Saxon troops in Upper Lusatia. In addition, there was a general discontent with Frederick's Letter of Majesty which had sanctioned Calvinist religious practice. If he had expected more tolerance in Silesia – the presence of Calvinism there was greater than in Bohemia – he had miscalculated gravely.[1] He tried to win the burghers' allegiance by granting them access to the royal castle and to his person, but his efforts were in vain. Against his pleas that all live together peaceably despite their confessional differences, the Lutherans petitioned him to revoke his Letter of Majesty, though out of respect for his presence in the city they said that they would tolerate Calvinist services in the castle alone. To prevent inter-confessional strife from weakening his cause, Frederick complied readily, though regretfully. Nonetheless he began to attend Lutheran services in the Elizabeth Church both to show his Protestant ecumenism and increase the likelihood of receiving money from the burghers and the guilds for the war effort.[2]

Frederick's first priority was the war. From Breslau he informed the Union, the Dukes of Holstein, and the Kings of England and Denmark of the outcome of the battle at White Mountain and of his intention to continue the struggle.[3] He sent Volrad von Plessen and Camerarius to various princes and cities in northern Germany and another emissary, Paul Jesin, to Moravia and Hungary to secure support for the continuance of the campaign. Scultetus was sent back to Heidelberg, because his purported hand in the reformation of St. Vitus' cathedral had become a political liability for Frederick in Breslau.[4] But he would be quickly disappointed, because at about that time the Moravian Estates resolved to submit to the Emperor, despite Count Thurn's support for Jesin and Bethlen Gábor's threat to invade Moravia if they did so.[5] Gábor, meanwhile, double-crossed his allies a second time. While he promised to assist the Palatine, he negotiated a separate peace with the Emperor and withdrew his troops from Pressburg.

Frederick, however, was unaware of these developments in early December when he exhorted the diet of Silesian princes to remain true to the war effort on account of their promise to stand by him. He reminded them that they had supported his election as King of Bohemia, and that he had accepted the title for the sake of their religion and their rights and privileges. Complaining that he alone had borne the cost of the war and the embassies to various princes, and that now the Spaniards had invaded the Palatinate, he bid them to honor the terms of their confederation with the other rebel Estates. He warned that they were facing servitude under Spain or even a possible Turkish invasion. He recalled their oath of allegiance to himself and asked them to lead a counter-attack by Bohemia, Moravia, Lusatia, Hungary, and Protestants from the Union and abroad.[6]

The Silesian diet, however, did not share Frederick's zeal for the war. While they declared their readiness to render him further support, they offered him only a sixth of the sum of money that he requested.[7] When he objected, the Silesians asked him to accept the Elector of Saxony's offer to intercede and arrange a peace with the Emperor. Mutinies among the soldiery, the news of the Moravian submission to the Emperor, and the Saxon military presence in Lusatia contributed to the Silesian preference for peaceful measures of resolution. Frederick had no choice but to accept this decision. He consented to their embassy to Saxony, but he demanded nonetheless that they remain true to their confederation. After meeting once more with the Silesian princes, Frederick paid his debts and left Breslau shortly before Christmas, 1620.[8] When he left Silesia, the remnants of his influence departed with him. During the negotiations with Saxony, the Silesians would render their submission to the Emperor and sue for his mercy in February 1621. Frederick's departure, they would say, absolved them of their oaths to him.[9] From that point on, the last adherents of the Bohemian rebellion would be its King and Queen, the members of their court, and the detachments of armed forces still loyal to them.

Frederick would meet these developments with the resolution of his steadfast faith in God's design. When he learned of the Moravian Estates' submission to the Emperor, he wrote to Count Thurn,

> We entrust it to the Almighty and accept with patience the reprimand that he sent upon us. May he let everything occur for his honor and for the favor of his believers. ... We did not force ourselves on Bohemia and Moravia. We could have been well contented with our patrimonial lands, but we put that aside upon their request and honestly did everything in our power for their lands.

Now we receive the thanks, that they explicitly agree to a treaty – and after we put forward ours for their sake – and subordinate themselves to another. Now whether this is laudable and honest we let the whole world judge. Neither greed nor ambition brought us to Bohemia. Neither poverty nor suffering will make us desert our dear God or do something contrary to honor and conscience.[10]

Frederick would carry his conviction of righteousness and his devotion to God and honor till the end of his days.

Common Cause and Protestant Cause

Despite the disappointing outcome of his stay in Silesia, Frederick showed no sign of relenting. He went to join his wife in Küstrin in Electoral Brandenburg, where she delivered their fifth child and fourth son. Frederick, meanwhile, turned his efforts to mounting an alliance between Protestant German princes and estates and foreign powers against the Emperor. His primary targets were the United Provinces, the members of the Union, the Kings of England, Denmark, and Sweden, and the princes and estates of the Lower Saxon Circle.[11] Depicting his situation in the direst of terms, he urged unity for the sake of their own security and that of their religion. In this diplomatic effort, Frederick was trying to foment a war of religion in the Empire, 'the Protestant cause', in order to achieve the goals of 'the common cause', the recovery of the Bohemian throne and the defense of the Palatinate.

Through letters Frederick attempted to guarantee the Union's participation. He reported that the Silesians were committed to the common cause, despite their peace negotiations with the Elector of Saxony and the Emperor. The Silesians, he claimed, had allied with Bethlen Gábor and would work with the Dutch Estates General and the Kings of Great Britain, Denmark, and Sweden against the common enemy, the 'Papist League'. Frederick promised to devote his life to the common cause, and he asked the Union to maintain a constant correspondence with him so that nothing would go awry.[12] In another letter Frederick declared that he was going to fight for all Protestants' interests, so that the papists would not overcome those that were still free. Because he expected the Turks to join the war, he wanted the Union's advice on the direction of future policy. He exhorted the members

to open [their] eyes thenceforth, and not regard private interests so much as the public, but imitate the papist example, and faithfully assemble, and thus be all inclined to take precautions so that Spain and her followers do not increase in power and attain such advantages, the likes of which they never had before.[13]

Frederick concluded that negotiations for peace with the Emperor should not prevent all Protestants from working together to arrange the best conditions possible in a future settlement. Similar letters were sent to Joachim Ernst, Duke of Holstein, and to Duke Ulrich of Holstein, the Administrator of Schwerin, who had inquired about Frederick's condition after the misfortune in Bohemia.[14]

The initial reaction to Frederick's Protestant and common causes was resoundingly negative. Georg Wilhelm, the Elector of Brandenburg, as a Calvinist and Frederick's brother-in-law, seemed the most likely candidate to help the royal Bohemian exiles, but the Lutheran Estates of Brandenburg were reluctant to do anything on their behalf. Georg Wilhelm lacked the financial means to act independently, and the public debt of his electorate was already among the largest in Germany.[15] Shortly after the pair came to Berlin, an expression of Imperial displeasure did arrive as expected, and Frederick had to leave the city at the end of January.[16] He was no more successful at his next destination, Wolfenbüttel, where he hoped to meet Friedrich Ulrich, the Duke of Braunschweig-Wolfenbüttel. The Duke, however, had left town, and no one would disclose his whereabouts.[17] Despite these patent rejections, Frederick remained undaunted. He commissioned Count Mansfeld as Field Marshall of Bohemia, issued specific instructions on troop recruitment, allotted 30,000 fl., and ordered him to correspond regularly about his activities.[18] Frederick also wrote to Maurits, the Prince of Orange, to get the Estates General to grant 200,000 Guilders, resume payment of monthly subsidies, and supply military assistance.[19] Perhaps Frederick hoped that naming his new baby, Moritz, would make the Prince feel a greater obligation to be of assistance to the family.

His wife and his faith buoyed his spirits on the rough seas of political reality. In Breslau the separation from Elizabeth, the dismal winter weather, and the magnitude of his failure as King of Bohemia had depressed his spirits.[20] On some days he had not left his chamber at all, and he had said that he would enjoy no peace of mind until he had learned of his wife's safe arrival in Brandenburg.[21] In a letter he had exhorted Elizabeth 'to take with patience all the misfortune that God send [them]', and in these words he had not so much given advice as shared with her the source of his consolation.[22] To his uncle, the King of Denmark, Frederick had written of his desire to carry out God's will, his hope for God's protection, and his prayer that God would send him the means to redress the dire situation he faced.[23] After rejoining Elizabeth and her new-born in

Brandenburg, Frederick's morale had improved. During their next separation, while he was in Wolfenbüttel, he could take pleasure in the beauty of the ducal mansion and the company.[24] Nevertheless he longed to see Elizabeth again, because being with her, he wrote, 'is indeed the most precious company that I can have in this world'.[25]

While in Wolfenbüttel Frederick decided not to return to the Lower Palatinate with his family but settle instead in the Low Countries, most likely because he heard about the Emperor's formal declaration of the Imperial ban against him, which had been expected for some time. In a solemn ceremony in Vienna on 29 January 1621, Ferdinand II had banned Frederick and, at the same time but in a separate declaration, the Count of Hohenlohe, the Margrave of Jägerndorf, and Christian of Anhalt. Frederick was banned for breaking the Imperial peace, for crimes of *lèse-majesté*, and for rebellion against the Empire, because he had accepted the crown of Bohemia, illegally offered to him, and had made himself the head of the rebellion. Because the nature of Frederick's rebellious crimes was determined to be 'notorious', Ferdinand was entitled constitutionally to proclaim the ban without going through the normal process of summons and hearings.[26] The resolution to ban an Imperial elector in this manner had taken fourteen months to settle, and it was controversial both in and beyond the Emperor's court.[27] Frederick dismissively regarded the ban as yet another Habsburg breach of the Imperial constitution, but nonetheless it entailed a sharp reduction in his safety in the Empire. No one was allowed to aid him, and anyone could attack his lands or his person with impunity. He therefore resolved to go to the United Provinces of the Netherlands, the region of the Empire where people were least likely to obey the Emperor and where he would find the greatest measure of safety for himself and his family. He planned to stay in Wolfenbüttel until Elizabeth arrived, and he requested a convoy from Prince Maurits to lead them to The Hague in safety.[28]

The declaration of the ban did not lead Frederick to revoke his plans for a new alliance. Indeed it gave him more proof that the Habsburgs were determined to corrupt the Imperial constitution and oppress Protestant princes such as himself.[29] From Wolfenbüttel he decided to attend a meeting of Protestant princes in Segeberg in Holstein – that he had not been invited did not deter him – called by Christian IV, King of Denmark, whose goal was to prevent the war from spreading to northern Germany.

Segeberg

At first glance the Segeberg conference was a partial success for Frederick's common cause. The assembly, which included delegates from the Lower Saxon Circle, the Union, Brandenburg, the United Provinces, England, and Denmark, resolved to send Emperor Ferdinand II the following demands: the revocation of the Imperial ban against Frederick V and the restoration of his lands and titles, the dissolution of Maximilian's and Ferdinand's armed forces, and a guarantee for Bohemian and Imperial constitutional religious freedoms. Should the Emperor not comply, these Protestants potentates resolved to muster an army of 30,000 and force him to do so.[30] The assembly, however, would not commit to restoring Frederick as King of Bohemia, nor would they mobilize any forces until they heard the Emperor's response. The outcome of the conference was a merely diplomatic gesture, because the delegates generally preferred containing the war to escalating it on behalf of Frederick's causes. The Emperor's triumph over the Bohemians, the Imperial ban against Frederick, and Spínola's invasion of the Palatinate had engendered a fear that the war might extend itself from the Upper Rhine and Bohemia into northern Germany.[31]

The Danish King, however, was willing to fight to rid the Empire of the Spanish soldiers. He sent words of encouragement to the Landgrave Moritz of Hessen-Kassel – Spínola was pressuring him to abandon the Union – telling him to hold out against the Spanish and wait for help from Denmark. He told Anstruther, the English ambassador, that it had become necessary to turn to arms in the interests of Protestantism, and, laying his hand on Anstruther's shoulder, added that the time for words had gone by. In addition to mustering an army, Christian planned to send an ambassador to tell the Emperor to make peace at once or expect war with Denmark. Unfortunately for Frederick, this embassy was the only resolution taken at Segeberg that was actually carried out.[32]

Christian IV was at best ambivalent towards his nephew's situation, and he did not support either of his causes unconditionally. The King would not fight alone, and he found the Lower Saxon princes unreliable. He was also wary of the Dutch connections with his rivals, the Hanseatic cities and Sweden.[33] Moreover Christian held his nephew responsible for the current crisis in the Empire. When the two princes met at Segeberg in March 1621, he blurted, 'Who advised you to drive out kings and to seize kingdoms? If your councilors did so, they were scoundrels'.[34] He advised Frederick to renounce his claim to the Bohemian crown, which could have led to a settlement with the Emperor and to an end to the war in the Palatinate.[35]

Frederick rejected the suggestion as unconstitutional. He could not give up the Bohemian crown, because, in his view, it belonged to him by law. The problem was the injustice of the House of Austria. Until, he said, Ferdinand II made good his promise to maintain Bohemian freedom and uphold the Letter of Majesty, Frederick was unable to break the vows that he had made to his confederates. In addition, he said that he would not make an apology to the Emperor, because his actions had 'had absolutely nothing to do with the Imperial Majesty as a Roman Emperor, but only as a duke of Austria'.[36] The distinction was one of jurisdiction. Frederick admitted to having a conflict with Ferdinand Habsburg only in his capacity as Archduke of Austria. By this logic, Frederick had committed no crime against the Holy Roman Emperor, and therefore the Imperial ban against him was invalid. It was rather the Emperor who owed Frederick an apology.[37] He did not take this position in order to protect only his pride. He too looked on his Bohemian episode as a complete failure, referring to the Bohemian crown as a 'crown of thorns', but he would not compromise his vows.[38]

The Segeberg meeting failed to produce a Protestant alliance, above all because a wide diveristy of local and international interests impeded progress. Gustavus Adolphus, King of Sweden, did not send a representative, and no delegation from Mecklenburg appeared, which were taken as refusals to participate. Only Duke Friedrich Ulrich of Braunschweig and Duke Christian of Lüneburg would assist in the war, and both had begun to ready their arms before the Segeberg meeting began. The old rivalry between Denmark and the cities of the Hanse undercut the alliance, because the cities feared that Christian IV might use the alliance's forces to attack them. The cities also threw up a barrier between Denmark and their traditional protector, the Dutch. Nor did England, the Union, or the Lower Saxon Circle rise to the occasion. King James I shared none of Christian IV's militarism. When Anstruther appeared at Segeberg, he was not empowered to act as England's representative to the meeting, and when he requested a loan from Christian for the Palatines, it was to be in the form of a gift to his niece, Elizabeth. More participation from England did not appear to be forthcoming.[39] Except for Frederick, Christian, and the Dutch, the powers involved were hesitant to open hostilities against the Spanish army on the Rhine, and neither Denmark nor the United Provinces would act alone. The appeal to the Protestant cause was not able to overcome the basic interest of state security. Obviously the Protestants at Segeberg did not believe that the existence of their religion was at stake.

After the conference, Frederick traveled with his family to safety in Holland, where his uncle, the Prince of Orange, received them ceremoniously in mid April 1621. They took up residence in The Hague (s' Gravenhage), which served the seat of the Estates General, the national assembly of the seven Dutch provinces.[40] Though dispossessed, the pair did not live without means. The Estates General granted them 10,000 Guilders per month and the use of the Hof te Wassenaer, a large mansion in the town, and from England they received another 26,000.[41] In the summer of 1621 the Estates would loan Frederick another 150,000 for his forces in the Palatinate.[42] Furthermore, the pair did not have to support a large body of retainers and courtiers. For all those capable of bearing arms among Frederick's followers, military commissions in the Prince of Orange's army were made available.[43] Nonetheless, expenses would exceed income in a matter of months, and creditors would plague the Palatines for years afterwards.[44]

In The Hague Frederick established his court-in-exile, of which he was unequivocally the leader. Christian of Anhalt had abandoned the Palatines altogether.[45] Abraham Scultetus, after a brief return to Heidelberg, would go to preach in Emden.[46] Count Thurn had applied to the Emperor for mercy, been rejected, and then fled to Hungary, but he would assist the common cause in the coming years in Venice.[47] Volrad von Plessen continued as Palatine adviser, though his taking residence in Leiden a couple of years later must have reduced his influence on Frederick's policy. Camerarius, who had failed to persuade Frederick to relinquish the Bohemian crown, was on various diplomatic missions for much of 1621.[48] When he was in The Hague, Camerarius mainly worked as a correspondent and publicist, composing letters, reports, and polemics, either at Frederick's behest or with his permission. Finally, there is little reliable evidence that indicates that Elizabeth either determined her husband's policy or contributed substantively to its formation.

The Hof te Wassenaer rapidly became the center of a communication network that relayed Palatine diplomatic correspondence, secret military information, and general news from one end of Europe to the other, from Edinburgh to Istanbul. There Frederick would work to obtain Dutch and English assistance to prevent the conquest and possible dismemberment of the Palatinate. Already the Emperor had laid claim to the town of Oppenheim, and the Elector of Mainz had claimed the districts of Pickelheim and the Bergstrasse.[49] Frederick was in danger of losing his Palatine estates as he had Bohemia and the incorporated lands.

The English Dimension

Everything now seemed to depend on England. Just as Frederick arrived in the Netherlands, the Twelve Years' Truce between Spain and the United Provinces expired. These two powers were again, officially, at war, and both were allied in one way or another with England. Neither took up the offensive immediately, but a large portion of the Spanish Army of the Netherlands was in the Lower Palatinate. As long as England remained an ally of Spain, no alliance of Protestant powers was likely to form on Frederick's behalf. Frederick's task was to persuade his father-in-law to abandon his pacific policy and turn against the Habsburgs. It was to be a lengthy, tiresome struggle but, in the end, not totally futile.

Though James I had roundly condemned his son-in-law's adventure in Bohemia, he had promised on more than one occasion to defend the Palatinate, should it become necessary. James wanted to stop the war and to see Frederick's full restoration to his patrimony, but the King preferred to use negotiations instead of hostilities. For James, a negotiated settlement placed the burden of the solution unilaterally upon Frederick: he had to reconcile himself with the Emperor if the Imperial ban was to be retracted and the Palatinate restored. The first, vital step was that Frederick had to renounce his claims to Bohemia. James had never acknowledged his son-in-law as King of Bohemia and usually addressed him in their correspondence as 'Monsieur mon tres cher fils le Prince Electeur Palatin du Rhin'.

After the King had heard about the outcome at White Mountain, he had dispatched Jacob Morton to the Union and Robert Anstruther to Christian IV to enlist their assistance in resolving the crisis in Bohemia and in arranging Frederick's reconciliation with the Emperor. James had also sent Sir Edward Villiers to urge Frederick to rely totally on his father-in-law's advice and to renounce his claim to the Bohemian crown. In hopes of influencing Frederick, the Marquis of Buckingham had sent a similar message to Elizabeth, informing her that James, Prince Charles, Viscount Doncaster, Sir John Digby, the two secretaries of state, and other important figures in the English government were also in favor of a formal renunciation.[50] In response Frederick said that he had not given up hope of regaining what was lost, but he would comply with James' wishes. This was typical of communication between James and Frederick; the former made requests, and the latter agreed to comply, though he usually, in fact, did not.

King James wanted Frederick to return to the Lower Palatinate immediately, despite the fact that much of it was occupied by Spanish troops, where he could lead its defense and care for his subjects. It was no secret that Frederick's tour across the north of the Empire had been devoted to recruiting assistance for his wars, which would only make James' plans to obtain peace through negotiations more difficult. Frederick had attributed the necessity of staying in The Hague to the Imperial ban, which had placed him and his family in danger throughout the Empire. Furthermore, his presence in the Palatinate would only encourage Spinola and his troops. Frederick had complained that if the princes of the Union abandoned the Palatinate, then the full burden of war would fall upon him, guaranteeing his ruin, the total loss of all estates, friends, and allies, and the decimation of his honor. Frederick had asked the King to approve his stay in the Low Countries, though he had added that, supplied with an army, he would make his return to the Palatinate with his honor intact.[51]

In his letters of reply, he had tried to persuade James to uphold the Protestant and common causes. Since all prior constitutional arguments had only elicited the King's derisive skepticism, Frederick had appealed directly to his Protestant sympathies. He had explained that he had accepted the Bohemian crown first for 'the advance of the glory of God', and that though his misfortune had also been due to God's inscrutable will, this did not deny the righteousness of the Bohemian adventure.[52]

> If it had pleased God to give happy issue, all the party of the religion would have had relief, but since this has not been the will of God, it is for me to take both the good and the evil from His hand.[53]

He begged his father-in-law not to attribute his actions to disobedience but to a sincere desire to perform the will of God and to aid Protestantism. Frederick pointed out that he still held parts of Silesia and various towns in Bohemia, and he disclosed his hope of recovering his losses with aid from James and other Protestant princes. He expressed his certainty that James would take up the defense of his grandchildren's patrimony, return peace to the Palatinate and all the Empire, guarantee the true religion and liberty, and put an end to Spínola's campaign.[54]

James proceeded, perhaps somewhat resentfully, with his plans to negotiate a settlement to the Palatine war. First and foremost, he wanted to secure a suspension of arms in the Palatinate. If the hostilities there could be brought to a halt, then the opposing parties would have a greater chance of settling their differences free from the pressure of desperation and war. James' efforts to procure and then secure this suspension of arms would last for nearly five years, almost until his death in 1625.[55] The main reason why this project would fail is because he would be unable to tame the Winter King. In all James' negotiations with Spain, the Archdukes, and the Emperor, he claimed that he would bring Frederick into line and guarantee his good behavior for the future. It would prove impossible to accomplish either. During the course of the campaign in the Palatinate, Frederick would continue his pleas for James' assistance and yet disobey most of his requests. James would never manage even to persuade Frederick to abandon his claim to Bohemia, which was the first condition of James' intercession on his son-in-law's behalf.

Nonetheless, there were powerful motions in favor of peace in the Palatinate in the first months of 1621. The Twelve Years Truce between

Spain and the United Provinces was set to expire in April 1621, and
Archduke Albert needed to have as much of the Army of the Netherlands
as possible to defend his borders. In March 1621 Sir John Digby had
conducted a successful embassy to the Archdukes in Brussels for a
suspension of arms.[56] Archduke Albert had then recommended the
suspension to Spínola and the princes of the Union.[57] In February Spínola
had warned the Union not to defend the Palatinate. He had explained that
his assignment was to make sure that the Emperor received his due respect
and obedience, to insure that neighboring lands were not destroyed by
further war, and to return peace to the Empire. Spínola had denied that the
King of Spain was seeking to win power in the Empire by means of force.
He had directly contradicted one of Frederick's main accusations against
the Spanish by insisting that the King of Spain intended no infringements
of German liberties or the Empire's religion and constitution. The Union
members, he had claimed, would suffer no harm if they simply obeyed the
Emperor.[58] This offer had thrown them into turmoil. Confusion and
dissension had reigned at the Union meeting in February at Heilbronn, as
the members had quarreled about the publication of the Imperial ban and
the constitutional liberties of Germany.[59] By the end of February, it had
appeared that the Union would not challenge Frederick's ban, or those
against the Margrave of Jägerndorf, Christian of Anhalt, and the Count of
Hohenlohe either.[60]

  The Union soon dissolved despite English efforts to shore it up in the
last minute. At the end of February Sir Albert Morton had brought to the
Heilbronn meeting £30,000, which had been collected in England, and a
promise from James to defend the Palatinate, if Frederick followed the
King's advice.[61] If this meant a formal renunciation of Frederick's claim
to Bohemia, such was not forthcoming. Another English ambassador, Sir
Isaac Wake, had negotiated with Mansfeld about defending the Upper
Palatinate, 'when Bohemia should be restored to the Emperor'.[62] These
offers, however, had not provided the required reassurance against the
danger of defending a banned prince. The Union princes had thanked
James for the money and agreed that Frederick should obey all his
commands.[63] Nevertheless, when Spínola had offered a two-month cease-
fire, under the condition that they defend neither Frederick nor the
Palatinate if he did not make his peace with the Emperor, the leader of the
Union forces, the Margrave of Ansbach, had accepted.[64] The Treaty of
Mainz was signed on 12 April 1621 under the mediation of Landgrave
Ludwig of Hessen-Darmstadt and the Elector of Mainz. King James'
preference for a suspension of arms had only encouraged the Union's
acceptance, and the members blamed England fully for the current crisis
and their capitulation.[65] In May the Union formally dissolved itself at

Heilbronn, leaving only the small detachments of British volunteers and the local Palatine forces guarding the land. Spanish dominance over the area seemed unquestionable. At James' behest, and under orders from Archduke Albert, the Spanish forces in the Palatinate agreed to a three-month cease-fire, and Spínola returned to the Spanish Netherlands with a large part of the army, leaving Don Gonzalo Fernández de Córdoba with 17,000 infantry and 2,500 cavalry in the Palatinate.[66] The collapse of the Union and the cease-fire in the Lower Palatinate removed two major obstacles to peace. The next was Frederick.

He utterly refused to give up his royal Bohemian title or sue for the Emperor's mercy, and he insisted on his right to defend his Palatine lands by all means available. He probably had a measure of confidence that his strongholds could weather the current storm, if he shared Sir Horace Vere's opinion. At Frankenthal, Vere reported that the Margrave of Baden-Durlach was 'solicitous', that the Dutch companies would 'be reinforced to their former strength', and he added, 'neyther are wee (the English I meane) soe weake as is generally believed'.[67] He and his men mocked the Emperor's supporters for their overconfidence, 'that they dare dispose not only of what they have, but even of what they have not, building Castells in the aire as yf victory were theire handmaide'. Frankenthal, Vere said, was 'in the hope of supply owt of England ... and ... in daily expectation to have comfortable newes from thence'.[68] Frederick was in general hesitant to support any embassy in favor of a peace treaty. According to Elizabeth's secretary, Francis Nethersole, Frederick was 'unwilling to do any thing which may shew that he hath any trust of being restored to the Palatinate by a treaty, till there be something done by force'.[69]

Frederick's response to the Treaty of Mainz was to warn Christian IV that the Palatinate lay open to Spanish invasion and papist encroachment and that German liberty and Protestantism lay vulnerable to irreparable harm.[70] This plea fell on deaf ears. When the Lower Saxon Circle met in late April, they declared their neutrality in the Palatine war, and even the Danish representatives agreed with this resolution. Christian IV would later reply that he was resolved to render some form of assistance for the Palatinate, but he recommended that Frederick actually not defend his lands, nor unite with other Protestants, nor, under any circumstances, make an alliance with other princes.[71] Apparently the Danish King and the northern German Protestants looked at the war as an affair between Frederick and Emperor Ferdinand.

Frederick's and Elizabeth's pleas to James I were somewhat more effective. Immediately after arriving in The Hague, Elizabeth humbly entreated her father to help them soon, 'otherwise I fear that all will be lost'.[72] Frederick protested,

I will live happily, not being able to look to anyone, after God, for the remedy of my evils than Your Majesty, in whose hands I put myself entirely, desiring to submit my will to his, knowing well that he take to heart the conservation of his children.[73]

Frederick's submission, however, was only available on his terms, and because he would not damage his honor or admit any fault, and it was hardly submission at all. Only a few days later, on hearing news of the Treaty of Mainz, they both informed James that some princes of the Union had blamed their dissolution on his inactivity, and they begged him to show the world that he would not abandon them.[74]

Before these pleas reached James, he had sent Dohna to Frederick to tell him that he would receive £14,000 for the most urgent necessities of the army in the Palatinate and £6,000, at his discretion, for those suffering the deprivations of war.[75] He must have interpreted this grant as a tacit approbation of his political stance, because his thanks to James was a request for £50,000![76] Frederick stated that the Emperor would make no restitution unless force was used. He asked James to commission an ambassador to obtain security for the Upper Palatinate from the Duke of Bavaria. The Emperor had to be pacified by force, Frederick argued, because his acts were 'so extreme, that they can only incense further the wrath of God on the general public'.[77]

On 5 May Frederick received James' announcement of the continuation of Sir John Digby's embassy to the Archdukes and to the Emperor, this time to arrange the full restoration of the Palatinate. James had declared that he was obligated 'by the law of honor and of nature to see [Frederick] restored'.[78] For the success of this embassy, James required his son-in-law to obey and to render all due respect to the Emperor. But Frederick put no faith in the efficacy of this embassy and instead continued to work on the war effort. Later in May he would ask James to make a military pact with Denmark and the Lower Saxon Circle to prevent them from laying down their arms.[79] Frederick also commissioned the Margrave of Jägerndorf to fight on his behalf in Bohemia and the incorporated lands.[80]

James, however, despite the grant of £20,000, had not changed his policy toward the war in the Palatinate. He stuck firmly to his plan to use negotiations in order to bring Frederick to submit to the Emperor. As long as his son-in-law remained recalcitrant, James would be relieved of the responsibility to procure a restoration by force of arms. This plan is revealed in his elusive or dismissive answers to a number of propositions from Frederick, delivered in May by Francis Nethersole. To a request for money and men to enable Frederick to return to the Palatinate, James said that such a measure was impossible given the Treaty of Mainz and the peace negotiations at Brussels. When Frederick asked James to appeal to the Kings of Denmark and France to aid the common cause, he answered that he had done so and would continue to do so, but he would only ask for diplomatic support of the treaty negotiations. To a request for approval and support for Mansfeld's army, James said that it would only be granted if all of Frederick's forces would not attack either the Emperor, the Duke of Bavaria, or any member of their party. Frederick demanded a full, unconditional, unrestricted restitution, with indemnities for his and his allies' expenses, for which he would neither renounce his alliances nor deprecate himself to the Emperor. James said that he would never ask Frederick to accept conditions that were prejudicial to his honor, nor to make a submission to the Emperor that was beneath his status as a prince of the Empire of his rank, but the King did not specify which rank his son-in-law rightfully held, that of king, elector, or merely count palatine. When Frederick demanded a full restitution and indemnification for the unjust deprivation of his brother, Duke Ludwig Philipp, James replied that the Duke's restoration would most likely follow Frederick's, but there was nothing to be done for the reimbursements, especially considering that the Duke had supported his brother in the Bohemian war. To the request that James procure an amnesty for the Dukes of Saxe-Weimar, the Margrave of Jägerndorf, Christian von Anhalt, the Count of Hohenlohe, and other German and Bohemian supporters of Frederick, James merely stated that the present negotiations were committed to procuring Frederick's restitution alone. Finally, when Frederick asked what he should do about the promise he had made to Bethlen Gábor not to make a separate peace with the Emperor, James merely observed that Gábor had already violated that pact on his own, thus freeing Frederick from any obligation.[81]

The Defense of the Palatinate

Despite James' clear desire for an end to all hostilities while his peace negotiations were in progress, Frederick had no intention of giving up the struggle. He had some arms and money at his disposal.[82] After the Union members had withdrawn their forces, Frederick still had 5–6,000 armed men in the Lower Palatinate in mid May.[83] This force was hardly a match for the 21,000 Spanish troops under Don Fernández de Córdoba, but Frederick's men controlled the three main strongholds of the Palatinate, Frankenthal, Mannheim, and Heidelberg. With the 2,000 British volunteers, they had a chance of resisting the Spanish for some time. Moreover, Georg Friedrich, the Margrave of Baden-Durlach, had decided to muster a force for the defense of the Palatinate.[84] Frederick repeatedly appealed to Christian IV and the Dukes of Braunschweig and Lüneburg for military assistance against the invaders who, he proclaimed, intended to wipe out German freedom and the Protestant religion.[85] Frederick intensified his description of the dire consequences that would befall Germany if the Protestants laid aside their arms or refused to act in unison. He was sure that England would send military assistance, and he wanted Christian to count on it as well.[86] Frederick was convinced that the English and Danish embassies to the Imperial court were useless, because the Spanish and the Jesuits had taken full control of the Emperor's will.[87]

What confidence Frederick may have had in the early spring of 1621 probably decayed during the months of the cease-fire. By May it had become common knowledge that Maximilian of Bavaria and Wolfgang Wilhelm, the Duke of Pfalz-Neuburg, had made formal, rival claims to the Palatinate and its electorate.[88] Frederick's potential allies, England, Denmark, and the Lower Saxon Circle, were devoting their resources to conducting embassies instead of sending arms. Still worse, he heard from his council of state in Heidelberg that the Lower Palatinate was facing a catastrophe. His subjects were in turmoil, and his soldiers were mutinous. A famine was incipient. From all sides there was great pressure for Frederick's submission to the Emperor. The Palatinate, his council ruled despairingly, was impossible to defend.[89] King James, meanwhile, acknowledged his son-in-law's statement of submission to his counsel and reaffirmed his dedication to restoration of the Palatinate. James told Frederick 'to rely only on the favor of God and on our assistance'.[90]

Frederick, however, primarily hoped for military assistance from England, and it indeed appeared to be a distinct possibility. As he watched the progress of the Parliament of 1621, he must have noted with pleasure that the House of Commons attempted to persuade the King to contribute to the war with an argument that was similar to his own. In June, at the end of the first session, the House of Commons declared that they were

> considering seriously the present state of the King's children outside the realm and the general affliction of those in other lands who profess truly the same Christian religion that is received by the Church of England, and being touched by a true sentiment and compassion of their distress as members of the same body.[91]

The Commons expressed their exuberant readiness for a war, if James resolved to commit himself to one, and promised to pledge their lives and properties to the effort. Perhaps on the same day, however, Frederick received from James the copies of Archduke Albert's and Spínola's letters that expressed their ready compliance with James' request to abstain from hostilities in the Palatinate till the end of June, provided that the Spanish forces received no provocations.[92] Elizabeth, though she was pleased with the sentiments in Parliament, did not believe that any help would come from England unless James took action on their behalf.[93] The English Parliament wanted war, and the English King wanted Palatine pacification.

Frederick, however, wanted war and English participation. He fervently believed that Ferdinand was tightening a tyrannous grip on the Empire. In June 1621 the Emperor's officials executed twenty-eight alleged leaders of the Bohemian rebellion, including a Catholic, in Prague, and made numerous retributions and confiscations throughout Bohemia, the incorporated lands, and Austria.[94] Still worse, it was common knowledge that the Emperor intended to hold an Imperial diet in Regensburg formally to transfer Frederick's electorate to Duke Maximilian.[95] Frederick sent Andreas Pawel in the early summer of 1621 to England to continue efforts in favor of the common cause, but Pawel's embassy was as unsuccessful as Achaz von Dohna's. When Pawel forwarded one of Frederick's requests for an astounding sum of money, James stormed out of the room and said to some English lords who were standing nearby, 'See this man here', indicating Pawel, 'he desires £30,000 instead of my oath; if I had to save my own Kingdom, I wouldn't be able to round up £30,000!'[96] James still wanted Frederick to go to Heidelberg as soon as it could be done safely.[97] Furthermore, in his intercession with the Emperor, James refused to insist on the invalidation of the Imperial ban, because, he said, it was 'necessary that he proceed by means that are feasible', and such a demand was 'a thing which cannot be hoped for'.[98] When Pawel left England, he said in disgust, 'the King of England leads a godless life, is a blasphemer, an adulterer, and ... he always has the Spanish ambassador near him'.[99]

James remained unmoved by his son-in-law's latest efforts to alter his political stance. In mid July Frederick received a statement of James' confidence in Digby's embassy to Ferdinand II, though there was no guarantee of compliance with its demands. James had recently received a promise from Philip IV, the new King of Spain, that he would intercede with the Emperor on England's behalf. James then ordered Frederick to abstain from all hostilities and provocations during the negotiations, because the slightest offense would ruin everything. The King further recommended that his son-in-law relinquish control the few towns in Bohemia that still resisted Imperial rule. James announced that the cease-fire in the Palatinate had been extended for a couple more weeks, and he promised that the Emperor would consent to a general suspension of arms within that time.[100] These wishes were not to be granted.

The steady worsening of his affairs was driving Frederick to desperation, but his faith gave him stability and bestowed consistency on his policy. In late June, in a letter to Bethlen Gábor, Frederick said that his affairs 'more and more by the disposition of God's wroth incline to utter ruine, so that continually the one mishap followes the other which hitherto tormented us many manner of wayes'.[101] His troops had not been paid since February, and there had been terrible acts of violence in the Upper and Lower Palatinates by both the defending and the invading armed forces.[102] Worst of all for was the recent loss of Pilsen and the other garrison towns in Bohemia that had been in his possession. Frederick had sunk all the money that he extracted from the Palatinate into Mansfeld's army, and the result had been victory for the enemy and near rebellion in the Palatinate. He had been forced temporarily to give up his hopes and designs for regaining Bohemia.[103] The Bavarian threat to the Upper Palatinate, the Spanish conquest of the Lower, and the dissolution of the Union had plunged Frederick a 'great pitt of misery'.[104] Still, he would continue his efforts to bring together an international alliance of Protestant potentates. Frederick pledged, '[we will] so order all our actions, that either we make peace or warre, we may alwayes be found ready to give an accompt before God and the whole worreld'.[105]

Digby's Embassy

Sir John Digby, meanwhile, embarked on his embassy to Emperor Ferdinand II. His instructions asked the impossible. Digby was to request Frederick's full restitution *status quo ante bellum* by way of offering James' mediation. Digby was not to threaten, as the Danish ambassador had, that Frederick's restoration and the revocation of his ban would be carried by force if not by the Emperor's fiat.[106] James acknowledged that it was unlikely that Emperor would grant the restitution 'simply for our Respect and friendshippe', so he offered a guarantee of his son-in-law's future good behavior. Digby was to promise that Frederick would renounce the Bohemian crown, both for himself and for his son who had been named successor, and would do all that the Emperor required in accordance with his birthright and rank in the Empire. In addition, Digby was to secure some unspecified security for Protestantism in Bohemia and the Empire and plead for mercy for the princes who had supported Frederick. If the Emperor failed to comply, Digby was to indicate the beginning of 'an immortall and an irreconcileable quarrell' and then go to Spain and make the same demands.[107] James summarized the goal of the mission as follows:

Our meaning briefly and plainly is, that in case heerein satisfaction shal bee denied us, you endeavor to fix the quarrell, as well upon the King of Spaine as upon the Emperor. But this wee would have you do rather solidly then by any words of threatning or menace; And rather to give us a just and good ground, when wee shall see occasion, to enter into a warre, then suddainly to imbarque us in it.[108]

This embassy was meant to save face for James, fulfill his promise to restore Frederick by all means feasible, and shift the responsibility for his fate onto his own shoulders.

The embassy began rather well. His first modest success came in the Lower Palatinate, when he obtained a promise from Córdoba to refrain from hostilities unless he were provoked or received contrary orders.[109] Digby was fully aware of the motions to transfer the Palatine electorate to a Catholic prince, but since he was armed with letters from the Archdukes in favor of a restitution and expected to receive similar letters from the King of Spain, he did 'not utterly dispaire'.[110] By early July, Digby had his reception at the Emperor's court.[111] Ferdinand welcomed Digby cordially, offered him lodgings, and proposed that they turn to business only after he was well rested after his long journey.[112] But during his negotiations, word arrived that Mansfeld's army in the Upper Palatinate, which new recruits and Dutch money had increased to about 20,000 men, had attacked a town across the Bohemian border and had made other strikes against the bishoprics of Bamberg and Würzburg and the landgraviate of Leuchtenberg. Maximilian immediately complained to the Emperor, who issued a commission for the Duke to invade the Upper Palatinate in pursuit of Mansfeld.[113] The Duke readily complied. Meanwhile the Margrave of Jägerndorf, under Frederick's commission, had invaded Moravia and Silesia, and his irregular ally, Bethlen Gábor, had rearmed and fought against Ferdinand's troops, killing General Bucquoy in the process.[114] In August Gábor besieged Pressburg and raided the area around Vienna, and Emperor Ferdinand could actually see the nearby villages in flames.[115] Worst of all, Vere moved his troops onto the Bishop of Speyer's lands, claiming that the Duke of Zweibrücken and the council of Heidelberg ordered him to lodge his men there. Córdoba immediately resumed his offensive, taking the castle at Stein and laying siege to Frankenthal.

The sudden resumption of violence made a mockery of James' pacific desires and of his promise to control Frederick. Digby did what he could under the circumstances. He tried to alleviate Frederick's fears that his electorate had been promised absolutely to Maximilian; such a belief was 'contrary to the receavede opinion of most of the Courts of Christendom'.[116] Digby described the situation as open, and he thought that the Emperor was inclined to make a deal. Indeed, most of the princes who had declared against Frederick had also asked Ferdinand to make no 'private or suddaine resolution in these businesses but so to proceede as therby an universall and durable peace may be settled in the Empire, and an absolute reconciliation and oblivion of matters in all parts'.[117] Digby told Frederick to have patience and added, 'the late proceedings of the Marquis of Jaghendorf and Count Mansfeld have rather hurt and retarded your Majesty's affaires then any way advantaged them'.[118] Digby begged him to abide by James' will and to keep the peace during the treaty negotiations.

Digby's impression from Vienna was that there was a chance for Frederick's restoration. Ferdinand's councilors said that the Emperor would do all he could 'with honor and conscience' to satisfy James. His requests, however, they said, 'concerned not the Emperor alone, but the Dignity of the Empire, [which] by these unjust proceedings [had] beene reduced unto so great straights', forcing Ferdinand to depend on other princes, namely the Duke of Bavaria, for help.[119] The councilors all emphasized the great importance of Frederick's immediate submission and lasting obedience in the future. When Digby asked if the transfer of the electorate to Maximilian was set in stone, their elusive answer shifted the burden from the Emperor: 'the Duke of Bavaria is a Prince that will loose nothing that is to be gott'.[120] It was said that Maximilian accepted that the other electors had to be consulted and that Ferdinand could not and would not sacrifice his honor. Indeed, Digby came to understand that the Emperor, his councilors, and many princes of the Empire, including those who were friendly toward England,

> have sett downe positively, that whatsoever else shall be condescended unto, it must be with the upholding of the honor and dignity del imperio Romano, which I assure you is so often here in theyr mouthes, as if the imperatore romano were in better estate then Augustus Cæsar.[121]

Ferdinand resisted supporting a suspension of arms in the Palatinate because of Mansfeld's and Jägerndorf's belligerence. It would be 'no equall motion', Digby reported, 'to have a Cessation in the Count Palatines Territoryes, when the Emperor was first assayled in his, by virtue of the Count Palatine's Commissions'.[122] Still, Ferdinand agreed to halt the Spanish execution of the Imperial ban if Frederick would show at least 'an inclynation to Peace' and would 'take such order that it may appeare to the world, that these new attempts of assayling Bohemia and Silesia were not by his direction'.[123] In other words, Frederick had to revoke his commissions to his generals.

Digby came to recognize that the Emperor was in an intractable situation. In his reports to England he explained the hopeless difficulty of the situation and proposed that they turn to Spain for a solution, 'for that the Buisines is so full of Accidents, and severall Interests, as there wilbe a necessitye of applying ones self to that part, where the Buisiness sticketh'.[124] Digby had greater expectations of success in Spain, where he expected to encounter less difficulty than in Vienna, because he found

> the interest of State to be very litle betwixt [King James] and the Emperor; So that what is to be wrought here, is rather to be done by way of reflection from Spayne and Brussells then that any thing that wee can do in England can be of much consideration with them here.[125]

Nonetheless, Digby recognized that peace was impossible without Frederick's submission, and all those who thought otherwise would, Digby said, 'in the end finde themselfes mistaken'.[126] But since there was no sign of a submission from Frederick, the prospects for peace were not good.

Frederick did not partake in any of Digby's measured sympathy for the Emperor's circumstances. 'The opposing party', Frederick declared, 'was not inclined to a reasonable improvement, but meant to delay everything in legal disputes to his advantage and, in the meantime, wear us out'.[127] In fact Frederick had instructed his emissary to Vienna, Andreas Pawel, to obstruct the English embassy to the Emperor! In August Digby tried to persuade Pawel that Frederick's submission was absolutely necessary for a revocation of the Imperial ban. Pawel, however, retorted that no revocation was necessary, because the ban was already 'naught and invalide' due to its alleged illegalities.[128] He also carried an order from Frederick not to remit the Bohemian towns of Tábor and Třeboň to Ferdinand.[129] Digby concluded in disgust,

> I think they would have the Emperor aske them forgivenesse for having wronged them with so injurious a Ban, and in recompence of the wrongs hee hath done them, to do all that shal bee required.[130]

At the same time Frederick sent Digby several objections to his peace negotiations. The main problem, Frederick said, was the ban, which had laid all his lands open to any aggressor, in violation, he claimed, of the Golden Bull, the Imperial capitulations, and the constitution of the Empire. He refused to revoke his generals' commissions in the interest of his own defense. He bade the ambassador to bear three points in mind: firstly, that all his actions have been in accordance with the service of God, the prosperity of the Empire, and respect for Emperor Ferdinand, as long as he abided by the Imperial constitution; secondly, Frederick wanted a good peace settlement for all princes of the Empire; and thirdly, he would be well-inclined toward the House of Austria as long as its members would not harm him and his posterity.[131] Such obstinance guaranteed that Digby's embassy would come to nothing, which had been Frederick's plan from the beginning.[132]

In September Count Oñate advised Digby to 'lose no more time here, for that the Emperor was now so incensed against the Count Palatine for that his Ministers should be the Aggressors in all parts'.[133] Baron Strahlendorf, the Imperial vice-chancellor, informed Digby that Ferdinand was resolved to have 'either a generall Peace or a generall warr'.[134] Digby was told that with the renewal of hostilities in and around the Upper and Lower Palatinates, a suspension of arms was impossible.[135] During his final audience, he explained that honor and familial obligation had motivated King James to intervene in the Palatine war, which 'was very like to sett a generall combustion in Christendome'. Ferdinand answered 'very gratiously' but said he would make no resolutions without consulting the princes of the Empire. He announced that he would soon send an ambassador to give satisfaction to the King of England.[136] As Digby left Vienna, he analyzed the situation as follows:

> if yet a constant hand may be held, the businesse wilbee overcome to the Kings satisfaction, but if the King of Bohemia will suffer his Name to bee used by those that hetherto hee hath done, and take those middle wayes, of neither relying upon a Treaty, nor avowedly making of a warre, hee wilbee ruined irrecoverably, And his enimies have the advantage of doing all things against him upon justifiable pretext.[137]

The ambassador's estimation of the state of affairs was mostly correct. But because Frederick did not have the resources to conduct his wars on his own, he had to rely on 'those middle wayes'.

Digby's embassy had been doomed to fail from the beginning because of Frederick and Ferdinand's competing, conflicting, and contradicting notions of Imperial justice. The two princes' accusations ironically mirrored each other. Each accused the other of destroying the peace and unity of the Empire, violating the fundamental law and the Golden Bull, abusing religious freedom, and attempting to alter the composition of the electoral college. Each regarded the other's legal argumentation as preposterous casuistry. While Frederick would admit no wrong, Ferdinand would grant no concessions where no submission was forthcoming. The result was the devastation of the Empire, its lands, its population, its dignity, and its honor through civil war.

Between War and Peace

During Digby's embassy Frederick's relations with his father-in-law soured considerably. He was coming under greater pressure as the situation in the Palatinate decayed. In July the lack of money threatened to cast the army and the whole territory 'into a total confusion, from which [could] only ensue the ruin of the cause and of all the Palatinate, if God did not miraculously remedy it'.[138] At the same time his father-in-law was commanding him to lay down his arms. When James received news of the renewed hostilities, he complained bitterly to Frederick and reminded him of his promise to abide by his father-in-law's will.[139] This letter crossed paths with a plea from Frederick for money to pay his mutinous troops. He suggested that the King send the two subsidies that Parliament had granted him to pay for the garrisons in the Palatinate.[140] He warned, however, that neither his conscience nor his honor could allow the King to oblige him to assist the Emperor against Bethlen Gábor, because, Frederick added, with more than a hint of insolence,

> as much as for the solemnly sworn confederation as for [Gábor's] being a prince who has always professed the same religion, of which Your Majesty is the Defender, and that by doing so I would be helping deliver many thousands of souls under the tyranny of the antichrist.[141]

James had never proposed such a double-cross, though one could have been inferred if Frederick had dissolved his alliance with Gábor, submitted to the Emperor, and then obeyed an order to render assistance against the Transylvanian prince. Frederick most likely distorted his father-in-law's advice on purpose to demonstrate his disgust with its dissonance with his own policy.

This letter incensed James, who proclaimed that 'the displeasure that we feel from this is such that we see ourselves bereft of means to relieve it'.[142] He mocked the impertinent request for the two parliamentary subsidies. It was impossible, he said, to supply such assistance, 'nor with all the revenues of our crown', would it be possible to carry out all the designs that were asked of him.[143] He was astounded at the misinterpretation of his recommendation to dissolve the confederation with Bethlen Gábor, and James blamed Frederick personally for the distortion. James had only insisted that Frederick break off his alliance with Gábor. The King then attacked the attempts to enlist Turkish forces in defending or retaking Bohemia, a move which obligated every Christian prince to support the Emperor immediately and unconditionally. James warned Frederick that such an alliance 'could only render him a surfeit of dishonor'.[144]

Frederick defended himself by warning James that the enemy would be as faithless to his treaties as they were to the Imperial constitution. The recent executions of the condemned rebels in Prague were yet more proof of Ferdinand's vindictiveness and injustice. A third of those executed were 'such aged men that it had been a small degree of clemency to have suffered their naturall death'.[145] According to Frederick, the Emperor and his party had 'then made their intentions exhaustively recognizable' through these bloody retributions.[146] As to Bethlen Gábor, Frederick claimed that it was uncertain whether or not he would bring Turkish forces into the continuing war in Moravia and into Bohemia.[147] Gábor and Count Thurn had informed The Hague that the Turks had mobilized 60,000 men that May, though it was not clear whether they were headed against the Empire or for war against the King of Poland.[148] Frederick was waiting to see if any such campaign would actually take place.[149] Finally, he justified Mansfeld's incursion across the Bohemian border as necessary for the defense of the Upper Palatinate against the encroaching enemy forces.[150]

While Digby was concluding his negotiations in Vienna, the news of the Spanish refusal to renew the truce in the Palatinate had thrown Frederick into a state of consternation. Elizabeth observed that her husband was 'much more troubled at the newes more then ever I saw him'.[151] Frederick indignantly defended Mansfeld's actions to James I: 'I do not hold it necessary for me to justify all his actions as I know of none of his proceedings that are not for my service and according to the reason of war'.[152] Frederick protested that the King's negotiators had failed to condemn Maximilian's invasion of the Upper Palatinate. The enemy, Frederick argued, had used the cease-fire to reinforce their troops and to hinder his own defense efforts, and they were negotiating with the King of England out of polite respect alone. He asked James to help him to obtain troops from the King of Denmark and the Dukes of Braunschweig and Lüneburg. As usual, Frederick had answered his father-in-law's call for peace with pleas for war.

His relations with his uncle, King Christian IV, were nearly as counter-productive as those with his father-in-law. None of Frederick's arguments could move the King to fulfill the intentions that he had stated at Segeberg. The Danish embassy to the Emperor had been fruitless.[153] Christian had subsequently taken offense at his nephew's doubts about his sincerity, and the repeated requests that he take up war single-handedly and immediately, without long and weighty consideration, were equally irksome. Christian considered Bethlen Gábor scarcely or not at all reliable, and found England unlikely to do anything on Frederick's behalf. Still, Christian IV confirmed that he would do all that he could for his nephew when it was possible.[154]

In reply, Frederick tried to promote closer relations between Denmark and England. He asked Christian to be patient with James. To decrease Christian's dubiousness, Frederick sent word of Parliament's declaration in his favor and for the good of Protestantism. Christian's ambassador to England, Sir Andreas Sinclair, had likewise recommended mobilizing forces in order to win a favorable settlement from the Emperor.[155] To encourage Danish assistance, Frederick sent Achaz von Dohna to Christian IV in mid summer 1621, and in The Hague the Palatines were hopeful that Dohna would find the King well-disposed toward them.[156] On an afternoon in late August, Dohna had a three-hour, private conversation with Christian IV at his palace at Friderichsburg, but the King effectively excused himself from fighting on Frederick's behalf.[157] Christian bemoaned the sad and dangerous state of the Empire and declared that he would muster a force of 6000 horse and foot for three months, but he would not allow it to go to the Lower Palatinate, because the march there and all possible retreats were problematic and insecure. He recommended that Frederick seek help from the Lower Saxon Circle, Britain, the United Provinces, and France. He said that King James had made it known to all that he wanted the war ended through peaceable means. Frederick, being a reasonable man, Christian added, should readily notice that the French and English assistance was uncertain, and that the Hungarian and Turkish aid was quite dangerous. Christian recommended that Frederick should look to saving his Palatinate himself.[158]

News from eastern Europe led Frederick to return to his wars. His hopes for returning eventually to Bohemia were rekindled by a report that Jägerndorf's army had grown to 10,000 strong, and that he intended to join it to Gábor's in Hungary.[159] Frederick heard that Gábor, Jägerndorf, and Count Thurn might bring a force of 40,000 together at Pressburg, so a march on Vienna or Prague was not beyond the realms of possibility.[160] Moreover, Mansfeld related that Gábor might make a claim to Bohemia if Frederick were to abandon his. The Count advised Frederick to defend his rights and his estates with the sword, especially against the Duke of Bavaria, whose obvious ambition was to take possession of the Palatinate.[161] At this time, it is fair to say, Frederick was not 'so much moved toward a repentance by the hopes he might frame out of the present conjuncture of a fayre possibility to recover his Crowne agayne'.[162] The Palatinate, however, was once more in immediate danger, because Spínola had refused to extend the truce.[163] Frederick was considering leading a detachment from the Dutch army to the Palatinate.[164] Earlier in August he had tried to obtain money from the Marquis of Buckingham and from funds that Elizabeth had deposited at Nürnberg. If no money came from England, Frederick was resolved to pawn his jewels and lead an army himself.[165] On 26 August he left The Hague for Emmerich to join the Prince of Orange and the Dutch army against encroaching Spanish forces. Elizabeth expressed their optimism: 'our affaires in Bohemia beginne to mend, the King of Hongarie is maistre of the feeld, Mansfeld and Yegendorf do daylie prosper, the King is with the Prince of Orenge at the armie'.[166]

A couple of days later, while Frederick was in Arnhem, he enlisted the services of a unique soldier of fortune, Christian of Halberstadt. Christian, the administrator of the diocese of Halberstadt and the brother of the Duke of Braunschweig-Wolfenbüttel, was an outlandish, twenty-two year old chivalric adventurer who had been a fervent supporter of the Bohemian-Palatine regime since 1619. In the interim he had begun to profess a passionate, somewhat abstract love for the exiled Queen of Bohemia. The motto on his battle standards was 'All for God and for her'. Though it is not known when he first caught a glimpse of Elizabeth, it is most likely that he saw her sometime during her and Frederick's journey from Wolfenbüttel to The Hague.[167] That was apparently enough for Christian. He would fight for the common and Protestant causes till the end of his days. He is perhaps the only other German prince to have taken the Winter King's cause as his own. In addition to Frederick's and Elizabeth's restoration, Christian's main interest was to protect German constitutional liberty and Protestantism from the perceived Habsburg bid to transform the Empire into a Catholic, absolute monarchy after the Spanish style.[168] Scruple about Lutheran-Calvinist antagonism did not inhibit him; indeed, nothing seemed to. At Arnhem he announced his intention to raise 1,000 cavalry and march to the Palatinate. Frederick was at first receptive: 'I believe that it would only be good for my affairs, and maybe not bad for him; but all is in the hand of God'.[169]

Frederick did not manage to persuade the Prince of Orange to give him troops to take to the Palatinate, and threatening missives from his infuriated father-in-law quickly drove him back to The Hague.[170] James had rejected all excuses for Mansfeld's military action and refused to supply any more money.[171] The King acknowledged no valid reasons against Frederick's submitting to the Emperor and was appalled at his decision to join the Prince of Orange on campaign. James threatened to end his intercession and publicly blame Frederick for its failure.[172] For the time being these letters tempered Frederick's lofty aspirations. It was observed that 'his flying thoughts of a possibility of returning agayne to Prague are quite fallen to the ground, although there want not still a fayre gale to hold them up'.[173] Emissaries from Jägerndorf and Gábor had come and delivered their renewed oaths of fidelity to Frederick, and that was enough to prevent the dream of a return to Prague from dying altogether.

James' threats had done nothing to undermine Frederick's sense of his own justness; to him they were yet another example of his father-in-law's flawed conception of the situation. Though to Frederick the retrieval of Bohemia was a hope, the defense of the Palatinate was an undeniable obligation. When he returned to The Hague in early October 1621, he and his advisers produced a document meant to persuade James of the constitutionality of the common cause and the futility of his peace negotiations. Because all former pleas in favor of a Protestant cause had failed to work a positive effect, the Palatines once again returned to the constitutional tack. The original version of the document contained an article that explained that the main cause of the present conflict lay in the dispute over the nature of the Bohemian constitution: was it an hereditary or an elective monarchy? This question 'still not being legitimately decided, it follows that there has not been a single reason to pass condemnation against the King of Bohemia without a preliminary cognizance and a decision on the cause'.[174] Because the whole political body of the Empire had not resolved the legal question, they reasoned, the House of Austria had decided the issue in accordance with its ambitions. When this draft was presented to Dudley Carleton, the English ambassador to the United Provinces, he struck out this article, and Frederick and his advisers, probably with great reluctance, accepted the change. This argument, though true in their minds, would not have helped to persuade James.[175]

The letter that James received argued that a submission was impossible, because it would require Frederick's confession of the crime of lèse-majesté and cast infamy upon himself and his posterity.[176] The Imperial ban, he complained, had reduced his status in the Empire to that 'of a simple peasant', and a submission would be tantamount to an approval of this unjust persecution.[177] Another letter protested that his enemies had misrepresented his actions. In fact, he argued, only Ferdinand was acting in bad faith. He had agreed to a suspension of arms and then commissioned Maximilian to invade the Upper Palatinate. Frederick tried to persuade his father-in-law that the Emperor intended his total ruin.[178] Nonetheless he reiterated that he would obey all James' orders, including one to make a submission, as long as they did not compromise his conscience and honor.[179]

The Palatines believed that if their cause prospered in the war, then there was a greater chance that they could gain more allies, and that their negotiators could arrange a peace in their favor. Reports that Mansfeld, Halberstadt, and Jägerndorf were fighting competently for Frederick's cause raised expectations in The Hague that the Emperor's contingent at the Brussels treaty negotiations would be more inclined to peace than hitherto, 'when all the water ran on their side'.[180] Following Frederick's orders, Mansfeld abandoned the Upper Palatinate to Maximilian in late

October and marched to the Lower to drive Córdoba away from Franken-thal.[181] The Count had some 17,000 foot and 5,000 horse in the field, who, receiving little and infrequent pay, were perpetually on the edge of mutiny. From their actions these mercenary troops appeared more apt for theft, arson, rapine, and murder than for battle, but they still managed to raise the Spanish siege at Frankenthal.[182] At the end of October, it is claimed, they serendipitously intercepted one of the Emperor's couriers headed for Brussels and his cache of correspondence.[183] In a letter to Don Balthasar de Zúñiga, Emperor Ferdinand had allegedly written in his own hand that he had verbally promised Frederick's electorate to Duke Maximilian. Moreover, the letter added, 'it is not necessary to trust the King of Great Britain, as much as that he is of the religion, and that one can neither remedy nor make secure these affairs, only if the religion called Calvinism be totally exterminated'.[184] It is uncertain whether these letters were genuine or forgeries. The bluntness of the language in a diplomatic document is uncharacteristic of Ferdinand, and that fact that no cipher was used for such sensitive material raises suspicions about the letters' verisimilitude. Mansfeld immediately sent copies of the letters to The Hague, saying that he would hold on to the originals until it was safe for him to hand them over as well, but since they have yet to be located and examined thoroughly, nothing conclusive can be said about their veracity.

Frederick, at any rate, swore by them, and he regarded the find as a sign of divine favor. 'God', he wrote, 'the Director of all things and the protector of the innocent, has miraculously discovered the source and the most secret counsels' that unequivocally revealed the Emperor's pernicious designs against him, his posterity, and the members of his religion.[185] Just as Maximilian had allowed the publication of the Palatine-Bohemian secret correspondence, Frederick directed Camerarius to publish the intercepted letters in a work promulgating the common and Protestant causes.[186] It was a warning to Lutherans as well as Calvinists that the Emperor, the pope, and their supporters were pursuing a war of religion aimed at the extirpation of Protestantism in the Empire, and a crucial step in that project, the argument ran, was the transfer of the Palatine electorate to the Duke of Bavaria. The Imperial ban against Frederick was declared a violation of Ferdinand's election-concessions, an infringement of religious freedom, and a potential weapon against all Protestants. The House of Austria was said to be determined to make the Imperial throne a possession of their heritable patrimony as a part of the Spanish goal to establish an absolute monarchy over the whole of Europe. As soon as the Palatinate was subdued, all forces would be turned against the United Provinces.[187]

The criss-crossing movements of emissaries, armies, and missives intensified until winter sent all forces into their seasonal quarters. In November
Digby had suffered his last humiliation in Brussels before returning to
England. Because of the fighting, it was said, he 'was mostly mocked and
laughed at with his suspension of arms'.[188] Vere ensconced his men in
Mannheim, and Mansfeld planted himself on the Bishop of Speyer's lands,
because the land around Heidelberg was unable to sustain the depredations of
his army.[189] At the same time Tilly, the general of the Bavarian forces, issued
an ultimatum against Heidelberg, but the city refused to capitulate.[190] Those
forces quickly reached the Lower Palatinate and approached Heidelberg.[191]
By 19 November Frederick had received no word from the Palatinate since
Tilly's arrival and no reports from England since Digby's return. Despite the
lack of information, Frederick was still 'in heart for the present, but full of
anxiety for the future'.[192] He then received another blow; an assembly of
Lower Saxon Circle insisted that he give up his royal titles, lay down his
arms, make amends with the Emperor, and abstain from all further hostilities.
Frederick's submission, the Circle asserted, would ameliorate the conflict and
save many souls from the slaughter; if things were to continue in the present
course, the Palatinate would be ruined, and the whole of the Empire with it.[193]

Shortly afterwards, however, Frederick received new encouragement
from England. His return to The Hague appeared to have satisfied his
father-in-law. Suddenly James offered to send £30,000 to maintain forces
in the Palatinate if Frederick signed a treaty for a suspension of arms and
ceased all hostilities. In an amazing about-face, the King announced that
he was preparing himself for war and that he had recalled Parliament for
that purpose.[194] For Frederick this news was more a confirmation of his
tactics than a correction. He responded to the Lower Saxon Circle's
request in full defiance. He protested his desire for peace and his constant
obedience to the Imperial constitution, and he told them about the
intercepted letters, which 'God [had] miraculously sent'.[195] He wrote, 'we
have the steadfast confidence in God, the just knight, he will certainly
know our innocence in his time, [to] whom we, however, want to hold still
with Christian patience in his fatherly afflictions'.[196] In the interest of the
common and Protestant causes, he would not relinquish his royal titles.
Frederick warned that if the Spanish conquered the Lower Palatinate, they
would soon take control of the entire Rhineland. The King of Great
Britain, he said, was fully resolved to restore him and had reconvened
Parliament, which had also declared in his favor. He asked the Circle to
revise its policy; it should help protect the Palatinate from the Duke of
Bavaria and the Catholic League.

Despite James' offer of £30,000, his peace treaty was a bitter pill. By
signing Frederick would have to agree to renounce the Bohemian crown,

submit himself to the Emperor's mercy, and remain peaceable, and in return he would receive an amnesty. He found this treaty embarrassing and dangerous to his cause.[197] Under duress, Frederick gave his seal and signature, but he did not sign the copy that was sent to him; he altered the conditions to his own satisfaction.[198] He and his advisers produced a new version, including a phrase such that Frederick 'would be restored with all his dominions and rights', and he claimed that it was in total conformity with James' intentions.[199] Frederick also sent his father-in-law copies of the Emperor's intercepted letters, which, he hoped, would demonstrate unequivocally the truth of his position. These letters, he asserted, revealed Ferdinand's intentions against the glory of God, the well-being 'of the orthodox churches', and the safety of the Empire and its neighboring princes and realms.[200] He confessed that as first secular prince in the Empire he could not remain silent on the subject without wounding his conscience. He highlighted the Emperor's secret promise of the Palatine electorate to Maximilian and the latter's machinations to usurp the Upper Palatinate.[201] Days later Frederick sent James a verbose complaint about the ever-increasing number of reported atrocities in the Palatinate, the calumnies against his honor, and the conspiratorial assaults on his constitutional rights.[202]

King James made no reaction to the intercepted letters. They did not change his mind about the current crisis, because, not unreasonably, he suspected that they were forgeries.[203] His reply was a simple expression of his royal pleasure that Frederick had signed the treaty, saying nothing about the changes he had made. James said that he was working to procure French support for the Palatine defense and to include a restoration of the Palatinate in the negotiations for the Anglo-Spanish marriage treaty.[204] He would send no more forces to the Palatinate that winter, but he was content with providing occasional payments for the maintenance of Vere's force of volunteers. James had only resolved to enter the war in the Palatinate, 'so long as he shall perceave from thence that his Cowncell and advise is truelie and exactlie followed'.[205] This caveat once again made the settlement of peace entirely contingent on Frederick's willingness to submit to his father-in-law's will.

With the onset of winter, Frederick and his regime turned to preparations for the next campaign season with a mixture of uncertainty and hope. Despite Mansfeld's attestations of loyalty, it was well known that the Count had willingly negotiated with the Archdukes and Maximilian about joining the Emperor's service.[206] At the end of December Mansfeld agreed to accept an annual pension from the Venetians in return for his readiness to raise and lead an army of 5,000 horse and 20,000 foot against an enemy of the Republic, presumably Spain. He could continue to serve the Palatines for the time being, but if the Republic were to call on him, he was supposed to give them priority.[207] In late December, 2,000 men and 200 cavalry from the city of Hamburg and the King of Denmark increased the troops under Christian of Halberstadt.[208] Frederick continued to encourage the Margrave of Baden-Durlach to join the conflict and tried to obtain his help in resurrecting the Union and in obtaining new allies.[209]

* * *

The course of the Palatine crisis during 1621 reveals that Frederick's ardent attachment to his 'common cause' was the principal cause for the continuation of the Thirty Years' War at this early stage. Of his greatest prospective allies, the Kings of Great Britain and Denmark and the Lower Saxon Circle had declared that Frederick first had to relinquish his claim to the Bohemian throne if he wanted to be restored. But because Frederick considered himself the rightful King of Bohemia according to the constitution of the Holy Roman Empire and the will of God, he could not renounce the crown. To admit to having done wrong was an offense against his honor. For Frederick, the war would continue until the Emperor made amends for his errors. Under these presumptions it is nearly impossible for him to have come to terms.

Frederick wanted to incite a war of religion to effect his restoration, but for almost all other princes of consequence, the ends did not justify these means. No state leader wanted the Palatine war except for Frederick. For the King of Spain and the Archdukes, it was a diversion and a threat to their relations with England; for James I, it was a violation of his pacific policy; for Christian IV, it alone did not warrant solo intervention; for the princes of the Union and the Lower Saxon Circle, it was constitutionally unsound and bad for the Empire; for the Dutch, it may have been a welcome diversion for the Spanish, and as such, it warranted some subsidies; for Emperor Ferdinand II, the longer it continued, the deeper he was indebted to Duke Maximilian of Bavaria, who, with his eye on Frederick's lands and electorate, was perhaps the only prince of consequence who saw the merits of continuing the war.

Frederick's few supporters were mostly adventurers who lived and profited from the spoils of war, or they had separate motivations for fighting on Frederick's behalf. Mansfeld and Jägerndorf were first and foremost *condottiere*. Halberstadt was living out a fantastic career of devoted chivalric service for the Winter Queen. Bethlen Gábor, though not an adventurer, was naturally devoted to his ambitions in Hungary. As long as it was convenient for him, helping Frederick was another way of hurting the Habsburgs. The Palatine success in 1621 was simply survival against

the combined forces of Spain, the Catholic League, and the Emperor. The
failure of all peace settlements and the continuation of hostilities, in
accordance with Frederick's will, actually reduced his chances of
restoration and escalated the war in the Empire. His obstinacy was based
in his conviction that his decisions were in accordance with the will of
God, and that to revoke his allegiances was a dishonor to God and to
himself, no matter at what price. Frederick's politics brought neither
complete success nor total failure, but they kept the war going. He was to
lose his lands and titles in the process nonetheless.

Notes

1. The Silesian principalities of Liegnitz, Wöhlau, Öls, Brieg, Münsterberg, and
   Beuthen had all officially adopted the Calvinist Reformation by 1616. Henry J.
   Cohn, 'The Territorial Princes', ip. 137.
2. van Eickels, *Schlesien*, pp. 382–4.
3. Duke Joachim Ernst of Holstein was to go as Frederick's emissary to inform the
   King of Denmark. BHStA, KB, 121/3a, fols 8–12: 15/25 November 1620,
   Instructions.
4. van Eickels, *Schlesien*, p. 387.
5. Gindely, *Geschichte*, i, pp. 230–1.
6. van Eickels, *Schlesien*, pp. 390–1.
7. Ibid., pp. 393–4.
8. Ibid., pp. 394–9.
9. Ibid., pp. 485–6.
10. 'Wir befehlen es dem Allmächtigen, und nehmen in Gedult an, die Straff, so er uns
    zugeschickt, der wolle, alles zu seiner Ehr unnd seiner Gläubigen Gnaden
    außschlagen lassen. ... Wir haben uns zu Böhmen unnd Mähren nicht getrungen,
    hätten uns wol mit unsern Erbländern contentiren können, haben aber solches auff
    ihr Ersuchen, hindan gesetzt, und uns ihrer nach all unserm Vermögen treulich
    angenommen, nun empfangen wir den Dank, daß sie sich absonderlich in Tractat
    einlassen, und nachdem wir das unserige ihrentwegen auffgesetzt verlassen, und sich
    einem andern untergeben, ob nun solches rühmlich und ehrlich, lassen wir die ganze
    Welt urtheilen, kein Geiz oder Ehrgeiz hat uns in Böhmen gebracht, kein Armuth
    noch Elend soll uns von unserm lieben Gott abtrünnig machen, noch etwas wider
    Ehr und Gewissen thun lassen'. AP, ii, 243.
11. AR, #6054, 23 December 1620/2 January 1621, Frederick V to Estates General of
    the United Provinces.
12. 'Päpistichen Liga'. BHStA, KB, 121/3a, fols 50–1: 23 December 1620/2 January
    1621, Frederick V to Princes of the Union. This letter was received in
    Heidelberg on 19 January 1621 and presumably distributed to the Union mem-
    bers thereafter.
13. '... nunmehr die augen auffthun undt nicht so sehr auff das privatum als publicum
    sehen, sondern der Päpstlichen exempel nach, auch getreülich zusamb setzen, undt
    also ins gesambt geneigt sein werden, mit Verhuten zu helffen, damit Spanien, undt
    sein anhang, ja nicht noch mehrern, undt solchen vorthel erlange, dergleichen sie

zuvor noch niemahlen gehabt'. BHStA, KB, 121/3a, fol. 66: 8/18 January 1621, Frederick V to Princes of the Union.

14. BHStA, KB, 121/3a, fols 22–3: 25 December 1620/4 January 1621, Frederick V to Duke Joachim Ernst of Holstein. BHStA, KB, 121/3a, fols 14–8: 2 December 1620, Duke Ulrich to Frederick V, and 23 December 1620/2 January 1621, Frederick V to Duke Ulrich.

15. Parker, *The Thirty Years' War*, p. 54.

16. van Eickels, *Schlesien*, p. 399.

17. Frederick sarcastically noted the affront as 'une courtoisie extraordinaire'. Aretin, 'Sammlung', p. 174: 23 January/2 February 1621, Frederick V to Elizabeth.

18. AR, #6054, 2/12 February 1621, Frederick V to Mansfeld. For an English translation see PRO, SP, 81/20, fol. 7: 2/12 January 1621, Frederick V to Mansfeld. The date on this document cannot be correct, because Frederick did not reach Wolfenbüttel till February. The correct date is 2/12 February 1621.

19. AR, #6054, 4/14 February 1621, Frederick V to Prince of Orange.

20. Elizabeth was on her way to Küstrin. See note 10.

21. Aretin, 'Sammlung', p. 171: 6 December 1620, Frederick V to Elizabeth.

22. 'de prendre en patience tout le malheur que Dieu nous envoye'. Aretin, 'Sammlung', p. 172: 10 December 1620, Frederick to Elizabeth.

23. BHStA, KB, 121/3a, fols 8–12: 15/25 November 1620, Instructions to Duke of Holstein.

24. Aretin, 'Sammlung', p. 174: 23 January/2 February 1621, Frederick V to Elizabeth. There may have been some political considerations in his efforts to maintain good cheer. He observed, 'On trouve bien peu d'amitié, quand on est en malheureux'. Ibid.

25. 'certes c'est la plus chere compagnie que je puisse avoir en ce monde', Aretin, 'Sammlung', p. 174.

26. The nature of Frederick's crimes was described as 'notorisch, weltkündig, beharrlich', and classified as 'notorium crimen rebellionis'. Kampmann, *Reichsrebellion*, pp. 48, 53.

27. For a discussion of the juristic considerations of this resolution see Ibid., pp. 49–70.

28. Aretin, 'Sammlung', p. 175: 6 February 1621, Frederick V to Elizabeth.

29. For the full range of Palatine objections against the legality of the Imperial ban against Frederick V, see Johann Joachim von Rusdorf, *Consilia et negotia politica, ubi diversi tractatus et consilia, diverso tempore, [prout res in deliberationem cadebant, aut proponebantur, scripta & rerumpublicarum in Europa statum concernentia], continentur. Accedit Epistolarum familiarium ipsius autoris ad viros illustres & amicos scriptarum, collectio ex Bibliotheca Loeniana* (Frankfurt am Main, 1725).

30. Lockhart, *Denmark*, pp. 90–2.

31. Jaroslav Goll, *Der Convent von Segeberg, 1621* (Prague, 1875), p. 6.

32. Ibid., pp. 26–8. The ambassador was to represent the Lower Saxon Circle as well, and he carried a written declaration from Frederick.

33. Lockhart, *Denmark*, p. 91.

34. S. R. Gardiner, *History of England from the Accession of James I to the outbreak of the Civil War, 1603–1642* (London, 1883), iv, p. 180.

35. BHStA, KB, 121/1/II, fol. 5: 2/12 March 1621, Christian IV's conditions at Segeberg.

36. 'mit der Kay. May. alß einem Röm. Kaiser gantz nichts, sondern nur alß mit einem

Hertzoge zu Österreich zuthun gehabt'. BHStA, KB, 121/1/II, fl. 8: 4/14 March 1621, Frederick's reply at Segeberg.

37. BHStA, KB, 121/1/II, fol. 9: 5/15 March 1621, Frederick V to Christian IV.

38. 'eine Dornenkrone', Goll, *Segeberg*, p. 25.

39. Ibid., pp. 22–8.

40. Oman, *Elizabeth*, p. 246. The Hague was dubbed 'the largest village in Europe', because it did not enjoy the title or privileges of a town.

41. Ibid., pp. 250–1.

42. Thereafter, despite Frederick's repeated requested for more money and despite Prince Maurits' frequent support, the Estates General would only recommend his requests to King James and Venice. Mout, 'Der Winterkönig', p. 260.

43. Oman, *Elizabeth*, pp. 250–1.

44. For Camerarius' complaints in the late summer of 1621, see Söltl, *Der Religionskrieg*, iii, pp. 130–5.

45. After the Segeberg conference, Anhalt traveled to Sweden and eventually settled in Denmark, where Christian IV gave him permission to live quietly. Anhalt would later appeal to the Emperor for mercy in June 1621 and receive his reconciliation in Vienna in 1624. He would then retire to his patrimonial estates in Bernburg. v. Heinemann, 'Christian I., Fürst von Anhalt', ADB, iv, pp. 148–9. For pleas from Anhalt and his wife to the Emperor for mercy, see PRO, SP, 80/4, fols 26–33, 39–42.

46. BHStA, KS, 16745, fol. 71. He began serving in Emden in early 1622 and would die two years later, at the age of 58.

47. PRO, SP, 81/20, fols 77–8: 19/29 January 1621, Nethersole to Secretary Naunton.

48. He had recommended Frederick's transferring his claim to the Bohemian crown to Bethlen Gábor, without any constitutional grounds, and clearing the Palatinate of its invaders, hopefully with English assistance. Söltl, *Der Religionskrieg*, iii, p. 108. Camerarius spent the first half of 1621 away from Frederick, mostly in Heidelberg and at Union meetings in Heilbronn. Schubert, *Camerarius*, pp. 89–99.

49. Arthur W. White Jr., 'Suspension of Arms: Anglo-Spanish Mediation in the Thirty Years War, 1621–1625', PhD Thesis, Tulane University (1978), p. 140.

50. S.R. Gardiner, ed., *The Fortescue Papers, Camden Society* (London, 1871), pp. 147–8.

51. BHStA, KS, 9254/2, fols 6–7: 14 February 1621, Declaration to Edward Villiers.

52. 'l'avancement de la gloire de Dieu'. BHStA, KS, 9254/2, fol. 23: 4/14 February 1621, Frederick V to James I.

53. 's'il eust pleu a Dieu de donner heureuse issue tout le parti de la religion en eussent du soulagement mais puis que ce n'a este la volonte de Dieu c'est à moi de prendre de sa main et le bien et le mal'. BHStA, KS, 9254/2, fol. 23: 4/14 February 1621, Frederick V to James I.

54. BHStA, KS, 9254/2, fol. 23: 4/14 February 1621, Frederick V to James I.

55. For a full account of these negotiations, see White, 'Suspension'.

56. Robert Zaller, ''Interest of State': James I and the Palatinate', *Albion*, vi, 2 (1974), p. 156.

57. White, 'Suspension', p. 166.

58. BHStA, KB, 146/4: 6 February 1621, Ambrosio Spínola to Union.

59. PRO, SP, 81/20, fol. 181: 16/26 February 1621, Bilderbeck to Naunton.

60. PRO, SP, 81/20, fol. 188: 19/29 February 1621, Bilderbeck to Naunton.

61. PRO, SP, 81/20, fol. 63: 14/24 January 1621, James I to Princes of the Union.

62. PRO, SP, 81/20, fol. 301: c. March 1621, Memorial of Albert Morton.

63. PRO, SP, 81/20, fol. 170: 7/17 February 1621, Princes of the Union to James I. The letter is signed by the Duke of Zweibrücken, the Margrave of Brandenburg, and the Duke of Württemberg.

64. There had been complaints about the Union forces' poor discipline since the autumn of 1620. It was said that they were doing more harm than good in occupying the Palatinate. Söltl, *Der Religionskrieg*, iii, p. 106.

65. Söltl, *Der Religionskrieg*, iii, p. 121.

66. Egler, *Die Spanier*, pp. 60–1.

67. PRO, SP, 81/20, fol. 231: 3/13 March 1621, Sir Horace de Vere to Secretary of State.

68. Ibid.

69. PRO, SP, 81/20, fol. 264: 19/29 March 1621, Nethersole to Secretary of State.

70. BHStA, KB, 121/3a, fol. 62: 12/22 April 1621, Frederick V to Christian IV.

71. BHStA, KB, 121/3a, fol. 71: 2 May 1621, Christian IV to Frederick V.

72. 'autrement ie crains que tout sera perdu', PRO, SP, 81/20, fol. 313: 7/17 April 1621, Elizabeth to James I.

73. 'Je viveraÿ content ne pouvant apres Dieu attendre de persone le remede à mes maux que de V. M.ste entre les mains de laquelle je me remets entierement desirant soubmestre ma volonte à la siene sachant bien quelle aura à coeur la conservation de ses enfans'. PRO, SP, 81/20, fol. 315: 7/17 April 1621, Frederick V to James I.

74. PRO, SP, 81/20, fol. 329: 12/22 April 1621, Elizabeth to James I, and fol. 331: 12/22 April 1621, Frederick V to James I.

75. BHStA, KS, 9254/2, fol. 33: 16/26 April 1621, James I to Frederick V.

76. BHStA, KS, 9254/2, fols 37–8: 24 April/4 May 1621, Frederick V to James I. Frederick's request for money would be summarily dismissed. James forwarded it to the King of Denmark and gave no guarantee that it would go farther. BHStA, KS, 9254/2, fol. 43: 13/23 May 1621, James I to Frederick V.

77. 'pour rallentir des persecutions tant extremes, qui ne peuvent qu'enflammer d'avantage l'ire de Dieu sur tout le general'. BHStA, KS, 9254/2, fols 37–8: 24 April/4 May 1621, Frederick V to James I.

78. 'par la loy de l'honneur & de la nature de vous voir restabli'. BHStA, KS, 9254/2, fol. 35: 19/29 April 1621, James I to Frederick V.

79. BHStA, KS, 9254/2, fol. 41: 11/21 May 1621, Frederick V to James I.

80. AP, ii, pp. 437–8.

81. PRO, SP 81/21, fols 9–11: 7 May 1621, SV, Nethersole's proposals for the King of Bohemia, and James I's answers.

82. Despite the threat felt by the Estates General, Prince Maurits had pled on Frederick's behalf in the first months of 1621, and the Estates had sent a commissioner (Cornelis van Hoogenhouck) to meet Frederick in Braunschweig to discuss his needs. Just before Frederick had reached The Hague in April 1621, the Estates General had resumed their monthly grant to Mansfeld of 50,000 fl. Mout, 'Der Winterkönig', pp. 259–60.

83. BHStA, KB, 121/3a, fol. 66: 7/17 May 1621, Frederick V to Christian IV. Copies were sent to the Dukes of Braunschweig and Lünenburg. It is uncertain whether this numbered included the Dutch companies under the command of Colonel Obertraut. See PRO, SP, 80/4, fols 11–12: 29 April/9 May 1621, John Carpenter to Secretary Calvert.

84. BHStA, KB, 146/5, 24 February 1621, Georg Friedrich to his son, Friedrich.

85. BHStA, KB, 121/3a, fol. 69.

86. BHStA, KB, 121/3a, fol. 63: 26 April/ 6 May 1621, Frederick V to Christian IV; fols 75–6: 22 May/1 June 1621, Frederick V to Christian IV.

87. BHStA, KB, 121/3a, fol. 79: 22 May/1 June 1621, Frederick V to Christian IV and the Dukes of Braunschweig and Lüneburg.

88. A few universities approved the validity of Wolfgang Wilhelm's claim. BHStA, KS, 3682, 3681, and 3684.

89. PRO, SP, 81/21, fol. 34: 25 May 1621, Palatine Council of State to Frederick V.

90. 'de vous reposer seulement sur la faveur de Dieu et sur nostre assistence'. PRO, SP, 81/21, fol. 18: 13/23 May 1621, James I to Frederick V.

91. 'considerans serieusement l'estat present des enfans du Roy hors le Royaume, & l'affliction generale de ceux qui en autre pays font vrayement profession de la mesme Religion Chrestienne qui est receue par l'Eglise d'Angleterre, & estans touchez d'un vray sentiment et compassion de leurs detresses comme membres du mesme corps', BHStA, KS, 9254/2, fol. 51: copy of the declaration in Parliament, dated 4 June 1621.

92. BHStA, KS, 9254/2, fols 45–9.

93. Baker, *Letters of Elizabeth*, p. 58: 11/21 May 1621, Elizabeth to Thomas Rowe.

94. The Elector of Saxony had arranged for a general amnesty in Lusatia and Silesia, and in Moravia and Austria only one death sentence was carried out. ADB, vi, pp. 650–1.

95. PRO, SP, 80/4, fols 17–18: 13/23 May 1621, Carpenter to Calvert. PRO, SP, 81/21, fol. 49: 1/11 June 1621, Frederick V to James I.

96. 'Sehet ihr disen Mann zugegen (dadurch den And: Pavel mainendt) der begehrt vor mein Ayden 30M £ Sterling, wann ich mein aigen Königreich salvieren müest, so gethraut ich mir nicht 30M £ Sterling aufzutreiben'. BHStA, KS, 16745, fol. 75, #138.

97. BHStA, KS, 9254/2, fol. 70: 20 June 1621, James' response to Andreas Pawel's memorial.

98. 'il fault qu'elle y procede par des moyens qui soyent faisables, . . . c'est chose qui ne se peut pas esperer'. BHStA, KS, 9254/2, fol. 72: 20 June 1621, James' response to Andreas Pawel's memorial. 'Elle' refers to 'Sa Majesté'.

99. 'der König auß Engellandt ein gottloß leben führe, sei ein blasphemator, adulter, und daß er den Spanischen ambassator stets umb sich hab'. BHStA, KS, 16745, fol. 75, #138. Pawell made this statement to Tschernembl.

100. BHStA, KS, 9254/2, fols 61–2: 23 June/3 July 1621, James I to Frederick V.

101. PRO, SP, 81/21, fol. 84: 13/23 June 1621, Frederick V to Bethlen Gábor. Normally their correspondence was carried on in Latin, so this English translation either comes from an intercepted letter or was prepared for and sent to the English court.

102. PRO, SP, 81/21, fol. 100: 22 June 1621, Duke of Zweibrücken to James I.

103. PRO, SP, 81/21, fol. 85: 13/23 June 1621, Frederick V to Bethlen Gábor.

104. Ibid., fol. 86.

105. Ibid., fol. 87.

106. PRO, SP, 80/4, fols 22–3: 23 May 1621, SV, James' Instructions to Digby; fols 19–21: 20/30 May 1621, Carpenter to Carlo Vittorini; fols 43–8: Report about the Danish embassy in Vienna.

107. PRO, SP, 80/4, fols 22–4: 23 May 1621, SV, James' Instructions to Digby.

108. Ibid., fol. 25.

109. PRO, SP, 80/4, fols 63–4: 14/24 June 1621, Digby to Calvert.

110. PRO, SP, 80/4, fols 37–8: 28 May/7 June 1621, Digby to ?

111. PRO, SP, 80/4, fols 97–8: 2/12 July 1621, Digby to Calvert. For an account of this embassy, see Zaller, 'Interest of State.'

112. PRO, SP, 80/4, fols 99–100: 4/14 July 1621, Digby to Calvert.

113. White, 'Suspension', pp. 179–80.

114. Gindely, *Geschichte*, ii, pp. 22–5.

115. White, 'Suspension', p. 181.

116. PRO, SP, 80/4, fol. 124: 20/30 July 1621, Digby to Frederick V.

117. Ibid., fols 124–5.

118. PRO, SP, 80/4, fols 140–2: 26 July/5 August 1621, Digby to Frederick V.

119. PRO, SP, 80/4, fol. 127: 26 July/5 August 1621, Digby to Calvert?

120. Ibid., fol. 129.

121. PRO, SP, 80/4, fol. 133: 26 July/5 August 1621, Digby to Carleton.

122. PRO, SP, 80/4, fol. 136: 26 July/5 August 1621, Digby to ?

123. Ibid., fol. 137.

124. Ibid., fol. 138.

125. Ibid.

126. PRO, SP, 80/4, fol. 148: 26 July/5 August 1621, Digby to Carleton.

127. 'der gegentheil zu keiner billigmeßigen güte geneigt, sondern alles zu seinem vorthel uff die lange banck zu verschieben und underdeßen unß in mehr und mehr abzumatten gemeint', BHStA, KB, 121/3d, fol. 17: 12/22 July 1621, Frederick V to Christian IV.

128. PRO, SP, 80/4, fol. 163: 12/22 August 1621, Digby to Calvert.

129. White, 'Suspension', p. 212.

130. PRO, SP, 80/4, fol. 163: 12/22 August 1621, Digby to Calvert.

131. PRO, SP, 80/4, fols 178–80: 13/23 August 1621, Frederick V to Digby.

132. 'Mr. Digby n'obtiendra rien à Vienne'. Aretin, 'Sammlung', p. 180: 11/21 September 1621, Frederick V to Elizabeth.

133. PRO, SP, 80/4, fols 203–4: 5/15 September 1621, Digby to the Lords' Commission.

134. Ibid., fol. 205.

135. Ibid., fol. 206.

136. Ibid., fols 206–7.

137. PRO, SP, 80/4, fol. 216: 5/15 September 1621, Digby to Calvert. Deciphered version of fols 212–15.

138. 'en une confusion totale, dont il ne s'en peult ensuivre que la ruine de la cause, et de tout le Palatinat, si Dieu miraculeusement n'ÿ remedir'. PRO, SP, 81/21, fol. 148: 18 July 1621, Plessen to Nethersole.

139. PRO, SP, 81/21, fol. 127: 6/16 July 1621, James I to Frederick V.

140. PRO, SP, 81/21, fol. 129: 7/17 July 1621, Frederick V to James I.

141. 'tant pour la confoederation si solennellement juree que pour estre un prince qui à fait tousjours profession de la mesme religion dont V. M.ste est defenseur et que par la J'ayderois à remettre tant de milles ames soubs la tÿrannie de l'entechrist', PRO, SP, 81/21, fol. 130: 7/17 July 1621, Frederick V to James I.

142. 'le desplaisir que nous en re[ss]entons est, quand nous nous voyons desnuer des moyens d'y satisfaire'. BHStA, KS, 9254/2, fol. 80: 22 July/1 August 1621, James I to Frederick V.

143. 'ny avec tous les revenus de nostre couronne', BHStA, KS, 9254/2, fol. 80: 22 July/1 August 1621, James I to Frederick V.

144. 'ne pourroit que redonder à vostre grand deshonneur'. BHStA, KS, 9254/2, fol. 81: 22 July/1 August 1621, James I to Frederick V. In April Bethlen Gábor had asked

the Turkish Sultan to intervene in the war against the Habsburgs. Frederick's response was a mere complaint about his predicament and a request for Gábor's true adherence and constant support. AP, ii, pp. 434–7.

145. PRO, SP, 81/21, fol. 152: 20/30 July 1621, Nethersole to Secretary of State.
146. 'ihre intentiones genugsam zu erkennen geben'. BHStA, KB, 121/3a, fol. 143: 28 July/7 August 1621, Frederick V to the Dukes of Braunschweig and Lünenburg.
147. PRO, SP, 81/21, fol. 152: 20/30 July 1621, Nethersole to Secretary of State.
148. BHStA, KB, 121/3a, fols 100–3: 20/30 June 1621, Frederick V to Christian IV.
149. The Palatine regime was not wholly in favor of an association with the Turks. Johann Joachim von Rusdorf and Count Palatine Johann of Zweibrücken were nervous about its potential for damage to the common cause and, indeed, to all Christendom. Johann Joachim von Rusdorf, 'Bericht Jo: Joachim Russdorfs gewester churpflaz rath; was er anno 1621 zu Wien weger seines herrn negotiert. Von wort zu wort auss der heidelbergischen geheimben registratur und cantzley ausszifferten originalien', (1624).
150. PRO, SP, 81/21, fol. 152: 20/30 July 1621, Nethersole to Secretary of State. According to Mansfeld, he had been instructed to attack Bohemia. PRO, SP, 80/4, fol. 292: 3/13 October 1621, Digby to Lords.
151. She asked the Marquis to keep this disclosure a secret between himself, James I, and Prince Charles. Baker, *Letters of Elizabeth*, p. 61: 28 July/8 August 1621 [sic], Elizabeth to Buckingham.
152. 'Je ne tiens a moy necessaire de justifier touttes ses actions encores que je ne sache rien de ses procedures qui ne soyent pour mon service et selon raison de guerre'. BHStA, KS, 9254/2, fols 78–9: 30 July/9 August 1621, Frederick V to James I.
153. For this embassy's demands for the revocation of Frederick's ban and the restitution of his estates, see PRO, SP, 80/4, fols 19–21.
154. BHStA, KB, 121/3a, fols 94–99: 2 June 1621, Christian IV to Frederick V.
155. BHStA, KB, 121/3a, fols 100–3: 20/30 June 1621, Frederick V to Christian IV.
156. PRO, SP, 81/22, fol. 6: 1/11 September 1621, Nethersole to Calvert. On the way Dohna recruited fourteen captains and their companies, each 200 men strong, for Palatine service. PRO, SP, 81/21, fol. 233: 22 August/1 September 1621, Nethersole to ?
157. BHStA, KB, 121/3a, fols 83–6: 5/15 September 1621, Dohna to Frederick V.
158. BHStA, KB, 121/3a, fols 104–9: 22 August 1621, Christian IV to Frederick V.
159. PRO, SP, 81/21, fols 203–4: 13/23 August 1621, Nethersole to Calvert.
160. PRO, SP, 80/4, fols 182–3: 15/25 August 1621, Digby to Calvert.
161. AR, #6055: 2/12 August 1621, Mansfeld to Frederick V.
162. PRO, SP, 81/21, fol. 204: 13/23 August 1621, Nethersole to Calvert.
163. PRO, SP, 81/21, fol. 179: 1/11 August 1621, Vere to Calvert. James had procured extensions of the truce through June and July. White, 'Suspension', pp. 184, 191, 215.
164. PRO, SP, 81/21, fol. 205: 13/23 August 1621, Nethersole to Calvert.
165. PRO, SP, 81/21, fol. 201: 7/17 August 1621, Nethersole to ?
166. PRO, SP, 81/21, fol. 216: 21/31 August 1621, Elizabeth to Roe.
167. 'Tout pour Dieu et pour elle'. Hans Wertheim, *Der tolle Halberstädter: Herzog Christian von Braunschweig im pfälzischen Kriege, 1621–1622* (2 vols, Berlin, 1929), i, p. 200. It has been argued, however, that Christian first met Elizabeth in The Hague, and not during her journey there. Karl Wittich, 'Christian der Halberstädter und die Pfalzgräfin Elisabeth', *Separatabdruck aus der Zeitschrift für*

Preußische Geschichte und Landeskunde (August 1869), pp. 1–20.

168. Wertheim, *Der tolle Halberstädter*, i, pp. 205–7.

169. 'Je crois que cela ne seroit que bon pour mes affaires, et peut être pas mal pour luy; mais tout est en la main de Dieu'. Aretin, 'Sammlung', p. 177.

170. PRO, SP, 81/22, fols 51–3: 22 September/2 October 1621, Nethersole to Calvert.

171. BHStA, KS, 9254/2, fols 82–3: 30 August/9 September 1621, James I to Frederick V.

172. 'sans en brouiller les moyens'. BHStA, KS, 9254/2, fols 86–7: 30 August/9 September 1621, James I to Frederick V.

173. PRO, SP, 81/22, fols 51–3: 22 September/2 October 1621, Nethersole to Calvert.

174. 'n'estant pas encores legitimement decidé, il s'ensuit, qu'il n'y a eu aucune raison de passer condemnation contre le Roy de Boheme, sans prealable cognoissance & decision de cause'. BHStA, KS, 9254/2, fol. 92: 3/13 October 1621.

175. BHStA, KS, 9254/2, fol. 91: 3/13 October 1621. The marginal note explains how the draft was corrected and approved.

176. BHStA, KS, 9254/2, fols 91–8: 3/13 October 1621, 'La Resolution du Roi de Bohème'. Also see PRO, SP81/22, fols 62–8: 29 September/9 October 1621, 'Brieve Deduction'.

177. 'd'un simple payssant'. BHStA, KS, 9254/2, fol. 92: 3/13 October 1621.

178. BHStA, KS, 9254/2, fol. 132: 12/22 October 1621, Frederick V to James I.

179. PRO, SP, 81/22, fols 93–4: 3/13 October 1621, Frederick V to James I.

180. PRO, SP, 81/22, fol. 131: 20/30 October 1621, Nethersole.

181. PRO, SP, 81/22, fols 110–12: Frederick V to Mansfeld. At the end of October, the Prince of Orange had promised Mansfeld 50,000 fl. and praised him for his continuing resolve to fight for Frederick and to defend the liberty of the Protestant religion. PRO, SP, 81/22, fols 121–2: 26 October 1621.

182. By August Mansfeld's army had 'absolutely ruined and wasted' the Upper Palatinate so that it could no longer stay there. PRO, SP, 80/4, fol. 154: 26 July/5 August 1621, Digby to Carleton.

183. For copies of these letters, see PRO, SP, 80/4, fols 294–306.

184. 'il ne se faut pas fier au Roy de la Grande Bretagne, d'autant qu'il est de la religion, et qu'on ne peut remedier ni rafermir les affaires, si ce n'est que la Religion nommée Calvinistique soit du tout exterminée'. PRO, SP, 81/22, fol. 126: 28 October 1621, Mansfeld to Frederick V.

185. 'Dieu Directeur de toutes choses et protecter de l'innocence a miraculeusement descouvert la source et les plus secrets' BHStA, KS, 9254/2, fol. 121: November 1621, Frederick V to James I.

186. Camerarius' *Cancellaria Hispanica* would appear in early 1622. This publishing war would continue throughout the 1620s. See Reinhold Koser, *Der Kanzleienstreit* (Halle, 1874). For comments on *Anhaltische Kanzlei* and *Prodromus* by Camerarius and many other anti-Habsburg pamphlets, see Karl Nolden, 'Die Reichspolitik Kaiser Ferdinands II. in der Publizistik bis zum Lübecker Frieden 1629', *Inaugural-Dissertation zur Erlangung der Doktorwürde der philosophischen Fakultät der Universität zu Köln*, (1957).

187. Schubert, *Camerarius*, pp. 122–30.

188. 'der werd mit seiner suspension d'armes mehrtheils verspott und außgelacht'. BHStA, KS, 16745, fol. 70: 7 November 1621, 'Der Straßburg correspondent bericht.' William Trumbull faired no better. He had applied for an extension of the truce in late September, but the Infanta could not grant it. The authorization that she

had received from the Emperor stipulated the necessity of the Duke of Bavaria's concurrence, and he had been busily executing the ban in the Upper Palatinate. The Infanta had authorized Córdoba to continue his conquest of the Lower, and she refused to grant a suspension of arms on the grounds that she had no authority to do so. White, 'Suspension', pp. 262–3. BHStA, KB, 121/3f, 8 November 1621.

189. PRO, SP, 81/22, fols 146–7: 31 October/10 November 1621.

190. PRO, SP, 81/22, fol. 143: 29 October/8 November 1621: Tilly to Heidelberg Council. PRO, SP81/22, fol. 144: 30 October/9 November 1621.

191. Low river levels assisted the Bavarians' march, allowing easier and more frequent crossings. PRO, SP, 81/22, fols 158–9: 5/15 November 1621.

192. PRO, SP, 81/22, fol. 165: 9/19 November 1621, Nethersole to Calvert.

193. BHStA, KB, 121/3a, fols 158–61: 20 October 1621, Lower Saxon Circle to Frederick V.

194. BHStA, KS, 9254/2, fols 115–16: 12/22 November 1621, James I to Frederick V.

195. 'hatt es Gott wunderbarlich geschickt', BHStA, KB, 121/3a, fol. 149: 22 November/ 2 December 1621, Frederick V to Lower Saxon Circle.

196. 'Wir haben aber die veste zuversicht zu Gott dem gerechten ritter, er werde unsere unschuldt zu seiner zeitt wol zu [verthendig] wißen, dem wir indeßen in seiner vätterlichen heimsuchung mitt Christlicher gedullt still hallten wollen'. BHStA, KB, 121/3a, fol. 153: 22 November/2 December 1621, Frederick V to Lower Saxon Circle.

197. He asked James not to show the treaty to anyone if the Emperor did not accept it, because it would only encourage Palatine enemies. BHStA, KS, 9254/2, fol. 121: Frederick V to James I. The Palatines labeled the document 'das außgepreste Instrument', BHStA, KS, 9254/2, fol. 119.

198. Marginal note: 'Nota Engellandt hatt für sich selbsten solche offerta dem Kaiser gethan, undt den könig in Böhem schrifftlich und durch seinen Gesandten inständig ia betrohlich ermahnet nicht allein dieselbe einzugehen, sondern auch ihme darüber dis instrument in Pergament, under seiner des konigs in Boham handtunderschifft und Sigel zum furderlichsten zu uberschickten'. BHStA, KS, 9254/2, fol. 113: 25 November/5 December 1621. 'j'ay entendu plus particullierement par la bouche de Son. Ambass'. BHStA, KS, 9254/2, fol. 122: Frederick V to James I.

199. BHStA, KS, 9254/2, fol. 120: Frederick V to James I. 'cum omnibus ditionibus et juribus restituerit'. BHStA, KS, 9254/2, fol. 113: 25 November/5 December 1621.

200. 'des Eglises orthdoxes', BHStA, KS, 9254/2, fol. 121: Frederick V to James I.

201. BHStA, KS, 9254/2, fol. 122: Frederick V to James I.

202. PRO, SP81/22, fols 192–3: 26 November/6 December 1621: Elector Palatine to James I.

203. Weiß, *Die Unterstützung*, p. 45.

204. BHStA, KS, 9254/2, fol. 123: 31 December 1621/10 January 1622, James I to Frederick V. James confirmed that the £30,000 was sent to Frederick by 'lettre de change'.

205. PRO, SP, 80/4, fol. 345: 16/26 November 1621, Digby to Nethersole.

206. White, 'Suspension', p. 180. PRO, SP, 81/21, fol. 193: 3/13 August 1621, Mansfeld to Captain Ferenz. PRO, SP, 81/21, fol. 195: 5/15 August 1621, Mansfeld to Frederick V. PRO, SP, 80/4, fol. 242: 19/29 September 1621, Simon Digby to ? Sir John Digby had accosted Mansfeld with this information and warned him that if he abandoned his defense of the Palatinate, his honor and reputation 'would from one of the most renowned Cavagliers of Christendome become the most vile and

infamous'. PRO, SP, 80/4, fol. 282: 2/12 October 1621, Digby to Lords.

207. Zwiedineck-Südenhorst, *Die Politik*, i, pp. 192–3, 206–7.

208. PRO, SP, 81/22, fol. 224: 10/20 December 1621.

209. BHStA, KS, 7052: 13/23 December 1621, Frederick V to Georg Frederick, Margrave of Baden-Durlach. The Margrave had made efforts to refound the Union since July 1621, but because the Elector of Saxony stayed aloof, the Duke of Württemberg would make no alliance without him. There were further ideas and attempts to forge some sort of alliance to protect the Lutherans of the Empire, but these too, without Saxony's participation, came to nothing. Gotthard, '"Politice"', pp. 300–1.

Chapter 6

Frederick at War, 1622

In 1622 Frederick V would leave The Hague and make a daring journey incognito across France to join his forces in battle against the enemy in the Palatinate. Arriving at his general's headquarters in Germersheim, he would proclaim in a loud voice, 'I will have nothing to do with a suspension of arms, for that will be my ruin. I must have either a good peace or a good war'.[1] Unfortunately he would have neither. Though he would taste the thrill of victory, in the end he would have to swallow the shame of defeat. Too few princes would rally to his common cause, while King James I continued to negotiate with the Habsburgs for a suspension of arms and tried to coerce Frederick into changing his tactics. Yet despite international pressure in favor of a cease-fire, neither he nor Emperor Ferdinand II would relinquish their arms. Though James would manage to score a partial victory in his fight to gain control over his son-in-law's actions, Frederick's conscience rendered his convictions unalterable. At the year's end he would lose all of his lands apart from a single town, but a solution to the Palatine crisis would still be no closer at hand. The war could not be stopped because the main contenders' perceptions of the situation were essentially incommensurable and their mutual demands impracticable.

For Frederick, defending his patrimonial estates by force of arms was his lawful obligation, and he was convinced that the opposing party would never agree to a just settlement unless it were soundly defeated in battle. He was certain that his enemy was bent on suppressing all of his rights and on removing him from the community of princes and estates under the Imperial constitution. The Emperor's correspondence, actions, and secret promises were proof of his utter lack of trustworthiness. From Frederick's standpoint, Ferdinand had stated his intention to extirpate Calvinism, had savagely crushed the Bohemian rebellion, and had perverted Imperial law by authorizing the Spanish and Bavarian invasions of the Palatinate, by declaring the ban against Frederick, and, above all, by promising the Palatine electorate to Duke Maximilian. Frederick believed that he had no reasonable choice but to demand his full, unrestricted restitution before he agreed to peace with the Emperor, and that the only way to procure this arrangement was to defeat him in battle.

Ferdinand faced a similar situation. It had been his lawful obligation to relieve his lands of the burden of sedition, and as Emperor it was his duty to restore peace to the Empire. The enemy had usurped his territories and his royal crown, had ignored his Imperial commands to end the fighting, and had even denied his constitutional authority to referee the conflict. Frederick seemed dedicated to the downfall of the Habsburg dynasty in the Empire. He had accepted no defeat, admitted no error in his ways, and continued to support all rebels against Habsburg rule. Foreign potentates negotiating on his behalf had been unable to make him abide by any of their terms for peace. While Ferdinand had expressed his willingness to consent to a cease-fire and offer his mercy in return for the Palatine's submission, Frederick had brazenly authorized the continuation of violence in the eastern and western reaches of the Empire and had invited England and France to intervene militarily. He had even welcomed a Turkish invasion on his behalf. Ferdinand believed that he had no legitimate option apart from quelling this bellicose prince, and that because he lacked the means to do so alone, he had to commission other princes for the task, necessarily granting them the spoils as compensation.

Between these two extremities stood James I with the ostensible backing of the King of Spain and the Infanta Isabella. James wanted both sides to end the fighting together at the same time, even if temporarily, and settle their differences through negotiations for a final treaty. He saw that the war would only create more causes of complaint the longer it lasted, and that it would put more pressure on him to abandon his self-proclaimed status as Europe's *rex pacificus* and to resort to arms on behalf of his children. His sympathies, however, despite his familial obligations, were decidedly with the Emperor. Above all James believed that the best chance to restore peace to the Empire lay in restraining his son-in-law.

Palatine Tactics

Throughout the first half of 1622 Frederick would take personal command of the forces defending the Lower Palatinate. He was devoted to procuring a military victory in the Lower Palatinate, not because he was averse to peace, but because he had decided that the only way to bring Ferdinand to acceptable terms was to defeat his forces in the field. Frederick resolved to fight during his father-in-law's negotiations in order to secure a favorable settlement, a policy articulated by Camerarius as 'arranging peace under the shield'.[2] A more immediate goal was to relieve the Palatinate of the burden of war, preferably by shifting it onto the enemy's lands. In January 1622 he was weighing the option of leading Mansfeld's and Halberstadt's armies out of the Palatinate towards Bavaria or into the bishoprics of Würzburg and Eichstätt, leaving behind Vere and his regiments to protect Palatine strongholds. At the same time Frederick thought of continuing peace talks, advertising his readiness for a just peace, and protesting that he was engaged in war against his will. He should proclaim himself ready to pay the Emperor all due respect in accordance with the Imperial constitution.[3]

The status of Frederick's affairs in early 1622 called for such desperate measures. The move formally to bestow his electoral dignity on Duke Maximilian was well underway. After Ferdinand had refused to grant Digby's demands in the late summer of 1621, the Electors of Mainz, Cologne, Trier, and Saxony had been approached to give their consent for the transfer. While the Elector of Cologne had given his immediate assent, Mainz and Trier had advised against the measure and counseled peace instead. Still, they had made it understood that if an electoral diet were held, they would comply with the Emperor's demands. The Elector of Saxony had said that he would not object.[4] Moreover, it was suspected that the Palatinate was to be partitioned, the Emperor receiving Oppenheim and the Elector of Mainz the Bergstrasse.[5] And finally Frederick lost a bellicose ally. On 6 January 1622 Ferdinand signed a treaty whereby Bethlen Gábor agreed to renounce his claims to the crown of Hungary and return the crown jewels in return for grants of land and money and a title of an Imperial prince.[6] Following this truce the Margrave of Jägerndorf's forces were disbanded.[7] Fewer potentates than ever appeared to be on the Palatines' side.

A new offensive was organized to counteract this situation. On the diplomatic front Frederick resolved in January 1622 that the Electors of Mainz and Trier had to be persuaded that peace was impossible as long as he remained expelled from his lands.[8] Duke Johann of Zweibrücken was ordered to browbeat the two spiritual Electors with an exaggerated depiction of the consequences of an electoral transfer. Emissaries were sent to urge the King of Denmark, the Duke of Württemberg, and other sympathetic Lutheran princes to dissuade the Elector of Saxony from endorsing the transfer.[9] Frederick warned the Doge of Venice of the general Habsburg threat to the Empire and Italy and asked for funds to assist the King of England's defense of the Palatinate.[10] Similar entreaties were sent to the Duke of Savoy and the Dukes of Braunschweig and Lüneburg.[11] Frederick urged Margrave Georg Friedrich of Baden-Durlach to take up the common and Protestant causes, despite the Emperor's recent threat to subject him to the Imperial ban.[12] Only the last of these pleas obtained the desired response.

On the military front the numbers and movements of armies rallying to the common cause gave Frederick plentiful cause for wishful thinking.

Baden-Durlach, instead of bowing to the Emperor, threw down the gauntlet for the sake of the restoration of the Palatinate. Georg Friedrich abdicated his entire estate to his son in order to free his family from the dangers of the Imperial ban and tried to raise a force of 20,000 men.[13] In full agreement with Frederick's declarations, the Margrave claimed that their only goal was peace, and that the means to this goal was a restoration of the electoral college as it stood before the war, with the Count Palatine in possession of his electorate.[14] Another 15-20,000 men under Christian of Halberstadt would be ready to fight in the spring.[15] He had been gathering his forces in Padernborn and Lippstadt, and intended to lead them to the Palatinate as soon as the weather permitted it.[16] The Landgrave of Hessen-Kassel was arming as well, though in self-defense; he hesitated sending his troops to the Palatinate.[17] But still better, King James informed Frederick that an English army of 8,000 foot and 1,600 horse would be sent to the Lower Palatinate, despite the recent dissolution of Parliament.[18] At the end of January he thanked James profusely both for the army and his agreeing to correspond with other princes on Frederick's behalf.[19] Nethersole heard that James was 'resolute to recover the Palatinate', and that a royal council 'breath[ed] nothing but warre and vengeance'.[20] The King, the Palatines heard, was supposed to raise his standard on 10/20 March 1622.[21]

While Frederick watched the formation of these armies, which were numerically comparable to the Spanish and Bavarian forces, his concern for his honor soon compelled him to return to the Lower Palatinate. In February, Nethersole said that Frederick was 'fully resolved' to do so, 'esteeming this to be a course though no whit more safe, yet much more honorable' than his other options.[22] He saw no advantage in a cessation of arms. The reports from the Upper Palatinate about Maximilian's occupation and Ferdinand's intercepted letters had made Frederick

> fixed in opinion that his enemyes ayme is onely to ridde him of the assistance and themselves of the feare of the forces of the Count Mansfelt and [Halberstadt], which can neither be held together in a truce, nor the like be drawne easily together agayne if these should be licensed upon a deposition of armes.[23]

A truce would only enable Emperor Ferdinand to call an Imperial diet, as he had already tried to, and ratify the translation of the Palatine electorate through a majority vote of the princes and estates. The problem was that James I, despite his war-like words, was as committed to his negotiations for a suspension of arms as ever.

Rex Pacificus

Military assistance from England remained doubtful, and Frederick knew it. He was warned against trusting James because of his friendly inclinations toward Spain. The council of Baden advised Frederick in March 1622 not to depend on England, because James seemed to act in accordance with Spanish interests.[24] Frederick's emissary, Johannes Joachim von Rusdorf described assistance from England as 'subject to the wind of traverses and procrastinations', because of James' ardent desire for an Anglo-Spanish marriage alliance.[25] In reference to Spanish assurances of an eventual restoration of the Palatinate, Rusdorf admonished

> the traverses and amusements authorized by the title of parent and by the good offices under the pretext of a certain marriage are the most suspect and injurious. It is a grave error to esteem flimsy words and courtesies more than actions and effects.[26]

Nonetheless, Frederick's agent in London, Abraham Williams, reported in March that the privy council was meeting almost daily and that money and men would be provided. Even James was said to be unhappy with the slow pace of progress in the affair, but he continued to negotiate nonetheless. Digby would soon go to Spain, and another ambassador, Lord Chichester, the President of the council for the war in the Palatinate, was expected to go negotiate with the Emperor.[27] But at the same time James granted Philip IV permission to recruit a force of 8,000 men from England and Scotland to serve in Spanish armies. In the following month James sent a preacher to the Tower for publicly comparing the Palatinate to a soul in hell and Spínola with the devil, from whose clutches the soul could not escape.[28] It has been suggested that Frederick might have received some aid from the Turkish Sultan had James' ambassador at the Turkish court, Sir Thomas Roe, not worked against it.[29] In 1622 James I remained as firmly against an escalation of the Palatine war as he had been in the years preceding.

Negotiations remained his preferred means of resolving the Palatine crisis. In January and February James had considered a Spanish plan for the restitution of the Palatinate, whereby Frederick would send his eldest son, Friedrich Heinrich, to be raised at the Emperor's court in Vienna, later to marry a daughter of the Emperor. When he reached his majority, he was to inherit the Palatinate and its electoral dignity. Naturally Frederick refused outright, but other negotiations progressed. In mid January Emperor Ferdinand was willing to empower the Infanta Isabella to arrange a suspension of arms in the Palatinate and then to preside over a conference for a general peace treaty.[30] In response to Digby's embassy in the summer of 1621, Count Georg Ludwig von Schwarzenberg was selected to go to Brussels and then to England, but this embassy was merely a matter of form.[31] Schwarzenberg was instructed to convey the Emperor's inclination to restore the Count Palatine but not to negotiate in detail about either the restitution or granting Frederick mercy.[32] According to Simon Digby, the English agent in Vienna, the purpose of this embassy was merely

> to cumplye in the matter of Ceremony and Complement in regard his Majestie [James I] hath sent so many Ambassadors hither, and especially to amuse his Majestie with hopes of a peaceable accommodation, and to retard, yf not absolutely to hinder his sending over forces for the defence of the Palatinate.[33]

Digby found Schwarzenberg a poor choice for the task, because he was neither sufficiently informed to handle the matter, nor had he ever 'beene much ymployed in the Affaires of State and . . . was absolutely retired to a Country lyfe'.[34] Digby warned, if King James 'expect any just dealing or satisfaction to his demands for any other respect then for his owne conservation, and by constraint he will I feare in the end fynde himself much deceaved'.[35]

But James was more than satisfied with Schwarzenberg's embassy. On his arrival in London on 6/16 April 1622, he was welcomed with festivities and honors equivalent to those shown the French ambassador.[36] He was greeted by the Marquis of Buckingham, who, upon forwarding his King's greetings, asked 'if he would be allowed to visit [the ambassador] at any time and to use the same familiarity as with the Count of Gondomar', the Spanish ambassador.[37] There was not to be enough time, however, for him to develop a working relationship with either the King or Buckingham; Schwarzenberg had his audience with James I on the next day and went back to Brussels after a couple of weeks. The ambassador's speech – few could have understood it, because it was delivered in German – exonerated the Emperor's actions in the Palatine crisis and tried to assuage James' concerns. Schwarzenberg flattered the King's wisdom, justice, and moderation and said that the Emperor shared his desire for peace. Without naming Frederick, Schwarzenberg blamed him and his adherents for the failure of the King's efforts to conclude a peace-treaty.[38] The ambassador declared that the Emperor was ready to lay down his arms as soon as his adversaries did the same, and that he had dealt with James honestly, without fraud, and sincerely intended to grant him satisfaction, 'especially at the earnest interposition of the Kings Maiestie of Spaine'.[39] At another audience Schwarzenberg and Gondomar tried to dissuade James from assisting in a renewal of the violence in the Palatinate. The Emperor's embassy to England ended with the mutual agreement that further negotiations should continue in Brussels under the Infanta's mediation.[40]

Despite James' prior declaration about sending an army to defend the Palatinate, none went. There had been expectations that Lord Chichester would bring 8,000 foot and 1,600 horse to the Palatinate, but the budgeted £250,000 were not to be had.[41] Instead of an army Horace Vere received a new commission to become Commander-in-Chief of the Palatine-English-Dutch forces already in the Lower Palatinate, which numbered roughly 9,000 men, one third of whom were British soldiers. Vere then restricted his men to the defense of the three main fortress-towns in the Lower Palatinate: Mannheim, Heidelberg, and Frankenthal.[42] Immediately there were complaints about this arrangement. One Colonel Merven, stationed in Heidelberg, had informed The Hague that many German soldiers, captains, and officers were deserting daily because they were receiving much less pay than the British. Frederick asked General Vere to pay all equally to rid the regiment of jealousy.[43]

On Campaign

In March 1622 Frederick left The Hague to take personal command of the forces in the Palatinate. He probably went with dreams of victory in his head as well as a sobering awareness of the inherent dangers of the journey and of the battlefield. Though firmly convinced of the righteousness of his cause and the correctness of his tactics, he was neither willing nor able to make himself either a martyr or a cold-blooded soldier of fortune. During the campaign he would be unable to overcome his humanity, and soon defeats in the field, barbarism among the soldiery, renewed pressure from England, and a longing to see his wife would send him back again. In these events he showed that he lacked the heartlessness of other princes as opportunistic as himself.

Traveling incognito with Nethersole and five others, Frederick made for the Lower Palatinate at first by sea to Boulogne and then by post to Paris. The party selected this detour for its safety and because of Frederick's desire 'to cast his eye en passant on that famous citty which he was never agayn like to have such ready opportunity to see'.[44] He did some sight-seeing, and, already missing his wife, he bought some costume jewelry and other gifts for her, though their modesty embarrassed him.[45] After Paris, Frederick left his companions – they wanted to take a less direct, longer, and safer route – and traveled alone through Lorraine to the Palatinate, accompanied only by a merchant.[46] He was unafraid of the risks, because he was certain that God would grant him a good voyage.[47] In the north-eastern edge of Lorraine, at the town of Bitsch, the two men encountered twelve Habsburg soldiers, some of whom recognized the merchant, but luckily not Frederick. The merchant entertained them and asked them to convoy him and his companion to Frankfurt, but, not coming to an agreement on the price, the two parties went their own way.[48] On another occasion, as Frederick and his companion rode on horseback, a gentleman in a coach passing by said loudly to his fellow travelers, 'There goeth the King of Bohemia', and 'passed without further enquiry'.[49] Apart from these two encounters, the journey was probably uneventful.

On 12 April Frederick reached Mansfeld's quarters in Germersheim, brimming with confidence. Marshal Ravile, the Lieutenant-Governor of Luxembourg, whom the Infanta had sent to induce Mansfeld to abandon Frederick and switch sides, witnessed his arrival and heard his loud proclamation that he would settle for nothing less than 'a good peace or a good war'.[50] Frederick soon observed with pleasure 'great joy of [his] poor subjects' at his being in his homelands once again.[51] His soldiers were likewise encouraged. They believed 'that God was with him in this journey, and that as he shewed it manifestly by preserving their King from that perill in his way to them, so he will also continue to manifest, as much by preserving them, and his countryes thorough his comming'.[52] In all likelihood Frederick was of the same mind.

Marshal Ravile feared that the Palatine's presence could turn his army into a more formidable force than it had been, and the prediction proved correct.[53] In late April Frederick and Mansfeld, joined by Vere and the Margrave of Baden-Durlach, crossed the Rhine, invaded the lands of the Bishop of Speyer, and then defeated the Bavarian army in an engagement near Wiesloch.[54] Frederick at first retreated, setting a village on fire, and then attacked, taking Tilly's men by surprise and killing 2,400.[55] Not long before Tilly had allegedly put the entire population of Hilsbach, a small town south-east of Heidelberg, to the sword – men, women, and children – so for the Palatines his defeat was a sign that God 'had forsaken the enemy as displeased with their unchristian massacring of innocent women and children and that upon cold blood'.[56] Moreover, because Frederick's army had been 'then upon the very point of breaking in it selfe', his victory appeared all the more to be 'the especiall and indeede wonderfull, if not miraculous working of our Almighty God'.[57] Frederick probably espoused the same interpretation of these events. On hearing the news of the victories, Vere declared optimistically,

> There could nothing have happened more seasonably to give luster to the kinge of Bohemia's retourne, to comfort his subiects, confirme his frends, discourage

his enemyes and consequently reestablish his affayres having that assistance he expects.[58]

After this successful engagement, Frederick went to Heidelberg.

The thrill of victory confirmed the righteousness of his current course of action. After Wiesloch he seemed all the more convinced 'that a truce [was] the high way to the ruyne of his affayres'.[59] Frederick wrote,

[The Almighty] already let us see his grace impressively in the past battle, for which we cannot duly say enough praise and thanks to him. We should pray to him that he may want to stand by us further. I go now toward the enemy. I hope with God's help for good success in our affairs.[60]

For Frederick, the victory at Wiesloch was a sign of God's favor, and he resolved to continue his campaign in spite of the negotiations in Brussels. Indeed, he wished that James' project would soon fail:

I do not want to hope that His Majesty (James I) will have my enemies brought to a treaty, this being the means for me to lose entirely. Even the impossibility can be easily seen, and the inequality. The enemy has the means to maintain his army with supplies and money. We are in a ruined land and do not have the mines of the West-Indies. During the treaty the enemy has the means to increase his army. Mine can only diminish. It is better to treat for peace with arms in hand.[61]

This was to be Frederick's policy for as long as he possessed 'the means'.

Unfortunately they did not remain at his disposal for very long. After Wiesloch Tilly had retreated to Wimpfen, a few miles north of Heilbronn, while Mansfeld and Frederick went north to take Ladenburg and its passage over the Neckar. Leaving the Margrave of Baden-Durlach in the rear, their plan was to destroy Córdoba's bridge over the Rhine at Oppenheim.[62] On 6 May 1622 Tilly, bolstered by Córdoba's forces, avenged himself on the Margrave, who lost most of his men, supplies, artillery, and cache of money.[63] One week later, while Frederick was at Frankenthal, he received orders from King James to retire to one of the cities garrisoned by the English forces and wait, peaceably, for the results of the negotiations in Brussels.[64] Frederick was ordered to have Mansfeld stay where he was and commit no acts of hostility on the neighboring princes, otherwise, the King warned, full blame for the conflict would fall on Frederick directly.[65] James had also written to Mansfeld and Christian of Halberstadt to persuade them to restrain themselves in similar manner. The King promised to incorporate them and their interests in the general peace treaty, but first the suspension of arms had to be settled and obeyed.[66] Frederick also received a copy of a letter from the Infanta Isabella, in which she said that Córdoba was ready to comply with a truce and that Frederick's restoration was ready to be completed at the pleasure of King Philip IV of Spain.[67] But these measures were not enough.

There was no chance that Frederick would comply. A suspension of arms at this point would have caused him to lose his largest force of arms. Still worse, he was threatened with 'the eternall losse of his credit with all military men if he should now shift of his soldiers dishonorably, and by consequence, the everlasting disabling himself to rayse an army agayne'.[68] Because Frederick had more prestige at this point than money, a sharp reduction of the former would have reduced his already limited capacity to call men to his service. Mansfeld himself was firmly against disarming, because 'there cann nothing happen so pernitious unto him as a Cessation of Arms, the reason whereof is too obvious'.[69] Furthermore, according to Vere, some princes of the former Union and some towns were 'no lesse enimies to a Truce' than Mansfeld.[70] He had been paying his troops whenever he received money, but there had not been enough even to cover the costs of quartering.[71] It would have been impossible to maintain the army in the field if it did not plunder neighboring lands for its subsistence. Even the Estates General advised Frederick to continue the war and stay in the field, and they warned him away from peace negotiations or a truce with the enemy.[72] In his response to his father-in-law's orders, he politely expressed a wish that the treaty could be settled, but admitted that he saw small chance for it. He protested his desire to obey the King's commands, but he feared that the enemy would only use a suspension of arms to further their cause. Still he agreed to accept a one-month truce if his army could be provided with pay and proper garrisons. Then, to render the treaty completely impossible, Frederick requested that James include Mansfeld in its terms and satisfy his particular demands.[73]

Frederick continued his campaign with his hopeful energy unabated. From Frankenthal he rode south with his army toward Hagenau, a town in Further Austria, the lands along the Rhine belonging to the Habsburg Archduke Leopold. On 17 May Frederick personally led an attack against the Archduke's cavalry and even took two shots on his cuirass. The charge sent the rest of Leopold's troops into flight, pitching their artillery into the Rhine, and leaving behind a cache of RT100,000 among other booty. Six officers from Leopold's cavalry switched to Frederick's side.[74] In nearby Bischweiler his men found that the Archduke had left sixty soldiers, massive amounts of powder and fuses, musket balls, and other materials.[75] During this time he was in the field from morning till night, and he could hardly find time to write to his wife. Once, when he finally did, he was interrupted more than six times.[76]

1 Gerrit van Honthorst, *Frederick V, King of Bohemia*, 1635. By courtesy of the National Portrait Gallery, London.

2 Unknown artist, *Elizabeth, Queen of Bohemia*, 1613. By courtesy of the National Portrait Gallery, London.

3 Daniel Mytens, *James I of England and VI of Scotland*, 1621. By courtesy of the National Portrait Gallery, London.

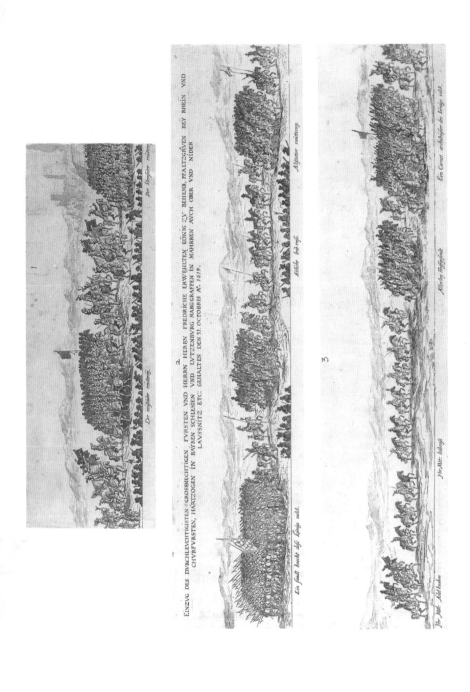

EINZVG DES DVRCHLEVCHTIGSTEN GROSSMECHTIGEN FVRSTEN VND HERRN HERRN FREDRICHE ERWEHLTEN KÖNIG ZV BEHEMB PFALTZGRÄVEN BEY RHEIN VND CHVRFVRSTEN, HARTZOGEN IN BAYRN SCHLESIEN VND LVTZENVRG MARGGRAFFEN IN MAHREN AVCH OBER VND NIDER LAVSSNITZ ETC: GEHALTEN DEN 31. OCTOBRIS A°. 1619.

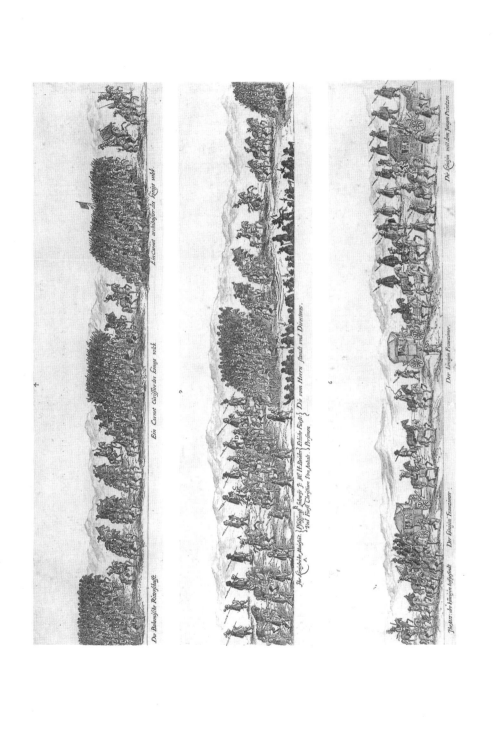

Die Böhmische Ritterschafft.   Ein Carnet Cüriffier der königl. volck   Ein Carnet antelidyfor des königs volck

Im Fürstlichs Staflat. } Officiret F: Schwip F: M^r H:Beider } Etliche Fauft } Die vom Herrn faust und Directores.
                                                          } Vnd Pofst Uberpfawn Vnd Anhalt. } Profssmen

Theatre: der königin hofgefindl.   Der Fürstin Frawenmer.   Der königin Frawenmer.   Die Fürstin mit dem jungen Printzem

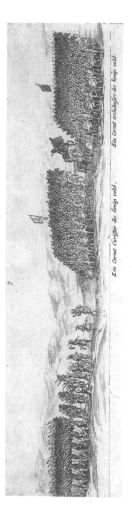

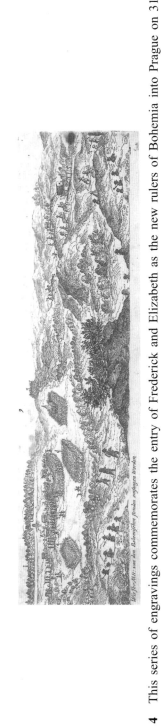

4 This series of engravings commemorates the entry of Frederick and Elizabeth as the new rulers of Bohemia into Prague on 31 October 1619, accompanied by their eldest son, Frederick's brother, various lords and ladies of the Palatine court, the Bohemian directors, and hundreds of supporters. By kind permission of the Staatliche Museen zu Berlin, Kunstbibliothek.

5 Eberhard Flugblatt, *The Coronation of Frederick V and Elizabeth in Prague.*
Reproduced by kind permission of Kurpfälzisches Museum, Stadt Heidelberg.

6 Frederick, King of Bohemia, on horseback with a view of Prague in the background. Reproduced by kind permission of Österreichische National-bibliothek, Vienna.

SERENISSIMVS, POTENTISSIMVS, ET INVICTISSIMVS PRINCEPS AC DOMINVS,
DN. FERDINANDVS II. ROMANORVM IMPERATOR SEMPER AVGVSTVS, GERMANIÆ,
HVNGARIÆ, BOHEMIÆ REX, &c. ARCHIDVX AVSTRIÆ, DVX BVRGVNDIÆ, &c.

Wolf Kilian sculpsit et excudit 1622

7 Holy Roman Emperor Ferdinand II, in full imperial regalia. Reproduced by
kind permission of Österreichische Nationalbibliothek, Vienna.

8 Matthäus Merian, *Die Schlacht bei Hoechst*, 1622. A representation of the battle at Höchst in 1622, one of the more notable defeats of Christian of Halberstadt. Reproduced by kind permission of Westfälisches Landesmuseum für Kunst und Kulturgeschichte, Münster.

9 Pieter Snayers, *Die Schlacht bei Stadtlohn*, 1623. An oil painting of Christian of Halberstadt's greatest defeat, the battle of Stadtlohn, 1623. Reproduced by kind permission of Koninklijke Musea voor Schone Kunsten van België, Brussels.

10 Pieter Molijn, *de Plundering van een Dorp*, 1630. This painting shows the routine plundering of a village by soldiers. No attempt is made to highlight the cruelty. All removable items are heaped on the right, while fire consumes the houses in the background. The inhabitants are rounded up and led away. This was standard practice for all belligerents during the Thirty Years' War. Frans Hals Museum Haarlem. Photo: Tom Haartsen, Fotografie Beeldende Kunst.

11 Sutherland Collection, *Der pfälzisch Bilgram*. 'The Palatine Pilgrim' (c.1621) is an example of the libel literature published about the Winter King. It depicts him as a poor, lonely wanderer in search of help, being refused by Moravia, Silesia, Brandenburg, the Hanseatic cities, and England, until, falling on his knees, he manages to persuade the Dutch Republic to give refuge to him and his family. Reproduced by kind permission of Ashmolean Museum, Oxford.

His heart was lifted even higher when he received word from his wife about her delivery of their sixth child and second daughter, Louisa Hollandina. 'I praise God for it with all my heart' he said, because the good delivery of a child was 'a great grace that God gives [one]'.[77] He reckoned that she had gone to the delivery bed on the day he and his army had defeated Tilly at Wiesloch.[78] Elizabeth's news must have counteracted Frederick's disappointment over Baden-Durlach's recent defeat, which, he wrote, 'did us much harm and has broken a great many good plans'.[79] But he remained committed to his campaign nonetheless, giving directions to Heidelberg for maintaining supplies, bolstering the defense works, and repairing the bridge.[80] He and Mansfeld soon led the army north to relieve the Palatinate of the burden of its presence and to join up with Christian of Halberstadt.

Their destination was the lands belonging to the Elector of Mainz and the Landgrave Ludwig of Hessen-Darmstadt, a Lutheran prince who had supported the Emperor's cause from the beginning of the conflict and had mediated the Treaty of Mainz in April 1620. Rather than making an attempt to resist the Palatine army, the Landgrave let them into his main town when they arrived in the first days of June. Frederick had earlier blamed the Landgrave for inciting the Union to dissolve and turn against the common cause, and now he accused him of providing material, financial, and political assistance to the enemy and of preventing troops favorable to Frederick from passing through Darmstadt to the Palatinate. While the Palatine troops sated themselves on the town, Frederick demanded that the Landgrave behave in accordance with his self-pronounced neutrality.[81] Ludwig, for his part, tried to persuade his visitor to submit to the Emperor for the sake of peace. Frederick took the opportunity to correct the Landgrave: his struggle, he insisted, was not against Ferdinand as the Holy Roman Emperor but as an Archduke of Austria, and peace was not possible without a full restoration of the Palatinate, a guarantee for the rights and liberties for Bohemia, and money for his soldiers' arrears. Frederick then demanded that Ludwig hand over his fortress on the Main at Rüsselheim, where the army had planned to make a crossing. The Landgrave refused.[82] That night he fled with his son toward Mainz, but Frederick's soldiers caught them and brought them back. To make sure that there would be no further trouble, he resolved to keep the pair with him, under his protection, so to speak, until a peace treaty were settled.[83]

English Intercession

At the same time Lord Chichester, who, against his will, had been selected to oversee the English King's defense of the Lower Palatinate, arrived in

Mainz.[84] He brought no new forces, but he did have money to pay the troops in Vere's service. Unfortunately it was not nearly what was necessary, in part because English pounds had lost much of their value in the Palatinate.[85] Based on his observations, Chichester reported to James that £192,000 per annum were needed at the very least, and perhaps a quarter again as much, to mount and maintain James' promised army of 8,000 men and 1,600 horse. Regular payment was essential, because without it the soldiers, being mostly mercenaries, would readily resign, defect, or mutiny. Chichester recommended that James send three or four months' pay at once, if he indeed wanted to raise such a force.[86]

The real purpose of the mission, however, was not to provide Frederick with a new army, but to bring him to abandon his own. The Elector of Mainz, who had received reports about his ravaged lands and the abducted Landgrave of Hessen-Darmstadt, had complained bitterly to Chichester, who then begged the Winter King to return to the Palatinate. Frederick agreed, but only if Landgrave Ludwig and the Elector of Mainz would provide sustenance for the Palatine army, and if the opposing side refrained from attacking in the meantime.[87] Before such arrangements could be finalized, Tilly's return with reinforcements induced Mansfeld and Frederick to return to Mannheim, bringing the Landgrave with them. Chichester, now joined by Nethersole, followed Frederick to Mannheim and encouraged him to give up all use of force and submit himself entirely to James' will.[88] Chichester had been instructed to tell Frederick to remain in the Palatinate and refrain from any acts of aggression against his neighbors for the sake of the negotiations in Brussels.[89] Nethersole was ordered to criticize Frederick for his 'excessive defiance and doubt in the reality and candor of the procedures of the Emperor and the King of Spain'.[90] Frederick was urged to put his fate entirely in James' hands and send an emissary to Brussels.[91] James wanted his son-in-law to accept his judgment of the situation and make no conjectures, because, he claimed, Frederick was not as well informed.[92] To sweeten the demands, Chichester and Vere offered Frederick 60,000 fl. to pay his soldiers for ten weeks while the treaty in Brussels was being settled.[93]

At first Frederick refused to do his father-in-law's bidding.[94] He said that he would gladly lay down his arms if the Emperor would revoke his promise to transfer the Palatine electorate to the Duke of Bavaria. Above all he feared that a period of truce would allow an Imperial diet to convene, where the electoral transfer would most likely be pushed through. He mentioned that the Elector of Saxony and the Duke of Bavaria had both refused to acknowledge a general peace treaty made at Brussels 'as being a matter of the Empire, and therefore ought to be treated with the Empire by the constitutions thereof as they pretend'.[95] For them, a diet was the essential part of the settlement process. Despite the fact that Ferdinand II had told both James I and Philip IV that nothing had been promised to Bavaria irrevocably, and that a full restitution for the Elector Palatine was still within the realms of possibility, Frederick found it most difficult to believe that 'the Emperor may not as well deceyve the King of Spayne' in addition to James.[96]

Frederick was in turmoil. He did not understand how his father-in-law could want him to remain in the Palatinate but not to contribute to its defense. He was 'badly tormented' with the request that he quit the field and thereby render his presence all but useless.[97] 'I am so very annoyed', he wrote to his wife, 'that I do not know how to express it to you enough'.[98] Furthermore, he had recently promised the Margrave of Baden-Durlach that, in return for the use of 7,000 of his soldiers, he would not make a separate peace, and now the Margrave was also in Mannheim with his army.[99] To Chichester, however, the Margrave had asserted his allegiance to James I and stated his intention to abide by a treaty from Brussels conference.[100]

The greatest impediment proved to be that Frederick refused to compromise his honor. During the negotiations, Chichester observed, 'hee is so curious of the opinion of his Honor, as I can hetherto litle prevayle with him in that point'.[101] Nethersole too saw that 'the poynt of honor be of hard digestion with him'.[102] For Frederick, his princely honor served as a justification for political opportunism. Why should he submit now, after all, when he had an army in the field and when he was absolutely certain that his opponents would not abide by the treaty under consideration?

James, meanwhile, was growing ever more furious with Frederick. His military actions, to say nothing of the abduction of the Landgrave, was enough to drive the King into a fit of rage. On 3/13 June, James dispatched a letter that again repeated his threat to abandon Frederick completely and to declare to the world that his inconstancy had forced the King to do so. He accused Frederick of breaking all his promises, reallocating men and money given for the defense of Mannheim and Frankenthal to his own forces in the field, and refusing to send an emissary to Brussels even when safe-conducts had been supplied.[103] Once again the King demanded Frederick's obedience and reaffirmed the promise to restore him. This time, however, to add force to the demands, James added that he had ordered Vere to withdraw with his troops from the Palatinate if Frederick did not comply immediately. Vere was also to issue the King's command to all British subjects among the various Palatine forces that they were not allowed to fight for Frederick again.[104] Such measures, however, did not become necessary.

Steps Toward Peace

After the meeting with Chichester, however, Frederick decided to give his father-in-law a degree of satisfaction, but, for his honor's sake, he would not comply with all his wishes. On 13 June he resolved to remain in Mannheim for some time, though, as he told his wife, 'it breaks my heart'.[105] He could sustain his army for a while with the money from Chichester, but Christian of Halberstadt would remain in the field, acting on his own authority. Frederick, Mansfeld, and Baden-Durlach all agreed to a three-week abstention from hostilities, provided they were not attacked. Invitations were then sent to Halberstadt, Tilly, and Córdoba to do the same.[106] Frederick also agreed to send Andreas Pawel to Brussels to work with Richard Weston and the other English negotiators, but Pawel was to prove more obstructive to the process than otherwise.

Pawel was instructed to introduce the thorniest of all constitutional issues into the discussion, to declare that 'the most important above all disagreements which [the present conflict] concerns consists in the fact that the King of Bohemia has in reality accepted the crown that was offered him'.[107] In addition to a suspension of arms Pawel was to demand a general amnesty, the complete restitution of the Palatine estate and electorate, full reimbursement of war reparations, and a cancellation of the Imperial ban. Only after this were done would Frederick deprecate himself in full knowledge of his innocence and with full security for his honor. Writing to Brussels directly, Frederick reaffirmed his desire to abide by the dictates of a peace treaty, reminding Weston to take care of the well-being and honor of the Palatine dynasty.[108] Halberstadt and Mansfeld soon sent a representative of their own, one Captain Weiss, to demand the astounding sum of 500,000 gold ecu for each in return for their disarmament.[109]

Nevertheless, a rational consideration of the chances of success in the present war seems to have led Frederick to change his attitude toward his father-in-law's demands. The time spent campaigning through his homelands had dampened his initial, fervent enthusiasm. His conviction that God was on his side could not disguise the fact that the troops were in a terrible state. Discipline had never been good, but by then it had so decayed that Chichester concluded,

> I might conceive that kingdoms and principalities for which they shall fight to be in great danger and hazard ... and how can it be better or otherwise wher men are raised out of the scume of the people by princes who have no dominion over them, nor power for want of paye to punish them, nor meanes to reward them, livinge onely upon rapine and Spoyle as they do.[110]

As the army withdrew from Darmstadt, it had skirmished with Tilly's troops near Lorsch and suffered some losses. It could not remain in Mannheim, because of the lack of provisions to support it.[111] Even Mansfeld had told Frederick to give in to his father-in-law's demands, because the situation in the Palatinate did not show much likelihood of improvement.[112] It was soon decided that Mansfeld, who was suffering from gout, would cross the Rhine and lead them to Alsace, leaving behind 4–5,000 sick men. For his own protection Frederick decided to put the rest of Baden-Durlach's troops into garrisons and to remain in Mannheim for several days.[113] During that time, he waited earnestly for word from Christian of Halberstadt.

Consenting to James' cease-fire appears to have been fatal to Frederick's military campaign. On 20 June the Margrave of Baden-Durlach suddenly left Mannheim, leaving his troops there, without saying a word either to his colonels or to Frederick, who believed that the lack of money was the Margrave's main reason for leaving in such a scandalous manner.[114] The Margrave left Frederick 'in a tyme when he most needed him', and after some days Georg Friedrich would actually withdraw his troops from Palatine service entirely.[115] Also on 20 June Frederick heard that Halberstadt and his army had suffered a terrible loss.[116] While retreating from the combined forces of Tilly and Córdoba, Halberstadt's makeshift bridge over the Main at Höchst had collapsed, pitching the baggage into the river. In the ensuing panic as many as 4,000 were killed from fighting in the rear or by drowning in the Main in the attempt to escape. Many who successfully crossed the Main fled to Mannheim, where they arrived empty-handed and hungry.[117] Frederick feared that Christian had died as well, until word came on 21 June that he had survived and regrouped the greater part of his cavalry and some of his infantry. Frederick wrote to his wife, 'I want to hope that God will deliver him soon and give us our revenge. ... We fear nothing more than the lack of provisions'.[118] After Christian arrived on 22 June, he met with Mansfeld, and the two decided to leave Mannheim on the next day, because there were not enough supplies to sustain them any longer. Frederick resolved to go with them.[119]

On catching wind of this plan, Chichester tried to talk him out of it, and when he proved resistant, he was presented James' menacing letter of 3/13 June.[120] Chichester had received it earlier and read it, but he had decided not to show it to Frederick because of his recent bout of compliance, 'and besides the greife it woulde have brought unto the distressed prince'.[121] Chichester had also wanted to reserve the letter for a time of need. Frederick read the letter 'with great observance', and after an extended silence, said that James, if he knew what state Frederick was in, would not forbid his going with the army, because 'he had submitted himselfe to the treatie at Bruxells'.[122] He said that he would not engage in any hostile act unless the enemy attacked him, and because there was no sign that Tilly and Córdoba would refrain from doing so, it was better for Frederick to leave. He explained to Chichester: 'seeinge what he did was for his honor and preservation of his person, he hoped [James I] would not be displeased with him for his departure hence at this time'.[123] Chichester's further attempts to persuade Frederick to stay were futile. Frederick handed him a letter for James I which made the usual promise of obedience and the usual argument that the enemy was averse to peace and would refuse to accept a truce. Frederick explained that because of the utter lack of supplies he hoped that it would not be taken amiss if he went with the army away from Mannheim until the results of the negotiations were known. Because enemy forces were rapidly approaching, he added, it would not be of much help to the treaty if he allowed them to entrap him, as they apparently intented to do.[124]

On 23 June Frederick began to undo his recent deeds. He released the Landgrave of Hessen-Darmstadt and began to retrace his steps out of the Palatinate.[125] From Mannheim Frederick, Mansfeld, and Halberstadt crossed the Rhine and rode south toward Landau, where Frederick composed a full answer to his father-in-law's letter of 3/13 June. In it he expressed his dismay at the King's outrage and described his resolutions as having been 'as pacific as made in service and obedience'.[126] He probably meant these words in all sincerity. Vere believed as well that Frederick's suspicion toward the suspension of arms derived from the 'opinion that he might sooner and surer attayne to the peace projected by the King his father thorough his Majestyes treating for that immediately without any preceding Truce'.[127] He had seriously believed that his chances for winning a favorable peace would have been greater if he had been able to deal his opponent a significant or crippling blow in the battlefield while James had pushed for a restitution of the Palatinate instead of bargaining for a temporary cease-fire.

During the march the indiscriminate barbarism of the rank and file became intolerable to Frederick, and on 28 June he resolved to abandon his army. As he wrote to Chichester,

> as for this army, it has much such disorder, and I believe that there are people [in it] possessed by the devil, who take pleasure in setting fires everywhere, that I will be much relieved to be away from it. There is a distinction between friend and enemy, [but] they ruin one as well as the other.[128]

The excesses of the soldiery afflicted Frederick with regret, and he feared that they would be imputed to him. He desired nothing more than to get away.[129] On 29 June Frederick went to Drusenheim in the southern extremity of the Palatinate and reaffirmed his promise to comply with the suspension of arms.[130] Meanwhile his predictions about his enemies' resistance to peace soon came true when Chichester tried to prevent Tilly and Córdoba from invading the Palatinate. Córdoba argued that according to the Infanta's instructions he was not allowed to do anything 'prejudicial' to Catholic princes, so as long as Frederick's army was imposing itself on other princes' lands, Córdoba had to continue.[131] Tilly insisted that he would only desist if he received express orders from the Emperor.[132] These forces bore down on Heidelberg, and because Mansfeld had taken so many soldiers from General Vere, he did not think the city had a chance of withstanding.[133]

Instead of attempting to relieve his capital, Frederick decided to entrust himself to his father-in-law's will, in spite of contrary pressures in his army. In early July he formally discharged Mansfeld and Halberstadt, abandoned the army, and retired to Sedan at the court of his uncle, the Duke of Bouillon, a leader of the French Huguenots, who had remained neutral in the Palatine war. Not a single soldier followed Frederick, and on his journey only two servants accompanied him. Even his squire left him after a few days and went back to the army.[134] When Frederick reached Sedan, he beseeched James to prevent the enemy from taking advantage of the peace.[135] He also wrote to his wife, 'May God touch [the King's] heart, certainly I do everything to content him, but I obtain so little with it'.[136] In accordance with the King's demands, he even issued a full power for negotiations in his name, which did not identify him as an elector.[137] He thereby agreed to be represented at Brussels as a banned prince, dispossessed of his electorate.

While Frederick waited in Sedan for the results of the negotiations in Brussels, he looked forward with ambivalence to his eventual return to The Hague. Though he knew that he would be subject to even more ridicule than before, he longed to see his wife.[138] Elizabeth never left his thoughts, and he gazed at her portrait often, wishing to see the original. He was more than satisfied with the hospitality that his host offered, and when he did not keep himself busy writing letters, he passed the time playing tennis and swimming afterwards to cool off. 'For the rest I am doing very well', he wrote, 'if my affairs would do so well, I would be very happy'.[139] He received word from England of the King's pleasure about his withdrawal to Sedan, especially because there could be no more pretexts for attacks against the Palatinate.[140] Frederick responded with a complaint that his enemies were still on the offensive, and he also disclosed his fear that Mansfeld's coming to Sedan with the army might induce the King of France and other enemies of the Duke of Bouillon to launch an attack.[141]

Violence Prevails

Despite James I's best intentions to the contrary, there was to be no peace as long as there were armies in the field. After Frederick had discharged Mansfeld and Halberstadt, they offered their services to the Infanta and the Kings of France and England, but the terms were too extreme to warrant serious consideration. After looting Alsace, Frederick's former army burned and plundered its way through the Duchy of Lorraine. In its wake Archduke Leopold returned to the Rhineland in later July and quickly retook Hagenau and other towns that Mansfeld had occupied, and Córdoba crossed the Rhine and took Neustadt in the Palatinate. In August Leopold ravaged Germersheim and other Palatine towns and villages, and his forces even looted Speyer, though the bishopric was certainly not an enemy territory, concentrating on Protestant households and those which had supplied soldiers for the Palatine service.[142] Leopold then moved on to Heidelberg, which Tilly's forces had surrounded, cutting off the town's supply routes from the countryside. Chichester, who was still in the Palatinate, condemned the unrestrained savagery inflicted upon the general populace by the bands of Cossacks and Croats fighting in the Emperor's service.[143] The utter devastation of the landscape made it appear that the enemy thought 'of nothing but an absolute conquest of this State by famyne rayther then by the sword'.[144]

Mansfeld and Halberstadt reached Sedan in August, and their presence was highly disruptive. When the former settled a deal to serve the King of France, the latter and three regiments of cavalry mutinied, because they wanted to return to Germany instead. Frederick was disconcerted, because Louis XIII blamed him for trying to stir up the Huguenots, and the Duke of Bouillon accused him of endangering them both.[145] Frederick wrote to Elizabeth, 'I am very embarrassed here because no matter what one does, there is no sympathy for me'.[146] He protested that he did not want to meddle in local affairs, and that he had not wanted his former army to come to France. Mansfeld was then trying to persuade Frederick to accompany the army once again, but he found the Count's efforts offensive. He felt no regrets about his earlier decision to discharge the two *condottiere* and abandon his army. 'God', he said, 'granted me a great favor in my not being associated with this army any more'.[147] The condition of the army was catastrophic; the troops were nearly dying from hunger. 'If God does not extend his hand to them', Frederick warned, 'we will see a bad end to this army'.[148] Bouillon wanted to give them supplies, but he feared retaliation from the King of France. To make matters worse, Mansfeld's and Halberstadt's quarrelling had come so far that the two were on the verge of settling their differences in a duel. Frederick heard that Mansfeld wanted 800 men 'to make headway against the crazy Duke of Braunschweig [Halberstadt], who wanted to seduce the army to his side'.[149]

Frederick had actually developed a measure of hope for the Brussels peace conference. While he wanted the army to leave Sedan, he did not want it to return to Germany or attack the Spanish Netherlands, both of which would have disrupted the peace negotiations. 'I confess', he told Elizabeth, 'that I would have rather preferred that [the army] had taken another resolution to serve the [Huguenot] Churches of France, and I believe that this could have been better for my affairs, but the soldiers did not want to'.[150] The dilemma was solved when the Dutch Republic commissioned Mansfeld and Halberstadt to raise Spínola's siege at Bergen-op-Zoom, and in later August they left Sedan, provided with munitions and ten cannon from the Duke of Bouillon. After they entered the Spanish Netherlands, Córdoba quickly engaged them at Fleurus near Namur. Both sides inflicted roughly 2,000 casualties on the other, and the two *condottiere* managed to continue on their march. Due to a wound at Fleurus, Halberstadt had his left arm amputated, but he refused to give in to his disability, and, as a sign of his resolve, adopted the motto, *Alter Restat*, 'the other remains'. The army would actually relieve Bergen-op-Zoom in early October, drawing Córdoba out of the Palatinate. Tilly was left to take the three main strongholds at his leisure, and he had an Imperial order to do so. The siege of Heidelberg commenced in late August.[151]

Given the relentless violence, the inexorable conquest of the Palatinate, and the negotiators' helplessness, Frederick withdrew in the face of his own powerlessness. He so desired to see his beloved 'Astre' once again that he declared, 'God may well send me afflictions and it is not the least thing to be far for so long a time from my dear heart, whose portrait I carry so very carefully', and, in his imagination, he kissed her lips a 'million' times.[152] His desire to flee his fate and retreat with his wife from the affairs of the world increased as rapidly as his affairs declined. At the end of August, as the conquest of the Palatinate continued unabated, he disclosed to her his deepest wishes: 'may it please God to give us a little corner of the world, to live there happily together, it is all the good fortune that I wish'.[153] For Frederick, this 'little corner' was not to be found in The Hague. It was filled with his creditors, his dependents, ambassadors from his hesitating allies, and his unwilling hosts, the Estates General of the United Provinces, but it was home to his wife and family.[154] He would have to wait longer in Sedan before he could see them once again.

The negotiations in Brussels, meanwhile, because of delays, miscommunication, and fundamental disagreements, failed to produce a suspension of arms. The Emperor's party demanded that Frederick first 'submit, humiliate, and deprecate' himself, before the truce began.[155] Thereafter he would have to relinquish permanently all claims to Bohemia, give up his Palatine electorate as well, renounce all alliances with princes and estates in and beyond the Empire, and refrain from conducting all correspondence or arranging any plans with anyone against the Emperor, the Empire, its electors, princes, and estates.[156] Naturally Pawel and Weston could not accept these conditions. Much time had been wasted, because the Infanta would not accept the credential letters for the English commission because they referred to Frederick as an elector.[157] Afterwards there were other wearisome arguments about whether Heidelberg was actually being besieged or not, and whether the suspension of arms pertained to the Palatinate alone or to the Empire in general.

Mansfeld's and Halberstadt's invasion of the Infanta's lands only made the situation worse. The Emperor's delegates immediately blamed Frederick for it, and the fact that his former army continued to used his artillery pieces and battle standards settled the issue.[158] While Weston maintained that the two mercenaries were acting independently, the Infanta complained that the armies that Frederick had brought together were wasting her lands and going to the aid of Spain's archenemies. She expected either the English ambassador or the English King to halt the invasion, but for Weston, this was a separate issue. Conversely, he demanded that Tilly and Archduke Leopold lay down their arms, because Frederick had relinquished the use of force in the Palatinate, but the Infanta protested that she did not have the power to give such orders. Nonetheless she sent letters urgently requesting that both to break off the siege at Heidelberg. The city fell in mid September, just after the pay for the defending garrison ran out, on the same day that Chichester received the Infanta's letters. When he forwarded them to Tilly, the courier was sent back with no reply.[159] Heidelberg capitulated on relatively merciful terms; most of the defending soldiers were allowed to march out of the city unmolested.[160] According to custom, the town was sacked and plundered, and shortly after this news reached Weston, he left Brussels and returned to London.

During the siege Frederick had observed once again the ineffectiveness of his father-in-law's peace negotiations. In his perspective, the Habsburgs had flouted James' efforts and wantonly abused his and Frederick's peaceable intentions in their renewed assaults on the Palatinate. James had formally taken Heidelberg, Mannheim, and Frankenthal under his protection, but he made no move to break off the sieges by force. Despite his frustration, Frederick promised his patience, but after news of the city's fall arrived, he lost all restraint.[161] No longer afraid of offending the pacific sensitivities of his father-in-law, he told James that all the enemies' fine words had resulted in the fall of Heidelberg, and that Mannheim and

Frankenthal were now threatened and needed help desperately. After God, Frederick added, no one could help him more than James, whose own honor was at stake in the defense of the two towns.[162] Early in September Buckingham had assured Frederick that England would not tolerate what had just occurred, in which case, James would declare war on the Emperor and take up the common cause as his own.[163] But what annoyed Frederick the most was how 'they continue still in England to make a distinction between the Emperor and the King of Spain, and yet both of them take everything from me'.[164] Because of the lateness of the season, Frederick recommended that the best solution would be for an English army to invade Flanders and for a Danish army to attack the Catholic bishops in northern Germany. Such a move, he argued, would inspire the King of Spain to give in to peace.[165]

Because the negotiations in Brussels had failed, there was no more reason for Frederick to stay in Sedan. Though he did not particularly want to return to The Hague, he longed to be with his wife again and escape his current circumstances entirely, 'because', he wrote,

> I would be better able to serve my God. I would have a happier spirit in the smallest corner of the world than the greatest monarch in the largest palace, and certainly, if I had it my way, I would withdraw from everything and leave all for the King of England to do.[166]

These words show the extent of the conflicting forces in Frederick's mind. He wanted to withdraw from worldly worries to be a better Christian, and yet he would not submit to the Emperor, which would have been the necessary first step in that process. Furthermore, he absolutely refused to relinquish his claim to the Bohemian crown, acknowledge the legality of the Imperial ban, and tolerate the transfer of his electorate. His honor and the righteousness of his cause compelled him to abide by these resolutions, despite his conviction that his God could be served better in more modest venues. He would not betray his conscience when all seemed lost already, because he still had his honor and the interests of his children to defend. Burdened with his helplessness and his yearnings, he would wait in Sedan until he received the necessary safe-conducts and his father-in-law's approval for his return to The Hague.[167]

The Loss of the Palatinate

While he waited, Tilly besieged Mannheim. Vere was defending the fortress with no more than 1,700 men, many of them sick and all of them unpaid, because no more money had come from England. Resistance was pointless; there were not enough men to cover all the defenses, some of which had not even been completely prepared. Vere wanted to abandon the town and withdraw to Frankenthal, but the Mannheim burghers would not allow it.[168] After Vere retreated his troops into the castle, Tilly gave him the option to march out freely. On James' orders they surrendered to the Bavarian forces. They were allowed to retreat to Frankfurt to await further instructions. James forbade Vere to make another entry into the Palatinate with his men. He then marched them to the United Provinces and returned to England.

By November Frederick was back in The Hague, certainly relieved to be with his wife, but embittered and completely disillusioned at the loss of Mannheim. He complained to James, Charles, and Buckingham that the conquerors of the Palatinate had already begun to force its inhabitants to convert to Catholicism, which was fully in line with the Emperor's alleged ambition to extirpate Calvinism, as revealed in the intercepted letters. Frederick's response was to ask for a return to arms. He requested money to sustain Mansfeld's and Halberstadt's troops and muster a new army for the defense of the Palatinate once again.[169]

James' apparent faith in the King of Spain, however, was not to be so easily shaken. During the siege of Mannheim, Philip IV had ordered the Infanta not to allow the city to fall into Bavarian hands, but these orders had arrived after the deed had already been done.[170] In an attempt to pacify Frederick, Secretary Calvert reaffirmed the King of Spain's promise to restore the Palatinate, by force if necessary. Calvert sent Frederick copies of Philip's order to the Infanta to give James all satisfaction possible, and of the Infanta's recent order that Tilly not attack Frankenthal.[171] But Frederick could not have been content with these letters, because he did not distinguish between the interests of the King of Spain and the Emperor. In his eyes, he was the victim of a grand Habsburg conspiracy to wipe out his dynasty and, with it, Protestantism in the Empire.

Willingness to trust the Habsburgs remained the major point of contention between the King of England and his son-in-law. By the winter of 1622–1623 Frederick had only Frankenthal formally in his possession, and James, unwilling and unable to defend it, arranged with the Infanta to have the town deposited under her protection until a peace treaty could be arranged with the Emperor. Frederick had already sent Pawel to England to plead for money for Halberstadt and Mansfeld so that they might keep Frankenthal from falling into Spanish hands, and in mid February 1623, Frederick received James' expression of shock at the proposal. The King wrote that it sounded like Frederick had been listening to bad counsel and pernicious flattery which was leading him down the road to ruin. Peace, said the King, was the only way to work a restoration, and to sequester Frankenthal into the Infanta's safe-keeping was the only way to keep the town out of Tilly's hands. James insisted that Frederick put his faith in the King of Spain, because Philip had supposedly given his word to restore the Palatinate, by force of arms if necessary, even in the event of a war between England and the Duke of Bavaria and the Emperor. It was better, James added, that Spain occupy the Palatinate instead of Bavarian forces.[172] He ordered Frederick to make a decision on the sequestration of Frankenthal after three days. His requests for money for Manfeld's army James dismissed as pure 'exorbitance and impossibility'.[173]

To Frederick, however, peace according to his father-in-law meant the total deprivation of all that belonged to him. The previous year's defeats had done nothing to alter his understanding of the Palatine crisis. In mid February 1623 he reminded James of Heidelberg's fate and described the process of re-Catholicization that was already under way there.[174] After a long description of the suffering in the Lower Palatinate, Frederick concluded that peace *sub clypeo* was a wiser path than credulous negotiations.[175] And indeed, little more than one week after he wrote this letter, Ferdinand publicly bestowed the Palatine electorate on Duke Maximilian. The Emperor had convened a diet of Imperial princes at Regensburg, and objections from Count Oñate, the Electors of Saxony, Brandenburg, and Mainz, and Duke Wolfgang Wilhelm of Pfalz-Neuburg had only resulted in the restriction of Maximilian's possession of that dignity for the duration of his life.[176] Nonetheless, Ferdinand reiterated his willingness to bestow his grace upon Frederick if he would just submit humbly, acknowledge his guilt, and engage in no more machinations. His full restoration could take place after Maximilian's death, and then the Kings of Spain and England would be satisfied.[177] On 25 February 1623 Maximilian received his new dignity after the Emperor's vice-chancellor excoriated the crimes of Frederick V in a long harangue. Though the Palatine's defeat at this moment appeared complete, it was not without consequences.

Because James had promised to take care of Frederick's affairs for him, the Palatine crisis became an affair of English domestic and international politics. In the next year it would become a dominant issue that would inspire unprecedented events in English history. While Frederick remained peaceably but impatiently in The Hague, the Palatine crisis would lead to the failure of the negotiations for the Anglo-Spanish match, temporarily divide the English royal family against itself, and eventually break the peace between England and Spain.

Notes

1. Gardiner, *History of England*, iv, p. 309.
2. 'sub clypeo negotium pacis tractiren', Söltl, *Der Religionskrieg*, iii, p. 109.
3. BHStA, KB, 122/3b, fol. 191: 3/13 January 1622, anonymous memo.
4. Gindely, *Geschichte*, ii, pp. 40–1.
5. PRO, SP, 81/23, fol. 76: 24 February 1622, SV, Nethersole to Naunton.
6. Gindely, *Geschichte*, ii, p. 27.
7. Two of the Margrave's regiments were said to have joined Tilly's service. PRO, SP, 81/23, fol. 143: 1/11 April 1622, Vere to Carleton?
8. The idea was suggested to Frederick, who found it 'sehr gutt'. BHStA, KB, 122/3b, fol. 192: 3/13 January 1622, anonymous memo.
9. At the end of January Zweibrücken took over negotiations with the Electors of Mainz, Triers, and Saxony, and the Duke of Neuburg, and in February instructions were sent to Johann Kasimir Kolben von Wartenberg for negotiations with Kulmbach, Ansbach, Württemberg, Baden, Straßburg, Nürnberg, and Ulm. BHStA, KB, 122/3b, fol. 194: 7/17 January 1622, council deliberations. In February Frederick sent Camerarius to Hamburg on an embassy to the Lower Saxon Circle and the King of Denmark. BHStA, KB, 122/3b, fols 219, 262.
10. PRO, SP, 81/23, fol. 69: 21 February/3 March 1622, Frederick V to the Doge of Venice.
11. BHStA, KB, 122/3b, fol. 348: 7 March 1622, Frederick V? to Duke of Savoy. BHStA, KB, 121/3a, 16/26 March 1622, Frederick V to Dukes of Braunschweig and Lüneburg.
12. BHStA, KS, 7052: 14 March 1622, Frederick V to Margrave of Baden. Georg Frederick also received a copy of a letter by Emperor Ferdinand disclosing the intention to grant the Palatine electorate to Duke Maximilian. BHStA, KS, 7052, 25 March 1622, Margrave of Brandenburg to Margrave of Baden-Durlach; March 1622, Emperor Ferdinand to Papal Legate Extraordinary, Fabrizio Verospi.
13. Gindely, *Geschichte*, ii, pp. 32–3. PRO, SP, 81/23, fol. 41: 6 February 1622, SV, Nethersole to Calvert.
14. BHStA, KS, 7052: 1 April 1622, Margrave of Baden to the Elector of Saxony.
15. White, 'Suspension', p. 322.
16. PRO, SP, 81/23, fol. 41: 6 February 1622, SV, Nethersole to Calvert.
17. Gindely, *Geschichte*, ii, p. 33.
18. The original source for this disclosure does appear to be extant. According to Arthur White, Nethersole brought Frederick the news at the end of January. White, 'Suspension', p. 306. Gondomar knew about this plan in early January 1622. Ibid., p. 284. According to Elmar Weiß, it was merely rumored, in March 1622, that Chichester would lead this army to the Palatinate. Weiß, *Die Unterstützung*, pp. 50–1. In May 1622, Simon Digby, still in Vienna, mentioned that James had granted Vere a commission to raise such an army. PRO, SP, 80/5, fol. 148: 8/18 May 1622, Simon Digby to Calvert.
19. PRO, SP, 81/23, fol. 22: 19/29 January 1622, Frederick V to James I. Frederick had supplied James with a list of potential allies in the Palatine war. The first was the King of France, who was not expected to intervene directly, but to interest the Duke of Lorraine and the Count Vaudemont in the Palatine war. Next on the list were the King of Denmark, the King of Sweden, the Elector of Brandenburg, the Duke of Braunschweig, the Duke of Lüneburg, the two Dukes of Mecklenburg, the two

Dukes of Pommern, the Dukes of Holstein, the Duke of Coburg, the Dukes of Eisenach, the Marquis of Kulmbach, the Margrave of Ansbach, the Duke of Württemberg, the Margrave of Baden, the Landgrave Moritz of Hessen, and Venice, the Swiss cantons, the Princes of Anhalt, the towns of the Hanse, and the principal cities of the Empire. PRO, SP81/22, fol. 244: 'La liste des Rois, Electeurs, Princes et Estats, envers lesquels sa Majeste de la Grande Bretagne est suppliée de faire ses bons offices en faveur du Roy de Boheme son Beaufils'.

20. PRO, SP, 81/23, fols10–11: 13 January 1622, SV, W. Peaseley to Nethersole.
21. PRO, SP, 81/23, fol. 43: 6 February 1622, SV, Nethersole to Calvert.
22. Ibid., fols 38–9.
23. Ibid., fol. 43.
24. BHStA, KS, 7052: 9 March 1622, the Baden council to Frederick.
25. 'subjette au vent de traverses et procrastinations'. BHStA, KS, 16745, fol. 6: 20 February/2 March 1622, Rusdorf's report.
26. 'les traverses et amusements autorisés du tiltre de parente et des bons offices soubs prætext d'un mariage in certain, sont les plus suspects et nuisibles. C'est grand abus d'estimer plus les paroles legeres et courtoises que les actions et effects'. BHStA, KS, 16745, fol. 6: 20 February/2 March 1622, Rusdorf's report.
27. BHStA, KS, 16745, fol. 71: 15/25 March 1622.
28. Weiß, *Die Unterstützung*, p. 46.
29. Ibid., p. 50.
30. PRO, SP, 80/5, fol. 11: 7/17 January 1622, Simon Digby to Trumbull.
31. PRO, SP, 80/5, fol. 28.
32. StACK, #5, 5 February 1622, Ferdinand II to Schwarzenberg.
33. PRO, SP, 80/5, fols 36–7: 30 January/9 February 1622, Simon Digby to ?
34. Ibid.
35. Ibid., fol. 38.
36. Nevertheless, his accompaniment and appearance were subject to ridicule; it was said 'that he hired a fair jewel to wear in his hat'. Elizabeth M. Thomson, *The Chamberlain Letters* (New York, 1965), p. 263: Letter 405, 13 April 1622, SV.
37. 'das er zu allen studen zu mir khomen, unnd die familiarita, gleichwie mit dem Grafen Gondomar, gebrauchen dorffe'. StACK, #7, 16 April 1622, Schwarzenberg to Ferdinand II?
38. PRO, SP, 116/286, fol. 211.
39. PRO, SP, 116/286, fol. 212.
40. For his efforts Schwarzenberg received a chain of diamonds worth £2000 at the end of April and then traveled with Richard Weston to Brussels to work on forging a suspension of arms. Weiß, *Die Unterstützung*, pp. 47–8. White, 'Suspension', p. 315.
41. Weiß, *Die Unterstützung*, pp. 50–1.
42. Ibid., p. 49.
43. BHStA, KS, 16745, fol. 8: 4/14 March 1622, Frederick V to General Vere.
44. PRO, SP, 81/23, fol. 157: 4 April 1622, SV, Nethersole to Calvert.
45. Aretin, 'Sammlung', p. 182: 4/14 April 1622.
46. White, 'Suspension', p. 329.
47. Aretin, 'Sammlung', p. 182: 4/14 April 1622.
48. PRO, SP, 80/5, fol. 139: 2/12 May 1622, Lord Digby to Carleton?
49. PRO, SP, 80/5, fol. 140: 2/12 May 1622, Lord Digby to Carleton?
50. Gardiner, *History of England*, iv, p. 309. The Infanta had lavishly offered the Count

a general pardon, the titles of Prince of the Empire and Grandee of Spain, land and a pension from the Duchy of Luxembourg, an army of 20,000 subject to herself and not to Spínola, and RT300,000 to pay Mansfeld's debts, but this offer had been only a fraction of his even more extravagant demands. PRO, SP, 81/23, fol. 240. For Mansfeld's demands, see fols 244–5.

51. 'grande joye de mes pauvres subjects'. BHStA, KS, 9254/2, fol. 234 and PRO, SP, 81/24, fol. 119: 3/13 May 1622, Frederick V to James I.

52. PRO, SP, 81/23, fols 202–3, 209–10: 18/28 April 1622, Nethersole to Calvert.

53. White, 'Suspension', p. 331.

54. Gindely, *Geschichte*, ii, p. 35. Gindely says that this battle took place at Mingolsheim, but Elmar Weiß (*Die Unterstützung*, p. 51) and Geoffrey Parker (*The Thirty Years' War*, p. xxviii) refer only to an engagement at Wiesloch. Discrepancy about the date – Weiß cites 22 April and Gindely 27 April – may indicate that Frederick scored two victories in the same week, but the original sources I consulted speak of only a single, successful battle for the Elector Palatine.

55. PRO, SP, 81/23, fol. 194: 17/27 April 1622, Nethersole to Frederick V.

56. PRO, SP, 81/23, fol. 165: 6/16 April 1622, Vere to Calvert. PRO, SP, 81/23, fol. 221: 19/29 April 1622, Nethersole to Calvert.

57. PRO, SP, 81/23, fol. 221: 19/29 April 1622, Nethersole to Calvert.

58. PRO, SP, 81/23, fol. 238: 20/30 April 1622, Vere to Calvert.

59. PRO, SP, 81/23, fol. 203: 18/28 April 1622, Nethersole to Calvert.

60. 'Ich zwiefele nicht der almechtige werde ewer und soviel erfromen Christen gebet erhoren, er hatt uns schon in vergangenem treffen sein gnadt ansehnlich sehen lassen darfuhr wir Ihm billich nicht gnug lob undt dancksagen künnen, er ist zu bitten er wolle auch ferners uns beystehen, Ich ziehe itzander dem feindt nach, hof mitt gottes hülf gutten succes unserer sachen'. BHStA, KS, 16745, fol. 18: 20/30 April 1622, Frederick V to Baron Tschernembl. The commas are mine. The manuscript says that the letter was written in Brussels, but this was impossible. 'Brussels' must have been a code-word to disguise Frederick's whereabouts if the letter were intercepted. He was in the habit of using code-words. Baron Tschernembl, for example, was also known as 'Windeck'.

61. 'Je ne veux esperer que sa Majesté se lairra port[er] de mes ennemis a une trefve; cela estant le moyen de me perdre entierement, mesme l'impossibilié se peut aisement voire, et l'inegalité. L'ennemi a les moyens de contenter son armée avec vivres et argent. [N]ous sommes en un païs ruiné, et n'avons les mines des West-Indes. Durant la trefve l'ennemi a les moyens d'accroistre son armée. La mienne ne peut que diminuer. Il vault mieux traicter de la paix les armes en main'. PRO, SP, 81/24, fol. 57: 25 April/5 May 1622, 'Extraict d'[un]e lettre du Roy de Boheme, escri[t] de Heydelberg le 5me de May, 1622, st: no'.

62. Gardiner, *History of England*, iv, p. 310.

63. Gindely, *Geschichte*, ii, pp. 35–6.

64. In mid April Vere had received James' commands to make no hostilities and no difficulties for the treaty negotiations. PRO, SP, 81/23, fols 164–6: 6/16 April 1622, Vere to Calvert.

65. BHStA, KS, 9254/2, fols 229–230: 22 April/2 May 1622, James I to Frederick V. Also see PRO, SP, 81/24, fol. 42: 22 April 1622, SV, James I to Frederick V.

66. PRO, SP, 81/23, fol. 232: 19/29 April 1622, James I to Mansfeld. BHStA, KS, 9254/2, fol. 231: 22 April/2 May 1622, James I to Christian of Braunschweig. PRO, SP, 81/24, fol. 40: 22 April 1622, SV, James I to Christian of Braunschweig.

67. PRO, SP, 81/24, fol. 29: 21 April 1622, SV, Nethersole to Frederick V.
68. PRO, SP, 81/24, fol. 132: 5/15 May 1622, Nethersole to Calvert.
69. PRO, SP, 81/23, fol. 166: 6/16 April 1622, Vere to Calvert.
70. PRO, SP, 81/23, fol. 111: 15 March 1622, SV, Vere to Calvert.
71. PRO, SP, 81/23, fol. 143: 1/11 April 1622, Vere to Calvert.
72. Mout, 'Der Winterkönig', p. 263. After Frederick's victory at Wiesloch, the Estates planned to grant him another 150,000 Gulden.
73. BHStA, KS, 9254/2, fol. 234: 3/13 May 1622, Frederick V to James I.
74. PRO, SP, 81/24, fol. 199: 21/31 May 1622, Chichester to Carleton.
75. Aretin, 'Sammlung', pp. 192–3: 8/18 May 1622, Frederick V to Elizabeth.
76. Ibid.
77. 'J'en loue Dieu de tout mon coeur', 'une grande grace que Dieu vous fait'. Aretin, 'Sammlung', p. 191: 8/18 May 1622, Frederick V to Elizabeth.
78. This would locate the date of the battle at 28 April, since Louisa Hollandina, according to one source, was born on 18/28 April. See BHStA, KB, 89/3c.
79. 'nous fait beaucoup de tort et a rompu force bons desseins'. Aretin, 'Sammlung', p. 192: 8/18 May 1622, Frederick V to Elizabeth.
80. BHStA, KS, 16745, fol. 27: 10/20 May 1622, Frederick V to Johann Christof von der Grün; fol. 23: 6/16 May 1622, Frederick V to Johann Christof von der Grün.
81. PRO, SP, 81/25, fols 262–4: June? 1622, 'Brefve Deduction'.
82. Gardiner, *History of England*, iv, pp. 313–14.
83. PRO, SP, 81/25, fol. 34: 2/12 June 1622, Chichester to James I.
84. Weiß, *Die Unterstützung*, pp. 50–1. White, 'Suspension', p. 348. Chichester had said that he would rather give £500 to the benevolence than to go to the Palatinate. White, 'Suspension', p. 288.
85. The money had been collected from the benevolence, which brought in £88,000 instead of the expected £200,000. Gardiner, *History of England*, iv, p. 295. £45,000 would go to Vere's forces. PRO, SP, 81/25, fol. 196: 23 June 1622, SV, Chichester to James I. By the summer of 1622 prices had tripled, and exchange rates were extortionate. PRO, SP, 81/24, fol. 60: 26 April 1622, SV, Vere to Calvert; fols 144–5: 6/16 May 1622, Vere to Lords of the Council. PRO, SP, 81/25, fol. 54: 6/16 June 1622, Vere to Calvert.
86. PRO, SP, 81/24, fol. 277: June? 1622, Chichester to James I. For an itemized accounting in florins, see PRO, SP, 81/25, fols 56–8: 6 June 1622, SV, Burlamachi to Calvert?
87. White, 'Suspension', pp. 351–3.
88. BHStA, KS, 9254/2, fol. 236: 27 May 1622, Nethersole to Frederick.
89. Weiß, *Die Unterstützung*, p. 50.
90. 'trop de deffiance & doubte de la realité & candeur des procedeures de l'Empereur & du roy d'Espagne'. BHStA, KS, 9254/2, fol. 238: Calvert to Nethersole.
91. PRO, SP, 81/24, fol. 257: 27 May 1622, SV, Nethersole to Frederick V.
92. BHStA, KS, 9254/2, fol. 238: Calvert to Nethersole.
93. PRO, SP, 81/25, fol. 64: 6/16 June 1622, Nethersole to Calvert.
94. Weiß, *Die Unterstützung*, p. 51.
95. PRO, SP, 81/25, fol. 6: 2/12 June 1622, Nethersole to Calvert.
96. Ibid., fol. 5.
97. 'bien tourmenté', Aretin, 'Sammlung', p. 183: 3/13 June 1622.
98. 'J'ay tant d'ennuy que je ne le vous saurois assé dire'. Aretin, 'Sammlung', p. 183: 3/13 June 1622.

99. Gardiner, *History of England*, iv, p. 313.
100. PRO, SP, 81/25, fols 35–6: 2/12 June 1622, Chichester to James I.
101. PRO, SP, 81/25, fol. 28: 2/12 June 1622, Chichester to Carleton.
102. PRO, SP, 81/25, fol. 24: 2/12 June 1622, Nethersole to Calvert.
103. In May Vere reported that the Palatine ministers in the towns had done nothing to help him, and that the best men were being taken for military service in the field, leaving 'the poorest men that ever I saw putt in their places' to defend the towns. PRO, SP, 81/24, fol. 226: 23 May 1622, SV, Vere to Carleton?
104. BHStA, KS, 9254/2, fols 226–7: 3/13 June 1622, James I to Frederick V. Also PRO, SP, 81/25, fols 39–40. Weiß, *Die Unterstützung*, p. 52. White, 'Suspension', pp. 354–5.
105. 'ce m'est un grand crevecoeur'. Aretin, 'Sammlung', p. 183: 3/13 June 1622.
106. White, 'Suspension', p. 365.
107. 'Le Chef de tout le Different dont il s'agit consiste en ce que le Roy de Boheme à accepté reellement la Couronne qui luy a este offerte'. BHStA, KS, 9254/2, fol. 222: Instructions for Andreas Pawel.
108. PRO, SP, 81/25, fol. 74: 6/16 June 1622, Frederick V to Weston.
109. PRO, SP, 81/25, fol. 87: 7/17 June 1622, Christian of Braunschweig to Captain Weiss.
110. Quoted in White, 'Suspension', p. 384.
111. PRO, SP, 81/25, fols 35–6: 2/12 June 1622, Chichester to James I.
112. Weiß, *Die Unterstützung*, p. 52.
113. PRO, SP, 81/25, fol. 52: 6/16 June 1622, Chichester to James I.
114. Aretin, 'Sammlung', p. 186: 11/21 June 1622.
115. PRO, SP, 81/25, fol. 195: 23 June 1622, Chichester to James I.
116. The three-week cease-fire did not incorporate Halberstadt.
117. White, 'Suspension', p. 373. Gindely, *Geschichte*, ii, pp. 36–7.
118. 'Je veux esperer que Dieu le remettra bientot et nous donnera notre revanche. ... Nous ne craignons rien plus que faute de vivres'. Aretin, 'Sammlung', p. 185: 11/21 June 1622.
119. PRO, SP, 81/25, fol. 195: 23 June 1622, SV, Chichester to James I.
120. For Frederick's copy of the letter, see BHStA, KS, 9254/2, fol. 226: 3 June 1622, SV, James I to Frederick V.
121. PRO, SP, 81/25, fol. 125: 11/21 June 1622, Chichester to Calvert.
122. PRO, SP, 81/25, fol. 195: 23 June 1622, SV, Chichester to James I.
123. Ibid.
124. BHStA, KS, 9254/2, fol. 220: 12/22 June 1622, Frederick V to James I. Also PRO, SP, 81/25, fol. 127.
125. Frederick had tried to show Ludwig the best hospitality possible, and Nethersole observed that the Landgrave was 'only in libera custodia, for he eatest, and converseth with his Highnes, and they live together like friendes'. PRO, SP, 81/25, fol. 67: 6/16 June 1622, Nethersole to Calvert.
126. 'autant pacifiques que portées au service & obeyssance', BHStA, KS, 9254/2, fol. 218: 16/26 June 1622, Frederick V to James I. The copy of this letter in the PRO, SP, 81/25, fols 78–9, bears the incorrect date of 6/16 June 1622.
127. PRO, SP, 81/25, fol. 117: 11 June 1622, SV, Vere to Nethersole.
128. 'Quant à cet armée elle fait tant de desordre & croy qu'il ya des gens possedez du diable qui se plaisent à mettre le feu par tout, que Je seray bien aise d'en estre esloigné. Il y a distinction d'amy et d'enemy Ils ruinent aussi bien l'un que l'autre'. PRO, SP, 81/25, fol. 145: 18/28 June 1622, Frederick V to Chichester.

129. PRO, SP, 81/25, fol. 147: 19/29 June 1622, Frederick V to Chichester.

130. BHStA, KS, 9254/2, fol. 216, and KS, 8701, fol. 1: 19 June 1622, SV.

131. White, 'Suspension', p. 386.

132. PRO, SP, 81/25, fols 160–1: 23 June 1622, SV, Beecher to Chichester?

133. PRO, SP, 81/25, fol. 203: 24 June 1622, SV, Vere to Carleton?

134. The squire had become so bored, not being able to talk to anyone, that Frederick gave him his freedom. Aretin, 'Sammlung', p. 187: 14/24 July 1622.

135. BHStA, KS, 9254/2, fol. 210: 6/16 July 1622, Frederick V to James I. Also see PRO, SP, 81/26, fol. 29: 6/16 July 1622, Frederick V to James I.

136. 'Dieu luy veuille toucher le coeur, certes je fais tout mon possible pour le contenter, mais je gagne fort peu avec'. Aretin, 'Sammlung', p. 189: 7/17 July 1622.

137. BHStA, KS, 9254/2, fol. 209:14/24 July 1622, Frederick V to James I. The power to negotiate is at fol. 207.

138. Aretin, 'Sammlung', p. 187: 14/24 July 1622.

139. 'Je me porte au reste très bien: si mes affairés se portoient si bien, je serois fort heureux'. Aretin, 'Sammlung', p. 188: 14/24 July 1622.

140. BHStA, KS, 9254/2, fol. 197: Calvert to Frederick; fol. 199, 19 July/29 July 1622, James I to Frederick V.

141. BHStA, KS, 9254/2, fols 192–3: 4/14 August 1622, Frederick V to James I. Also see, PRO, SP, 81/26, fols 181–2: 4/14 August 1622, Frederick V to James I.

142. PRO, SP, 81/26, fols 209–10: 10/20 August 1622, Nethersole to Calvert.

143. PRO, SP, 81/26, fol. 185: 5 August 1622, SV, Chichester to Carleton. Also see fol. 233.

144. PRO, SP, 81/26, fol. 299: 13/23 August 1622, Vere to Calvert.

145. In 1622 a royal military campaign was underway against the Huguenots through the west and south of France.

146. 'Je suis bien sou icy car quoy qu'on faict il n'y a grand gramercy pour moy'. PRO, SP, 81/26, fol. 179: 4/14 August 1622, Frederick V to Elizabeth.

147. 'Dieu m'a faict une grande grace de n'estre plus aupres de ceste armée'. PRO, SP, 81/26, fol. 180: 4/14 August 1622, Frederick V to Elizabeth.

148. 'Si Dieu n'y met la main nous verrons une mauvaise issue de cest' armée'. PRO, SP, 81/26, fol. 180: 4/14 August 1622, Frederick V to Elizabeth.

149. 'pour faire teste au fol Duc de Braunswick qui luy vouloit desbaucher son armee'. PRO, SP, 81/26, fol. 180: 4/14 August 1622, Frederick V to Elizabeth. Frederick sympathized with Halberstadt in the conflict, observing his passionate affection for the Palatine cause, and that it was 'bien son malheur de s'estre joinct a Manfeld'. Ibid.

150. 'je confesse que j'eusse mieulx aymé qu'ils eussent pris autre resolution de servir les Eglises de France et cro[ie] que cela eust peu estre mieux pour mes affaires, ma[is] les gens de guerre n'ont pas voulu'. PRO, SP, 81/26, fol. 180: 4/14 August 1622, Frederick V to Elizabeth. See note #145.

151. Gindely, *Geschichte*, ii, pp. 38–9.

152. 'Dieu m'envoye bien des afflictions et n'est pas la moindre d'estre si long temps esloign[e] de mon cher coeur, dont le pourtraict est bien soigneusement porté de moy'. PRO, SP, 81/26, fol. 180: 4/14 August 1622, Frederick V to Elizabeth.

153. 'plut à Dieu qu'eussions un petit coin au monde pour y vivre contents ensemble, c'est tout le bonheur que je me souhaite. Mais la demeure de la Haye ne m'agrée guére'. Bromley, *Collection*, p. 16: Letter 8, 20/30 August 1622, Frederick V to Elizabeth.

154. He had left a mountain of debts behind in March: 'im hag khan er nit lenger bleiben, wegen großen unkhostens, der sich auf dise stundt so zu bezahlen in die 30,000 [fl?] belauft, und die Leuth wollen fast nicht mehr borgen'. BHStA, KS, 16745, fol. 71: 15/25 March 1622.
155. 'submittiren, humilieren unnd deprecirn', PRO, SP, 81/25, fol. 265: Conditions to the English and Palatine ambassadors.
156. PRO, SP, 81/25, fol. 265: Conditions to the English and Palatine ambassadors.
157. Later Frederick supplied a credential which did not bear his title as 'elector'. See note 137.
158. White, 'Suspension', p. 449.
159. Ibid., pp. 471–2.
160. Weiß, *Die Unterstützung*, p. 53.
161. BHStA, KS, 9254/2, fol. 186: 11/21 September 1622, Frederick V to Buckingham. Frederick did not write to James directly 'de peur de l'importuner'.
162. BHStA, KS, 9254/2, fol. 187: 15/25 September 1622, Frederick V to James I.
163. Weiß, *Die Unterstützung*, p. 54.
164. 'On continue encore en Angleterre à faire distinction entre l'Empereur & le Roi d'Espagne; & cependant l'un & l'autre me prennent tout', Bromley, *A Collection*, Letter 9: 20/30 September 1622, Frederick V to Elizabeth.
165. BHStA, KS, 9254/2, fol. 190: Memoire for Schönberg. BHStA, KS, 9254/2, fol. 184: 15/25 September 1622, Frederick V to Buckingham, and fol. 191: 14/24 September 1622, Frederick V to Charles.
166. 'car je pourrois mieux servir à mon Dieu, aurois l'esprit plus content en le plus petit coin du monde, que le plus grand monarque au plus grand palais: & certes, si je suivois mon humeur, je m'en retirerois de tout, & laisserois faire le Roi d'Angleterre'. Bromley, *A Collection*, Letter 9: 20/30 September 1622, Frederick V to Elizabeth.
167. Aretin, 'Sammlung', p. 191: 3 October 1622.
168. PRO, SP, 81/27, fol. 76: 23 September 1622, SV, Vere to Calvert.
169. BHStA, KS, 9254/2, fols 180–3: 5/15 November 1622, Frederick V to Buckingham, James, and Charles.
170. Weiß, *Die Unterstützung*, p. 54.
171. BHStA, KS, 9254/2, fol. 178, 20 November 1622, Calvert to Frederick V; fol. 174: 29 October 1622, King of Spain to Infanta; fol. 176: 16 November 1622, Infanta to Tilly.
172. BHStA, KS, 9254/2, fol. 166: 23 January/2 February 1623, James I to Frederick V.
173. 'exorbitance & impossibilité'. BHStA, KS, 9254/2, fol. 165: 23 January/2 February 1623, James I to Frederick V.
174. The Spanish had begun the process of reintroducing Catholicism into the Lower Palatinate as soon as they conquered the territory. Egler, *Die Spanier*, p. 117. In March 1623 Tilly would order the expulsion of all Protestant ministers from Heidelberg, by force if necessary. PRO, SP, 81/28, fols 101–2: 6/16 March 1623, Nethersole to Calvert.
175. BHStA, KS, 9254/2, fol. 170: 4/14 February 1623, Frederick V to James I.
176. Albrecht, *Maximilian I.*, pp. 567–9.
177. Gindely, *Geschichte*, ii, pp. 51–2. Also see PRO, SP, 80/6, fols 26–7: 23 February/5 March 1623, Ferdinand II to James I, and PRO, SP, 81/28, fol. 91: 25 February/7 March 1623, Bachoffen to Calvert.

Chapter 7

Undermining the Anglo-Spanish Peace, 1623

The Palatine crisis might have been resolved in 1623, or so it was hoped by King James and the Prince of Wales. At the very least they sought to draw nearer to the Spanish Habsburgs by means of a marriage treaty that would have supported a lasting peace between England and Spain. In late February 1623 Charles and the Marquis of Buckingham, accompanied by a single servant, left England in secret and traveled across France on horseback toward the Spanish court in Madrid. There they hoped to restore the Palatinate and then return to England in triumph with the Infanta María at the prince's side, but they would fail on both accounts. The Palatine crisis had produced irreconcilable differences that would poison the marriage negotiations. The great irony of Charles' and Buckingham's remarkable voyage to obtain a Spanish bride is that it actually proved to bring the twenty years of peace between the two nations to an end.

Palatine Policy

Naturally Frederick V was dead set against an Anglo-Spanish marriage alliance and was determined to do everything in his limited power to make sure it would not succeed. Since about 1619 it had been a goal of Palatine diplomacy to prevent the conclusion of the Anglo-Spanish match.[1] Frederick had never believed that such a marriage would or could result in his restoration, nor had he ever put much faith in his father-in-law's efforts to end the crisis by negotiations. In 1622 he had submitted to the resolutions of the Brussels conference when it seemed that no other option was left to him. Because the fall of Heidelberg and Mannheim had brought that conference to an end, Frederick had been relieved of his promise to submit to the Emperor, which he had never intended to do anyway.

The news of the electoral transfer to Maximilian had confirmed for Frederick that war was the only way to deal with the Habsburgs. Nethersole reported that the deed 'hath finally cut off all hope of [the Palatine's] restitution by treaty', the King of Spain's promises and intercessions notwithstanding.[2] That the transfer had been done without including Frederick in a trial or process of law merely reinforced his conviction that the Habsburgs were determined to pervert Imperial constitution and 'reduce everything to an extreme servitude'.[3] The Emperor's offer to restore the Palatinate after the Duke of Bavaria's death in return for Frederick's supplication for mercy struck the Palatine government-in-exile as 'palpable deceits', and, as with the Imperial ban, they planned to publish and distribute an attack on the Emperor's unconstitutional proceedings to all Protestant Imperial princes and estates.[4] Frederick resolved to resume his correspondence with the King of Denmark and the Lower Saxon Circle in order to procure their military intervention in the Palatine crisis.[5] He figured that the international protestation against the electoral translation might bring him new supporters, and, if he had had the means, he would have commissioned Mansfeld and Halberstadt once again to resume the war in the Palatinate.[6]

Safely lodged in The Hague, Frederick redoubled his efforts to establish an international alliance in his favor. The goal of this alliance was still to procure his full restitution, but this time the designated means was to attack the lands of the Habsburg dynasty from all sides, irrespective of their proximity or immediate strategic relevance to the Palatinate. In 1623 Frederick expanded his search for allies to include non-Protestant powers that were traditionally inimical to Habsburg interests: France, Venice, Savoy, and the Ottoman Empire. On 7 February 1623 the first three of these powers formed the League of Lyons, the goal of which was to expel the Spanish from the Valtelline, the pass through the Alps between the duchy of Milan and Tyrol, and Mansfeld was commissioned to make a diversionary attack on Habsburg territories.[7] Despite the Venetians' resolute neutrality since the beginning of the Bohemian rebellion, it was in the Republic's interest to support campaigns against the Austrian and Spanish Habsburgs, whose lands encircled Venice.[8] Frederick continued to plead for financial assistance, not for himself, but for Bethlen Gábor, who, assisted by the Margrave of Jägerndorf, once again turned against Emperor Ferdinand and tied down his forces. Since the end of 1622 Frederick expected Gábor to return to war against the Emperor, but this time he was supposed to have the support of a Turkish army, 30,000 strong.[9] Frederick fully encouraged this venture and would try to maintain his own connections with the Turkish sultan in Istanbul.

He sought Turkish assistance for his struggle against the Habsburgs, either in the form of support for Bethlen Gábor or as a Turkish campaign against the Habsburg lands directly. Clearly for the Winter King, the Habsburgs posed a greater threat to the Holy Roman Empire than the Turks. His ambassador to the Turkish Sultan was Count Thurn, the leader of the defenestration of Prague in 1618, who had been subsequently exiled from Bohemia in 1621. Throughout 1623 Thurn resided in Galata, just across the Golden Horn from the city of Istanbul and the Tokapi palace, and he negotiated with the Turks so that 'the King of Hungary (Bethlen Gábor) may accelerate his secretly planned military campaign against the House of Austria'.[10] In addition to Thurn, Frederick had three other contacts in Istanbul during the mid 1620s: his own agent, Abraham Cormano, the Dutch agent at the Ottoman court, Cornelius Haga, and his steward, Lamberto Verhaer. These men aided Thurn in his negotiations on Gábor's behalf and informed Frederick about the Turkish regime's warm inclinations toward him, despite the Emperor's obstructive tactics. Haga reported that a legation from Vienna had done considerable harm to Palatine interests by disseminating falsehoods and creating considerable irresolution in Istanbul. Nonetheless, Haga found the regime well-inclined towards Frederick and his cause. 'The Grand Vizier Hussain Passa', wrote Haga, 'shows in all his words and actions an extraordinary affection and inclination toward the royal person of Your Majesty and your interests'.[11] He recommended that Frederick send the vizier ingratiating letters directly, but the vizier would actually be removed from power before this recommendation could be carried out.[12]

In addition to his hopes in Gábor and the Turkish Sultan, Frederick had cause to believe that more Protestant princes and estates of the Empire would come to his aid in 1623. By the end of 1622 the Lower Saxon Circle had decided to muster an army of 18,000 men to defend the territory against the rising tide of warfare that threatened to enter its borders. Though officially they were arming themselves against any invaders, be they Tilly's troops or Mansfeld's, the Circle revealed its preferences by letting Christian of Halberstadt march his forces into its territories.[13] In January 1623 Frederick received word, after a silence of several months, from Christian IV, King of Denmark, who said that he would contact the Lower Saxon Circle and the Electors of Brandenburg and Saxony to discuss ways to restore the peace. Christian said that James I would come to realize that all negotiations were in vain, but the Danish King added that the best solution to the crisis was still Frederick's submission to the Emperor.[14] And indeed the Electors of Brandenburg and Saxony appeared more likely to abandon their support for the Emperor's policies. Both Electors had protested the transfer of Frederick's electorate, and Johann Georg had strenuously objected to the Emperor's expulsion of Lutheran preachers from Prague, a part of the retribution against those responsible for the Bohemian rebellion. Moreover, Saxony disbanded a force of 5–6,000 men that he had raised for the Spanish against Mansfeld and Halberstadt. Though Johann Georg had never respected Palatine claims to the Bohemian crown, he did not fail to continue referring to Frederick as a 'Prince Elector'.[15]

Ironically, the act of Frederick's dispossession had more influence with these two Protestant electors than had his clarion call to save Protestantism. He had repeatedly tried to persuade Johann Georg of the grave threat that the Habsburgs posed, not just to Calvinists in the Palatinate, but to all Protestants in the Empire, but these warnings had had no effect.[16] Both Saxony and Brandenburg, however, expressed their objections to the transfer in constitutional terms. They did not deny that a guilty prince could be punished like other men, but he needed to have a trial or some process of law that was 'according to the fundamentall lawes and constitutions of the Empire'.[17] The Elector Palatine, they said, should have been tried by his peers and the Emperor.

Frederick, for his part, was convinced that only a return to arms could procure his restoration, and a resumption of hostilities was certainly possible if not immediately probable. Mansfeld and Halberstadt were still at large, armed, and available for hire if Frederick could just obtain the money. Christian of Halberstadt remained resolutely on the Palatine side. According to one of Frederick's informers, the wild Duke was 'resolved rather to die, or live imprisoned, or live miserably under the Turkish Emperor, than to change his own mind: to re-establish German liberty and to set up the Queen again as Empress in Prague'.[18] In an extended meal-time tirade, the Duke asked one of Frederick's secretaries to challenge Tilly to a duel and blamed the whole of the Palatine disaster on King James I:

> In comparison with Alexander, M. Julius Cæsar, and Henry IV the Great, esteemed and celebrated as the most outstanding heroes of the world, then the old pants-shitter, the old English bed-shitter is, because of his stupidity, is the greatest ass in the world.[19]

In his own way Halberstadt managed to articulate the main problem with all Frederick's negotiations: the King of Great Britain would not take up arms on his behalf, and without English participation, no alliance of Protestant powers could be formed.

Despite the failure of the Brussels negotiations for a suspension of arms in the fall of 1622, James remained convinced that the best way to solve the Palatine crisis was through negotiations, and he was determined to quell Frederick's belligerence in peace treaties and blockade his military alliances. In March 1623, to avoid having to pay for the garrison at Frankenthal, the King decided to hand the town over to the Infanta Isabella and the King of Spain for safe-keeping. James tried to obtain his son-in-law's acquiescence in the sequestration, though it meant effectively surrendering the fortress to its besiegers without a respectable fight.[20] He promised nonetheless that all Palatine lands and dignities would be restored to Frederick by one means or another, asking him to rely on his faith: 'with God's help we surmount everything'.[21] Negotiations proceeded in London for a suspension of arms, and throughout 1623 James pursued multiple marriage treaties to re-establish peace in central Europe and to keep England from joining the conflict. By far the most important and the one most likely to succeed was a marriage between Prince Charles and Philip IV's sister, the Infanta María.

The project of forging an Anglo-Spanish match had a history of its own. The idea was nearly as old as the Treaty of London, which had brought an end to the years of hostilities in 1604, and it had become a serious issue when Charles had been left the sole male heir to the throne after the death of his older brother in 1612. While the negotiations had slowly progressed, the main sticking point had been religious: the fact that Catholicism was banned in England and its followers were a persecuted minority. The Spanish tended to want to make freedom of worship for English Catholics a necessary condition of the match, but they did not demand it because James had often said that he would break off the negotiations if they did. The complexity of the match and its unpopularity in England had increased exponentially after 1618. James preferred peace with Spain over war on behalf of his reckless son-in-law. An Anglo-Spanish match would have increased his influence with Europe's most powerful dynasty, and a massive dowry of Spanish silver would have made his penurious government less dependent on Parliament. Above all he wanted to use the match to lead to a resolution of the Palatine crisis, which might have brought the Thirty Years' War to an end and reduced the tension between Christian confessions in Europe.

The Spanish also preferred peace over war with England. The Spanish monarchy desperately needed English neutrality to allow its armed forces to pacify Germany and resume active pursuit of the war against the United Provinces, and thus far James had been willing to provide it. There were compelling reasons for both monarchies to agree to a marriage treaty, but a glaring contradiction remained: why should there be a union between Prince Charles and the Infanta María when Spanish and Austrian Habsburg arms had deprived his only sister, Elizabeth Stuart, Electress Palatine and Winter Queen, and her family of their hereditary lands and titles?

The Journey to Spain[22]

When Charles and Buckingham made their way to Madrid their prospects of success appeared considerable. English and Spanish negotiators had agreed on most of the terms, and they were waiting for the pope to issue a dispensation. James' emissary, Sir John Digby, was optimistic, and for his good work, James made him the Earl of Bristol. The young king, Philip IV, seemed open to the idea and had urged the pope to expedite the process, adding that it would be better if James were succeeded by Charles and the Infanta María and their heirs than by Frederick and Elizabeth.[23] And when Charles and Buckingham arrived, they were met with euphoria. Madrid pulsated with festivities, and the King and his servants treated the visitors with the greatest courtesy and honor. They were thoroughly impressed with the Prince's gallantry and the unprecedented nature of the visit, but they also hoped that Charles would convert to Catholicism. Bristol had the same suspicion, but it seems never to have occurred to the Prince and the Marquis. The pair remained hopeful despite their hosts' obvious disappointment.

James, meanwhile, was trying to keep the Palatine crisis from ruining his son's chances. As mentioned, Frankenthal was simply turned over to the Infanta Isabella. The Emperor was left out of the arrangement, because James refused to deal with him directly, 'he having thrice broken all his promises'.[24] Nonetheless James reacted favorably toward a new plan to settle the future of the Palatinate by means of a marriage between Frederick V's eldest son and Emperor Ferdinand's second daughter. Without insisting on knowing the details, James endorsed the idea in principle, and he praised its potential practicality to Charles and Buckingham: 'if either that way, or any other, this business be brought to a good end'.[25]

Frederick, however, remained implacable. The news of Charles' journey gravely worried him, and when he heard about what his father-in-law had done with Frankenthal he was livid with rage. He left The Hague in fury without telling his wife about his plans or whereabouts, but he returned after his temper subsided.[26] He dispatched directions to his new agent in England, Johann Joachim von Rusdorf, to communicate formal objections. Rusdorf was instructed to complain about the injustice of the electoral translation, the danger any peace with the Emperor would imply for the constitution of the Empire and his own restitution. Rusdorf was to remind James that even the King of Spain had objected to the translation. James was asked to second that protest and defend Protestantism and German liberty. Apparently both the Electors of Saxony and Brandenburg had invited James to join them and the King of Denmark 'in their opposition against the Emperor and his proceedings'.[27] In addition, Frederick requested a secret monthly allowance of £20,000 for independent military operations.[28] Palatine bellicosity had obviously not subsided.

James, however, preferred to stick to all of his negotiations. In London talks had resumed for a suspension of arms in the Palatinate, and the King intended to arrange a general peace treaty at another conference in the future.[29] He told his son-in-law merely to trust in the honor of Philip IV, which would inspire him to keep his promises.[30] James blamed Frederick for his own predicament, observing that it was he who provoked the Emperor and not vice versa.[31] The negotiations in London had the best chance of success, because they needed only to confirm the reality of the situation. Both parts of the Palatinate had been successfully overrun by Spanish and Catholic League forces. James had handed over Frankenthal, and Frederick had no commissioned forces in the region. On 1 May 1623 a treaty was signed that guaranteed peace for fifteen months, during which time the Infanta Isabella would oversee a round of negotiations in Cologne for a final settlement.[32] Even the Emperor ratified the treaty and proclaimed the cease-fire to the Imperial princes.[33] At this point more than any other thus far, it looked like there was an actual chance for quiet order to return to the Holy Roman Empire. Only Frederick failed to comply.

When he received a copy of the treaty, read its contents, and saw yet another promise from his father-in-law to restore him, he sighed deeply.[34] He refused to partake in James' negotiations and resolved not 'to let ourselves be bound through such slippery means'.[35] Instead of turning away from military means, he was 'rather much more resolved to pay attention and to use all good occasions that God may lay in our hands for the maintenance of our righteous causes'.[36] Instead of signing, he sent James a litany of objections: his enemies were still waging war against him; the Palatinate was being partitioned; there was no guarantee of restitution for him or his mother, the Electress Dowager, and his brother, the Duke of Simmern, who had lost everything; the Spanish were poised to attack the United Provinces; and the Emperor and the Duke of Bavaria only wanted to hurt Protestantism. Frederick said that he saw no reason to sign the treaty and added, by way of explanation, that he was absolutely dedicated to 'the conservation of my honor, which I am and will remain until the last breath of my life'.[37] Two secretaries were then sent to Spain to explain to Prince Charles the justice of Frederick's intransigence. The Palatines' message would find the Prince's ear much more sympathetic than the King's.

In Madrid, meanwhile, things had taken a turn for the worse. The papal dispensation had indeed arrived, but it was not followed by a wedding ceremony. It contained a new codicil that demanded freedom of conscience and worship for English Catholics, and Philip IV was designated to guarantee compliance by the English. Charles and

Buckingham were appalled, but while the Prince took it in stride, the Marquis became belligerent. Buckingham blamed the new delay on Philip's favorite, Count Olivares, and in their ensuing debates they came to hate each other intensely. Their enmity hardened Olivares' skepticism against the match. Buckingham also quarreled with other members of the Council of State and even threatened the papal nuncio that English Catholics would be made to suffer if the marriage did not go through. During this time he received word that James had elevated him to a ducal title, which did not improve his behavior. The new Duke of Buckingham even attacked Bristol and excluded him from the negotiations. Charles soon restored Bristol but failed to mollify the Duke.

Throughout June Charles did his best to have the terms of the dispensation altered, and James sent word that he would agree to the new conditions, requesting that Charles return to England at once. The Spanish then said that Charles could wed the Infanta in September and that she would be sent to England the following March. Charles strenuously objected, threatened to leave, and then buckled on 17 July, accepting the latest terms. Madrid was lit once again with celebratory bonfires, and by the end of the month, James and his privy council had sworn to abide by the articles that Charles had accepted, effectively promising to effect toleration of Catholicism in England, Scotland, and Ireland. James sent an official commission to Charles and Buckingham to negotiate the restoration of the Palatinate.

There was, however, no peace to be had on the issue. Throughout June and July Frederick and James engaged in a war of words that grew increasingly bitter. James had dismissed all of Frederick's complaints and reissued the old threat to abandon him completely if he refused to sign the suspension of arms treaty.[38] Frederick, for his part, did not back down. According to Camerarius, Frederick 'appear[ed] to want to bear rather the worst extremity than something dishonorable'.[39] Making peace, which demanded his backing out of all prior alliances, he said, would cast upon him 'an immortal hatred, to reach the summit of his misfortunes'.[40] His enemies, he claimed, would only flaunt the arrangement and violate the terms. Fifteen months of continuous abuse was unthinkable for him and his people.[41] To bring the point home, he even sent James a copy of the Emperor's intercepted note to the papal nuncio, in which he promised that the Duke of Bavaria would receive the Palatine electorate, whether the King of England liked it or not.[42] James simply disregarded it, and, having just signed the articles for the Anglo-Spanish match, he retorted that he had given his trust to the Emperor, the King of Spain, and the Infanta. He added that he would fulfill all his promises to Frederick, whether by treaty or force of arms.[43] Meanwhile Frederick continued to instruct his agents to lobby in Istanbul, with Bethlen Gábor and the Margrave of Jägerndorf about resuming war against the Emperor.[44]

Frederick's will to resist his father-in-law's cease-fire declined, however, when he received news of another military defeat. On 6 August 1623, Tilly attacked and demolished Halberstadt's army at Stadtlohn, in the bishopric of Münster. The Lower Saxon Circle had told Halberstadt to leave when Tilly threatened to invade in pursuit, and Halberstadt had then led his army of over 20,000 men to join with Mansfeld's, but Tilly caught the Duke. Of Halberstadt's army, 4,000 were killed, and 6,000 were taken prisoner, including Duke Wilhelm of Saxe-Weimar, who had raised a force on Frederick's behalf.[45] Halberstadt had not held a commission from the Winter King, but Frederick had hoped to be able to deploy that army against his enemies. In late August he broke down once again. He said that he would accept his father-in-law's treaty, but only if it could be changed from a suspension of arms to one procuring his immediate and complete restitution. By way of encouragement, he added that if James were to achieve the restitution, he would 'acquire the immortal glory to have done a deed worthy of his royal grandeur and promise'.[46] On 26 August 1623, the same day as the composition of this last letter, Frederick signed the suspension of arms, under the duress of his debts, according to Camerarius. Apparently all allowances from England, even those meant for Elizabeth and her children, would have been cut off if Frederick did not comply.[47] But there was nothing to fear from any peace conference; he had signed the document after the expiration of the three months allotted for the organization of the peace conference in Cologne. The Infanta in Brussels said that it was then necessary to appeal for the Emperor's affirmation once again.[48] There was no settlement to be had regarding the Holy Roman Empire.

In Spain efforts were similarly fruitless. The proceedings had been delayed again by the death of Pope Gregory XV, his dispensation having expired with him. The Spanish guaranteed Charles that a new dispensation would soon be forthcoming from Gregory's successor, but they would not alter the terms that Charles had agreed to. Meanwhile, Charles pressed for a treaty to restore the Palatinate to his brother-in-law, but he was to be gravely disappointed. He had already asked about the Palatinate, and Philip had avoided the issue, saying that the Palatine pair would be restored, without a treaty, when the marriage was over and done with.[49]

The young King's words seem to have contented Charles for some time, but everything changed in August, after the Council of State agreed, by a majority of one, to pursue the Palatine-Imperial match as the preferred solution to the Palatine crisis. The devil was in the details: Frederick would be liable to pay the astronomic sum of six million RT and send his eldest son to the Emperor's court in Vienna. The boy, upon attaining his majority, would receive the Palatine lands and electoral dignity and marry one of the Emperor's daughters. There was no word about his education, but it was obvious to all that it would not be Protestant.[50] The English delegation in Spain accepted and added that James would compel Frederick, Mansfeld, and Halberstadt to comply, by force of arms if necessary.

Charles, however, kept up the pressure. Philip was asked if he would make a similar promise regarding the Emperor: would he pledge to restore the Palatines by force if the Emperor's forces resisted? Some Spaniards were amenable, but Olivares seems to have been appalled by the suggestion.[51] When Charles pressed the issue, Olivares denied that there was any official negotiation in Spain at present regarding Frederick, his family, or the Palatine electorate, because they did not have a commission from the Emperor. 'And thirdly', the Count added, 'you should not think that His Royal Majesty is willing to leave His Imperial Majesty helpless in all incidental occasions, due to his sister's marriage'.[52] Charles' facial expression conveyed his deep displeasure, but he had nothing to say in reply but the following words, 'Buckingham and Digby will negotiate further about this'.[53]

This exchange may have been the moment in which he decided to leave Spain and forsake the negotiations, when, as Buckingham described it, they 'saw there was no more to be gained here'.[54] Charles had come to realize that there was no real possibility of fully restoring Frederick V and Elizabeth by treaty. The Spanish, the Prince found, despite their apparent wish to be compliant, would not take the necessary steps, and Frederick would never have consented to the terms of the Palatine-Imperial match at any rate. The journey had been in vain.

Charles left in September, probably more frustrated than he had ever been in his life. He had received word that James was ill and that a fleet was on the way to pick him up. He also heard than the new pope, Urban VIII, had been elected and that a dispensation would be soon be sent. But he would not wait to marry the Infanta as agreed. On 7 September he solemnly vowed to hold to the marriage contract as it stood and left documents allowing the wedding ceremony to be performed by proxy. During Charles' last two days in the company of the Spanish King, he asked Philip one last time to restore the Palatinate. The King promised to try to obtain it from the Emperor for Charles as a wedding present, but this answer was not satisfactory.[55]

As the party made its way from Madrid, it was met by Sir Francis Nethersole, Elizabeth's secretary, who delivered her plea to her brother that he not marry unless he had sufficient guarantees that she and her husband would be fully restored. Nethersole also conveyed Frederick's total rejection of the Palatine-Imperial match.[56] The mission seems to have served its purpose. Charles then composed a letter to Bristol, ordering him not to go through with the wedding 'until he had obtained security that the Infanta would not, subsequent to the formal betrothal, go into a monastery'.[57] This instruction was intended to impose a new, indefinite delay in the proceedings. The servant carrying the letter was told not to show it to Bristol until the arrival of the papal dispensation, and by that time the Prince would be long gone from Spain. This subterfuge indicates that Charles had decided to abandon the Anglo-Spanish match before he had left the country, but it could be that the bitterness of his disillusionment ran deeper. According to Nethersole, Charles 'resolved to make warre with Spayne, when he ... *was in Spayne*, rather then he would not see [the Elector and Electress Palatine] honourably repayred'.[58]

Unaware of all of this, his sister was on tenterhooks in The Hague. Her father's policies had produced absolutely no benefit for their cause, and for months her brother had been studiously endeavoring to marry into their greatest enemy's family. From her perspective, the perversity of the situation must have made it extremely painful. She wrote to the English Secretary of State, Sir Edward Conway, 'I hope his Majesty will one day see the falsood of our ennemies, but I pray God send my dear Brother safe in England againe and then I shall be more quiet in my minde'.[59] The Palatines could only wait and fervently hope that Nethersole's mission would succeed, that Charles, on his return to England, would alter his father's foreign policy. In that regard, at least, they were not to be disappointed.

The Match Dissolves

When Charles and Buckingham returned, it soon became clear that there had been a change of heart. Ten days before they had arrived at Portsmouth, Frederick had learned of their impending return and ordered Rusdorf to go greet the Prince on his and Elizabeth's behalf.[60] On 6/16 October 1623, the day of Charles' arrival in London, Rusdorf watched a city go mad with joy. Despite the drab, wet weather, bonfires blazed, church bells dinned, and countless rounds of healths produced 'an infinity of drunkards'.[61] It is doubtful that the reception would have been as jubilant if Charles had had a Spanish Habsburg bride at this side. Rusdorf also managed to obtain the secret information about the Prince's scheme to postpone the marriage.[62] Of all the ambassadors lined up to greet the Prince of Wales, Rusdorf alone was received; he congratulated Charles on a safe return, without mentioning any marriage. And again two days later at the palace at Royston, the Prince repeated this display of favor toward the Palatine ambassador.[63] Buckingham made a point of guaranteeing Rusdorf that the final outcome of the marriage negotiations would not in any way be disadvantageous to Frederick and Elizabeth.[64]

King James, however, did not show a new love for the Palatines. Rusdorf tried to extract an invitation for Frederick and Elizabeth to attend the King's formal reception of his son, but the answer was negative. James was not ready to let them come to England. Nonetheless the atmosphere at court was undergoing a transformation. Charles appeared more than usually grave, and in Buckingham Rusdorf observed a bitter grudge against Spain. People were openly criticizing the Spaniards, and Rusdorf soon learned that his masters would receive a lump sum of £3,000 in addition to their usual allowance.[65] This brief show of generosity, however, appeared to be an attempt to sweeten the terms of the Palatine-Imperial match, which remained for James the preferred way to resolve the Palatine crisis. James was planning to send Sir Dudley Carleton, the English ambassador to the Dutch Republic, to persuade Frederick of the wisdom of the plan and obtain a guarantee of his compliance before his father-in-law committed to negotiations with the Emperor and the King of Spain. James promised that Frederick's son would not be forced to convert to Catholicism, and, he added, because of the impending marriage of Charles and the Infanta María, the moment for a general settlement seemed especially propitious. Even the Emperor had congratulated the King on the match.[66] James had apparently not altered the direction of his foreign policy.

When Rusdorf sent Frederick word of these developments, he begged him to give the negotiations a chance and not issue the usual, quick refusal for the sake of his honor and conscience. The agent had received guarantees from Conway that no 'impossible or incompatible' stipulations would be included in the treaty.[67] Rusdorf's plea had no effect on Frederick whatsoever. In his reply to the King, he said that he would only follow the King's lead in so far as it pleased God, contributed to the public good, and improved his family's predicament. He said that he would certainly accept the proposed marriage, after he had been fully restored to his lands and titles.[68] To James, these words constituted 'a polite refusal'.[69]

Time, however, was on Frederick's side. In England, as autumn turned into winter, the match slowly, steadily met its demise. By the end of October James was complaining openly about Spain's failure to restore the Palatinate, but he persisted in his negotiations for the marriage and the delivery of the Infanta to England.[70] His ambassadors, meanwhile, were pressing Philip IV for an immediate, full restitution, saying that James had abandoned hopes of receiving anything from the Emperor.[71] By early

November James was blaming Bristol, Buckingham, and Charles for the bad state of affairs with Spain.[72]

Charles, however, pressed for a final resolution to the Palatine crisis before Christmas. He began looking abroad for support against Spain and told Sir Robert Anstruther to go to Denmark and add King Christian IV to the lists.[73] Charles also managed to have the full restitution of the Palatinate made a new condition for the marriage just before the date of the proxy wedding to which he had consented while in Spain. The timing was perfect if his intent was to cause indignation. In November Bristol had promised that the proxy marriage would take place if no one actively took measures to stop it.[74] After the papal dispensation was received in Madrid, the wedding was scheduled for 9 December. Just three days before the nuptials, Bristol received the new demand and submitted it to the Council of State. The wedding had to be delayed yet again, but no date was set for another try. It was impossible to recall invitations, so a degree of domestic humiliation was unavoidable. The dais was dismantled, and the Infanta quit her English lessons and rejected all subsequent letters from Charles.[75] It was clear to all that the match had expired.

But this does not mean that the match was a dead issue. The Spanish ambassador in England, Don Carlos Coloma, now joined by the Marquis of Hinojosa and Don Pedro de Mexías, tried their best to remove the new article regarding the Palatinate, if only for the sake of saving face. They produced various arguments against it and declared that Spain would not abandon peaceful negotiations unless England did first. James listened and kept the dialogue alive, because he was most unwilling to make war against Spain for the sake of his obstreperous son-in-law, who had frustrated all his peaceful efforts of the last four years.[76] If the King openly broke off the talks for the match, then pressure to declare war for the Palatinate would become practically irresistible. James was in turmoil. He wanted to continue negotiating, his council was still debating the issue, and his son and favorite were pushing for a complete break with Spain. He could hardly have dropped the new condition at this point, but he could have altered the text of the article to make the mere promise of a restitution, not its execution, satisfactory. That was the worst fear of the Palatine party, and that Charles and Buckingham would bow to the King's pacific inclinations.[77] The Prince, however, would have none of it. He asked James finally to admit to the King of Denmark that Spain had deceived him from the beginning. But James was not yet ready for war. No embassy was dispatched to Denmark because the King had issued no formal instructions.

At the end of 1623, despite the demise of the Anglo-Spanish match, it looked as if England would not wage war on behalf of the Palatinate as long as Frederick remained recalcitrant. In late November James requested that Frederick journey with a safe conduct to the Emperor and offer his submission. James claimed to have procured a guarantee for a full restitution of Frederick's son after the death of Maximilian, with Frederick acting as administrator of the Palatinate if he were still alive. The Palatine-Imperial marriage, James maintained, would secure amity between the houses, and he proposed that the two children be raised at his own court in the presence of Charles and the Infanta.[78] It does not appear that Frederick even bothered to respond to this idea. By December it was common knowledge that the Emperor had abandoned the idea of a peace convention at Cologne.

Yet Another Match

On 6 December a new marriage plan from London arrived in The Hague: the Palatine-Bavarian. A Capuchin monk, Alexander von Hales, alias Francesco della Rota, had come to London on Maximilian's behalf to negotiate the marriage of Frederick's eldest son with the Duke's niece. Maximilian had suggested a Palatine-Bavarian marriage between the two branches of the Wittelsbach dynasty to counter the Palatine-Imperial marriage and James' preference for Spanish mediation. Rota insisted that Frederick and James should trust the Duke of Bavaria more than the Habsburgs.[79] Rusdorf observed that few at the English court seemed to take this idea seriously, but, nonetheless, James found it appealing and was ready to consider almost any proposal apart from waging a war or calling a Parliament.[80] As discussions continued through December, bolstered by the participation of the Venetian and French ambassadors, Rusdorf became more convinced that the Duke of Bavaria, a natural opponent to Habsburg dominance of Germany, wanted to reconcile himself with Frederick.[81] Especially appealing was the opportunity for the Wittelsbachs to unite against the Habsburgs' expansionist tendencies in the Holy Roman Empire. Still there were significant problems, as no one at court was actually certain if Maximilian actually had a marriageable niece for Frederick's son, and the contested possession of the electorate seemed insurmountable.

In the summer of 1623, when James had first taken to the idea of the Palatine-Imperial match, he had suggested that a new electorate be created both to placate Maximilian and allow for Frederick's restoration, and now the Palatine-Bavarian marriage provided another opportunity to sound the idea once again. The representatives of both princes, however, refused to accept the indignity of their respective lord's receiving the new, eighth electorate, since both insisted that they had the better claim to the Empire's most prestigious secular dignities.[82] For both sides, at this stage of the conflict, altering the Imperial constitution in such a way was totally unacceptable.

The fundamental problem with James' negotiating in the Palatine crisis on his son-in-law's behalf was, as Rusdorf articulated it, his lack of appreciation and understanding for the constitution of the Holy Roman Empire.

> For our enemies know well that this King is not at all difficult, and that those who are not acquainted with the constitution of the Empire or the harmony of its pre-eminents, thus judge the affairs of the princes of Germany according to a consideration of the monarchy and absolute sovereignty under which they live; they let themselves be easily persuaded of things resistant to liberty and prerogative.[83]

Rusdorf therefore concluded that an eighth electorate was 'impracticable and incompatible in the Empire' and of such absurdity that it rendered serious negotiations impossible. He saw that to arrange such a Palatine-Bavarian treaty, which ran against the law of the Empire, had no hope of success.[84] It would take twenty-five more years of warfare and deprivation before the German princes involved would take up James' point of view on the matter. The creation of an eighth electorate was to be the component in the Peace of Westphalia that would bring the Palatine crisis to an end in 1648.

During the negotiations with Rota, the Palatines came to understand that England was finally going to join their cause after all. Frederick and Elizabeth were told that the English interest in the Palatine-Bavarian marriage was merely meant to divert time and energy from the Palatine-Imperial, which had been effectively abandoned.[85] On 9 December Frederick received word that James, Charles, and Secretary Conway were actually pleased with his negative response to the Palatine-Imperial marriage. Buckingham was wholly in favor of pursuing the restitution alone. Many of the lords at court gave Rusdorf assurances that things would soon look better for the Winter King and Queen. Rusdorf thought that most of the lords and Prince Charles himself gave no weight to James' various marriage negotiations, though not all made their opinions public, depending on their status and their interests at court. The partition of the Palatinate had outraged many, though some opined that the Elector of Mainz wanted peace more than anyone and would be compliant about Frederick's restitution.[86] Anstruther was finally made ready to go to Denmark, and Rusdorf actually heard Buckingham tell him to make haste. Anstruther was granted permission to make a stop at The Hague to obtain credential letters from Frederick and the princes of the Lower Saxon Circle for making plans for a common strategy.[87]

Despite all these hopeful indicators, Rusdorf took a wary view of the possibility of English assistance. He had come to the conclusion that as long as Frederick's affairs remained completely dependent on England's leadership, there was no hope for his restitution.[88] The bravado with which the English courtiers threatened to attack Palatine enemies struck Rusdorf as most unrealistic. 'They think that they alone are enough to ruin Spain and to put 100,000 men into Flanders, that all ought to obey them at once'.[89] But the divisions at court were plain enough. Rusdorf cautioned, 'when the dogs are unwilling, it is difficult to hunt'.[90]

* * *

With the coming of winter the campaigning season came to an end. There had been no military victories for either the Palatines or their allies in 1623. In August Bethlen Gábor had left Transylvania, joined by the Margrave of Jägerndorf and later Count Thurn, with a force of 20,000, mainly comprised of cavalry, and they were backed up by a Turkish army 30,000 strong. Frederick's ambassador in Istanbul, Court Thurn, went to Moravia, in charge of 8,000 cavalry.[91] But after having invaded Hungary and Moravia and raided Lower Austria for a couple of months, Gábor had decided to sue for peace before winter. On 18 November he had accepted an armistice from the Emperor and then withdrew to Transylvania.[92] Gábor had abandoned the Winter King yet again. Halberstadt's army had been decimated at Stadtlohn, and Mansfeld had not been active.

Frederick had seen no reason to expedite any negotiations for peace. In the last days of December he rejected his father-in-law's latest marriage and peace proposals because of their offensiveness to the Imperial constitution and to his honor. He first thanked James for his pains, which 'more so than any fear of human events, can make us become sorrowful or satisfied with recovering the loss of goods through the loss of honor'.[93] Out of concern for his honor, Frederick objected to each and every point. The requested submission to the Emperor in person, being merely a point of ceremony, should be done by proxy, and that only after his restitution, something of matter and substance, was successfully carried out. Frederick said that he would never accept the translation of his electorate to the Duke of Bavaria, which would 'ruin my cause for all time'.[94] He said that his acceptance of the suspension of arms had only helped the Emperor settle his armistice with Bethlen Gábor and intimidate the Electors of Saxony and Brandenburg and the Lower Saxon Circle into neutrality. Frederick warned that James' conditions for a lasting peace would never be accepted, because they were against the constitution of the Empire and 'a mark of infamy against me and my posterity'.[95] He said that all other marriages and treaties should not be considered without his first having sufficient assurance of his complete restitution. Both the Spanish and the Austrian Habsburgs, he argued, were simply using these negotiations to gain time and were conspiring to destroy his dynasty. He begged James to join with the King of Denmark, the secular Electors, the United Provinces, and other Protestant princes of the Empire to demand the restitution of the Palatinate, without which there could be no lasting peace in Germany.[96] Frederick instructed Rusdorf to continue negotiating with the French and Venetian ambassadors but not to enter into any treaty on his own.[97]

The main Palatine success of 1623 was that other disasters did not occur. All of James' treaties either foundered on their own, or Frederick was not forced to comply with the ones he had to sign. Above all the Anglo-Spanish alliance had foundered, and the Infanta María was not in London to prevent English military intervention in the Palatine crisis. In 1624, however, Frederick's and Charles' wishes would overcome those of King James and the Habsburgs, and the Palatine policy of resistance to Jacobean foreign policy would achieve its desired end. In 1623 the Palatine crisis had ruined the Anglo-Spanish match, and thereafter it would bring an end to the Anglo-Spanish peace as well. Frederick's stalwart protection of his honor would eventually contribute to the fruition of his old plan for an international Protestant alliance against the Habsburgs.

Notes

1. BHStA, KS, 3733, fol. 364: 19 August 1619, Memo from Amberg.
2. PRO, SP, 81/28, fol. 99: 6/16 March 1623, Nethersole to Calvert.
3. 'pour reduire le tout à une servitude extreme', PRO, SP, 81/28, fol. 69: 14/24 February 1623, Frederick V to James I.
4. PRO, SP, 81/28, fols 100–1: 6/16 March 1623, Nethersole to Calvert.
5. PRO, SP, 81/28, fol. 69: 14/24 February 1623, Frederick V to James I.
6. PRO, SP, 81/28, fol. 101: 6/16 March 1623, Nethersole to Calvert.
7. Parker, *The Thirty Years' War*, pp. 59, 61.
8. Zwiedineck-Südenhorst, *Die Politik*, i, pp. 100–5.
9. Frederick's secret informer in Transylvania kept him abreast of Gábor's actions and intentions and confirmed the reality of the impending support from the Sultan. BHStA, KB, 122/3c, fol. 180. News of the alliance may not have reached The Hague till December. PRO, SP, 81/27, fol. 192: 25 November/5 December 1622, Elizabeth to Roe.
10. 'der König in Ungern seine vorhabende impresen wider das haus Österreich accelerirn möge', BHStA, KB, 122/3c, fol. 291: 6 March 1623, to Count Thurn.

11. 'le Gran Vesir Hussain Passa montre en touts les discours et Actions une extraordinaire affection et inclination a la Royale personne de V. M.te et a son interest'. BHStA, KB, 122/3c, fol. 97: 19 August 1623, Cornelius Haga to Frederick V.

12. On 1 September 1623 Abraham Cormano reported that the vizier had just been replaced by another man who had been serving as pasha in Baghdad. BHStA, KB, 122/3c, fol. 99: 1 September 1623, Abraham Cormano to Frederick V. Despite the change in personnel, Frederick's agents were able to remain well informed about events in the Turkish capital. According to Lamberto Verhaer, 'Es ist aber gewiß, das bey den turchen nichts verhoelen bleibt, wer noer wil fleiß aenwenden, sulches zuwissen was sie hie mit alle herren Ambassadoren tracktieren', BHStA, KB, 122/3c, fol. 105: 9 December 1623, Lamberto Verhaer to Frederick V.

13. Gindely, *Geschichte*, ii, p. 56.

14. BHStA, KB, 121/3d, fols 24–5: 22 November 1622, Christian IV to Frederick V.

15. PRO, SP, 81/28, fol. 87: 15/25 February 1623, Nethersole to Calvert.

16. For the latest example see AP, ii, p. 653.

17. PRO, SP, 81/28, fol. 97: 2/12 March 1623, Electors of Saxony and Brandenburg to the Imperial Ambassador. English extract.

18. 'resolut apres plus toust mourir ou vivre prisonne, ou vivre miserablement apres l'Impereur de Turcs, que changer son propos assavoir; restablir la liberté germanicque e redresser la royne pour l'Imperatrice à Prage'. BHStA, KS, 8701, fol. 8: 11 July 1623, 'Frater tuus' to Johann Kasimir Streiff, Secretary to the King of Bohemia. This speech is printed in Wertheim, *Christian*, i, pp. 223–4.

19. 'Gleich wie Alexander, M. Julius Cæsar, und Henricus IV. le grand, die treflichiste helden von der Welt æstimirt und celebrirt worden, also ist der alte hosenschisser, der alte Englische Pettschisser wegen seiner couionerei der grösste couion von der Welt'. BHStA, KS, 8701, fol. 8: 11 July 1623, 'Frater tuus' to Johann Kasimir Streiff, Secretary to the King of Bohemia. Apparently Braunschweig continued to attack the English King and his pacific policies and negotiations in this scatological vein for some time. This speech is printed in Wertheim, *Christian*, i, pp. 223–4. I have treated 'couion' and 'couionerei' as a variation of 'couillon', which could mean 'testicle', 'fool', or 'idiot' in the seventeenth century. I have translated both words above to capture both the obscene tone and the denotation of foolishness.

20. BHStA, KS, 9254/2, fols 168–9: 13/23 March 1623, James I to Frederick V. Also see PRO, SP, 81/28, fols 116–7.

21. 'avec l'aide de Dieu nous surmonterons toutes', PRO, SP, 81/28, fol. 117: 13/23 March 1623, James I to Frederick V.

22. For an expanded version of this section, see Brennan C. Pursell, 'The End of the Spanish Match', *The Historical Journal*, (forthcoming).

23. AGS, EI, Libro 369, fol. 374: 4 March 1623, Philip IV to Pope Gregory XV.

24. Philip Yorke, Earl of Hardwicke, ed., *Miscellaneous State Papers. From 1501–1726* (2 vols, London, 1778), i, p. 404.

25. Ibid.

26. PRO, SP, 81/28, fol. 166, 26 March./5 April 1623, Nethersole to Calvert.

27. PRO, SP, 81/28, fol. 233: 26 April/6 May 1623, Calvert to Conway.

28. BHStA, KB, 122/3a, fols 5–7: 6/16 April 1623, Frederick V to Rusdorf. Frederick was currently receiving from James £3000 per month, from April to September, to cover his debts. BHStA, KB, 122/3a, fol. 8: 14/24 April 1623, Frederick V to Rusdorf.

29. PRO, SP, 81/28, fols 243–5: 1 May 1623, James I to Frederick V.
30. BHStA, KS, 9254/2, fol. 162: 18 April 1623, James I to Frederick V. PRO, SP, 81/28, fols 243–5: 1 May 1623, James I to Frederick V, and fols 247–8: 2 May 1623, James I to Electors of Brandenburg and Saxony.
31. PRO, SP, 81/28, fol. 243: 1 May 1623, James I to Frederick V
32. BHStA, KS, 9254/2, fol. 240: 21 April/1 May 1623. White, 'Suspension', p. 550.
33. BHStA, KS, 9254/2, fol. 248: 10 May 1623. White, 'Suspension', p. 554.
34. Söltl, *Der Religionskrieg*, iii, p. 179.
35. 'uns durch solche schlupffrige mittel binden zulassen', BHStA, KB, 122/3c, fol. 394: 11/21 May 1623, Frederick V to Achaz von Dohna.
36. 'sondern vielmehr resolvirt, alle gutte occasiones die Gott, zuerhaltung unserer gerechten sachen an die handt geben würde in acht zu nemmen undt zu brauchen'. BHStA, KB, 122/3c, fol. 394: 11/21 May 1623, Frederick V to Achaz von Dohna.
37. BHStA, KS, 9254/2, fols 258–9: 10/20 May 1623, Frederick V to James I. 'la conservation de mon honneur, qui suis et demeureray iusques au dernier souspir de ma vie', PRO, SP, 81/28, fol. 252: 10/20 May 1623, Frederick V to James I.
38. BHStA, KS, 9254/2, fols 252 and 256: June 1623, James I to Frederick V. PRO, SP, 81/28, fols 336–8: 27 June/7 July 1623, James' response. Also see BHStA, KS, 9254/2, fol. 261: 27 June/7 July 1623, James I to Frederick V.
39. 'scheint lieber das Äußerste als Unwürdiges ertragen zu wollen'. Söltl, *Der Religionskrieg*, iii, p. 181.
40. 'une hayne immortelle, pour achever le comble de mes malheurs'. BHStA, KS, 9254/2, fols 265–6: 10/20 June 1623, Frederick V to James I. Also see PRO, SP, 81/28, fol. 309.
41. BHStA, KS, 9254/2, fols 269–70: 12/22 July 1623, Frederick V to James I.
42. BHStA, KS, 9254/2, fol. 271. For a summary of this letter, see PRO, 81/28, fol. 350.
43. BHStA, KS, 9254/2, fols 272–3: 31 July 1623, James I to Frederick V.
44. For a list of Frederick's letters to Jägerndorf and Gábor, see BHStA, KB, 122/3c, fol. 603.
45. Gindely, *Geschichte*, ii, p. 57.
46. 's'acquerera la gloire immortelle d'avoir fait un oeuvre digne de sa royale grandeur et promesse'. BHStA, KS, 9254/2, fols 276–8: 15/25 August 1623, Frederick V to James I. Also see PRO, SP, 81/29, fols 82–4: 15/25 August 1623, Frederick V to James I. Frederick asked Rusdorf to seek the aid of as many sympathetic Privy Councillors and other supporters as possible. BHStA, KB, 122/3a, fol. 23: 26 August 1623, Frederick V to Rusdorf.
47. Söltl, *Der Religionskrieg*, iii, p. 183.
48. Gardiner, *History of England*, v, pp. 78–9.
49. Lockyer, *Buckingham*, p. 158.
50. Straub, *Pax et Imperium*, pp. 175–7.
51. Khevenhiller, *Annales*, x, p. 91.
52. 'und zum Dritten, daß Sie nicht gedencken wollen, daß Ihre Königl. Maj. durch die Heyrath seiner Schwester Ihre Kayserl. Maj. in allen vorfallendenden [*sic*] Occasionen Hülffloß zu lassen gesinnet seyn'. Khevenhiller, *Annales*, x, p. 96.
53. 'hierüber werde der Bugingam und Digbi weiter tractiren'. Khevenhiller, *Annales*, x, pp. 96–7.
54. Hardwicke, *Miscellaneous*, i, p. 451.
55. S.R. Gardiner, *Prince Charles and the Spanish Marriage, 1617–1623* (2 vols, London, 1869), ii, pp. 408–9.

56. John Rushworth, *Historical Collections* (8 vols, London, 1659–1701), i, p. 102.
57. Lockyer, *Buckingham*, p. 164.
58. PRO, SP, 81/34, fol. 115: 11/21 September 1626, Nethersole to Carleton? The italics are mine.
59. PRO, SP, 81/29, fols 120–1: 6/16 September 1623, Elizabeth to Conway.
60. BHStA, KB, 122/3a, fol. 30: 26 September/5 October 1623, Frederick V to Rusdorf.
61. BHStA, KS, 7552, fol. 16: 12/22 Oct. 1623, Rusdorf to Maurice.
62. BHStA, KS, 7552, fol. 8, 10: 6/16 October 1623, Rusdorf to Frederick V.
63. BHStA, KS, 7552, fol. 14: 11/21 October 1623, Rusdorf to Frederick V.
64. BHStA, KS, 7552, fol. 14: 11/21 October 1623, Rusdorf to Frederick V.
65. BHStA, KS, 7552, fol. 16: 12/22 October 1623, Rusdorf to Frederick V.
66. BHStA, KS, 9254/2, fols 160–1: 8/18 October 1623, James I to Frederick V. For the Emperor's letter of congratulation, see PRO, SP, 80/6, fol. 44: 27 August/6 September 1623, Ferdinand II to James I.
67. BHStA, KS, 7552, fol. 12: 12/22 October 1623, Rusdorf to Frederick V.
68. PRO, SP, 81/29, fol. 232: 20/30 October 1623, Frederick V to James I.
69. 'un civile refus', BHStA, KS, 7552, fol. 36: 22 November/2 December 1623, Rusdorf to Frederick V.
70. BHStA, KS, 7552, fols 18–19: 29 October/8 November 1623, Rusdorf to Maurice.
71. BHStA, KS, 7552, fols 31–3: 29 November 1623, Memo from English Ambassadors to Philip IV.
72. BHStA, KS, 7552, fol. 39: 12/22 November 1623, Rusdorf to Maurice.
73. BHStA, KS, 7552, fols 26–7: 1/11 November 1623, Rusdorf to Frederick V.
74. BHStA, KS, 7552, fols 22–3: 12/22 November 1623, Rusdorf to Frederick V.
75. Gardiner, *History*, v, p. 153.
76. BHStA, KS, 7552, fols 57–8: 26 November/6 December 1623, Rusdorf to Maurice.
77. 'Par tel eschappatoire le Roy espere, comme i'entends de tres bons lieu, de rompre les resolutions du Prince & du Duc de Buquingham, et se donner loisir de pouvoir continuer en ses procedures'. BHStA, KS, 7552, fol. 45: 30 November/10 December 1623, Rusdorf to Frederick V.
78. BHStA, KS, 9254/2, fols 156–7: 20/30 November 1623, James I to Frederick V. Also see PRO, SP, 81/29, fols 275–7: 19/29 November 1623: James I to Frederick V.
79. Albrecht, *Die Auswärtige Politik*, pp. 113–15.
80. BHStA, KS, 7552, fol. 35: 22 November/2 December 1623, Rusdorf to Frederick V.
81. BHStA, KS, 7552, fol. 57: 26 November/6 December 1623, Rusdorf to Maurice.
82. Albrecht, *Die Auswärtige Politik*, pp. 109–10.
83. 'Car nos adversaires sçavent bien, que le Roy n'est point difficile, & que ceux qui ne conoissent la constitution de l'Empire, ni l'harmonie de ses preeminences, ains iugent des aff.res des Princes d'Allemagne, selon la consideration de la monarchie & absolue souveraineté, soubs laquelle ils vivent, se laissent aisement persuader à des choses reluctantes à la liberté & prerogative'. BHStA, KS, 7552, fol. 70: 27 December/6 January 1623, Rusdorf to Frederick V.
84. BHStA, KS, 7552, fol. 72: 27 December/6 January 1623, Rusdorf to Frederick V.
85. BHStA, KS, 7552, fol. 59: 24 November/4 December 1623, Rusdorf to Maurice?
86. BHStA, KS, 7552, fols 22–3: 12/22 November 1623, Rusdorf to Frederick V.
87. BHStA, KS, 7552, fol. 24: 16/26 November 1623, Rusdorf to Frederick V.
88. BHStA, KS, 7552, fol. 68. Undated, unsigned, but in the hand of Rusdorf's French secretary.

89. 'ils pensoient que seuls estoient bastants de ruiner Espagne, et mettre 100M hommes en Flanders, que tout leur debvoit obeyr incontinent'. BHStA, KS, 7552, fol. 69: Undated, unsigned, but in the hand of Rusdorf's French secretary.

90. 'Sed invitis canibus venari difficile est'. BHStA, KS, 7552, fol. 39: 12/22 November 1623, Rusdorf to Maurice.

91. BHStA, KB, 122/3c, fol. 605: 28 October 1623.

92. Gindely, *Geschichte*, ii, pp. 59–60.

93. 'plus qu'aucune crainte des evenements humains, nous peut attrister ou nous rendre contents de recouvrer la perte des biens par la perte d'honneur'. PRO, SP, 81/29, fol. 315: 20/30 December 1623, Frederick V to James I. Also see BHStA, KS, 9254/2, fols 151–5, 158: 20/30 December 1623, Frederick V to James I.

94. 'ruyner ma cause a tout jamais', PRO, SP, 81/29, fol. 316: 20/30 December 1623, Frederick V to James I.

95. 'une marque d'infamie à moi & à ma posterité'. PRO, SP, 81/29, fol. 316: 20/30 December 1623, Frederick V to James I.

96. PRO, SP, 81/29, fols 317–18: 20/30 December 1623, Frederick V to James I.

97. BHStA, KB, 122/3a, fol. 41: 20/30 December 1623, Frederick V to Rusdorf.

Chapter 8

The Rise and Fall of The Hague Alliance, 1624–1626

The events of the next two years would give rise to soaring hopes for the Palatines in their struggle against the Habsburg dynasty. A direct result of the failure of the Anglo-Spanish marriage alliance would be a resurgence of warfare over the Palatine crisis. The match had been one of the highest barriers to Palatine plans for the formation of an international alliance against the Habsburgs, but Frederick's patient defiance would reap its benefits for his common cause. England's return to belligerence, however, would not be immediate. Though Prince Charles, the Duke of Buckingham, and the English Parliament would succeed in breaking the Jacobean peace, the King would resist their efforts and frustrate the military campaign until his death in March 1625. The new King of England would then lead the charge, endeavoring to draw the Habsburgs' traditional enemies and other powers, Catholic and Protestant, into the fray, and this effort would culminate in an alliance, sealed at The Hague, between England, Denmark, and the United Provinces. But it too was destined to fail. The goal of replacing Frederick in his former position in the Holy Roman Empire was the only interest that his many potential supporters had in common, but it alone would not be strong enough to pre-empt individual considerations of domestic security, expense, and, in some cases, religion. Moreover, in order to restore Frederick unconditionally – he would accept nothing less – the Emperor, the King of Spain, and the Duke of Bavaria had to be vanquished on the battlefield, but this was too formidable a task for a loose coalition of potentates who would not take extraordinary measures on behalf of a common project located outside their borders.

War or Negotiations?

At the beginning of 1624 the Palatines placed their hopes on England for a resumption of war. There can be no doubt that the English general public was ready and waiting for war against Spain on behalf of the dispossessed

Palatines.[1] Charles and Buckingham were also firmly in the Palatine camp, but King James' preferences remained peaceable. In January Frederick received news from London that reinforced his suspicion that his father-in-law had little intention of effecting his restitution by force of arms. In the previous month a Dutch emissary had been at court, complaining of his nation's suffering at the hands of the Spanish, and Charles and Buckingham had been pushing James to ally with the Dutch and enlist their strength against Spain. The King, however, was still holding on to Spanish offers, which were 'fewer and harder' than those emanating from the Empire. James wanted Spain to provide the restitution, despite the fact that the Anglo-Spanish match had been indefinitely suspended. A majority of his councilors found such a restitution highly unlikely. Meanwhile negotiations for the Palatine-Bavarian marriage had not been abandoned and actually seemed to be making some progress. James appeared to favor this settlement, although Buckingham and the two Secretaries of State were in adamant opposition.[2]

Frederick ordered Rusdorf to negotiate with Francesco della Rota about the settlement with Bavaria, although, from the Palatine perspective, the project was worthless. The Duke of Bavaria's behavior towards Frederick had been, as he put it, 'so unfriendly', that he had to doubt his cousin's motives fundamentally.[3] He wanted to know whether and how Maximilian was supposed to negotiate or settle an agreement without the Emperor's knowledge or permission, particularly when he had overrun Frederick's lands in the Emperor's name. The Duke's earlier seizure of Upper Austria, his conquest of the Upper Palatinate, and his plundering of Heidelberg provided ample evidence of the intentions behind his methods.[4] Frederick directed Rusdorf to negotiate with the French and Venetian ambassadors about the match and insure that no harmful resolutions came out of it. He was to reject immediately all conditions disadvantageous to Frederick's 'honor, conscience, and reputation', and, above all, the suggestion that his son would be raised at the Bavarian court.[5] In addition, Frederick ordered Rusdorf to encourage the foundation of an alliance between the Dutch and the English, with the goal of restoring the Palatinate.

Negotiations between Rusdorf, Conway, and Rota for the Palatine-Bavarian match continued while Charles and Buckingham pushed for war against Spain and prepared for the upcoming Parliament. James, however, was still entertaining the Palatine-Bavarian match as a solution to the Palatine crisis. The papal nuncio in Brussels had assured the King that Maximilian's desire for settlement was genuine, and James was to send an agent to The Hague to negotiate with Frederick directly.[6] An advantage of a Palatine-Bavarian marriage settlement was that the two branches of Wittelsbachs could have helped England to form a front against the

Habsburgs, but there were two major points of disagreement: the guarantee for the security of the children to be married and the full restitution of the Upper Palatinate. Furthermore, sending Frederick's son to Munich would mean that the boy would be raised a Catholic, which for the Palatines was totally unacceptable. For Maximilian the prospect of his niece being raised a Calvinist in Heidelberg was likewise unthinkable. In addition, Maximilian would only return the Upper Palatinate to Frederick's son in exchange for an immense sum of money, because the province had been granted to the Duke to remit his military expenses on the Emperor's behalf.

Rusdorf was convinced that the Duke of Bavaria and his supporters did not intend to do any good despite their many protestations to the contrary. To him negotiations with Maximilian had been mere chicanery, conducted to buy the time to secure all that he had won.[7] Rusdorf warned Frederick that Maximilian was certainly in league with Pope Urban VIII in the affair, though Rota swore that the Duke, and not the pontiff, had not been the author of the propositions. The papal nuncio, for his part, swore by his baptism that he was not working in collusion with Spain and that Maximilian was sincere in his intentions. The nuncio guaranteed that Frederick's son would not be forced to change his religion.[8] Because Munich and Heidelberg were immediately rejected by the opposite parties, Maximilian insisted that the children be brought up at the court of another Wittelsbach relative, Duke Wolfgang Wilhelm of Neuburg, who had converted to Catholicism in 1613. Rusdorf, however, warned Frederick that conversion was still the aim nonetheless.[9] The fact that a capuchin and a nuncio were conducting the Duke of Bavaria's negotiations provided enough evidence that the talks were 'rather for the cause of religion than for reason of state or of peace'.[10] Nevertheless Rusdorf advised Frederick not to break off the discussion, because it was preferable to keep Maximilian 'favorable and standing by' than to repulse his overtures. If they did, Rusdorf said, 'the Catholics would presume that we intended a war of religion, also no Catholic prince would enter in any confederation with you without incorporating the said Duke in it'.[11] The implication behind this statement is that Rusdorf did not view the current conflict as a 'war of religion'.

As the negotiations continued, Frederick instructed Rusdorf to voice a genuine desire for peace and a willingness to make amends with the Duke of Bavaria despite the many offenses against the Palatinate and himself. Frederick knew that a reconciliation would return tranquillity to the Empire, and he wanted the ambassadors of France, Venice, and Savoy to see that it would be advantageous for their principalities, because, he said, of the Spanish and Austrian Habsburg plan to establish a universal domination in Europe.[12] Rusdorf had declared the Spanish 'impudent prostitutes, who seek nothing but a general conflagration and despair, since they know that they are the most powerful among the Catholics'.[13] According to recent responses from Spain to English demands for the restoration of the Palatinate, 'it was as clear as the sun' to Frederick that the Spanish monarchy was content to make promises only in vague terms. He said that the King of Spain had never been serious about returning the Palatinate, 'something which we', he said, 'for our part have always thought, though [King James] has been persuaded of something else'.[14]

Frederick wanted his father-in-law to continue to negotiate with Bavaria, but he wanted the King to increase his sensitivity about Imperial constitutional issues. The affair, observed Frederick, actually concerned the whole Empire, 'which has its particular constitutions and fundamental statutes, the preservation of which each and every Estate is obligated and responsible'.[15] He knew that James and Charles favored the settlement of the Palatine crisis by means of the creation of an eighth electorate, and Frederick ordered Rusdorf to inform them of the constitutional ramifications of this and other proposals before they made agreements based on them.[16] Frederick warned that any acknowledgment of Bavaria's occupation of his electorate would be damaging to him, because the Golden Bull, the core of the Imperial constitution, only allowed for seven, and he was sure that Maximilian would never voluntarily relinquish his electorate. Finally, while Frederick agreed with Rota's claim that reconciliation between the Palatine and Bavarian branches of the Wittelsbach dynasty would indeed be beneficial to the maintenance of German common liberties, Frederick had to ask, 'then why did Bavaria not consider it better previously, when better means were available for attaining such an goal?'[17]

Frederick's ardent belief in his own blamelessness was stronger than ever at this stage. He remained completely convinced that he had not been the author of the recent wars and misery in the Empire. He insisted that he had always wanted and still continued to desire nothing but peace. He was fully aware that many libels had been published against him, and he marveled that they portrayed him, he said,

> as if we had, from the beginning until this hour, not given or made known a single sign that we may be inclined to peace, but rather that we had much more rejected all means offered to us and, as it were, presently endured for an amicable settlement, and had only sought war alone and persecution of other Estates.[18]

His natural response was to order a counterattack. He had Camerarius compose and publish a Palatine 'Apologia' of 1624, which addressed Frederick's detractors and attempted to parry their most vicious blows.[19]

Rota's coming to The Hague in March actually marked the end of the negotiations, not their consummation. Before the Capuchin left England, Rusdorf warned that if the negotiations failed, 'one would impute the obstruction of the peace to Your Majesty', but this consideration did not intimidate Frederick.[20] He received Rota in The Hague, showed him the child in question, and dealt with him attentively. Frederick refused, however, to make any concessions in letting Maximilian take responsibility for his upbringing. While Frederick favored reconciliation with Bavaria in principle, he would never have allowed his first-born son to be sent away from his family to a place where he would be under constant pressure to forsake them and their religion. Because Rota would make no concessions either, nor offer sufficient security for the children, the project came to nothing, almost as a matter of course. When he returned to Brussels, the Venetian ambassador resident in The Hague, Marco Antonio Morosini, summarized the opinion of the Palatine court toward the Bavarian plan: '[the Bavarians] want only the children and give nothing for them'. Frederick, meanwhile, had put his hopes for restitution in the English Parliament.[21]

The opening of the Parliament of 1624 in late February had occasioned the end of the negotiations in England for the Palatine-Bavarian marriage. Frederick was kept aware of the progress of the Parliament of 1624 through a constant stream of personal reports, copies of speeches and resolutions in Parliament, and other material that Rusdorf sent to The Hague.[22] Frederick understood that Charles and Buckingham were steadfastly in support of the Palatine cause and that 'the King [was] also genuinely stirred'.[23] James wrote to the Electors of Saxony and Brandenburg, the Duke of Württemberg, the Landgrave of Hesse, and other princes of Brandenburg to secure their support against the electoral transfer.[24] Furthermore, it seemed that the English monarchy would finally adopt the Palatine policy of *pacem sub clypeo* and use military power to force the Habsburgs to alter their policies toward Frederick and the Palatinate. Behind Charles and Buckingham gathered a 'Patriot' coalition that wanted a war to restore Frederick V and Elizabeth to their Palatine inheritance. Frederick knew about the 'good Patriots in England' and their desires, and he ordered Rusdorf to support their interests with the King.[25] Because the 'Patriots' managed to work with Parliament, this group was able to displace the 'Spanish' faction that had been favored at the English court for so many years.[26]

This transition, however, did not occur smoothly, and in the end it did not bring the desired results. After King James invited Parliament to discuss his foreign policy, the Lords and Commons advised him to break off negotiations for the Anglo-Spanish match and the restitution of the

Palatinate, but they would not grant him funds for a war until he declared one. The Commons wanted a war against Spain for the sake of Protestantism, but James wanted merely to restore the Elector Palatine and avoid direct conflict with Spain in doing so. Charles and Buckingham moved the King to terminate the talks, but not all diplomatic relations, with Spain, and they encouraged the Commons to pass the subsidy bill. The Prince and the Duke also began work on an alliance with the Dutch Republic and arranged to hire Count Mansfeld to lead an Anglo-French expedition to the Palatinate.[27] But affairs only progressed hesitantly because of James' reluctance to declare war against Spain. Delays annoyed and depressed the Dutch emissaries who were working on the proposed alliance. 'It seems', said Rusdorf in April, 'that the English advance one step and go three backwards, seeing that they are not so inflamed anymore to declare war against the Spaniards'.[28] Because there were no preparations as yet for war, and the campaign season was just around the corner, it was unlikely that 1624 would see much done for the recovery of the Palatinate. Rusdorf explained, 'The King would not risk his state by declaring war, being unprovided and unprepared'.[29] James would not commit to war against Spain, that is, without French support.

Count Mansfeld, who had disbanded his army in January 1624, traveled between France and England to settle terms for a joint expedition against the Habsburgs. In Paris he received a guarantee of French subsidies for a new army, if England also provided contributions, and thereafter he went to England.[30] King James and Prince Charles received Mansfeld honorably, making him a Knight of the Garter and lodging him at the Prince's court, in the quarters that had been prepared for the Infanta María, a gesture meant to anger the Spanish ambassador. Charles publicly displayed his esteem for Mansfeld, and entertained him liberally and courteously, making him an attraction for the many people of high and low social standing who came to see him.[31] On the day he arrived, James reaffirmed his intention to recover the Palatinate by military means. For such a campaign, Mansfeld agreed to accept 10,000 infantry, 3,000 cavalry, six cannon, and £20,000 per month, but James insisted that the King of France provide a force of equal strength.[32] He also bid the Count not to attack the lands of the King of Spain, the Infanta Isabella, or their allies.[33] Mansfeld warned James, however, that 'the King of France would do nothing, if [James], as the most interested party, did not begin first and that in fact'.[34] Mansfeld soon departed for Paris to complete the arrangements for the expedition, and Charles' own carriage took the Count to Dover.[35] Afterwards James broadcast that he had commissioned Mansfeld to lead an expedition for 'the advancement of common liberty and principally for the recovery of the Palatinate'.[36] Rusdorf, however, invested no hope in these plans. 'This year', he told Frederick, 'will be lost like the others, and even the Count of Mansfeld is of the opinion that nothing significant will happen this year'.[37]

The month of May revealed the lack of unity behind King James' call for a war on Frederick's behalf. In early May the court was in turmoil over Spanish rumors that Buckingham was plotting James' deposition in favor of Charles.[38] Then a showdown between Buckingham and Lord Treasurer Middlesex unsettled the royal government. And finally, when the subsidy bill was finished in late May, it provided a fraction of what was needed to restore the Palatinate by force, and the bill's text did not even mention that goal. Instead the money was supposed to support the defense of England, the security of Ireland, assistance for the United Provinces, and the mobilization of the royal navy.[39] The alliance concluded with the Dutch turned out to be only for mutual defense, and responses from Christian IV and the Elector of Saxony to James' call for support brought more disappointment than satisfaction. No money was forthcoming for Bethlen Gábor because of inadequate assurance of its use or effectiveness.[40] After James signed the subsidy bill, making his displeasure fully known, Parliament issued him a list of grievances. In indignation he prorogued Parliament until November.

Frederick, meanwhile, did all he could to exploit the changing political situation in England, though his participation was not directly solicited. In the spring and summer of 1624 he recruited English support for a bid to obtain a company of cavalry from the French crown as a present for the baptism of his latest son, who had been born in August 1623 and christened 'Louis' (Ludwig) in honor of the King of France.[41] In June, when Frederick heard that four ships from Dunkirk had been seized on the English coast, he asked that they be turned over to him as compensation for the damage that Spain had wrought on his land.[42] Out of caution he ordered Rusdorf not to consult with the Prince directly to the extent that the King could take offense, and he should not insist that the English use Frederick's royal Bohemian titles in official declarations that concerned him.[43] After the conclusion of Mansfeld's negotiations, Frederick sent Rusdorf special credentials to partake in discussions for the restoration of the Palatinate, though the King had not requested Palatine participation.[44] Frederick noted that it was 'not a little odd' that no one had asked his opinion or advice in an affair that was practically identical to his interests.[45]

In the summer of 1624, James' actions showed nonetheless that he was serious about recovering the Palatinate, but that he would not lead his nation into war unaccompanied. Charles and Buckingham worked on Mansfeld's expedition and on an offensive and defensive marriage alliance with France while the campaign season ran its course. A defensive alliance was sealed with the Dutch Republic, whereby England would send and support 6,000 soldiers in Dutch service, intended to benefit the fortunes of the Elector Palatine.[46] Meanwhile Isaac Wake departed on his embassy to Italy, and Sir Robert Anstruther and Sir James Spens traveled to the Kings of Denmark and Sweden with strong requests from James to obtain their assistance in Frederick's restoration. James also wrote again to the Elector of Saxony, this time with more force. In July he assured his son-in-law that the principal goal of his military levies and his negotiations was, as it had always been, Frederick's restoration.[47]

At the same time, however, James refused to correspond with Bethlen Gábor or to send letters of reprisal to Spain. Frankenthal received no aid, and on one occasion, Secretary Conway met Rusdorf's appeal on the town's behalf with an exasperated outburst. 'What, he [said], do you want us to do about it? This town will cost the King more than it is worth!'[48] Only three months remained before the expiration of the cease-fire stipulated in the treaty of sequestration. Thereafter, because no general peace had been established, the town could be lawfully exposed to plunder and destruction by the Spanish troops that occupied it. Moreover, when Mansfeld's emissary, Captain Weis, came to obtain a guarantee for the Count's commission, Charles said that Mansfeld had to be patient while negotiations for a French match and alliance were underway.[49] Captain Weis waited till early August and then, having accomplished nothing, returned to the continent.[50] Later that month, Frederick saw that there would in fact be no military campaign on his behalf in that year. The King of France gave nothing to Mansfeld as the Palatines had hoped. 'His commission', Rusdorf reported, 'is going up in smoke'.[51] Secretary Conway said that James could not raise an army to go on campaign this year because of the lack of time and money.[52]

The Quest for an Alliance

The need for a firm alliance was paramount. None of Frederick's potential allies, acting alone, could hope to challenge effectively the Habsburgs and their supporters. Only a combination of forces fighting on multiple fronts could hope to bring Ferdinand to accept that peace in the Empire was contingent upon Frederick's restoration. The appearance that neither England nor France would put armies in the field in 1624 made Frederick fear that the Emperor would solidify his currently advantageous position in the Empire. He heard that Ferdinand planned to obtain a general resolution of the Imperial diet (*Reichsabschied*) to confirm the transfer of the

Palatine electorate to Duke Maximilian. This measure would have ratified the transfer in the name of the whole Empire, and thereafter all complaints against its constitutionality would be redundant.

Preventing a ratification was a daunting project. Recently the Elector of Mainz had thrown his full support behind the transfer and tried to persuade the Elector of Saxony, who had objected in 1623, to shift his inclinations. And since the rupture of the Anglo-Spanish marriage negotiations, the Spanish ambassadors at the Imperial court would probably not intercede on Frederick's behalf. Moreover, the Palatine suspected that the Emperor was going to try to gather support for a war against the Dutch.[53] Though the best way to disrupt the diet would be to send an army into Germany, Frederick hoped that James would divert the proceedings by procuring an extension of the sequestration treaty or some other measure to stay the Emperor's hand. Frederick appealed to James

for the sake of his children, his honor, reputation, and promise ... because we have followed His Majesty's will and strong threats out of dutiful and filial respect not only in the point of the said sequestration, but also in all other impositions applied to us, which has, as it were, bound our hands and feet and made the business so burdensome.[54]

According to Frederick, his father-in-law was obligated to take some measure to prevent the Emperor from destroying the Palatine dynasty in the Empire entirely.

Frederick's arguments for Anglo-French intervention mainly referred to the Imperial constitution. He asked James to dispatch an army into the Empire with Mansfeld at its head, and added that the King would win great glory by aiding his children, 'who have been dispossessed so unjustly of all that belongs to them irrefutably by virtue of the Golden Bull and the fundamental law of the Empire'.[55] Frederick was certain that James, joined with Louis XIII, could procure a complete restitution of the Palatinate, preserve German liberty, and rid the Empire of Spanish forces. Over the following months, he instructed Rusdorf to reiterate this argument and request to James I.[56]

The English responded coolly to Palatine constitutional arguments for intervention. They had to weigh a military intervention against the concerns of English domestic and international interests. James said that he would wait to act till he heard from Denmark and France.[57] His aim, for the time being, was to extend Frankenthal's sequestration and obtain neutrality for the town through negotiations. Conway recognized that the upcoming Imperial diet was set against Frederick, but the secretary was sure that its resolutions could be altered when an English army would eventually enter Germany. Conway declared categorically that the 'fundamental laws and constitutions were not at all adamantine, that one could always abolish them and have them revoked; in the same way that experience had amply shown'.[58] Rusdorf, however, decried this view: 'He does not understand these laws at all. He has always been of the opinion that arms will do it, and words, letters, and embassies not at all. The Prince and the Duke of Buckingham will second him in this'.[59] Conway also told Rusdorf bluntly 'that England had no other interest in Germany apart from the Palatinate, it does not matter to them whether all Germany is set in flames, provided that they might have the Palatinate'.[60] It was necessary for England, Conway said, because 'if we lose the Palatinate first, next we will lose the Low Countries, then Ireland, and finally ourselves'.[61]

Throughout the autumn of 1624 Frederick tried to harness the various motions in favor of war on his behalf. Despite the lateness of the campaigning season, he continued to apply pressure in England for the execution of Mansfeld's commission, especially for the delivery of the monthly payments that had been allotted to the Count.[62] In October Frederick suddenly made a trip to Berlin, presumably to bolster the new resolve of his brother-in-law, Elector Georg Wilhelm, to abandon his neutrality and to join the Palatine cause. In the summer the Elector had dispatched his adviser, Christian von Bellin, to Denmark, Sweden, the United Provinces, and France to add Brandenburg's weight to the alliance plans.[63] Though the content of political discussions during Frederick's visit is not known, their outcome did not entail immediate substantive assistance for Mansfeld's expedition.[64] When he returned to The Hague in November, he was vexed to find that few or none of the promised subsidies had reached the Count, and he asked instead that they be sent to him, because, as he said, 'we would like to try our luck with it'.[65]

Indeed it appeared that the King of England wanted to hinder the expedition, despite the fact that Louis XIII had agreed to give Mansfeld six months' pay. James altered the commission so that the Count was not allowed to harm either the land or the people under the King of Spain or the Infanta Isabella. This codicil appalled Frederick. The restriction made no sense to him, given the fact that Spanish forces had been the first to attack Palatine lands and people, and he feared that James' alteration would lead to a change in the French commission for Mansfeld.[66] Frederick decided to allow the Count to use the cannon that he had left in Sedan in the summer of 1622, provided that Mansfeld paid for it.[67] He no longer trusted Mansfeld, knowing from experience that he would follow his own interest over that of his current employer.[68] At the time Mansfeld was in communication with the towns of Zürich and Bern, perhaps offering them his services, because it still was not clear to him whether he would receive any forces from England or France and, if so, what the joint commission would be.[69]

Diplomatic efforts to establish an alliance were pursued with greater energy than the military campaign to wrest the Palatinate from Spanish and Bavarian hands. As usual King James was more supportive of the former than the latter. In September he wrote to the Lower Saxon Circle, the town of Emden, and the Count of East Friesland to procure aid for Mansfeld. The King dispatched ambassadors to Denmark, Sweden, France, Savoy, Venice, and the Netherlands to enlist support for his efforts to recover the Palatinate. Frederick established contacts with each of these ambassadors, and he used England's mobilization to enhance his information of affairs and to bolster his own diplomatic efforts to recruit other powers with interests in an anti-Habsburg war.[70] Frederick also tried to send special letters of recommendation with the Earl of Carlisle on his mission to France, and special thanks and promises of future rewards were promised to the French ambassador to England for his pains on behalf of the Palatine cause.[71] Frederick established contacts with Sir James Spens, who led an embassy to Sweden, and with Isaac Wake, the English ambassador dispatched in 1624 to Savoy and Venice.[72] For the Palatines the most important of these English embassies was to northern Germany and Denmark by Sir Robert Anstruther, who was a confidant of Rusdorf.

Anstruther's embassy marked the change in the neutrality of the northern Protestant princes toward the Palatine crisis. His mission was to procure military support from the King of Denmark and the greater northern German Protestant princes for England's war to recover the Palatinate. In Anstruther's instructions there was no mention of a Protestant alliance against Catholic aggression; the goal of the campaign was 'the peace of christendome, the particular preservation of States and the politique maintayning of every Prince and state in their own souveraynitie: leaving the worke of faith to God, the onely lord of that kingdome'.[73] Anstruther's first stop had been The Hague, where he had met with Frederick and had discussed the goals of the embassy. In Denmark Anstruther had found Christian IV 'well affected, yet very circumspect', because of his dubiousness about Mansfeld. Immediately after Anstruther had left, Christian had issued calls for Frederick's full restitution and embarked on an 'unusually positive, even belligerent' correspondence with other Protestant princes.[74] Though the Danes supplied no military assistance in 1624, they would in the years thereafter. Anstruther had had similar success in Berlin, where Elector Georg Wilhelm had given his full agreement to the project and had dispatched his adviser, Christian von Bellin, to Copenhagen, Stockholm, The Hague, London, and Paris to add Brandenburg's voice to the calls for a pro-

Palatine, anti-Habsburg alliance.[75] The Elector of Saxony, however, who had recently recognized the Duke of Bavaria as the legitimate holder of the Palatine electorate, had refused to partake in another attempt to plunge Germany back into war.[76]

Most favorable was the news that Sir James Spens brought on his return from Sweden in December 1624. He stopped in The Hague and reported that King Gustavus Adolphus was favorably inclined toward the Palatine cause.[77] What the King really wanted was an anti-Habsburg alliance that encompassed France, Venice, and Savoy, as well as Protestant powers, to bolster his war against Poland. He had spoken about mounting and leading an army of 50,000 into Germany, mainly paid for by his allies. It was clear, however, that the Swedish plans hardly included the restitution of the Palatinate.[78] At about the same time Christian von Bellin arrived in The Hague, bringing statements of support from Georg Wilhelm. Frederick instructed Rusdorf to assist both Spens and Bellin in England.[79]

With such reports Frederick probably looked to the future with perhaps a hint of contentment, certainly more so than in recent years. In the winter of 1624–25 there was no serious attempt afoot to forge a peace settlement, and Frederick heard choruses of voices across Europe and Scandinavia in support of a grand military alliance in his favor. At the same time, however, Mansfeld's expedition accomplished none of its goals. Despite the many delays and hindrances, the campaign did actually get underway, but its inauspicious start presaged an ignominious end. Frederick had prayed, 'God give him constancy and good resolve', but that did not help the Count and his new army.[80] Because too few volunteers joined, recruiters turned to impressment, and when the force made its way to Dover, it plundered and pillaged the local inhabitants mercilessly. There were already so many deaths and desertions among the soldiery that the Privy Council ordered another 2,000 to be gathered. In January 1625, 3,000 German soldiers arrived from the cities of the Hanseatic league, and Christian of Halberstadt came to London to join the expedition – he planned to take over the command of the cavalry divisions from France – but the force could not depart as there was nowhere to send it. King James adamantly refused to permit a landing in the Spanish Netherlands, and at the last moment the French King retracted his permission for the army to land in France and cross French territory toward the Palatinate. James then forbade them from raising the Spanish siege at the town of Breda, despite Frederick's special plea to the contrary.[81] In February Mansfeld's army finally embarked for Zeeland, where they landed on a small island and began their training. But the lack of money and adequate shelter and the rampant spread of disease quickly decimated the army. By the end of March Halberstadt declared the force too weak to campaign in Germany.[82]

Days later, King James I himself succumbed to a final attack of disease, and with him fell the greatest barrier to war against the Habsburgs on behalf of the Palatinate.

James had been committed to restricting England's military activity to an absolute minimum, because he had been determined to avoid the inevitable domestic financial and political crisis that would have accompanied a full-scale war. He had not trusted his allies to provide sufficient support, and he had been wary of having to face the military might of Spain alone. His death was a relief to Frederick. When the Palatine wrote of his sorrow, he added immediately, 'nothing consoles us more than the new King's good affection toward us and the common cause'.[83] After only a couple of months, he would express his wish that James had been as heroic as his son, then, Frederick said, 'we would certainly never have come into this awful situation'.[84]

James' removal from the English throne did not make up for the other glaring weaknesses in the effort to form and coordinate an international alliance. The quiet withering of Mansfeld's destitute army must have shown Frederick that all plans, alliances, and resolutions would amount to nothing if men and money did not stand behind them, though in Mansfeld's case it was easy to blame the failure on James I for not supplying sufficient funds and for restricting the targets to non-Habsburgs. The main challenge was to transform diplomatic correspondence into armed action, despite the diversity of allies' interests and the scope of their potential distractions. Gustavus Adolphus' first interest at that time was besting the King of Poland; the restoration of the Palatinate was a mere argument for recruiting international assistance in the name of an anti-Habsburg alliance. Bethlen Gábor was reliant on the support of his Turkish liege, who was now engaged in an extended war with Persia. Fighting for Frederick, whether as dispossessed King of Bohemia or Elector Palatine, had previously provided Gábor with a useful justification for his repeated incursions into the Empire, but confessional sympathy – Gábor, like Frederick, was Calvinist – had apparently ended whenever the Emperor offered favorable terms for peace. The Dutch were more concerned with their old enemies, the Spanish, who had begun a siege at Breda in July 1624. The Republic simply could not afford to send a large force to the Palatinate on its own, but a significant invasion of that territory would have diverted the Spanish forces.[85]

The French, too, despite their interest, were easily diverted from making an effective assault on the Palatinate. France could have been Frederick's mightiest and most committed supporter against the Spanish and Austrian Habsburgs. In February 1624 the Marquis of La Vieuville, a notorious enemy of the Habsburgs, had become the minister of French foreign policy, and in April 1624 Armand-Jean du Plessis, Cardinal Richelieu, had joined the royal council of Louis XIII. That summer the French had signed the Treaty of Compiègne with the Dutch Republic and had loaned them money for their continuance of the war with Spain. In addition, France had revived her alliance with Savoy and Venice.[86] In August, Richelieu had replaced La Vieuville, and French forces had occupied the Valtelline. Frederick had argued that France should assist him for reasons of state and honor. The francophone Palatine Wittelsbach dynasty had rendered significant military and financial assistance on more than one occasion to Kings Henry II and IV, a fact which, Frederick had argued, was sufficient for the monarchs of France and Bohemia 'to contract a perpetual alliance between them'.[87] He had called on Louis XIII to join the drive to restore the Palatinate and the public peace.[88] French ambassadors had urged the Palatines to join their interests to those of France, so 'that [they] might not be the authors or drivers of a war of religion'.[89]

Obstacles, however, soon outnumbered and overpowered the Franco-Palatine connection. The French had favored the Palatine-Bavarian marriage settlement and had been involved in an extensive period of negotiations with the Bavarian Wittelsbachs.[90] The result was that France would prefer neither Maximilian nor Frederick. When the treaty for the Anglo-French match had been completed in December 1624, it did not include a provision for the restitution of the Palatinate.[91] Nonetheless, in the first months of 1625 Louis XIII promised to pay one million livres for two years to support campaigns by Mansfeld and Gustavus Adolphus for restoration of peace in Germany.[92] A new Huguenot revolt, however, soon made even indirect assistance for the dispossessed Elector Palatine impossible. France would do no more for the Palatinate than lay within her own interests.

Throughout this time Frederick's primary goal had been the recovery of his former status in the Empire, which he presented as a constitutional cause imbued with dynastic and religious significance. For this end he had fully supported any project that was directed against the Habsburgs primarily as well as the Catholic League, under Bavarian leadership. The predominantly anti-Habsburg intentions of France and Sweden had won his complete approval. Whatever their inclinations had been for the Palatinate, an attack on Habsburg lands would have increased the likelihood of their withdrawing troops from Frederick's territories. After March 1625 he could count on some form of assistance from England for a military effort restricted to the Palatinate alone, to which might be added the assistance of the Lower Saxon Circle, the King of Denmark, and the Elector of Brandenburg. For Frederick, international alliances against his enemies were the only means he had to procure his restoration, despite the many inherent difficulties. And after the death of James I, the prince who had tried more than any to force Frederick to accept a peace treaty without a complete restitution, the road to such an alliance lay open.

Annus Mirabilis, 1625

The year 1625 ushered in the greatest show of support for Frederick's cause during his lifetime, so great in fact, that he could even entertain hopes of returning to Bohemia.[93] By the end of the year an international alliance would devote itself to his restitution, and soon afterwards, the armies of the King of Denmark would enter Germany to face down those of the Catholic League and the Emperor. As in 1624, Frederick for the most part did not issue calls for an international Protestant alliance to fight for Protestantism in the Empire, and instead he sought an alliance irrespective of confession to attack his oppressors. His goal was to unite as many enemies of the Habsburgs as possible behind the goal of his own restitution. Ironically, this effort would result in an alliance of Protestant powers exclusively, which would then achieve nothing for Frederick because of the members' own fractiousness.

As spring approached, the Palatine court-in-exile was full of enthusiasm for military endeavors against their enemies. This belligerent tone was to remain the dominant voice in The Hague for the next several years. With the arrival of the English and French troops under Mansfeld, and at the news of further French, English, Danish, Swedish, German, and Transylvanian mobilizations, an exhilarated Camerarius reported, 'In short, a nearly universal war is going to take place this year in all Germany and Italy'.[94] In March Savoy, bolstered by France, invaded Genoa, an ally of Spain and an important communication link to the Empire.[95] Later in that month Frederick wrote to Bethlen Gábor and tried to incite him to arms again.[96] The likelihood that Gábor would indeed join the Palatine cause had increased by his marriage to Princess Katherine, sister of the Elector of Brandenburg, which made Bethlen a brother-in-law of Gustavus Adolphus. In the United Provinces, the Prince of Orange and members of the Estates General wanted to correspond with the Kings of Denmark and Sweden about their military plans, and Frederick saw a chance for a common Protestant coalition.[97] The King of Sweden soon offered to invade Silesia on Frederick's behalf.[98] In April 1625 the princes of the Lower Saxon Circle elected Christian IV as the commander of its military forces (*Kreisoberst*) and began to gather an army to drive Tilly's out of the Circle.[99]

Still there was cause for worry. In February the Palatine court had heard that the King of Poland had once again sent bands of Cossacks into the

Empire to attack Protestant estates, presumably in the Lower Saxon Circle, to benefit the Habsburg cause.[100] Frederick feared that his enemies would manage to frustrate his allies' efforts and then turn the full weight of the war against the United Provinces. The state of Mansfeld's army did not increase the feeling of security. Without good instructions and supplies, Frederick warned, this force 'might be completely ruined in a short time'.[101]

James' death at the end of March released the Palatines at once from all prior restrictions, but it also caused new delays. Perhaps in anticipation of the new reign, Frederick had ordered Rusdorf to keep the English monarchy and Parliament in close contact with Denmark and Sweden, so that the three kingdoms might one day forge an alliance.[102] When the news of James' passing arrived in April, Frederick was relieved to note, 'Now Mansfeld has a free hand once again'.[103] But Frederick recognized that the Count's withered army was in no shape to accomplish anything substantive, and the ceremonial conventions for ushering in the new reign would only postpone the preparations for further war.[104] Nonetheless, James' death unleashed a flurry of unrestrained Palatine politicking among influential members of the English government on behalf of a war against Spain and the Emperor for Frederick's restoration. Letters in favor of the Palatine cause were sent to Buckingham, Secretary Conway, the Archbishop of Canterbury, the Chancellor of the Exchequer, the Lord Treasurer, the Bishop of Lincoln, the Lord Privy Seal, Sir Richard Weston, and Viscount Mandeville.[105] In one week's time the Palatine-government in exile produced a new official mission statement, which Rusdorf received soon afterwards.[106]

After James' death Frederick was able openly to call for a war against the entire Habsburg dynasty, including both the Spanish and the Austrian branches, and their supporters. Since 1619 the contours of Frederick's pleas for an alliance had changed according to the needs of the times. His appeals in favor of the Protestant cause during the first years of the 1620s had failed miserably, and James I had repeatedly condemned Frederick for trying to incite a 'war of religion' in Christendom. Following his official divestiture in 1623, the failure of the Anglo-Spanish match, and the beginning of negotiations for the Anglo-French match, Frederick's message had rapidly lost much of its confessional overtones and had taken on a predominantly constitutional character. Reasons for his restitution lay primarily in the need to protect the rights and privileges of the Imperial electors and princes, as stipulated in the Golden Bull and the Imperial capitulations, from the insidious corruption supposedly perpetrated by Emperor Ferdinand II. Nonetheless, Frederick had continued to refer to common confessional interests where they were to be found between potential allies. Just before he received news of James' passing, Frederick had ordered Rusdorf to work toward an alliance between England, Denmark, and Sweden, because a bond between these three Protestant kingdoms and a group of German Protestant princes would greatly impress upon all of Germany the importance of Frederick's restoration to his former status in the constitution of the Empire.[107]

Nonetheless, from April to December 1625 the predominant Palatine goal was to assemble a coalition of all enemies of the Habsburgs, irrespective of confession, and to unify them behind the Palatine cause, despite their diverse individual interests.[108] At the core of the alliance would be the three main Protestant kingdoms of England, Denmark, and Sweden, supported by the Dutch Republic and various Protestant principalities of northern Germany, not failing to include France, Savoy, and the Venetian Republic too if possible, and Bethlen Gábor. The goal of the coalition was to wage a dynastic, not a religious, war for a constitutional end. Members were to fight the Habsburgs on all sides in order to effect Frederick's restoration to his former place in the Empire which, it was claimed, would put a stop to Habsburg designs for a universal monarchy over the Empire and Europe and to save traditional, German constitutional liberties. 'The principal goal', wrote Frederick, 'is to halt the ambitious designs of Austria and Spain, and to reconcile the affairs of Germany in their entirety, with the restitution of the Palatinate and of that which it depends on.'[109] He took it upon himself and his advisers to coordinate the project. That he continued to refer to himself as the King of Bohemia indicates his intention to entail Bohemia as well as the Palatinate in his restitution, but he was wise not to press this issue, because it involved a very different and more doubtful set of constitutional arguments and precepts. At any rate he wanted to leave The Hague as soon as possible and join an army in the field 'to serve the fatherland and the common cause', but he would not do so unless he could accompany an army that was well paid and well disciplined.[110] Otherwise, he said, he would earn 'more disgrace as honor from it'.[111]

Frederick quickly pressured the new King of England for assistance. He also appointed the Duke of Buckingham the general of Palatine armies and admiral of the navies acting in his name against Habsburgs.[112] He declared that England's and France's sudden alterations in the military strategy late in 1624 and their continued irresolution were weakening Danish and Swedish resolve. He reminded Charles I how damaging the wretched suffering of the Mansfeld's army was to English honor, but it was still worse for the honor of the King of Bohemia, because that army was mobilized for service in his name. Frederick did not want to take the blame for its misdeeds when he lacked the means to pay the soldiers properly, and when Mansfeld had not bothered to communicate with him.[113] Nevertheless, Frederick professed his total confidence in the new King and promised his compliance, but not his obedience, in Charles' deeds and negotiations. Frederick still said that he would not consent to any arrangement that derogated his conscience, honor, or posterity.[114]

In the summer of 1625 focus was shifted to the Lower Saxon Circle, where the King of Denmark was aiming to drive out Tilly's occupying army. Christian IV needed substantive financial and military assistance, and Frederick wanted potential coalition members to grant this aid before the alliance was formally sealed.[115] Time was a crucial factor, because after the Imperial diet planned for 1624 had not actually convened, the Emperor had called for a diet of deputies (*Deputationstag*) to meet in Ulm in August 1625. Though the stated purpose of the diet was to restore the common peace, Frederick denied that the Emperor actually wanted peace at all. The real purpose of the Diet, he argued, was to obtain a general consent for the transfer of the Palatine electorate to Duke Maximilian and ratify the Emperor's other unconstitutional practices against the rightful Elector Palatine.[116] The electoral transfer was a violation of the Golden Bull, 'which', Frederick declared, 'as a fundamental constitution neither should nor can be changed without the participation and approval of all Estates of the Empire'.[117] The Emperor's intention was 'to strengthen more and more the party of Austria, Spain, and the League for the oppression of German liberty'.[118] Frederick insisted, as ever, that he stood for peace.

> As for the King of Bohemia, as he has always protested, he also still protests sincerely that he thirsts only for peace, on the condition that it is founded not on the ruin and extirpation (such is the design of the opposing party) but on just and honest conditions, assured of his complete restitution, and of a uniform peace throughout all Germany, offering in this case everything that will not be contrary to his conscience, honor, to the fundamental laws and liberty of the Empire.[119]

He concluded with a declaration that the force of arms alone could restore the peace, liberty, justice, and equilibrium in the Holy Roman Empire.

At the same time Frederick requested that English, Danish, French, and German agents attend the diet of deputies and protest on his behalf, despite the fact that he was pursuing a resumption of war in northern Germany to disrupt it altogether.[120] Nonetheless he insisted that he was not opposed to negotiations in principle, just so long as they did not prevent his allies from using their arms. 'We would like to wish however', Frederick wrote, 'that the affairs could be brought to a good treaty, that arms continue, that negotiating be "under the shield", and our opponents could be turned to another and better way'.[121] Anstruther was duly instructed to attend the diet and bring along an emissary from Denmark for the same purpose.[122]

Just as Frederick was gathering his anti-Habsburg coalition and seeking for ways to disrupt the diet of deputies, Ferdinand II consented to partake in a new intercession, this time by Duke Johann Friedrich of Württemberg and Duke Charles of Lorraine, for negotiating a settlement to the Palatine crisis. In April the Emperor had informed these Dukes that he and Philip IV would consent to giving Frederick the portions of the Lower Palatinate then occupied by Spain, if he merely refrained from hostilities and submitted without opposition.[123] Because the electoral dignity had been bestowed on Maximilian, it could not be returned to the Palatine until the Duke's death. The Palatine restoration then under discussion would have been partial at best. The Dukes of Württemberg and Lorraine tried to persuade Frederick to abandon his current belligerent projects and come to terms for the sake of peace.[124] In responding to their invitations, he included lengthy arguments about the illegality and unconstitutionality of the Emperor's proceedings, from the Imperial ban to the impending diet of deputies. He tried to convince them of his own righteousness and the Emperor's desire to smother Germany in war and ruin.[125]

Württemberg's and Lorraine's intercession would continue throughout the next year, and though the correspondence between Frederick and Ferdinand was more accusatory than conciliatory in tone, it gave them a chance to engage in some form of dialogue and to express their mutual desires for peace above all. The two mediating Dukes acted as conduits for both sides rather than as proponents of either. The Duke of Württemberg feared that if they represented Frederick's case to strongly to the Emperor, their loyalty might become suspect. Lorraine despaired from the beginning that the mediation would go nowhere, because the Emperor demanded Frederick's unconditional submission and Frederick his unconditional restitution.[126] Because the combatants could not come anywhere near an agreement about the justice of their actions, war continued to ravage Germany and to intensify the suffering of the populace on an even greater scale than before.

The Hague Alliance

The course of events till the end of 1625 exposed the fissures running through Palatine plans for a grand anti-Habsburg alliance. Catholic powers rapidly fell out of the equation. France failed to assist Savoy against the Spanish and would soon abandon the Valtelline. After James' death

Venice quickly backed out of giving any money to Mansfeld, despite all previous arrangements, because it was clear that he would not contribute to the goals of the League of Lyons. Venice expressed its sympathy for Charles I and Frederick, but because of the prevailing threats to its own security, a gift of merely 200 Scudi was offered to Frederick's agent, Heinrich von Theiknau.[127] Nevertheless not every basis for hope vanished. In July Frederick heard that a French army 21,000 strong was approaching the German border, and he hoped that it would provide a diversion for the Habsburgs to the advantage of the King of Denmark.[128]

Protestants did not contribute much more than the Catholics. Among those Protestant powers that desired Frederick's restitution, a diversity of military interests kept them from unifying. In the summer of 1625 Gustavus Adolphus swept over Livonia and invaded Polish Prussia, and because of threats from the King of Poland, the Elector of Brandenburg quickly resumed his previous neutrality.[129] Mansfeld's army remained for a time in the Netherlands, where its numbers ebbed and flowed with the tides of desertions and arrivals of new recruits. That army seemed to be inherently problematic. Not trusting its leader, Frederick wanted it to be added to the Danish and German armies under Christian IV, because a single army was more secure than disjointed entities operating in different regions.[130] The Estates General, meanwhile, wanted to use it to defend Breda, but the town fell into Spanish hands in June 1625.[131]

The Dutch Republic seemed to be improving its inclinations towards Frederick and his cause, though little material support was forthcoming. By September the United Provinces would sign the Treaty of Southampton, an offensive and defensive alliance with England against the Habsburgs, the goal of which was to free the Netherlands from Spain and restore the Palatinate.[132] Frederick's relations with the Princes of Orange had usually been better than those with the Estates General, and, after the death of Maurits in April 1625, the new Stadholder, his brother, Frederik Hendrik, was an even closer connection. He had attended Frederick's and Elizabeth's wedding in London in 1613 and was the godfather of their first child. Frederik Hendrik married one of Elizabeth's ladies-in-waiting, Amalia von Solms, daughter of Frederick's deceased courtier, Johann Albrecht von Solms, and the Winter King and Queen had taken part in the ceremony of the marriage.[133] Perhaps because of the Stadholder's influence, the Estates General put another house at the disposal of Frederick's court.[134] For the time, however, little else was forthcoming.

The new King of England, Charles I, and his favorite, the Duke of Buckingham, were the most active supporters of a war against the Habsburgs on behalf of the common cause. Shortly after Charles' accession, he had sent Sir Henry Vane Sr. to The Hague to assure the Palatine pair that England would seek their restitution through force of arms. Nonetheless, Charles did not address the two with their royal, Bohemian titles, which reflected the limitations of his intended support. He had also dispatched a manifesto to the princes and estates of the Empire, declaring his intention to restore the Palatinate and thereby protect the fundamental law of the Empire, which had been jeopardized by the incursion of Catholic powers in the Palatinate. Emperor Ferdinand II and the King of Poland had received similar declarations. In June Charles decided to grant Christian IV a monthly subsidy of £30,000, and Anstruther was soon sent to Denmark bearing £46,000.[135] Charles wrote to his sister and brother-in-law about his commitment to their restitution and his intent to dispatch a great fleet against Spain 'in [Frederick's] name and under his commissions'.[136] Later that summer the expedition was assigned three tasks: destroy Spanish shipping, secure a foothold in that country, and capture the annual fleet bringing precious metals from the Americas as it approached its destination. This mission was supposed to force the Spanish to sue for peace and procure the Palatine's restoration as a concession to England, but a critical shortage of money crippled the venture.[137]

Domestic political troubles hampered Charles I's military ambitions. His first Parliament did not give adequate funds for his naval campaign against Spain. A terrible outbreak of plague in London and Charles' concessions to Catholics as stipulated in the Anglo-French match engendered severe qualms in the House of Commons. The members were outraged that Buckingham had loaned ships to France that had then been used to besiege the Protestant rebels at La Rochelle.[138] The members were more interested in discussing religion and other matters than in granting the King supply, and so Charles, despite his desire to intensify the war effort against the Habsburgs, dissolved it after a mere twelve days.[139] Though Rusdorf had tried to persuade the King that an attack in Germany would have been of greater use to the Palatines than a raid on the Spanish south coast, the King stuck to his plan.[140] Buckingham managed to dispatch the fleet, which actually flew Frederick's battle standard, but it accomplished none of its goals and instead ended in a total fiasco at Cádiz.[141]

The one achievement of the year was an international conference that established The Hague Alliance, between England, Denmark, and the United Provinces, in December 1625, with the ostensible purpose of procuring Frederick's restitution.[142] As a sign of success for Palatine politics it was rather limited. It included less than half of the targeted allies, and no Catholic powers joined. Brandenburg did not take part, and the Swedish ambassador had died during his journey to The Hague. France and Venice were content to be merely informed about the proceedings rather than become full members.[143] During the process the Palatines were restricted to the sidelines. The Estates General prevented Frederick from contributing to the discussions, but Camerarius was allowed to observe them.[144]

Beyond the common cause, the three delegations for The Hague Alliance had conflicting agendas. The English wanted to be relieved of the £30,000 monthly subsidy to Christian IV, yet they tried to procure declarations of war from Denmark and the Dutch against Spain and the Emperor. The Danes naturally wanted continued financial assistance for Christian's campaign to restore peace in the Lower Saxon Circle without such declarations. The Dutch did not want to give Denmark any money at all.[145] Despite these differences discussions proceeded quickly, and in the end the delegations managed to agree to contain the Habsburgs, rescue German liberty, and, despite initial resistance from the Danish delegation, restore the Palatinate to Frederick V.[146] The Duke of Buckingham and the Earl of Holland agreed, against instructions, to continue to pay £30,000 per month to Christian IV, and the Dutch were supposed to contribute £5,000. In return Christian IV was to enlarge his army and execute the stated military objectives. Mansfeld's army was to be joined to the Danish.[147] Though Frederick's name did not appear in the treaty, the three powers agreed to settle no separate peace without incorporating him into the terms.[148]

The alliance came together to Frederick's advantage but not for his sake alone. Each power had its own reasons for joining, and the Palatine cause was the only common interest shared between them. Frederick's influence with England was useful for the Dutch, but the Estates General did not let either him or his advisers influence Dutch negotiations with England and Denmark.[149] England and Denmark used the Palatine cause to extract promises of support from each other. All three delegations quarreled about the order of the signatures on the official documents, and none was pleased with the outcome.[150]

Frederick, at least, was more than satisfied. He had hoped that the conference would procure aid for the Danish–Lower Saxon military campaign, which he saw as the only venture with a fighting chance to procure his restoration. The terms of the treaty mentioned his restoration not only to the Palatinate but to Bohemia as well, and copies of the treaty's text were provided for Frederick and sent to Venice and Brandenburg.[151] Furthermore, France, Sweden, Savoy, Venice, Bethlen Gábor, and various German princes were called to join.[152] Frederick had wanted the alliance to be broader in extent, to encompass campaigns by the French and Bethlen Gábor against the Habsburgs in Alsace and in the eastern regions of the Empire.[153] Frederick had also wanted the field of battle to be shifted onto his enemies' lands and for Sweden and Brandenburg to be included in the treaty's articles. He voiced his assurance 'that God would give his blessing' to the alliance and that it would give courage to many other Imperial princes and estates.[154] He declared, 'they will see the beginning of a revolution'.[155]

Despite the inauspicious beginnings it appeared for a time that The Hague Alliance would indeed expand, and that Frederick's affairs would improve. In January 1626 Frederick accepted an offer from the Marquis of Baden-Durlach to raise an army of 10,000 and attack the Habsburgs.[156] In the same month Bethlen Gábor invaded Moravia, and soon afterwards his offer to become a member of the alliance reached The Hague. Gábor guaranteed that the Turks would not ratify the recent peace treaty signed with the Emperor, because the Grand Vizier in Istanbul, Gábor boasted, 'does nothing without him'.[157] He requested that the members urge Sweden to bring Muscovy into the war against Poland, sending 50–60,000 Tartars if possible. Moreover, Gábor wanted RT40,000 per month to maintain an army of 8,000 foot and 12,000 horse, which he would then lead to Bohemia and Silesia, where he would join with Mansfeld and still more cavalry from Moldavia and Wallachia. He then guaranteed that Turkish armies would be sent against Styria, Carinthia, and Austria.[158] If even half of what Gábor promised had come to pass, it would have been well worth the RT40,000. Frederick responded enthusiastically and tried for months to persuade Charles I to take up the offer.[159] The Duke of Saxe-Weimar and the King of Denmark added their voices in favor, and the latter sent an ambassador to England to procure Charles' acceptance.[160]

Despite these developments, the alliance neither expanded nor accomplished what it had set out to do. Brandenburg did not join. In February 1626 Bellin reported, 'All that Brandenburg can do at this time is to favor the army of the King of Denmark and of Mansfeld in secret'.[161] The Elector was actually in Prussia, preparing his defenses against the King of Poland, and could do nothing for the Danish war effort. The Dutch agent in Hamburg, Gaspar van Vosbergen, and the Duke of Saxe-Weimar kept Frederick informed of the uneven course of the Danish military effort.[162] Attention naturally turned away from the subjugated Palatinate to the currently active theater of war, the Lower Saxon Circle.

The foremost concern of Christian IV was not the restoration of the Palatinate but the safety of the Lower Saxon Circle and the protection of Lutheran confession especially. He and the Circle had armed to drive Tilly and the League army out of the Circle, and the two forces had skirmished in Hesse during the summer of 1625. Tilly had pressed his advantage after he heard that Christian had nearly been killed when a parapet had collapsed under him and his horse. While Christian had recovered, Tilly had advanced, and the Lower Saxon army had retreated in confusion. While political disunity had impeded the Circle's defense efforts, the

Emperor's new army, led by the Bohemian mercenary, Albrecht von Wallenstein, had slowly born down on the Circle.

Throughout the autumn of 1625 the Circle had held its own, while Duke Johann Ernst of Saxe-Weimar had driven Tilly back, and Mansfeld and Halberstadt had joined their troops to Christian IV's. All efforts to negotiate a peace had failed when the Circle had demanded the departure of Tilly and Wallenstein, an indemnity for their damages, and a guarantee of their possession of ecclesiastical territories secularized after 1555. The Emperor had responded with a demand for the Circle's disarmament, an indemnity, and full recognition for the transfer of the Palatine electorate.[163] Agreement was impossible.

In 1626 the Imperial forces crushed Mansfeld's army in April at Dessau Bridge, and the Count led what was left of his army to Silesia and drew away Wallenstein. But on 26 August Tilly decisively defeated Christian at Lutter-am-Barenberg and broke the will of many of the Circle's princes to resist any further. Mansfeld would manage to join with Bethlen Gábor in Silesia and hold off Wallenstein, but news of the Danish defeat at Lutter and of a Turkish débâcle at Baghdad would lead Gábor to sue, once again, for peace.[164] In December Gábor would come to terms with the Emperor at Pressburg (Bratislava), receive renewed concessions from earlier treaties, and disband the army of Count Mansfeld, who had just succumbed to a lethal illness a few weeks beforehand.[165] Another year saw no progress regarding the Palatinate.

During 1626 Frederick relayed reports from the battlefield to England and facilitated communications between the Kings of England and Denmark, the Prince of Orange, and Count Mansfeld, but to no avail.[166] After the first subsidy to Denmark, England contributed next to nothing to the effort for the rest of the year. According to Rusdorf, Charles simply did not have the money to help Denmark, Mansfeld, or Bethlen Gábor. Charles' total debts to the Danish King reached £240,000 by May 1626, and all he could offer was some of the crown jewels, which proved nearly impossible to pawn.[167] Mansfeld was given some Scottish regiments, but no money was provided for their pay.[168] English ships, meanwhile, tried to blockade the Elbe against Spanish trade with the towns of the Hanse, which did little or no harm to Spain but incurred bitter resentment against the English in Hamburg.[169] In England the crisis with France over the Huguenot rebellion at La Rochelle had brought hatred for the Duke of Buckingham to a fever pitch, and Parliament would grant no money to the King as long as it was not allowed to impeach the Duke. During the attack on Buckingham, a servant of the Earl of Bristol avowed 'that his master could prove that by the misconduct of the Duke of Buckingham, the Palatinate had been lost and that he had also been the reason why its restitution had not ensued'.[170] Frederick, knowing all about the uproar, observed regretfully, 'The revulsion in the land against the Duke is [so] great [that it] hinders much good'.[171]

In 1626 England proved totally unable to resolve the Palatine crisis by force of arms. Secretary Conway told Rusdorf that the government could do nothing without money, and that Parliament had refused to give it, despite the gravity of the danger and the King's good inclinations.[172] After Christian's defeat at Lutter, Frederick's please to Charles to uphold the terms of The Hague Alliance became more desperate.[173] In addition Frederick complained that the pension that James had promised two years earlier to his grandson, Karl Ludwig, had still not been paid.[174] Frederick even forwarded to Charles the appeals for help from the townspeople of Frankenthal, despite the utter lack of funds.[175] Charles' council advised him to impose a forced loan for Christian IV, and it was decided that they would send four regiments already in service in the United Provinces to Denmark. But since no money was sent with them, they were to prove more a liability than a contribution to the war effort. Propositions for supporting Bethlen Gábor and the Marquis of Baden-Durlach came to nothing. Faced with a war against Spain, a crisis in France, and a parliament inimical to the royal favorite, Charles could no longer embrace the restitution of the Palatinate as a vital interest of state or religion. His safety, after all, did not depend on it. In September 1625 the Duke of Buckingham had said succinctly, 'the loss of Germany will not touch the king here'.[176]

The fundamental problem between members of The Hague Alliance was the lack of willingness to take the necessary steps to achieve the stated common goal. By April 1626 almost none of the princes of the Empire, including the King of Denmark, had declared against the Emperor, though they wanted to see Frederick's restitution.[177] This was of no assistance to Charles I, who sought help for his war against Spain. Christian IV, who was desperate for financial assistance, had sent emissaries to compel England to send the promised monthly subsidies, but they were not confident that the two kingdoms would unite.[178] In England Dutch and Danish emissaries were told that there was no reason why Charles should pay for the Danish forces when Christian IV still refused to declare himself against the King of Spain and the Emperor.[179] The grave difficulties in coordinating an international military effort proved insurmountable. Frederick had tried to provide a link between all movements against the Habsburgs in Europe. But connecting The Hague Alliance with the league of France, Savoy, and Venice, and working in Bethlen Gábor as well was an all but impossible task.[180]

The 'Catholic' Side

The Catholic powers involved in this struggle were only marginally more successful in uniting their aims than the Protestants. A conference in Brussels in May 1626 had achieved less unity than the meetings for The Hague Alliance. Emperor Ferdinand had wanted Spain and the League to take on the expense of the war against Denmark and the Lower Saxon Circle, but Spain had wanted assistance from the League and the Emperor against the United Provinces by both land and sea, strangling the rebellious republic into submission by cutting off its trade. Duke Maximilian had wanted Spanish help against Denmark and the Lower Saxon Circle, but he had opposed any German participation in a war against the Dutch. Spanish and Bavarian antagonism had ruined the negotiations. Maximilian had refused to countenance the Spanish demand that he withdraw entirely from the Lower Palatinate so that Spain could offer it as a condition for peace with England. The Infanta Isabella had agreed only to send some troops to Münster and Hesse, but she would not assist Tilly unless the League and the Emperor would attack the Dutch rebels. After the victory at Lutter, Maximilian had discontinued negotiations. No Catholic alliance had formed.[181]

For both the Spanish and the Austrian Habsburgs, the coming of the Danish-Lower Saxon war had been an unwelcome development, but they had been unable to make the necessary provisions to stop it. Emperor Ferdinand II had wanted to prevent the war from proliferating into northern Germany. Throughout the first half of 1625 he had been convinced that Christian IV and the Lower Saxon Circle had been arming merely for their own security, without an intent to induce new hostilities. In the summer of 1625, however, repeated clarion calls from Maximilian, Tilly, and a few anti-Danish princes of the Lower Saxon Circle had changed Ferdinand's mind, and then he had commissioned Wallenstein to raise an army. When Khevenhüller had proposed forging a pact between Spain, the Catholic League, and all other Catholic princes who cared to join, the Spanish had been dubious but had given their consent to take part in the conference at Brussels nonetheless.[182]

During the mid-1620s, Spain had had no desire to subdue all German Protestant princes and oppress them under a Habsburg tyranny as Frederick and his supporters claimed, but they had been forced to intervene in German affairs for the safety of Habsburg possessions and of the Catholic religion. During the unraveling of the Anglo-Spanish match, Spain had pressured the Emperor to make peace with the Elector Palatine before England declared war, because having concurrent engagements in the Low Countries, Germany, and with England was most undesirable.[183] Olivares had seen clearly that the unifying force of the war-like motions against the Habsburg dynasty was the Palatine crisis. At the same time the Spanish monarchy had been against Maximilian's possession of the Palatinate and also against the creation of an eighth electorate to solve the problem.[184] Olivares had favored a settlement through a Palatine-Imperial marriage treaty, and he had tried to persuade Khevenhüller and the papal nuncio to accept the deal. Olivares had suggested that Frederick make the requisite submission and hand over his two eldest sons in Spain, because a journey to Vienna was too dangerous for the Palatines. Naturally Frederick had refused.[185] On the other hand Spain had not been able to induce Ferdinand to turn against Maximilian as long as the League's armies were defending the former against rebel armies in Germany. Moreover, the Catholic spiritual electors had called on Philip IV to protect them in the face of English and Danish mobilizations on behalf of Frederick V.[186] The Spanish King and Council of State had agreed to help the Emperor militarily, in order to prevent France from intervening supposedly to restore peace in Germany, along with Frederick V, by force.[187]

As long as Spanish arms had been successful, there had been no reason to bow to pressure to relinquish the Palatinate. For Spain, 1625 had been a real *annus mirabilis.* Spanish forces had taken Breda, successfully blockaded river trade in Westphalia to the United Provinces, protected Genoa from France and Savoy, expelled the Dutch from Bahía in Brazil, and repulsed the Anglo-Dutch naval attack on Cádiz. Nonetheless, Spain had wanted nothing to do with a war with Denmark, so terms had been offered to Christian IV in the late summer of 1625, which included the restoration of the Palatinate. When the Emperor and the League joined the talks, agreement had foundered on this last point. Ferdinand would not discuss Frederick's restitution until Christian dissolved his forces, which he had refused to do, presumably until the restitution was first carried out.[188] Though negotiations had failed in March 1626, Spain had still not been drawn into that conflict, and, still better, in the same month, Spain and France had signed the Treaty of Monzón, whereby Louis XIII and Richelieu had turned their backs on The Hague Alliance altogether and had allowed Spain to recover the Valtelline. Despite Spanish victories, however, Spain had not joined the League and the Emperor in their war against Lower Saxony and Denmark.

For Spain a restitution of the Palatinate in some form was still a possibility, even after the Emperor's victory at Lutter, but its significance for Spain only mattered in her relations with England. In the autumn of 1626 Olivares negotiated with an emissary of the Catholic League, about the future of the Palatinate, and explained clearly that a restitution of lands and titles to Frederick V was unthinkable at that point. Instead Spain wanted to be able to restore one of his children, provided he was raised as a Catholic, not for his sake, but for England's, should King Charles and England return to Catholicism, as the Spanish monarchy still hoped against all measure of reality. Spain continued to withhold its recognition of Bavaria's occupation of the Palatine electorate and would hold on to its portion of the Palatinate for as long as it was potentially useful.[189]

Frederick and his God

During the rise and fall of The Hague Alliance, Frederick had continued to rely on his seemingly limitless supply of faith and hope. He had often met good news with prayers such as the following: '[I] hope God our Lord will apply His blessing to all places'.[190] To bad news he had responded in a similar way. When he had heard about Lutter, he had blamed Christian's allies for not having lived up to their promises and prayed, 'May God prevent his ruin and bring him into better circumstances'.[191] But at times he had become frustrated with the series of catastrophes that God had inflicted upon the common cause. In the summer of 1625 when he had heard about the King of Denmark's near fatal fall and about the plague killing 4,000 in London, he had written, 'I hope [God] may throw the rod in the fire for once and let his enemies see his power'.[192] It would be in perfect keeping with this prince if he tended to see himself as an innocent victim instead of responsible perpetrator. Nonetheless, Frederick had never shown any sign of doubt about the identity of God's true people, church, and enemies.

Despite the events of recent years, he believed that God condoned his military aspirations, if not all his operations. Throughout the summer of 1626 he had trusted that God would keep the campaign afoot, despite its grave material needs: 'I live on the heartening confidence, [that] the Almighty will compensate for the shortcoming and confer beneficial means by some other way'.[193] After the defeat at Lutter, Frederick offered the Danish King his condolences in words that testify to his very war-like Christianity:

> Although God, the Most High Prince of War, often lets dark clouds cover his own, he also still tends to them finally, gladdening them once again with the loving rays of his sun, and release the weather of his wrath over the enemies of his church and the oppressors of common liberty; just as when you suppose to have brought your victories to the greatest extent, then you will either be ruined, or even at least will not continue, and you must recognize that you can do no more than what is allowed you from on High, as such things already in many places express the good hope [that] the Almighty will perhaps

compensate [Your Highness] for the loss suffered, to His honor, and for the consolation of so many hard oppressed souls, for thus then we pray to him with all our heart.[194]

Frederick remained as determined as ever to recover his lands and titles with whatever means were available to him. Because admitting to fault was not an option for him, he had no alternative but to wait for military forces friendly to his interests to restore him to power. At the beginning of 1625 Frederick had resigned himself to waiting for his deliverance: 'we must bear patiently our hardships, from which [God] will grant us the means to employ to redeem ourselves and await his blessing'.[195] As he looked back on the events of 1626, he wrote, 'one must let time run its course, until the Lord God may supply guidance and means for this purpose: for the good hope [that] he may not allow the common Protestant cause and those liberties, having been obtained at such great costs, to be oppressed.'[196] Faith gave Frederick a sense of righteousness, strength of conviction, consolation in defeat, and hope for future victory, with scant regard for the already uncountable miseries inflicted on the common people by marauding armies of all sides. This personal faith in a warrior God helped to perpetuate the Thirty Years' War.

* * *

Though 1626 had been a year of military disappointments, Frederick remained distrustful of peace negotiations that might jeopardize his cause. The diet of deputies at Ulm did not pose a problem, because after being twice delayed it never actually convened.[197] The defeat at Lutter, however, had raised the likelihood of a truce between all parties concerned. In September Frederick had believed that England was secretly negotiating a peace with Spain in return for a complete restoration of the Palatine lands and titles.[198] He had heard rumors to the same effect in the preceding summer and had ordered Rusdorf, should he enter into any such discussion, not to agree to any settlement based on promises alone; only deeds would have sufficed at that point.[199] The intercession of the Dukes of Lorraine and Württemberg had continued throughout the whole of 1626, and they had recommended that Frederick make a formal submission to the Emperor, and in November his own trusted adviser, Volrad von Plessen, had expressed the same point of view.[200]

Frederick, it must be said, was not against any settlement per se, but he was totally inflexible about the terms. Earlier in 1626 he had actually voiced a desire to submit to the Emperor in a manner appropriate to his rank as Elector Palatine, but he would only do so if it would entail his complete restitution.[201] During the summer of 1626, while the campaigns had raged across the Empire, Frederick had insisted that he had never wanted to induce great bloodshed or to rebel against the Emperor, but in order to effect his own restitution, his reconciliation had to be in accordance with the Imperial constitution. He had claimed that he was not being intransigent on this point for his own sake but for the rights of the electors and estates of the Empire.[202] After Frederick had signaled a willingness to submit, Ferdinand had wanted to discuss the arrangement in particular terms, but no settlement would be reached during the negotiations.[203] When the violence renewed in 1627, the archrivals' tentative steps towards a rapprochement, which had been so urgently desired throughout Europe and so long overdue, discontinued once and for all.

Notes

1. For a view of the popular response in England to the events surrounding the Anglo-Spanish match, see Thomas Cogswell, 'England and the Spanish Match', in Richard Cust and Ann Hughes, eds, *Conflict in Early Stuart England* (London, 1989), pp. 107–33.
2. BHStA, KS, 7552, fols 48–50: 11/21 December 1623, Rusdorf to Frederick V.
3. 'also unfreündtlich' BHStA, KB, 122/3a, fol. 46: 8/18 January 1624, Frederick V to Rusdorf.
4. BHStA, KB, 122/3a, fol. 47: 8/18 January 1624, Frederick V to Rusdorf.
5. 'ehren, gewissen undt reputation', BHStA, KB, 122/3a, fol. 47: 8/18 January 1624, Frederick V to Rusdorf. On 13 January, Frederick had told the resident Venetian ambassador in The Hague that he would never give up his son nor allow him to change his religion. CSPV, xviii, p. 193.
6. BHStA, KS, 7552, fol. 90: 21/31 January 1624, Rusdorf to Frederick V. The agent was William Alexander, the Master of Requests. For the nuncio's assurances about Maximilian, see PRO, SP, 81/30, fols 27–8.
7. BHStA, KS, 7552, fol. 90: 21/31 January 1624, Rusdorf to Frederick V.
8. BHStA, KS, 7552, fols 113–14.
9. BHStA, KS, 7552, fol. 117: 13/23 February 1624, Rusdorf to Frederick V.
10. 'plustost pour la religion que pour la raison d'estat où de la paix'. BHStA, KS, 7552, fol. 137: 27 February/9 March 1624, Rusdorf to Frederick V.
11. 'les Catholiques presumeroient, que pretendissions une guerre de religion, aussy nul Prince Catholique n'entreroit point en confoederation avec nous sans y comprendre led. Duc'. BHStA, KS, 7552, fol. 109: 22 February/3 March 1624, Rusdorf to Frederick V.
12. BHStA, KB, 122/3a, fols 54–5: 5/15 February 1624, Frederick to Rusdorf.
13. 'meretrici sfacciate, ne cherchoient autre, qu'une generale combustion et desespoir, à cause qu'ils scavent qu'ils sont les plus puissants entre les Catholiques', BHStA, KS, 7552, fol. 109: 22 February/3 March 1624, Rusdorf to Frederick V.
14. 'sonnenklar erscheinet' 'wie wir es unsers theils iederzeitt darfur gehaltten haben,

Seine Königliche Würde aber eines andern persuadirt gewesen'. BHStA, KB, 122/ 3a, fol. 56: 5/15 February 1624, Frederick V to Rusdorf.

15. 'welches seine gewisse constitutiones undt fundamental satzungen hatt, zu deren halttung ein ieder Standt verpflichtet undt schuldig ist', BHStA, KB, 122/3a, fol. 57: 5/15 February 1624, Frederick V to Rusdorf.

16. BHStA, KS, 7552, fol. 109: 22 February/3 March 1624, Rusdorf to Frederick V.

17. 'warumb Bayrn es dan nicht zuvor beßer erwogen habe, da beßere mittel zu solchem Zweckh zugelangen vorhanden gewesen?' BHStA, KB, 122/3a, fol. 59: 5/15 February 1624, Frederick V to Rusdorf.

18. 'alß ob wir von anbegin biß uff dießer stundt kein einzige anzeigung von unß gegeben oder mercken laßen, daß wir zue dem frieden geneigt seyen, sondern daß wir vielmehr alle unß offerirte undt gleichsamb endtgegen getragene mittel zu einer guttlichen composition außgeschlagen, undt nur lautter Krieg undt verfolgung der andern Stände gesucht hetten'. BHStA, KB, 122/3a, fol. 62: 5/15 March 1624, Frederick V to Rusdorf.

19. For the context of the 'Apologia' in the contemporary pamphlet war, see Koser, *Der Kanzleienstreit,* pp. 66–7.

20. 'l'on imputeroit l'empeschement de la paix à V. M'. BHStA, KS, 7552, fol. 140: 3/ 13 March 1624, Rusdorf to Frederick V.

21. 'Sie wollen nur die Kinder und geben nichts dafür'. Albrecht, *Auswärtige Politik,* pp. 116–17.

22. See BHStA, KS, 7552, fol. 115 and passim.

23. '... le Roy est aussy veritablement alteré'. BHStA, KS, 7552, fol. 93: 5/15 February 1624, Rusdorf to Frederick V.

24. PRO, SP, 81/30, fols 43, 49–59.

25. 'gutte Patrioten in Engellandt', BHStA, KB, 122/3a, fol. 48: 8/18 January 1624, Frederick V to Rusdorf. Also see fol. 70: 27 April 1624, Frederick V to Rusdorf.

26. For a full explication of this thesis, see Thomas Cogswell, *The Blessed Revolution: English Politics and the Coming of War, 1621–1624* (Cambridge, 1989).

27. Lockyer, *The Early Stuarts*, pp. 205–12.

28. 'il semble que les Anglois advancants un pied en reculent trois, veu qu'ils ne sont plus si eschauffez de declarer la guerre aux Espagnols'. BHStA, KS, 7552, fol. 170: 9/19 April 1624, Rusdorf to Frederick V.

29. 'le Roy ne pouvoit hazarder son Estat, en declarant la guerre estant despourveu et impreparé'. BHStA, KS, 7552, fol. 170: 9/19 April 1624, Rusdorf to Frederick V.

30. Weiß, *Die Unterstützung,* p. 67.

31. BHStA, KS, 7552, fol. 175: 21 April/1 May 1624, Rusdorf to Frederick V.

32. PRO, SP, 81/30, fol. 153: 24 April/4 May 1624.

33. Weiß, *Die Unterstützung,* pp. 67–8. For Mansfeld's consent, see PRO, SP, 81/30, fol. 176.

34. 'le R. de France ne fairoit rien, si le Roy comme le plus interessé ne commence le premier et ce reellement'. BHStA, KS, 7552, fol. 174: 21 April/1 May 1624, Rusdorf to Frederick V.

35. BHStA, KS, 7552, fols 178–9: 2/12 May 1624, Rusdorf to Frederick V.

36. 'l'advancement de la liberté commune & principalement le recouvrement du Palatinat' PRO, SP, 81/30, fol. 160: 26 April/6 May 1624. Also see, BHStA, KS, 7552, fol. 183: 24 April/4 May 1624, Rusdorf to Frederick V.

37. 'Ceste année se perdra commes les autres, & le Conte de Mansfeld mesme est d'opinion, que lon ne faira grande chose ceste année'. BHStA, KS, 7552, fol. 175:

21 April/1 May 1624, Rusdorf to Frederick V.

38.   BHStA, KS, 7552, fols 177–8: 2/12 May 1624, Rusdorf to Frederick V.

39.   Lockyer, *The Early Stuarts*, p. 213.

40.   BHStA, KS, 7552, fols 190–1: 14/24 May 1624, Rusdorf to Frederick V.

41.   BHStA, KB, 89/3c, and KB, 122/3a, fol. 64: 14/24 March 1624, Frederick V to Rusdorf. James ordered Secretary Conway to communicate with Louis XIII about this company. BHStA, KS, 7552, fol. 166: 4/14 April 1624, Rusdorf to Frederick V. When Ludwig died in January 1625, Frederick tried to have the company consigned to his youngest son, Edward, who was born on 6 October 1624. BHStA, KB, 122/3a, fol. 132: 6 March 1625, and KB, 89/3c.

42.   BHStA, KB, 122/3a, fol. 81: 10 June 1624, Frederick V to Rusdorf. Rusdorf immediately told Frederick that there was no hope of procuring these ships. BHStA, KS, 7552, fols 222–3: 11/21 June 1624, Rusdorf to Frederick V.

43.   BHStA, KB, 122/3a, fols 70–1: 27 April 1624, Frederick V to Rusdorf.

44.   BHStA, KB, 122/3a, fol. 76: 1 June 1624, Frederick V to Rusdorf.

45.   'nicht wenig fremd', BHStA, KB, 122/3a, fol. 75: 1 June 1624, Frederick V to Rusdorf.

46.   Weiß, *Die Unterstützung*, pp. 68–9.

47.   BHStA, KS, 7552, fol. 212: 17 June 1624, James I to Frederick V.

48.   'Qu'est ce, dit il, que vous voulés qu'en façions? ceste ville coustera plus au Roy qu'elle ne vaut', BHStA, KS, 7552, fol. 224: 12/22 June 1624, Rusdorf to Frederick V.

49.   BHStA, KS, 7552, fol. 239: 12/22 July 1624, Rusdorf to Frederick V.

50.   BHStA, KS, 7552, fol. 242: 26 July/6 August 1624, Rusdorf to Frederick V.

51.   'Sa Commission tourne totalement en fumée'. BHStA, KS, 7552, fol. 247: 3/13 August 1624, Rusdorf to Frederick V.

52.   BHStA, KS, 7552, fols 246–8: 3/13 August 1624, Rusdorf to Frederick V.

53.   BHStA, KB, 122/3a, fol. 84: 13/23 July 1624, Frederick V to Rusdorf.

54.   'wegen ihrer Kinder, ehre, reputation und versprüchnus … dieweill wir nicht allein in puncto bemeltter sequestration, sondern auch allen andern, unß beschehenen zuemutungen, Sr. Königl Wd. willen undt starcken vermahnung, auß schuldigen Söhnlichen respect gefolget haben, dadurch unß gleichsamb hände undt füeße gebunden, undt die sachen so schwer gemacht worden…'. BHStA, KB, 122/3a, fols 84–5: 13/23 July 1624, Frederick V to Rusdorf.

55.   'lesquels on a depossede si injustement de tout ce qui leur appartient irrefragablement en vertu de la Bulle d'Or et loy fondamentale de l'Empire', BHStA, KB, 122/3a, fol. 87: 13/23 July 1624, 'Memoire pour le sieur de Rustorff, De ce qu'il aura a exposer de bouche, et si besoing est par escrit, a Sa Majesté de la Grande Bretagne'.

56.   BHStA, KB, 122/3a, fol. 94: 9 September 1624, Frederick V to Rusdorf.

57.   BHStA, KS, 7552, fols 246–8: 3/13 August 1624, Rusdorf to Frederick V.

58.   'loix fondamentales et constitutions n'estoient point adamantines, que lon ne les pourroit tousiours abolir et les faire revoquer; ainsy que l'experience l'avoit assez tesmoigné', BHStA, KS, 7552, fol. 248: 3/13 August 1624, Rusdorf to Frederick V.

59.   'mais il n'entendoit point ces loix là. Il avoit touiours esté de l'opinion, que les armes le fairoient, nullement les paroles, lettres & Ambassades: Le Prince et le Duc de Buguingham luy en seroient tesmoings'. BHStA, KS, 7552, fol. 248: 3/13 August 1624, Rusdorf to Frederick V.

60.   'Que Angleterre n'avoit autre interest avec Allemagne que pour le Palatinat, il ne

leur chailloit, quoy que tout l'Allemagne fust en feu, pourveu qu'ils eussent le Palatinat'. BHStA, KS, 7552, fol. 248: 3/13 August 1624, Rusdorf to Frederick V.

61. 'nous perdissions ... premierement le Palatinat, apres nous perdrons les pays bas apres Irlande, en fin nous mesmes'. BHStA, KS, 7552, fol. 248: 3/13 August 1624, Rusdorf to Frederick V.

62. BHStA, KB, 122/3a, fol. 94: 9 September 1624, Frederick V to Rusdorf.

63. Lockhart, *Denmark*, p. 117. For Bellin's secret communications to Rusdorf, see BHStA, KB, 122/2II.

64. Aretin, 'Sammlung', p. 195.

65. 'wir unser Glück damit suchen möchten', BHStA, KB, 122/3a, fol. 96: 10/20 November 1624, Frederick V to Rusdorf. The King had arranged for Frederick to receive £20,000 under the direction of a commissioner to pay for the wages of some of the German colonels. BHStA, KS, 7552, fol. 267: 11/21 September 1624, Rusdorf to Frederick V.

66. BHStA, KB, 122/3a, fol. 101: 6 December 1624, Frederick V to Rusdorf.

67. BHStA, KB, 122/3a, fol. 104: 7/17 December 1624, Frederick V to Rusdorf.

68. Fiedler, 'Correspondenz', p. 385, 388.

69. BHStA, KB, 122/3a, fol. 110: 9/19 December 1624, Frederick V to Rusdorf.

70. BHStA, KB, 122/3a, fol. 98: 16/26 November 1624, Frederick V to Rusdorf. Frederick tried to obtain a separate recommendation letter for his agent, Paul Strasburg, on his embassy to Bethlen Gábor in Hungary.

71. BHStA, KB, 122/3a, fol. 90: 2/12 August 1624, Frederick V to Rusdorf. BHStA, KB, 122/3a, fol. 79: 1 June 1624, Frederick V to Rusdorf.

72. BHStA, KB, 122/3a, fols 112–13: 16/26 December 1624, Frederick V to Rusdorf. BHStA, KS, 7552, fol. 228: 8/18 July 1624, Frederick V to Isaac Wake. Also KS, 16745, fol. 120. Frederick's own agent in Venice from late 1624 to 1627 was Count Heinrich Matthias of Thurn. For a collection of Frederick's and Elizabeth's letters to Thurn, see Fiedler, 'Correspondenz', pp. 377–414.

73. Quoted in Lockhart, *Denmark*, p. 113, n. 20.

74. Lockhart, *Denmark*, p. 116.

75. Weiß, *Die Unterstützung*, p. 71. Nonetheless the general view in Berlin of English affairs was pessimistic. No one believed that England would accomplish what she claimed, and everyone doubted the outcome of the marriage and alliance with France 'du main dieu aidant'. BHStA, KS, 7552, fol. 251: 23 August/2 September 1624, Anstruther to Rusdorf.

76. Weiß, *Die Unterstützung*, pp. 71–2. The princes in Mecklenburg and Pomerania followed Saxony's word. BHStA, KS, 7552, fol. 250: 23 August/2 September 1624, Anstruther to Rusdorf.

77. BHStA, KB, 122/3a, fols 112–13: 16/26 December 1624, Frederick V to Rusdorf.

78. Weiß, *Die Unterstützung*, pp. 72–3.

79. BHStA, KB, 122/3a, fol. 113: 16/26 December 1624, Frederick V to Rusdorf.

80. 'gott geb Ihm bestendigkeit und gutte resolution' Fiedler, 'Correspondenz', p. 383. Also see p. 385.

81. PRO, SP, 81/32, fols 90–1: 14/24 February 1624, Frederick V to James I. PRO, SP, 81/31, fol. 145: 27 October/7 November 1624, James I to Mansfeld. PRO, SP, 81/31, fol. 174: 22 November/2 December 1624, Nethersole to Conway?

82. Weiß, *Die Unterstützung*, pp. 78–9.

83. 'nichts trost uns mehr als des itzigen Konigs gutte affection gegen uns und der gemeinen sach'. Fiedler, 'Correspondenz', p. 386. Frederick's letter of consolation

to Charles did not reflect this ambivalent attitude, but it had to be in accordance with propriety. PRO, SP, 81/32, fols 153–4: 12/22 April 1625, Frederick V to Charles I.

84.   'wir weren gewiss nie in den ubelen zustandt geraten' Fiedler, 'Correspondenz', p. 390.

85.   As it was, by 1624 Frederick had tired of making appeals to the Estates General that were constantly refused. Throughout that year, he had not appeared once before them and had written only on occasion. Mout, 'Der Winterkönig', p. 266.

86.   Parker, *The Thirty Years' War*, p. 63.

87.   'de contracter entr' eux une alliance perpetuelle'. BHStA, KB, 122/3a, fol. 87: 13/23 July 1624, Memoire pour le sieur de Rustorff, De ce qu'il aura a exposer de bouche, et si besoing est par escrit, a Sa Majesté de la Grande Bretagne. The French ambassador seconded this view by saying that Louis XIII and his predecessors 'avoient principalement cheri et cherissoient la maison Palatine devant toutes les autres en Allemagne, comme celle delaquelle la France avoit reçeu beaucoup de bons services, voire lon avoit tousiours estimé la maison Palatine en France, comme Françoise et nullement estrangere'. BHStA, KS, 7552, fol. 240: 18/28 July 1624, Rusdorf to Frederick V.

88.   BHStA, KB, 122/3a, fol. 87: 13/23 July 1624, Memoire pour le sieur de Rustorff, De ce qu'il aura a exposer de bouche, et si besoing est par escrit, a Sa Majesté de la Grande Bretagne.

89.   'que nous ne fussions auteurs & moteurs d'une guerre de religion'. BHStA, KS, 7552, fol. 188: 12/22 May 1624, Rusdorf to Frederick V.

90.   BHStA, KS, 7552, fol. 188: 12/22 May 1624, Rusdorf to Frederick V. See Albrecht, *Die Auswärtige Politik*, chs. 4 and 7, and idem, *Maximilian I.*, ch. 22.

91.   Weiß, *Die Unterstützung*, p. 77.

92.   BHStA, KB, 122/2II, Extract de la resolution donnée en France à M. Bellin, 1625. Another letter revised this sum to £100,000: 8 March 1625, Bellin to Rusdorf.

93.   Fiedler, 'Correspondenz', pp. 385, 387.

94.   'In summa universale fere bellum in tota Germania et Italia hoc anno futurum est'. BHStA, KS, 16745, fols 125–6: 4 March 1625. Proof for Camerarius' authorship of this letter is to be found at fols 123–4. For the report about the Marquis of Baden's and Bethlen Gábor's returning to arms, see BHStA, KB, 121/3g, fol. 3: 3/13 February 1625, 'De bon espoir' to Rusdorf.

95.   Parker, *The Thirty Years' War*, p. 68.

96.   BHStA, KS, 16745, fol. 127: 21/31 March 1625, Frederick V to Bethlen Gábor.

97.   BHStA, KB, 122/3a, fols 134–6: 3/13 March 1625, Frederick V to Rusdorf.

98.   PRO, SP, 81/33, fol. 61.

99.   Lockhart, *Denmark*, pp. 126–7.

100. BHStA, KB, 122/3a, fol. 125: 8 February 1625, Frederick V to Rusdorf.

101. 'in kurtzer zeit gantz und gar ruinirt werden möchte' BHStA, KB, 122/3a, fol. 130: 6 March 1625, Frederick V to Rusdorf.

102. 'daß das Parlament in Engellandt der sachen und allerseits Intentionen recht grundtlich informirt'. BHStA, KB, 122/3a, fol. 140: 2 April 1625, Frederick V to Rusdorf.

103. 'Manßfeld die handt nunmehr wieder frei hatt'. BHStA, KB, 122/3a, fol. 143: 15 April 1625, Frederick V to Rusdorf.

104. BHStA, KB, 122/3a, fol. 145: 11/21 April 1625, Frederick V to Rusdorf.

105. BHStA, KB, 122/3a, fols 152–4.

106. PRO, SP, 81/32, fols 175–7: 26 April/6 May 1625.

107. BHStA, KB, 122/3a, fol. 140: 2 April 1625, Frederick V to Rusdorf.

108. PRO, SP, 81/32, fols 175–7: 26 April/6 May 1625.

109. 'Le But principal ... est d'arrester les Ambitieux desseings d'Austriche et d'Espagne, et remettre les affaires d'Allemagne en leur entier, avec restitution du Palatinat et de ce qui en depend'. BHStA, KB, 122/3a, fol. 155: 6 May 1625, Frederick V to Rusdorf.

110. 'dem vatterlandt und der gemeinen sache dienen' Fielder, 'Correspondenz', p. 389.

111. 'mehr disreputation als ehr darvon' Fiedler, 'Correspondenz', p. 389.

112. BHStA, KB, 122/3a, fols 158–60: 31 May 1625, Frederick to Rusdorf.

113. BHStA, KB, 122/3a, fols 162–3: 2/12 June 1625, Frederick V to Rusdorf, and fol. 176, 178: 14/24 June 1625.

114. PRO, SP, 81/33, fols 53–4: 27 May/6 June 1625, Frederick V to Charles I.

115. BHStA, KB, 122/3a, fol. 155: 6 May 1625, Frederick V to Rusdorf.

116. BHStA, KB, 122/3a, fol. 170: 5 June 1625, Memo on the diet of deputies. Also see PRO, SP, 81/32, fols 190–1.

117. 'welche doch, alß ein fundamental verfassung, ohne alle Stände deß Reichs zuthun undt bewilligung nit geendert werden sol noch kan' BHStA, KB, 122/3a, fol. 255: sine dato, Memo for Anstruther regarding diet at Ulm.

118. 'fortifier de plus en plus le parti d'Austriche, d'Espagne et de la Ligue à l'oppression de la liberté Germanique'. BHStA, KB, 122/3a, fol. 170: 5 June 1625, Memo on the diet of deputies.

119. 'Quant au Roy de Boheme, comme il a tousjours protesté, aussy proteste il encores sincerement, ne respirer que la paix, moyennant qu'elle soit fondée non sur la ruine et extirpation (ainsi que ld. est le desseing de la contrepartie) ains sur des conditions equitables, honestes et asseurées de son entiere restitution, et d'une esgale tranquillité par toutte la Germanie, s'offrant en ce cas à tout ce qui ne sera contraire à sa conscience honneur, aux loix fondamentales et la liberté de l'Empire'. BHStA, KB, 122/3a, fol. 171: 5 June 1625, Memo on the diet of deputies.

120. BHStA, KB, 122/3a, fol. 167: 5 June 1625, Frederick V to Rusdorf, and fol. 177: 14/24 June 1625. For Frederick's instructions on these agents' negotiations, see fol. 189: 17 July 1624, Memo to Rusdorf.

121. 'möchten wir wunschen, daß underdessen, die sachen zu einem glucklichen tractat gebracht, die waffen continuirt, sub clypeo tractirt, undt unser Gegentheill uff einen andern undt bessern weg gelenckt werden könnte'. BHStA, KB, 122/3a, fol. 188: 7/17 June 1625, Frederick V to Rusdorf.

122. PRO, SP, 81/33, fols 121–2: 6/16 July 1625, Anstruther's instructions from Hampton Court.

123. BHStA, KB, 122/3a, fols 193–4: 23 April 1625, Emperor Ferdinand II to Dukes of Württemberg and Lorraine.

124. BHStA, KB, 122/3a, fols 195: 23 June 1625, Duke of Württemberg to Frederick V, and KS, 7053.

125. BHStA, KS, 7053, fols 102–5: 17/27 October 1625, Frederick V to Duke of Württemberg, and fols 110, 118–21. Also see KB, 121/3g, fols 10–11: 4/14 July 1625, Frederick V to Duke of Württemberg.

126. BHStA, KB, 121/3g, fols 12–28; KB, 121/1/II, fols 54–71; and KB, 121/3e.

127. Zwiedineck-Südenhorst, *Die Politik*, i, p. 53.

128. BHStA, KB, 122/3a, fol. 199: 18/28 July 1625, Frederick V to Anstruther.

129. Parker, *The Thirty Years' War*, p. 68.

130. BHStA, KB, 122/3a, fol. 155: 6 May 1625, Frederick V to Rusdorf; and fol. 136: 3/13 March 1625, Frederick V to Rusdorf.

131. Mout, 'Der Winterkönig', pp. 267–8.
132. Weiß, *Die Unterstützung*, p. 87. Lockyer, *Buckingham*, p. 278. Mout, 'Der Winterkönig', p. 267.
133. Mout, 'Der Winterkönig', pp. 258–9.
134. Mout, 'Der Winterkönig', p. 267.
135. Weiß, *Die Unterstützung*, pp. 81–3.
136. PRO, SP, 81/33, fol. 259: sine dato, Charles I to ?
137. Weiß, *Die Unterstützung*, p. 87.
138. Conrad Russell, *Parliaments and English Politics, 1621–1629* (Oxford, 1979), pp. 204–12.
139. Ibid., pp. 238–52.
140. Weiß, *Die Unterstützung*, p. 86.
141. Lockyer, *Buckingham*, pp. 281–5.
142. The Duke of Buckingham, the Earl of Holland, and Dudley Carleton led the English delegation, Jacob Ulfeldt and Christen Thomesen Sehested the Danish, and Count Floris of Culembourg the Estates General.
143. Lockhart, *Denmark*, p. 139. Lockyer, *Buckingham*, pp. 278–9. BHStA, KB, 122/3a, fol. 239: 5/15 October 1625, Frederick V to Rusdorf.
144. Mout, 'Der Winterkönig', p. 268.
145. Lockhart, *Denmark*, pp. 139–40. Weiß, *Die Unterstützung*, p. 88.
146. Lockyer, *Buckingham*, p. 279. Weiß, *Die Unterstützung*, p. 89.
147. Parker, *The Thirty Years' War*, p. 69.
148. Weiß, *Die Unterstützung*, p. 89.
149. Mout, 'Der Winterkönig', p. 268.
150. Lockhart, *Denmark*, p. 141.
151. Mout, 'Der Winterkönig', p. 268.
152. Weiß, *Die Unterstützung*, p. 89.
153. BHStA, KB, 122/3a, fol. 242: 18/28 November 1625, Memo to Buckingham.
154. 'que Dieu n'y donne sa benediction', BHStA, KB, 122/3a, fol. 245, sine dato, Memo.
155. 'ils verront le commencement d'une revolution'. BHStA, KB, 122/3a, fol. 245, sine dato, Memo.
156. The offer was contingent upon receiving money from England and France. BHStA, KS, 9251, fol. 1: 24 October 1625, Marquis of Baden-Durlach to Frederick V; and fol. 3: 1/11 January 1626, Frederick V to Marquis of Baden-Durlach. For a complete account of Baden's expedition, see Karl Obser, 'Markgraf Georg Frederick von Baden-Durlach und das Projekt einer Diversion am Oberrhein in den Jahren 1623–1627', *Zeitschrift für die Geschichte des Oberrheins*, 44, (1890), pp. 320–99.
157. 'ne fait rien sans luy' BHStA, KB, 122/3a, fol. 278: 3 March 1626, Frederick V to Rusdorf.
158. BHStA, KB, 122/3a, fols 278–9: 3 March 1626, Frederick V to Rusdorf.
159. BHStA, KB, 122/3a, fol. 276: 3 March 1626, Frederick V to Rusdorf; fol. 312: 26 August 1626, Frederick V to Rusdorf; fol. 314: 28 August 1626, Frederick V to Charles I; fol. 326: 22 November 1626, Frederick V to Buckingham; and fol. 331: 12/22 November 1626, Frederick V to Rusdorf.
160. BHStA, KB, 122/3a, fols 283, 289–92.
161. 'Ainsi tout ce que Brandenburg kan thun a ceste heure daß ist heimlich favorisiern tant die armée des K. in Den. des Mansfelts'. The Elector allowed Mansfeld to lead his army into the Altmark. BHStA, KB, 122/2II: 14 February 1626, El Conocido (Bellin) to ?

162. See BHStA, KB, 122/3a, fol. 181, 222, 265. It is not clear which Duke of Saxe-Weimar wrote to Frederick, Bernhard or Johann Ernst, but it is safe to assume that it was the latter. Both served in the armies of the Lower Saxon Circle, but only Johann Ernst had an independent command. Lockhart, *Denmark*, p. 135.

163. Gindely, *Geschichte,* ii, pp. 83–4.

164. Lockhart, *Denmark*, pp. 131–6, 144–50. Parker, *The Thirty Years' War*, pp. 69–70.

165. Gindely, *Geschichte*, ii, pp. 90–1.

166. BHStA, KB, 122/3a, fol. 273, 280–302.

167. BHStA, KS, 9251, fols 36–8: 4/14 February 1626, Rusdorf to Frederick V; fols 78–9: 17/27 March 1626, Rusdorf to Frederick V; fol. 131: 23 June/3 July 1626, Rusdorf to Frederick V. Adams, 'Protestant Cause', p. 376.

168. BHStA, KS, 9251, fols 51–3: 19/29 February 1626, Rusdorf to Frederick V; and fol. 134: 7/17 July 1626, Rusdorf to Frederick V.

169. Weiß, *Die Unterstützung*, p. 92.

170. 'que son maistre prouveroit que par la mesconduicte du Duc de Bughingam Palatinat avoit esté perdu et qu'il avoit esté aussy la cause que la restitution n'en estoit suivie'. BHStA, KS, 9251, fol. 100: 20/30 April 1626, Rusdorf to Frederick V.

171. 'der unwil Ist gross Im landt gegen den hertzogen so viel guts verhindert' Fiedler, 'Correspondenz', p. 401.

172. BHStA, KS, 9251, fol. 80: 17/27 March 1626, Rusdorf to Frederick V.

173. BHStA, KB, 122/3a, fol. 317: 10/20 September 1626, Frederick V to Charles I.

174. BHStA, KB, 122/3a, fol. 320: 3 November 1626, Frederick V to Rusdorf.

175. BHStA, KB, 122/3a, fol. 326: 22 November 1626, Frederick V to Rusdorf.

176. CSPV, xix, p. 155; quoted in Weiß, *Die Unterstützung*, p. 87. Weiß argues that England's primary interest was foreign trade, not the Palatinate.

177. BHStA, KS, 9251, fol. 86: 30 March/9 April 1626, Rusdorf to Frederick V; and fol. 121: 13/23 June 1626, Rusdorf to Frederick V.

178. BHStA, KB, 122/3a, fols 289–90: 12 March 1626, Christian IV to Frederick V; fol. 292: 3 April 1626, Frederick V to Rusdorf; and KS, 9251, fols 96–7: 11/21 April 1626, Rusdorf to Frederick V.

179. BHStA, KS, 9251, fol. 121: 13/23 June 1626, Rusdorf to Frederick V.

180. BHStA, KS, 9251, fol. 82: 15/25 March 1626, Rusdorf to Frederick V.

181. For a full discussion of these negotiations, see Straub, *Pax et Imperium*, pp. 205–51. Ritter, *Deutsche Geschichte*, iii, pp. 329–31. Gindely, *Geschichte*, ii, pp. 70–2.

182. Lockhart, *Denmark*, pp. 132–3. Gindely, *Geschichte*, ii, p. 71.

183. AGS, E. 2327, fol. 291: Consulta, 16 March 1624; and fol. 297: Consulta, 31 March 1624.

184. AGS, E. 2327, fol. 372: 'Parecer del Conde Duque'. Gindely, *Friederich V*, p. 13.

185. Gindely, *Friederich V*, pp. 11–12.

186. AGS, E. 2327, fol. 303: 28 May 1624, Catholic spiritual electors to Felipe IV. See Jürgen Kessel, *Spanien und die geistlichen Kurstaaten am Rhein während der Regierungszeit der Infantin Isabella (1621–1633)* (Frankfurt am Main, 1979).

187. AGS, E. 2327, fol. 301: Consulta, 27 June 1624.

188. Lockhart, *Denmark*, pp. 141–2.

189. BHStA, KS, 16539, esp. Olivares' answer to memo by Count of Frankenburg, fol. 46.

190. 'hof unser herr gott werde aller orten seinen segen verleihen'. Fiedler, 'Correspondenz', p. 397.

191. 'Ich beklag wohl den gutten Konig das Ihm das versprochene nicht besser gehalten wurdt gott verhutte seine Ruin bringe Ihn zu bessern zustandt'. Fielder, 'Correspondenz', p. 401.

192. 'ich hoffe er werde ein mahl die ruhte ins fewer werfen und seine macht gegen seine feindt sehen lassen'. Fielder, 'Correspondenz', p. 392.

193. 'Ich gelebebe aber der tröstlichen Zuversicht, es werde der allmächtige den mangell ersetzen, undt anderwerts erspriesliche mittell verleihen' BHStA, KS, 9251, fol. 127: sine dato, draft of Frederick V to Christian IV. Also see fol. 146: 17/27 July 1626, Frederick V to Christian IV.

194. 'ob wol Gott der Allerhöchste Kriegs fürst offtermals uber die seinige trübe wolken ergehen läßet, so pfleget er sie iedoch endtlich mitt den lieblich stralen seiner Sonnen wieder zu erfrewen, undt das wetter seines Zorns uber die feinde seiner Kirchen, undt undertrucker der gemeinen Libertet außzuschütten, also daß wan Sie vermeinen ihre victori uffs höchst gebracht zu haben, sie alßdan entweder zuschanden werden oder doch zum wenigsten gar stechen bleiben undt erkennen müßen daß sie nicht mehr vermögen als ihnen von Oben herab verhenget wirdt, wie dan solches sich albereit an vielen ortten erreuget der guttn hoffung es werde der Almächtige, E. L. den erlittenen verlust, zu seiner ehren, undt zum trost sovielen hartbetrangten Seelen, leichtlich ersetzen, wie wir ihn dan deßen gantz inniglich bitten'. BHStA, KS, 9251, fol. 173: 16 November 1626, Frederick V to Christian IV.

195. 'mussen wir unserr Trangsalen in geduldt ertragen, die mittel so er uns wurdt verleihen aus denselben uns zuerlosen an handt nemen und seinen segen erwarten'. Fiedler, 'Correspondenz', p. 381.

196. 'Man muss aber der zeit ihren lauff lassen, biss Gott der Herr hierzu rhat undt mittell schaffen wurdt, Der gutten Hoffnung, er werde dass gemeine Evangelische wessen undt die so theuwer erworbene Libertet nicht underdruckt werden lassen'. Fiedler, 'Correspondenz', p. 403.

197. BHStA, KB, 122/3a, fol. 276: 3 March 1626, Frederick V to Rusdorf; and fol. 305: 1/11 July 1626, Frederick V to Rusdorf.

198. PRO, SP, 81/34, fols 113–61: 11/21 September 1626, Nethersole to Carleton? See fol. 116. BHStA, KS, 9251, fol. 187: 29 November 1626, Frederick V to Rusdorf.

199. BHStA, KB, 122/3a, fol. 219: 15/25 August 1625, Frederick V to Rusdorf. Gondomar was said to have been in Brussels in the summer of 1626, negotiating a peace between England, Spain, and France, but nothing had materialized with regard to the Palatinate. BHStA, KS, 9251, fol. 141: 5/15 July 1626, Rusdorf to Frederick V; and fol. 152: 3/13 August 1626, Rusdorf to Frederick V.

200. Gindely, *Frederick V*, p. 22.

201. BHStA, KS, 7053, fols 128–9: 22 February 1626, Frederick V to Duke of Württemberg; and fols 141–2: 19/29 June 1626, Frederick V to Duke of Württemberg. Frederick asked George the new Elector of Mainz, Georg Frederick von Greiffenklau, to partake in the intercession and these negotiations. fol. 156: 16 November 1626, Frederick V to Elector of Mainz.

202. BHStA, KB, 121/3d, fol. 48: 20/30 June 1626, Frederick V to Christian IV.

203. BHStA, KS, 7053, fols 147–9: 21 September 1626, Ferdinand II to Maximilian I.

Chapter 9

Tragedy and Deliverance, 1627–1632

From 1627–29 the Danish-Lower Saxon war ended in failure, and in its wake victorious Imperial and League armies perpetrated a new series of retributions and dispossessions that posed new problems for the Holy Roman Empire. Concomitantly the Palatine crisis lost its pre-eminence as a point of constitutional contention. The continued presence and motion of large armies in northern Germany gradually shifted the entire scope of the conflict to that region. The Palatine crisis remained a problem, but it was not so compelling as the others that the war produced. As in a forest fire, Frederick had carried the flames from the lightning strike in Bohemia across Germany, and his supporters and their opponents had spread the blaze throughout the Empire and to other parts of Europe. But by the late 1620s the conflagration in northern Germany had only little to do with the smoldering ashes in the Palatinate. Yet Frederick did not relent on his constitutional position. He neither submitted to the Emperor nor acknowledged the loss of his electorate, though for a time he was inclined to do so. He had nothing left but his honor and his faith, and he refused to besmirch either. To Frederick V, Christian IV, and their supporters, the war brought on more injustices than it corrected, though the Emperor saw his victory as his great chance to correct the transgressions committed against the Peace of Augsburg since the mid sixteenth century. The Emperor's actions in the name of justice, however, only confirmed Frederick's and others' suspicions about the Habsburgs' designs on the Imperial constitution and Protestantism.

The End of the Empire's Wars

After the defeat at Lutter in August 1626, Christian IV had managed to regroup his forces, but his allies had abandoned the effort. Duke Friedrich Ulrich of Braunschweig-Wolfenbüttel had defected to the Emperor's side and had ordered all Danish-Lower Saxon troops out of his lands. The Dukes of Mecklenburg and other important nobles had pressured Christian to come to terms. Both sides might have agreed to peace had the Spanish not intercepted Christian's ambassador to Venice and obtained evidence of his ambitions against the Habsburg dynasty. Bolstered by local recruitments, a few British regiments from Charles I, and an army led by Frederick's old supporter, Margrave Georg Friedrich of Baden-Durlach, Christian had reassembled an army of over 30,000 men by spring of 1627, which was strong enough to hold off Tilly but not Wallenstein.[1]

In 1627 the commander of the Imperial army returned to northern Germany from Hungary and then, with Tilly, overran Pomerania, Mecklenburg, Holstein, and Jutland, but despite the fact that Wallenstein had over 100,000 men at arms, he could not conquer the Danish King completely. The Imperial army did not manage to take the Danish islands, let alone Norway or Scania, and therefore could not secure a total victory. Moreover, a Danish fleet and Danish, German, Scottish, and Swedish reinforcements drew Wallenstein out of Jutland and prevented him from taking the port of Stralsund in Pomerania during the summer of 1628. By 1629, because of expenses and loud complaints on all sides about the burdens of the war, both Christian and Ferdinand moderated their demands and ended the fighting. In the Peace of Lübeck, concluded in the summer of 1629, Christian agreed to withdraw his forces, renounce all claims over church lands in Germany, and never intervene in Imperial domestic affairs. He did not insist on the restoration of the Palatinate to Frederick V. Ferdinand stopped his plans for confiscating Holstein, Schleswig, and other lands under the King of Denmark. Neither side paid reparations to the other.[2]

During this time, England returned to peace. In 1627 and the years following England was unable to accomplish anything substantive for the Palatine crisis or the King of Denmark, despite Charles' sincere wishes to do so. Early in 1627, in response to the defeat at Lutter, Charles sent some regiments under Sir Charles Morgan to aid the Danish King.[3] Charles pawned a collar of rubies to cover some of their expenses, but desertion, disease, and the eventual discontinuation of pay helped to render this force almost totally ineffective.[4] At the same time the Spanish and French monarchies signed an alliance against the English and the Huguenots, and Spanish ships assisted in the assault on La Rochelle. England then faced the unique and terrifying situation of being at once at war with France over La Rochelle and with Spain over the Palatinate. Failure under such circumstances could hardly have been unexpected. An English expedition, led by the Duke of Buckingham, on behalf of the Huguenots at La Rochelle ended in disaster, and in April 1628 Morgan surrendered to Tilly and returned with most of the remaining men to England. In August a disgruntled officer assassinated Buckingham, and La Rochelle surrendered two months later. Because Charles had obtained some money from Parliament in the summer of 1628, he was able to send Morgan back to Germany with more men.[5] But neither this force nor Charles' ambassador,

Sir Thomas Roe, were able to persuade Christian IV to continue the war effort.[6]

Charles was still less able to persuade his Parliament. In early 1629 when he requested money to continue the war in Germany, Parliament petitioned him to declare a public fast 'upon the observation of the continued increasing miseries of the Reformed Churches abroad'.[7] Parliament would not give Charles money without the redress of its grievances, and, in protection of his royal prerogative, he would not satisfy them. The dissolution of Parliament in March 1629 demanded an end to England's participation in continental wars. One month later, Charles himself made peace with France, and, despite many pleas and protests from The Hague, he would do the same with Spain in November 1630. When formal peace negotiations between England and Spain began in 1629, the restoration of the Palatinate proved the major barrier to agreement. In 1627 Charles had declared that 'hee had no other originall quarrell with Spayne but the cause of his deare sister, which hee coulld no more distinguish from his own then nature had done theyr blouds, so woulld hee never lend eare to any tearms of Composition, without her knowledg consent and councell'.[8] The Spanish would only give assurances of a restitution and none in writing, which Frederick unsurprisingly found unacceptable. Finally the two sides solved the problem by expressly omitting him from the treaty.[9]

The third member of The Hague Alliance, the United Provinces, was fully embroiled in its war with Spain and would do nothing for Denmark or the Palatinate without the English, apart from allowing Danish army commissioners to recruit in their territory on occasion. The King of Sweden, who might have joined the alliance, continued to campaign in Prussia against the King of Poland from May 1626 till September 1629. France had first been tied down with the Huguenot rebellion and then with the war against England. When these were resolved, Louis XIII's forces invaded Italy, so fighting for the Palatinate was out of the question. Moreover Christian of Halberstadt had died after an extended fever in early June 1626, and Mansfeld had also succumbed to disease at the end of the following November.[10] Duke Johann Ernst of Saxe-Weimar had died one month later, and Bethlen Gábor passed away in November 1629. By the end of that year, Frederick would have lost almost every one of his sometime supporters.

Frederick V

Frederick began 1627 with the resignation that the preceding years had instilled in him. Because he feared that Christian IV would not be able to sustain the burden of the war alone unless the Dutch and the English helped him, Frederick prepared for another defeat by placing his hopes in God. 'Nothing is impossible for God', he wrote, 'One must entrust himself to His will in every way and hope for the redemption from this present distressed state of affairs from His merciful hand'.[11] Patience, however, did not mean passivity, and certainly not pacificism. Frederick was sure that 'there [were] still bold gentlemen left who [could] render the Fatherland useful service'.[12] He urged Charles I to support Christian IV in order to prevent the 'total oppression' of the Palatine dynasty and their common Protestant religion and of German liberty.[13]

Frederick spent most of the spring and early summer addressing the negotiations for a resolution to the Palatine crisis. The first talks would take place with the Emperor in Colmar in July 1627, which were to be the culmination of the intercession of the Dukes of Lorraine and Württemberg. The Dukes' goal had been to arrange Frederick's submission, and Christian IV had urged Frederick to use this opportunity to come to a peaceable resolution with the Emperor.[14] Frederick had answered according to his usual form: he was ready as always to do what was reasonable and practicable to settle the current conflict, but he was sure that the Emperor had only his ruin in mind.[15] He protested that he had only wanted peace all along.[16] He regarded Lorraine's and Württemberg's intercession as having 'no substance but consisting of only questions and answers for the most part'.[17] Frederick received a measure of support for his resistance from his brother-in-law, Charles I, who found the Emperor's conditions extreme. He told Frederick, 'we cannot but wonder that the duke would communicate them to you before they should bee formed with more Reason'.[18]

The negotiations at Colmar proceeded as had most others between Frederick and Ferdinand, but they showed that the former was ready to abandon some of his previous claims for the sake of peace. At first his delegates, Rusdorf and Andreas Pawel, began with a demand that the Emperor declare his intentions about the complete restitution of the Upper and Lower Palatinate. Württemberg's and Lorraine's deputies managed to turn the discussion to the Emperor's conditions, which had increased in severity over the years of war. This time, Frederick had to make an unconditional submission, renounce all claims to Bohemia, formally recognize Maximilian as Elector Palatine, grant toleration of Catholicism in the Lower Palatinate, and make amends for all the Emperor's expenses in the Palatine and Bohemian war. In accordance with instructions, the Palatine emissaries expressed their master's willingness to give up his claim to Bohemia, to make a submission but without humiliation, by proxy, and to let Maximilian bear the electoral title but only for his lifetime, and only if the two of them shared its duties. The Palatine agents declared the demand about toleration of Catholicism unconstitutional, but they said that they would try to persuade Frederick to accept the presence of at most three Catholic monasteries, leaving his secular and ecclesiastical authority untouched. They could not, however, even entertain paying reparations, because, according to their instructions, the damages and deprivations suffered in the Palatinate were of equivalent worth to the Emperor's expenses, so the one should recompense the other. The Palatines repeated that these offers were invalid if the complete restoration of the Palatinate were not guaranteed.[19] Rusdorf called the situation 'an inextricable labyrinth' and feared that the meeting would fail if no expedient were found to bridge the gap between the two sides.[20] No agreement was reached.

The outcome at Colmar infuriated Frederick, and he refused to take any blame for its failure. He had never been more pliable than at that meeting, and it was the Emperor who had refused to alter the demands.[21] Frederick protested that he had not taken up arms for his own defense in over five years, and that he had offended no one in the Empire for the same amount of time. Strictly speaking this was true, but the fact is that he had constantly encouraged others to fight on his behalf. He also claimed to have sought peace zealously through negotiations while Ferdinand had obstructed progress and made use of every negotiation for his own benefit.[22] The same could be said of Frederick, from the Emperor's standpoint. Facing an impending electoral diet in Mühlhause,n Frederick tried to persuade the Electors of Cologne and Trier to support his answers to the Emperor's demands.[23] He warned the Elector of Brandenburg that the Emperor's goal was none other than the destruction of their religion.[24] While the diet sat, the following statement was issued from The Hague: 'All orders in Germanie doe bend under the yoake of the domination of the house of Austria, without distinction nor exception of religion'.[25]

The electoral diet at Mühlhausen in October 1627 confirmed Frederick's worst expectations about his situation. Rusdorf, Anstruther, and Christian IV's German chancellor, were supposed to attend, but Wallenstein denied them safe-conducts. For Ferdinand, Palatine representation at the Colmar negotiations had been sufficient, and he no longer had any fear of English intervention in military affairs.[26] At the meeting the electors confirmed the Emperor's conditions for Frederick's submission, which had been put forward at Colmar. Moreover, the Elector of Brandenburg gave his acknowledgment of Maximilian's possession of the Palatine electoral dignity; the proximity of Wallenstein's massive army proved more compelling than Frederick's worn out tocsin. Georg Wilhelm indicated, however, that the electoral title should be rendered as promised to Frederick's children following Maximilian's death.[27] After the Mühlhausen Diet Frederick stood alone in his objection to the Imperial ban and in his claim to Bohemia and the Palatinate. There was nothing to comfort him but his faith: 'God can help when one expects it the least; we must trust Him and employ for His honor all human means that he may send'.[28] Given his assumptions, decisions, and priorities, there was little for him to do apart from hope and wait.

Throughout 1628 Frederick did what he could to resist the Habsburgs' apparently inexorable march to victory in the Empire. At the end of January 1628 he traveled to Wolfenbüttel, perhaps to persuade Duke Friedrich Ulrich to render some kind of aid to the King of Denmark. How long Frederick stayed and what exactly transpired is uncertain, but nothing substantively advantageous came of it.[29] After February he heard that Emperor Ferdinand had officially granted to Maximilian the Upper Palatinate and the portions of the Lower that lay on the right bank of the Rhine as his hereditary property. In return the Emperor had recovered Upper Austria and reimbursed the Duke for his RT10 million in expenditures for the Bohemian and Palatine wars.[30] In addition, Ferdinand secretly made the Palatine electorate a hereditary possession of Maximilian's dynasty, but Frederick did not learn this till much later. More than ever, Frederick was convinced that the Emperor desired his utter destruction.

Undaunted, he did his best to appear indefatigable. He continued to use his royal and electoral titles and to speak about 'the common Protestant cause'.[31] His chancery issued official declarations about the 'calamitous state' of Germany, attributing it to the Austrian and Spanish Habsburg desire to establish a universal monarchy over Germany, conduct a war of religion against all Protestants in the Empire, and extirpate Calvinists in particular. Catholics as well as Lutherans and other Protestants were suffering under the burdens of the war and were demanding peace, he claimed, but the Emperor would have none of it. He had rejected Frederick's offers of peace and had refused to grant an audience even to his brother, Duke Ludwig Philipp of Simmern, whose lands the Spanish had taken away and whose innocence the Emperor himself had acknowledged on previous occasions.[32] Furthermore, the recent transfer of the Upper Palatinate and the four right-Rhine districts of the Lower to the Duke of Bavaria meant that Frederick's subjects would have to convert to Catholicism or else lose their property and be driven from the land.[33] He wished that the Kings of England and France would settle their differences and turn against 'the common enemy', by which he meant the Habsburgs.[34] That war, he decided, had benefited no one but the King of Spain.[35]

None of these ominous developments, however, could bring as much pain to Frederick as the sudden loss of his eldest son, Friedrich Heinrich, on 17 January 1629. This one tragedy seems to have hurt him more deeply than all the others in his life. The two were traveling to Amsterdam in a passenger boat, when a much larger boat collided with their own and capsized it. Frederick managed to save his life by leaping from the sinking boat and grasping hold of a line that had been cast from the other boat into the water. When he was pulled on board, he begged the sailors to save his son and the other passengers, but the falling darkness and the opposing winds rendered their efforts ineffectual. They made three passes near the site of the wreckage, but hearing no voices or cries for help, they soon docked and put Frederick ashore where he could warm himself. On the morning of the next day the ebbed tides revealed the sunken ship and Friedrich Heinrich's drowned corpse, still clinging to the mast. Three other gentlemen of the court and others had died as well.

The accident devastated Frederick for months. He must have blamed himself, since initially he had not wanted to let his son accompany him on the journey, but others had persuaded him that the change of scene would amuse the boy and improve his appetite.[36] 'It having pleased God', he wrote, 'to add to my preceding hardships a new affliction, the pain of which cannot be expressed with the pen'.[37] Friedrich Heinrich had been, for his father, 'the one of all my children whom [he] loved the most'.[38] Only six months after the accident could he bring himself to inform Count Thurn, 'God has nearly destroyed me through the loss of my most beloved son, which has surpassed all previous agonies'.[39] Nevertheless Frederick's faith in God's providence remained unshaken. 'It is reasonable', he wrote, 'that I submit myself to it as to that which is always just and good, though human sense has difficulty comprehending it'.[40] He maintained his hope as well: 'since the hand of the one who governs all things has ordained it so, it is for me to adore Him and to submit myself, hoping His hand will strengthen me and change everything for the better'.[41] We will never know how effective these words of consolation were.

Throughout 1629 Frederick continued his diplomatic correspondence and supported the military effort against his enemies. He and his wife pressured Charles I not to make peace with Spain until he had fulfilled his promise to secure their complete restoration.[42] Frederick also urged Christian IV to incorporate the restitution of the Palatinate in his peace negotiations with the Emperor, because 'without a settlement', Frederick argued, 'and a fair, moderate agreement with regard to my affairs, no lasting peace is to be hoped for in the [Holy] Roman Empire'.[43] In June he returned to the field, to take part in the Prince of Orange's campaign against the Spanish Netherlands.

Throughout the summer and early autumn Frederick repeatedly visited the Dutch siege of the town of s'-Hertogenbosch, and he made a brief visit to Sedan in July, where there was other fighting nearby.[44] Frederick was more an observer than a participant in the fighting, and it was an opportunity for him to improve his knowledge of the techniques of warfare. He watched forces in action, examined several battlegrounds, and visited various princes, generals, and ambassadors.[45] He took breaks to join his wife and family at their summer residence in Rhenen, a former monastery, granted and partially furnished by the province of Utrecht, renovated under his personal direction.[46] He had no illusions about the marginal importance of his support for the Dutch military campaign. Since the failure of The Hague Alliance, the Estates General had only allowed Frederick to take part in their affairs in a ceremonial capacity.[47] He had equally little influence over English participation in the campaign. Though he wanted to recommend an officer for promotion among the English generals, he saw no point in writing since all his previous letters had elicited not a single answer.[48] His personal presence, however, still had a certain symbolic value: when s'-Hertogenbosch fell to the Prince of Orange in September 1629, Frederick stood next to him as they received the defeated General Grobbendonck.[49] For the Palatine and his cause, however, the victory meant next to nothing.

Ferdinand II

The good fortune of Emperor Ferdinand had meanwhile reached its zenith. Austria was once again fully in his possession, and Bohemia and the incorporated lands were completely subdued. The Count Palatine and his supporters were utterly defeated, and the King of Denmark had been forced to promise never to meddle in the internal affairs of the Empire again. Ferdinand's generalissimo, Wallenstein, had vanquished the rebels of the Lower Saxon Circle and enforced the Imperial ban against Dukes Johann Albrecht and Adolphus Frederick of Mecklenburg for aiding the King of Denmark. To Ferdinand, the time was ripe to enforce his vision of justice in the Empire.

In opposition to Frederick's accusations, Ferdinand naturally did not see himself as an ambitious tyrant. H.G. Koenigsberger has written, 'There is no evidence that Ferdinand wanted to destroy German Protestantism or to transform the Empire into an absolute monarchy', though to some Protestants it appeared that he did.[50] Nothing was more important to him than justice, secular and divine. His vision of the Imperial constitution and of his position in it was conservative. He saw himself as the divinely ordained supreme head of Christendom, and he wanted to lead the Empire back into the Catholic fold and to strengthen the Imperial throne in doing so.[51] He claimed, not without grounds, that he could dispose of many Protestant estates at will, because they had never possessed rights in the Imperial constitution. Still, he did not aspire to transform the Empire into a monarchy like that of France or Spain. He made no moves to centralize institutions and no attempt to administer Imperial government and finances without the assistance of various Imperial princes, secular and ecclesiastical.[52] Like Frederick V, when it came to important political decisions, Ferdinand often acted in accordance with his faith.

The Emperor was a zealous participant in the Counter-Reformation. His desire to benefit the Catholic church seems to have surpassed all other personal wishes. Declarations to his confessor reveal that confessional interest was closer to his heart than the interests of state, and he often sought theological advice before he made political decisions.[53] With predictable regularity he ordered the re-Catholicization of his own patrimonial lands and of the territories overcome by his victorious armies. As Archduke of Styria, Ferdinand had brought his own homelands into obedience by thorough repression and exile of the Protestants, and it was arguably his constitutional right, under the principle of *cuius regio eius religio*, to alter the religion of his lands according to his faith.

As King of Bohemia and Holy Roman Emperor he had identified the Protestant religion as the cause of the many rebellions in his reign, and after each victory against rebels, he had naturally wanted to insure that such uprisings would not occur in the foreseeable future.[54] After the battle at White Mountain, Ferdinand had punished the leaders of the rebellion and had expelled first Calvinist and then Lutheran ministers from the kingdom. When he had proclaimed a new constitution for Bohemia and the incorporated lands, he had acted in accordance with his right as conqueror, because the inhabitants had forfeited their privileges by supporting the rebellion. Under the new constitution, the succession became hereditary, as it was in the Palatine, Saxon, and Brandenburg electorates; the law protected Catholics alone; the diet of the Estates could only decide on matters of taxation; and the German language received legal parity with Czech. In Bohemia Ferdinand had imposed similar measures against Protestants and Protestantism as he had in Upper Austria, and he had been successful in his efforts to enforce his vision of divine and secular justice on those lands.[55] Sometimes, however, this earnest desire led him to make political errors of awesome magnitude.

The Edict of Restitution, issued on 6 March 1629, would prove to be Ferdinand's greatest mistake. After the victory at Lutter, Pope Urban VIII had exhorted Ferdinand to take advantage of his triumph over the rebellious Lower Saxon Circle and restore the church lands that had been alienated by Protestants, and Ferdinand had complied, despite circumspect hesitance at his own court in Vienna and resistance from the Electors of Saxony and Brandenburg at the Mühlhausen Diet. Ferdinand looked on the restitution of church lands as a legitimate opportunity to right former transgressions of the Imperial constitution's guarantees for the Catholic religion. The new Elector of Mainz, Archbishop Georg Frederick von Greiffenklau, had led the Catholic electors at Mühlhausen in their support for the Emperor's decision.[56]

In Ferdinand's estimation, the Edict of Restitution was a conservative document, legally defensible, and constitutional. The proclamation, published in late March 1629, opened with Ferdinand's claim that he was restoring the status quo of 1555 and, therefore, merely enforcing Imperial law. It provided for the restitution to Catholics of the hundreds of monastic and ecclesiastical foundations reformed since the treaty of Passau in 1552, the basis of the Peace of Augsburg. In accordance with the principle of *cuius regio eius religio*, the new lords of these lands then claimed the right to convert the inhabitants to Catholicism. Moreover, the edict officially prohibited all Protestant sects that had not been encompassed in the Peace of Augsburg, most notably, Calvinism. Lutheranism remained legal, and church lands in Electoral Saxony and Brandenburg were exempt, though for how long no one could say. In one year the commissioners enforcing the edict took back less than half of the designated number of properties, but, backed up by Tilly and the League army, they succeeded in the archbishoprics of Magdeburg and Bremen and the bishoprics of Halberstadt, Osnabrück, Minden, Verden, and Hildesheim.[57]

The decision to promulgate the edict in 1629 came towards the end of the campaign against the Lower Saxon Circle, not at the beginning. The Emperor had resisted viewing the Danish-Lower Saxon mobilization as a rebellion. Only when negotiations had ended in irreconcilable demands – Christian's for the restoration of the Palatinate, Ferdinand's for Danish-Lower Saxon disarmament – had it become clear to the Emperor that the Circle was in a state of rebellion. Ferdinand had not sent Wallenstein against the Circle primarily in order to recover the lands formerly belonging to the Catholic Church but to put down an uprising of belligerent rebels who had declared in favor of the banned Count Palatine. Once victory had been secured, however, Ferdinand was not likely to pass up the opportunity to take advantage of the situation. He saw the restitution of church lands as 'the great gain and fruit of the war'.[58] Moreover, he had been subject to severe pressure to carry it out. The Catholic League had demanded the restoration of church lands in the Lower Saxon Circle, and the four Catholic electors had endorsed applying the edict to the rest of Germany. As supreme judge in controversies about monastic institutions and communities, only the Emperor could make a ruling and issue an interpretation of that kind, but Maximilian had pushed Ferdinand to promulgate the edict as a piece of legislation.[59] Though some of his own councilors had warned him that the edict would transform the current constitutional conflict into a general war of religion, he had relied on his conscience and his faith and signed the document.[60]

A storm of protest greeted the edict. While it was legally defensible in the constitutional law of the Empire, it was an outrage against the parity between Catholic and Protestant confessions and between the Emperor and the Imperial estates that existed in constitutional practice.[61] Furthermore, the edict was more than an interpretation or clarification of pre-existing law. It was tantamount to a new law, which had to be ratified by an Imperial diet, and Ferdinand had never managed to convene one. Furthermore, according to the edict it was also possible to reclaim monastic foundations that had been subject to the Emperor alone and dissolved or secularized before 1552, which would have forced Protestant princes to accept Catholic institutions in their own territories, despite the privilege of *cuius regio eius religio.*[62]

There were other grounds for bitter complaint. In 1627 Spanish troops had carried out a ruling of the Imperial Supreme Court to dispossess the Calvinist Landgrave Moritz of Hessen-Kassel for having assisted Denmark and to render a portion of his lands to his cousin, Landgrave Georg of Hessen-Darmstadt, a Lutheran who had supported the Emperor since the beginning of the war.[63] Since the Mühlhausen Diet there had been increasingly vociferous complaints from the electors and various Imperial princes and estates, Catholic and Protestant together, about the size of the Emperor's army, which may have reached 120,000–150,000 in number, the degree of its exactions, and the arrogance of its general. In the spring of 1629 Ferdinand had sent 50,000 of Wallenstein's troops to northern Italy to assist Spanish forces in a war against Mantua.[64] It appeared to more and more Imperial estates that the Emperor was more interested in increasing the powers of the Habsburg dynasty than in restoring a manageable peace to the Empire. Members of both confessions condemned Ferdinand's bestowal of the duchy and ducal title of Mecklenburg on Wallenstein as compensation and reward for his services.

The problems between the Emperor, the electors, the estates, and the League grew still worse after the electoral diet in Regensburg in the summer of 1630, despite hopes to the contrary. Ferdinand wanted to procure support to help Spain subdue the Dutch Republic and to defend the Empire from anticipated attacks by Sweden and France, but the electors demanded Wallenstein's dismissal and a drastic reduction in the number of Imperial troops. Ferdinand also wanted his son to be elected King of the Romans to guarantee his eventual succession to the Imperial throne, but the electors demanded instead that Ferdinand relinquish his influence over the Imperial Supreme Court and declare no new wars without obtaining the electors' advice. Ferdinand lost in both cases. He dismissed Wallenstein but refused to mollify the severity of the Edict of Restitution, which even the Catholic electors had come to see during the preceding year as dangerously excessive.[65] Maximilian actually led the attack on the Emperor's policies and retreated from his prior support for the edict, considering the need for unity against the Swedish menace.[66]

The Emperor and electors did not disagree about the Palatine crisis, which was by then of minor concern to them. Despite pleas from Sir Robert Anstruther, the English ambassador – Rusdorf, the Palatine emissary, was not granted an audience – Ferdinand basically reiterated the conditions articulated at the Mühlhausen Diet.[67] The only difference was that he demanded no reparations but instead insisted that Frederick renounce all his alliances within and beyond the Empire and put a permanent halt to all his designs against the Emperor, the Empire, the electors, princes, and estates.[68] Frederick, however, would not retreat on any of his positions and had actually returned to his earlier, more stringent demands.[69] Frederick's instructions for Rusdorf said that the King of Bohemia would only deprecate himself, confessing to no crimes, if the Emperor would first revoke the Imperial ban and restore him to all his lands and titles.[70] Frederick's customary plea for mercy and restitution without having to comprise his sense of innocence or perform any acts of submission won little sympathy among the members of the assembly at Regensburg.[71] No progress was made toward a resolution of that tired controversy.

The Edict of Restitution would inspire more united resistance against the Emperor than the Bohemian rebellion or the Palatine crisis ever had. In 1629, Ferdinand's goal had been to secure the Empire from further violent upheavals. Unfortunately, his decisions eventually led the Elector of Saxony, who had been steadfast in his loyalty to the Emperor throughout the preceding years, to join with the Elector of Brandenburg in protest against the Edict of Restitution.[72] Following the Regensburg Diet, Johann Georg called a convention of Protestant estates in Leipzig in September 1630, which was a prelude to a conference of over 100 Protestant Imperial princes, estates, and Free Cities in early 1631. By April 1631 the Lutherans and Calvinists, overcoming their theological differences and long-standing enmities, formed a defensive alliance and provided for an army of 40,000 to defend and 'uphold the basic laws, the Imperial constitution, and the German liberties of the Protestant states'.[73] The formation of this

Protestant alliance coincided with an alliance between France and Sweden (the treaty of Bärwalde, January 1631) to pursue 'the restitution of the suppressed estates of the Empire'.[74] In May 1631, Louis XIII and Maximilian signed a secret pact of non-aggression and mutual defense, the treaty of Fontainebleau, in which France agreed to uphold Maximilian's status in the Empire, including his hereditary claim to the Palatine electorate, while recognizing at the same time his constitutional obligation to the Emperor.[75] Maximilian then felt a measure safer from the Protestant alliance and the Swedes, and Richelieu could silence the critics of his assistance for the Protestants for some time.

These various arrangements, all made to support their proponents' diverse conceptions of the Imperial constitution, reflect the depths of the rifts in that constitution. As at the beginning of the war, dynastic and confessional considerations together played a major role in determining each potentate's constitutional vision, and those who led the fighting did so to realize their own conception. The course of events during the next three years shows what might have happened had Frederick V been able to convert the campaign for his restitution into a genuinely 'common' or even an arguably 'Protestant' cause.

The Swedish Invasion

The King of Poland sued for peace with Sweden in 1629 and in September procured a truce of six years' duration. The terms and a promise of French assistance left Gustavus Adolphus free to intervene in Imperial affairs. In July 1630, while the Electoral diet was sitting at Regensburg, he landed in Pomerania with an army of roughly 10,000 men. This modest beginning did not presage the astounding string of victories that would follow.[76]

Gustavus Adolphus' stated purpose for the attack was to make retribution for past injuries and to restore the peace as guaranteed by the Imperial constitution. He declared that he was retaliating against Habsburg encroachments on Sweden's lucrative Baltic trade and against the Emperor's having sent 12,000 troops to assist the King of Poland in 1629. In addition Gustavus Adolphus wanted satisfaction for other minor complaints, such as having his letters intercepted. He also objected to the suppression of German liberties, but he insisted that the villain was not the Holy Roman Emperor. The Swedish King styled himself as the champion of the public peace in affairs of church and state, and, based on his words at the time and later statements from his chancellor, Axel Oxenstierna, there was no intention to conduct a crusade for Protestantism. Religion was an aspect of the public peace that needed protection.[77]

In the first year after Gustavus Adolphus' arrival, the number of his allies and his victories increased more and more rapidly. By the late summer of 1631, those supporting the King included the Dukes of Mecklenburg and of Saxe-Weimar, the Landgrave of Hessen-Kassel, the Elector of Brandenburg, and other princes, Magdeburg and other Imperial Free Cities, and the King of France. Earlier in 1631 Gustavus Adolphus had moved his armies slowly up the Oder, defeating the Imperial forces occupying towns in Electoral Brandenburg. In September, when Tilly led his army into Electoral Saxony to attack the Swedes, Johann Georg allied with Gustavus Adolphus and added 18,000 men to his army, which had grown to 23,000. These new allies exceeded the Imperial army in men and artillery and dealt it a crushing defeat, its first, on 17 September at Breitenfeld. Thereafter the Saxons invaded Silesia and Bohemia, and Gustavus Adolphus moved toward the Main and the Rhine, sending his enemies into flight, ravaging their lands, and extorting assistance from Protestant princes who had wanted to stay loyal to the Emperor. The proximity of a massive army would increase Gustavus Adolphus' number of Protestant allies at least as much as any constitutional and confessional interests they might have shared. In November 1631, the Saxon army would enter Prague, and in the next month the Swedes would cross the Rhine at Oppenheim and take Mainz.[78]

Frederick V was ecstatic. He had rejoiced at the Swedes' landing in northern Germany.[79] Gustavus Adolphus had made occasional contact with Frederick over the years, reassuring him in the summer of 1626 that Sweden was interested and well inclined towards the Palatine cause.[80] The Swedish victories and the ever increasing number of their allies had given Frederick the greatest hopes for his restitution yet. Throughout 1630 he had successfully resisted pressure from various princes and his own counselors to submit to the Emperor in accordance with the conditions from the Mühlhausen and Regensburg Diets, and during 1631, Frederick had become optimistic that he would be restored in the wake of the Swedes' victories, which, he was sure, had been divinely inspired.[81] While the campaign had progressed, Frederick had tried to gather more support for the King and for the cause of his own restitution from the princes and powers with whom he had a connection.

At first it appeared that nothing would be forthcoming from his hosts, the Dutch Estates General, which had been sharply divided in 1630 over accepting an offer of an unconditional truce from Philip IV.[82] During that year Frederick had tried to persuade them to grant him some lands in Jülich garrisoned by Dutch troops, by virtue of his rank of Count Palatine on the Rhine. Charles I had seconded this plea, but it had had no effect with the Estates, because they had not wanted to provoke Spain.[83] In 1631, however, the Prince of Orange returned to war, though the campaign against Flanders was abortive.[84] In October, after the Dutch had pulled back their forces, Frederick asked the Prince to put a corps at his disposal so that he could join it to Gustavus Adolphus' forces. The Prince of Orange replied that Frederick might have his own corps if he found the money to pay for it, or if he persuaded Gustavus Adolphus to divert some of the funds the Estates General had granted to the Swedish army.[85] Frederick also asked the Prince to pressure Charles I to aid the Swedes, but the answer was equally dismissive. Frederik Hendrik said that Frederick should go to England himself to persuade his brother-in-law.[86]

Though Frederick's efforts to keep England from making peace with Spain had come to nothing, Charles I, after signing the Peace of Madrid, had claimed that the new peace had not been meant to be prejudicial to Palatine affairs, and that he would continue to work for the long-awaited restoration.[87] He had then dispatched Anstruther to resume talks with the Emperor in Vienna in June 1631. With Rusdorf's assistance, Anstruther would negotiate for over a year at the Imperial court, and despite Spanish support for his terms for the restoration of the Palatinate, the talks would come to nothing.[88] In October 1631 Frederick and Elizabeth together pressured Charles I to contribute to the Swedish military effort, reminding him that his honor was at stake.[89] In the summer of 1631 Charles had authorized the Marquis of Hamilton to levy a few thousand troops and lead them, in the name of the Count Palatine, to northern Germany, but disease and desertion reduced this force to 500 men by December. Also in the summer, Charles had sent the Swedish King an ambassador, Sir Henry Vane, to arrange an alliance between the two kingdoms for the full restitution of the Palatinate.[90]

Vane had his first audience with the Swedish King in Würzburg in November, and there he learned that Frederick would have to go join the King in the field if he wanted to have his Palatinate returned to him. Vane saw that Gustavus Adolphus' successful campaign was indeed a two-edged sword: 'And for ought I know may be (if he prosper) in the Palatinats before Christmas, if not sooner; and then I feare it will be hard fetching it out of his hands without satisfaction'.[91] Vane did not recommend sending Gustavus Adolphus any monetary assistance due to what appeared to be a towering ambition. Whenever he received money, he apparently spent it on hiring more troops immediately.[92]

Gustavus Adolphus left Würzburg in November and moved down the Main. He was the first foreign conqueror to have taken Frankfurt in the history of the Holy Roman Empire. He then entered the Lower Palatinate and took Oppenheim before turning on Worms and then Mainz, which fell after a single day of siege.[93] Secure in Mainz, Gustavus Adolphus was positioned to make an assault on the Palatinate. In mid-December he proposed to Frederick's envoy, Baron Slavata, that the Palatine ally with the Swedes, but that he must first secure a monthly war subsidy for the campaign from the United Provinces.[94] Gustavus Adolphus saw that no peace in Germany was secure or feasible without Frederick's restitution.[95] He was also determined to use Frederick, his cause, and his connections for all they were worth.

Soon after this resolution arrived in The Hague, Frederick declared his intention to throw in his lot with the Swedish King. He had appealed to the Estates General to join with Gustavus Adolphus in November, and their initial reaction had been favorable. In early January 1632, Frederick informed them of the Swedish recovery of Oppenheim and asked for their assistance.[96] The Estates resolved to give him 150,000 Gulden, but they granted him a ceremonial audience before his departure only with reluctance and refused to pay his travel costs to the German border.[97] Many in that body were probably quite glad to see the departure of this perennially importunate guest.

For Frederick, God had provided him the opportunity to attend the conqueror, and the decision was fundamentally a matter of honor. Elizabeth wrote,

> when God and his honnour and frends call him there is no remedie; you know I love him not so little as to desire to be ridd of him, if necessitie did not make me to be content with it, his honnour being more deare to me then my owne contentment, of which I shall have but a little in his absence.[98]

For years Frederick had waited for an army to sweep his enemies out of the field so that he could retake control of the lands that belong to him by right of birth. For the first time, here was a force, led in person by a Protestant king, which showed no signs of weakness or impending decay as had those of Mansfeld and Halberstadt. If there was a time for Frederick's restoration, it was now. In late January he left his affairs in the hands of his secretary and asked Charles I to take responsibility for his wife and children during his absence.[99] When Frederick took leave of them, he was never to see them again.

The Last Campaign

As one would expect, the dispossessed King of Bohemia did not travel in royal style. He proceeded up the Rhine along terrible roads, stopping briefly in Wesel at the end of January, and then he followed the Lippe over

Dorsten and Marl, where he had to spend the night in a small, smoke-filled chamber. On the next day he lodged in an absent gentleman's house after his companions obtained offers of hospitality from the reluctant servants at gunpoint. On 4 February they passed near Dortmund through mild but rainy weather. Frederick feared that the journey would last a long time. Still, it must have been happily uneventful overall, considering that his only major cause of complaint was a malfunctioning pen that proved to be a significant annoyance when he composed his regular reports to his wife.[100]

Frederick reached Gustavus Adolphus in late February, perhaps just after he took Kreuznach in the Palatinate, having personally directed the siege. Its fall left only Frankenthal and Philippsburg as the major Palatine strongholds in Spanish hands. Other generals had taken other fortresses from Simmern in the northwest to Landau in the south.[101] He gave Frederick a royal reception and scolded Landgrave Georg of Hessen-Darmstadt for not addressing Frederick as the legitimate King of Bohemia. The Swedish King hosted his royal guest to numerous banquets and festive ceremonies and was pleased with Frederick's modest, affable bearing.[102] Over the course of the next few months, Frederick would be present at all military actions, and, thrilled with the Swedish King's boundless energy and excellent leadership, he would 'not thinck of resting, whiles he [was] in the feild'.[103] During this time, though Gustavus Adolphus treated his guest very honorably, Frederick often kept a discrete distance. He was observed to be in 'no way grievous to the King of Sueden', but he recognized the ambivalence of their relationship.[104] He wanted the Swedish King to be the instrument of his restitution, and for Gustavus Adolphus, having the dispossessed King of Bohemia and Elector Palatine in his party increased the legitimacy of his campaign. According to one astute observer, 'alwaies it is good, the two Kings should be together, for as Bohemia is protected by Sweden; so Sweden is justifyed by Bohemia'.[105]

Besides bestowing legitimacy, Frederick and his restoration proved a useful bargaining chip for Gustavus Adolphus as well. It had been a stated goal of Swedish designs for some time. Already in 1629 the Swedish King had named Frederick first in a list of princes whose restorations were essential to reestablishing the *status quo ante bellum* in the Empire.[106] In December 1631 Gustavus Adolphus had reiterated the necessity of the Palatine's restitution for achieving a lasting peace in Germany.[107] But at the same time he had used the Palatine crisis to negotiate assistance from England and to keep his enemies at bay. During talks with Sir Henry Vane, Gustavus Adolphus had demanded that the English provide him with complete command over an army of 12,000, a monthly subsidy of £25,000, and an alliance against Spain in return for Frederick's restoration to Bohemia and the Palatinate. Meanwhile, Gustavus Adolphus had been negotiating with emissaries from France, Bavaria, and the League about a partial restoration of the Palatinate as the cost of the League's neutrality. He had not given Frederick definitive terms for his restitution, though it quickly became clear that it would not be granted unconditionally. Gustavus Adolphus' reasoning was more militarily realistic than politically Machiavellian. There would have been no sense in clearing two territories for a prince who lacked the resources to defend them and whose enemies were still armed and in the field. Frederick's position in the Empire and his connections with Protestant powers necessitated that he receive a degree of satisfaction, but not if it jeopardized the Swedish military effort.[108] Before there could be any final arrangement about the Palatinate, Tilly first had to be soundly defeated.

In early March Gustavus Adolphus started to lead his army back up the Main. From Frankfurt Frederick wrote to Elizabeth that 'the King continues to show me plentiful affection; I am negotiating with him. I want to hope that all will go well'.[109] In mid March Frederick was handed conditions that he found 'very high', but not outlandish.[110] The King demanded freedom of worship for Lutherans in the Palatinate, the right to occupy all conquered fortresses for as long as the war would last, and a promise from Frederick that he 'like the rest of the princes', should acknowledge Gustavus Adolphus' absolute directory, and 'not depend upon any other king, prince, body or state, but only upon His Majesty.'[111] Only the first condition was constitutionally problematic, because it infringed on Frederick's privilege of *cuius regio eius religio*. The second and third terms were provisions for guaranteeing the security of the Swedish military position for the duration of the war. Gustavus Adolphus had not meant to force Frederick to dissolve his obligation to the Emperor and the Empire – not that he had ever been an obedient vassal of Ferdinand II – and make him a Swedish dependent. Gustavus Adolphus did want to make sure that Frederick would make no rival arrangements for his restitution with England, France, or the Dutch Republic that might undermine Swedish authority. Gustavus Adolphus did not demand absolute authority from Frederick in settling a peace but expected him first to assist the Swedish military effort and then be a good ally after the war's end.[112] Based on Frederick's initial impressions of his potential deliverer, however, he did not expect to settle a formal treaty with Gustavus Adolphus quickly. He wrote to his wife, 'The talks with the King of Sweden will be stretched out endlessly'.[113] Nonetheless he was still hopeful that they would come to a good arrangement, which might include his raising some troops and leading them under the Swedish King's general command.[114]

On 13 March Frederick heard that Tilly had attacked and defeated some Swedish troops. The Winter King then planned to leave Frankfurt and rejoin Gustavus Adolphus in Aschaffenburg, so that they could move together, Frederick hoped, against Bavaria. He was ambivalent about the campaign. He wrote to his wife, 'I would be much happier to be with you, but it is necessary to see what it will please God to arrange, to whom I entrust myself and my affairs'.[115] For the next few months he would accompany the Swedish army in its attack against his cousin and nemesis, Maximilian I.

Until 1632 Maximilian had been protected by the treaty of Bärwalde, but then Tilly, who had withdrawn his shattered army to Bavaria, had attacked Swedish troops at Bamberg on 28 February, and thereby violated the terms of the non-aggression pact.[116] Gustavus Adolphus mobilized his army and made for Bavaria. On 21 March he received a hero's welcome at Nürnberg, and at the evening banquet, Frederick occupied the place of honor, sitting directly across from Gustavus Adolphus.[117] They soon invaded Bavaria, ravaged Donauwörth, savaged its inhabitants, Protestant and Catholic alike, and destroyed Tilly's army, dealing a mortal blow to the seventy-three year old general.[118] Munich fell in May, and Frederick accompanied Gustavus Adolphus when he entered the city in triumph. To relieve pressure on Saxony from Wallenstein, whom Ferdinand had reinstated in December 1631, Gustavus Adolphus turned north toward Nürnberg. The Lower Palatinate remained quiet. In the summer of 1632 a Dutch assault on the Spanish Netherlands prevented the Spanish from trying to recover Frederick's lands, and the bulk of the Swedish army was busy besieging Wallenstein's stronghold near Nürnberg.[119]

The progress of arms was much more impressive than the negotiations regarding Palatine affairs, as Frederick had predicted. Gustavus Adolphus continued to give mixed signals about his restitution. Though showing Frederick all honor, Gustavus Adolphus had still never allotted a body of troops for his guest to lead. The continuous bargaining with the English ambassador about restoring the Palatinate in return for English military and financial assistance had only persuaded the Swedes that Charles I was more interested in negotiating than in coming to terms, but the same could have been said from the other side.[120] In late March Oxenstierna had told Sir Henry Vane that the Swedish King's intention was to force the revocation of the Edict of Restitution, settle a peace for Germany, and then go home, leaving Frederick to effect his own restitution. The Chancellor had implied that the whole war was Frederick's fault: the Bohemian war had only become a problem in Germany after he had accepted that crown.[121] Gustavus Adolphus had refused to promise to recover the Lower and Upper Palatinates and the electoral title by force of arms, which would have been 'to tye him to an impossibilitie'.[122] By June Vane concluded that it was useless to negotiate a restitution of the Palatinate with the Swedish King.

At first Frederick had been pleased with Gustavus Adolphus personally, though the former had quickly seen that negotiations would proceed slowly. For some months Frederick had followed the King resolutely and found him 'an excellent prince; one never becomes irritated being near him: may God preserve him for us!'[123] But with the passage of time, Frederick's enthusiasm waned. Above all, his desire to be with his wife and family again was replacing his excitement to be involved in the wars against his enemies. In his letters to his wife he said that he thought of her continuously, and nearly every one ended with a serious or even uxorious attestation of his love for her. Despite the repeated interceptions of their communications, they exchanged frequent letters, small presents, and portraits of themselves, their children, and their friends and relatives. Many of the people whom he met along the way spoke of how much they hoped to see Elizabeth again in Germany, 'but', he wrote, 'no one more than me!'[124]

While Frederick's negotiations continued to make no progress, his desire to see Elizabeth became an earnest yearning, and his patience vanished. By late July Gustavus Adolphus had lost his compelling appeal, though Frederick still spent hours with him in the field and on the march. He noted with regret how Germany was suffering more and more, even on a daily basis, under the continual burden of war.[125] Soon receiving news from The Hague became more important to him than the state of affairs on the front. He wrote to Elizabeth from Nürnberg, 'I confess that I am quite irritated here; principally because I so often may not have news from you'.[126] By August the lack of progress would become almost unbearable. 'The time', he would write, 'here hangs on me heavily, because nothing is happening'.[127] But Frederick's absence from his wife and family would be still harder for him to tolerate: 'I find nothing here so troublesome as having so little news'.[128]

In June Frederick had decided to permit the practice of the Lutheran religion in his lands. Though he could not subscribe personally to the Lutheran confession, he held no prejudice against Lutherans, even in the context of his own family. When his wife was looking for a caretaker to accompany their children, for example, Frederick recommended one Boniqua, despite the fact that he was a Lutheran, because his religion 'did not matter at all', considering that he would have nothing to do with the children's studies.[129] Nonetheless Frederick despaired when he heard that Gustavus Adolphus would only make firm arrangements for the Palatinate after he had consulted with the Elector of Saxony, who had never been sympathetic to the Palatine cause.[130]

Negotiations came to a head in July, when Charles had requested that Gustavus Adolphus send those British troops already in Swedish service to occupy the Palatinate, who would be supported by an English monthly subsidy of £10,000.[131] On hearing these terms, Frederick fell to pieces. 'With teares in his eies' and 'wishing himself out of the world', he complained to Vane and the Marquis of Hamilton that the treaty gave no advantage to England and would put the Palatine 'into an æternal subjection to bee slaves to the crown & king of Sweden'. Frederick preferred to have no treaty at all and declared that he would accept Gustavus Adolphus' offer to restore only those parts of the Palatinate then occupied by Swedish arms and no more.[132] Both Frederick and Gustavus Adolphus turned on the ambassador, declaring their grave displeasure. Vane tried to defend himself, insisting that his hands were tied in the negotiations, and he asked to be recalled.[133] By early August, Frederick accepted Gustavus Adolphus' offer of partial restitution, which entailed most of the Lower Palatinate, with the exception of Frankenthal, and only parts of the Upper. Nothing regarding the electoral dignity or Bohemia was guaranteed, and Frederick was visibly upset with the arrangement.[134]

He resolved to leave the company of the Swedish King in mid September. Gustavus Adolphus and Oxenstierna tried to keep Frederick with them by protesting their desire to give him satisfaction, but he had had enough of the Swedish wars. He preferred instead to attend the Frankfurt fair and return to his estates.[135] The two kings, one a hero, the other a pretender, took leave of each other towards the end of the month. As Frederick left, he received another set of terms for a Palatine-Swedish alliance, which were much the same as those from February, but which included still more rights and privileges for the Lutherans in the Palatinate. Considering that these conditions were not contingent upon any assistance from England, they were more generous than the first, but Frederick was still irked, because there was no provision for the restoration of either his electorate or Bohemia.[136]

He headed towards Frankfurt and reached the town at the end of September, where he heard that the negotiations were continuing without him and that the Swedish terms were growing worse. Now they wanted to retain the Bergstrasse, one of the best parts of the Palatinate, and remit the rest for a price, a demand that Frederick never expected to hear from the King of Sweden.[137] He became ever more depressed with his state of affairs and was losing hope in being restored by Swedish arms. 'It will be a true penitence', he said, 'that I will do here'.[138] Moreover, he found the Frankfurt fair a complete disappointment, and the lack of any nobles or gentlemen for company increased his melancholy.[139] In early October Frederick asked the Swedish King to accept his previous offer or simply to restore him with the same terms with which his brother, Ludwig Philipp, had regained Simmern. These entailed maintaining Swedish garrisons, tolerating Lutheranism, and recognizing the King as his benefactor.[140] Beyond that, Frederick was at a loss: 'If [Gustavus Adolphus] wants neither the one nor the other, I do not know what I ought to do'.[141] Frederick prayed that he could be together with his wife and family in the Palatinate by the following spring, and he sent a bitter letter of complaint to Charles I about the Swedes' unfair conditions and reneged promises.[142] The woeful poverty of Frederick's subjects and the paralyzed state of his affairs angered him.[143] He then decided to return to his homeland directly. From Frankfurt he entered the Lower Palatinate at Oppenheim, which lay in ruins, one half completely burnt.[144] As he went on toward Alsheim, he feared he would find himself there totally alone.[145]

Frederick's letter to King Charles I may have been instrumental in inciting the English King to action. In October 1632 Charles dispatched an ambassador to Frederick to announce he would be provided with an army of 8,000 infantry and 2,000 cavalry, under his personal command, to secure himself in the Palatinate. Charles allotted £16,000 for the costs of the embassy and the initial costs of the military force.[146] The timing could not have been better. The Lower Palatinate was all but cleared of the Spanish presence. Frankenthal remained in the hands of 800 sickly Spanish soldiers, and the Infanta was negotiating for the safe withdrawal of her troops and the town's possible return to Frederick.[147] Because the bulk of the Swedish King's armies were in eastern Germany, Frederick could have brought his mustered forces into the Lower Palatinate and, through intelligent negotiations, gradually obtained control of the strongholds.

After staying a few days in Alsheim, Frederick returned to Mainz, where Swedish ministers greeted him and wanted to resume their negotiations. Frederick, however, had no cause to be pleased. It seemed to him that the Swedish King wanted to hold him 'as low as he [could], ... but', Frederick reassured himself, 'he will only be able [to do] what God will permit him'.[148] He still found the demand for the toleration of Lutheranism offensive to his authority.[149] Moreover, the Swedish forces stationed in Heidelberg were making numerous sorties into the Bergstrasse, 'with great devastation and burning all about them'.[150] According to Henry Vane, the Palatinate was 'so ruined, that it [was] allmost a desert'.[151] There was no hope for peace in Germany, and there was only talk of more war. At that moment Frederick knew nothing of his brother-in-law's plan to restore him. Still, he had no viable alternative but to stay where he was.

Throughout late October and November 1632, Frederick's situation improved more quickly. In mid November he heard that the Swedish King was more pliable than he had been and was willing to articulate the treaty's stipulations in greater detail than in the past. Still better, Frederick heard that the governor of Frankenthal had agreed to hand the town over to him, but he was not sure if the Swedes would accept the arrangement, because the terms specifically named him as the beneficiary. The Upper Rhine was not threatened at that time, and neither Frederick nor his lands were in any danger of another invasion.[152] Safe in the castle in Mainz, his main comfort was to enjoy an increased correspondence with his wife. He wrote her about twice per week, and the post traveled relatively quickly between Mainz and The Hague, her letters taking about ten days to reach him. He was frustrated and wanted to see her again. '[I] would not stay eight days in Mainz', he wrote, 'being so extremely tired of it all'.[153] But when he wrote these words, he had no way of knowing that his life would be over in two weeks.

In late November Frederick developed a dreadful fever, delirium, constipation, and an inflammation in his lungs. His health had been good until that point, apart from an inflammation in his left ear that had temporarily deprived him of his hearing in early October.[154] Petrus de Spina, the physician of Landgrave Georg of Hessen-Darmstadt, attended Frederick, bleeding him and subjecting him to other early modern remedies. During the night of 29 November, he gradually lost his ability to breathe. By 7AM of the following day, he succumbed to his illness and was finally delivered of his worldly worries. An autopsy revealed no evidence of poison.[155]

News of Frederick's death broke his wife. Elizabeth confided in her brother, '[I am] the most wretched creature that ever lived in this world, and this shall I ever be, having lost the best friend that I ever had, in whom was all my delight'.[156] Without her children to care for, she would have rather been dead. In his condolences, Charles invited his sister to return to England, and she showed no offence that the invitation had not been given earlier, while Frederick had still lived, apparently a *persona non grata* in England. Nonetheless, she declined, citing the German custom that obliged a new widow to remain at home for a certain period of time. Even still she said she was not sure if she would come after that time until her children were 're-established in the Empire, or at least in a fair way of being so'.[157] She ended her reply with a request that Charles take her entire family into his protection. 'After God', she said, he was their 'sole resource'.[158]

Even in his obsequies Frederick was eclipsed by another. The death of Gustavus Adolphus on the battlefield at Lützen on 17 November had sent shock waves across Europe. There was no great, general mourning for the Winter King's passing twelve days later. To this day, the whereabouts of Frederick's remains are unknown. For years they were shuttled about from place to place until finally heading for Sedan, where it was presumed that they would find a safe and quiet place of rest.[159] But they vanished without a trace. If it is true that bandits attacked the caravan and stole the coffin, then it would have been the final, crowning humiliation.[160] Nonetheless several Dutch pamphleteers praised Frederick posthumously as a 'great and valiant king'.[161] Some of the rhetoric that bewailed the death of the two Kings spoke of the tragic loss to Protestantism of her two greatest leaders.[162] The combination, however, exemplified Protestantism's divisions as much as its unity. One king had been a Lutheran war hero 'obsessed with the dream of total victory', who had come very close to fulfilling it.[163] The other had been a Calvinist war victim, a mere pretender, obsessed with his own honor and conscience, always unwilling to accept his total defeat though he seemed incapable of achieving victory.

Notes

1. Lockhart, *Denmark*, pp. 149–53.
2. Lockhart, *Denmark*, pp. 173–7, 202–6. Parker, *The Thirty Years' War*, pp. 70–1, 89. Gindely, *Geschichte*, ii, pp. 131–2.
3. As many as 13,700 Scots soldiers joined the Danish forces, 1626–29. Murdoch, *Scotland and the Thirty Years War*, p. 10. Also see E.A. Beller, 'The Military Expedition of Sir Charles Morgan to Germany, 1627–9', *English Historical Review*, 43, no. 172 (1928), pp. 528–39.
4. PRO, SP, 81/34, fol. 276.
5. Beller, 'The Military Expedition', pp. 535–6.
6. Lockhart, *Denmark*, p. 200. In April 1629 Morgan and his men scored a modest victory against Imperial forces in Jutland. The Peace of Lübeck, however, put an end to his commission. Beller, 'The Military Expedition', pp. 538–9.
7. Quoted in Beller, 'The Military Expedition', p. 538.
8. BHStA, KB, 122/2I, 6/16 March 1627, Carlisle to Nethersole.
9. Weiß, *Die Unterstützung*, pp. 100–2.
10. PRO, SP, 81/34, fols 77–8: 6 June 1626, Friedrich Ulrich, Duke of Braunschweig-Lüneburg, to Charles I.
11. 'ist got nichts unmuglich. In dessen willen muss man sich allerseits ergeben und die erlosung von itzigen betrubten zustandt von seiner gnedigen handt erwarten'. Fiedler, 'Correspondenz', p. 406.
12. 'Es seindt noch tapfere Cavallier ubrig die den vatterlandt nutzliche dinst lesten kunnen'. Ibid., p. 405.
13. 'totale opression'. PRO, SP, 81/34, fol. 167: 11 February 1627, Frederick V to Charles I.
14. BHStA, KB, 121/3d, fols 55–6: 29 March 1627, Christian IV to Frederick V.
15. BHStA, KB, 121/3d, fols 53–4: 23 March 1627, Frederick V? to Christian IV; and fols 63–4: 14 May 1627, Frederick V to Christian IV.
16. BHStA, KB, 121/3d, fols 85–6: 19 June 1627, Frederick V to Christian IV.
17. 'von keiner substanz, sondern nur mehisten theils in fragen undt antworthen bestanden'. BHStA, KB, 121/3d, fol. 83: 19 June 1627, Frederick V to Gustavus Adolphus.

18. PRO, SP, 81/34, fol. 189: April 1627, Charles I to Frederick V. Also see BHStA, KB, 122/2I, 17 April 1627.
19. PRO, SP, 81/34, fols 215–16: 8/18 July 1627, Result of Conference at Colmar.
20. BHStA, KB, 89/3b, fol. 118: 5/15 July 1627, Rusdorf's report.
21. Frederick would continue to negotiate his reconciliation with the Duke of Lorraine in the next year. See PRO, SP, 81/35, fols 36–7, 48.
22. BHStA, KB, 89/3b, fol. 100: 1/11 October 1627, Frederick V to Duke of Württemberg.
23. BHStA, KB, 89/3b.
24. BHStA, KB, 121/3d, fols 91–2: 8 August 1627, Frederick V to Georg Wilhelm.
25. PRO, SP, 81/34, fol. 243: 22 October 1627.
26. BHStA, KB, 121/3d, fols 66, 67, 72, 78, 82. Weiß, *Die Unterstützung*, p. 102.
27. Gindely, *Geschichte*, ii, p. 115.
28. 'gott kan helfen wan man sich des am wenigsten versiehet auf Ihn mussen wir vertrawen und alle menschliche mittel so er zuschicken wurdt zu seiner ehr gebrauchen'. Fiedler, 'Correspondenz', p. 408.
29. Aretin, 'Sammlung', pp. 198–9.
30. Parker, *The Thirty Years' War*, pp. 84. Gindely, *Geschichte*, ii, pp. 122–3.
31. 'dem gemeinen Evangelischen wesen'. Fiedler, 'Correspondenz', p. 408.
32. PRO, SP, 81/35, fols 32–5: April 1628, 'the State of Affairs in Germanie'.
33. PRO, SP, 81/35, fols 55–6: 10/20 July 1628, Frederick V to Nethersole. These four districts were those of Heidelberg, Mosbach, Bretheim, and Bogsberg.
34. 'die gemeine feindt'. Fiedler, 'Correspondenz', p. 410.
35. Ibid., p. 411.
36. PRO, SP, 81/35, fols 123–4.
37. 'Aÿant pleu à Dieu adjouter à mes maux precedents une nouvelle affliction, dont la douleur ne se peut exprimer par la plume'. PRO, SP, 81/35, fol. 125: 10/20 January 1629, Frederick V to Charles I.
38. 'celuÿ de tous mes enfants que j'aÿmois le plus'. PRO, SP, 81/35, fol. 167: 6/16 March 1629, Frederick V to Charles I.
39. 'gott hat mich schwerlich heimgesucht durch den verlust meines liebstens sohn so alle vorige bekümmernis ubertroffen'. Fiedler, 'Correspondenz', p. 413.
40. 'il est raisonnable que ie m'y soubmette comme à celle qui est tousjours iuste et bonne, jaçoit que le sens humain aÿe de a peine de le comprendre'. Ibid.
41. 'puis que la main de celuÿ qui gouverne toutes choses en a dispose ainsi, c'est à moÿ de l'adorer et de m'ÿ submettre, esperant qu'elle me fortifiera et changera le tout en mieux'. PRO, SP, 81/35, fol. 132: 11/21 January 1629, Frederick V to Dorchester.
42. PRO, SP, 81/35, fols 194, 245–9. BHStA, KB, 89/3c: 18/28 May 1629, Frederick V to Charles I.
43. 'daß ohne hinlegung undt billich mäßiger vergleichung gedachten meinen sachen, kein beständiger friede im Römischen Reich zu hoffen'. BHStA, KB, 121/3d, fols 106–7: 8/18 April 1629, Frederick V to Christian IV.
44. Aretin, 'Sammlung', pp. 205–6, 261–3. Fiedler, 'Correspondenz', p. 413.
45. Aretin, 'Sammlung', pp. 199–209, 260–6.
46. Mout, 'Der Winterkönig', pp. 264–5. PRO, SP, 81/35, fol. 256: 24 October 1629, SV, Dorchester to Elizabeth.
47. Mout, 'Der Winterkönig', p. 272. As a member of the Order of the Garter, for example, he attended the ceremony for Frederik Hendrik's reception of the same honor in July 1627. Ibid., p. 268. Frederick's own decoration for the Order of the

Garter was in Munich, however, as part of the booty from Prague in 1620.

48. Aretin, 'Sammlung', p. 204.
49. Mout, 'Der Winterkönig', p. 269.
50. Trevor-Roper, *The Golden Age of Europe*, p. 138
51. Franz, 'Glaube und Recht', pp. 265–8.
52. Parker, *The Thirty Years' War*, pp. 77–8.
53. Franz, 'Glaube und Recht', p. 259.
54. Evans, *The Making*, p. 68.
55. Parker, *The Thirty Years' War*, pp. 80–4. Gindely, *Geschichte*, ii, pp. 99–103.
56. Bireley, *Religion and Politics*, pp. 51–5.
57. Michael Frisch, *Das Restitutionsedikt Kaiser Ferdinands. II vom 6. März 1629: eine rechtsgeschichtliche Untersuchung* (Tübingen, 1993). Parker, *The Thirty Years' War*, pp. 87–9. Gindely, *Geschichte*, ii, pp. 132–4.
58. Bireley, *Religion and Politics*, p. 54.
59. Albrecht, *Maximilian I.*, p. 698.
60. Asch, *The Thirty Years' War*, p. 95.
61. Frisch, *Das Restitutionsedikt*, pp. 126–7.
62. Asch, *The Thirty Years' War*, pp. 94–5.
63. Parker, *The Thirty Years' War*, p. 86. For Maurice's assistance to Christian IV, see Lockhart, *Denmark*, pp. 144–5.
64. Asch, *The Thirty Years' War*, p. 98.
65. Parker, *The Thirty Years' War*, pp. 100–2.
66. Albrecht, *Maximilian I.*, pp. 733, 743, 761–4.
67. Weiß, *Die Unterstützung*, pp. 103–5.
68. BHStA, KB, 122/2I, fol. 196: 31 September 1630.
69. BHStA, KB, 122/2I, fol. 70–2: 1/11 April 1630, Memo from Plessen, Rusdorf, and Camerarius.
70. BHStA, KB, 122/2I, fol. 6.
71. AP, iv, pp. 99–101.
72. Gotthard, 'Politice', p. 313.
73. Parker, *The Thirty Years' War*, pp. 104–6.
74. Parker, *The Thirty Years' War*, p. 107.
75. Albrecht, *Maximilian I.*, pp. 727–9.
76. Roberts, *Gustavus Adolphus*, ii, p. 442.
77. Parker, *The Thirty Years' War*, pp. 108–9.
78. Parker, *The Thirty Years' War*, pp. 110–14. Roberts, *Gustavus Adolphus and the Rise of Sweden* (London, 1973), p. 143.
79. PRO, SP 81/36, fols 44, 56–61: 10/20 June 1630 and 12/22 July 1630, Nethersole to Dorchester.
80. BHStA, KB, 122/3a, fol. 311: 27 July 1626, Gustavus Adolphus to Frederick V.
81. Gindely, *Frederick V*, p. 35. Mout, 'Der Winterkönig', p. 270. PRO, SP 81/37, fols 81–82: 9/19 October 1631, Frederick V to Charles I.
82. Israel, *The Dutch Republic*, pp. 508–12.
83. Mout, 'Der Winterkönig', pp. 269–70.
84. Israel, *The Dutch Republic*, p. 513.
85. BHStA, KB, 122/3b, fol. 413: 5/15 October 1631, Memo for Sieur du Pont; fol. 419: 11/21 October 1631. Extract of du Pont's report. The Estates General resolved to give money to Gustavus Adolphus in 1630. Mout, 'Der Winterkönig', p. 270. According to Michael Roberts, however, the Estates only agreed to grant three

monthly subsidies of 50,000 gulden in May 1631. They voted another two in December. Roberts, *Gustavus Adolphus*, ii, p. 596.

86. BHStA, KB, 122/3b, fol. 413: 5/15 October 1631, Memo for Sieur du Pont; fol. 419: 11/21 October 1631. Extract of du Pont's report.
87. BHStA, KB, 89/3c, fols 33–4, 56, 77.
88. Weiß, *Die Unterstützung*, pp. 106–7. See L.J. Reeve, 'Quiroga's Paper of 1631: a missing link in Anglo-Spanish diplomacy during the Thirty Years War', *The English Historical Review*, 51. 401 (1986), pp. 913–25.
89. PRO, SP 81/37, fols 81–82: 9/19 October 1631, Frederick V to Charles I. PRO, SP 81/37, fols 77–78: 7/17 October 1631, Elizabeth to Charles I.
90. Weiß, *Die Unterstützung*, pp. 107–12.
91. PRO, SP 81/37, fol. 123: 2/12 November 1631, Vane to Dorchester.
92. For Vane's detailed reports about the progress of the campaign, see PRO, SP 81/36–38.
93. Roberts, *Gustavus Adolphus*, ii, pp. 555–8.
94. PRO, SP 81/37, fol. 220: 15 December 1631. Gustavus Adolphus' resolution to Baron Slavata.
95. Roberts, *Gustavus Adolphus*, ii, p. 575.
96. BHStA, KB, 122/3b, fol. 416: 9 January 1632, Frederick V? to Estates General.
97. Mout, 'Der Winterkönig', p. 271.
98. PRO, SP 81/37, fols 226–7: 18/28 December 1631, Elizabeth to Dorchester.
99. PRO, SP 81/38, fol. 29: 15/25 January 1632, Frederick V to Dorchester. PRO, SP 81/38, fol. 34: 16/26 January 1632, Frederick V to Charles I.
100. Aretin, 'Sammlung', pp. 264–7.
101. Roberts, *Gustavus Adolphus*, ii, p. 675, n. 1.
102. Ibid., p. 611.
103. PRO, SP 81/38, fol. 178: 28 April/ 8 May 1632, Mr. Dinely 'alla Medesima'.
104. Ibid.
105. Ibid.
106. Schubert, *Camerarius*, pp. 374–5.
107. Roberts, *Gustavus Adolphus*, ii, p. 617.
108. Ibid., pp. 609–12.
109. 'Le Roy continue à me temoigner beaucoup d'affection, je suis en traité avec luy. Je veux esperer que tout ira bien'. Aretin, 'Sammlung', p. 267.
110. 'assé hauts'. Ibid., p. 268.
111. Roberts, *Gustavus Adolphus*, ii, pp. 612–13.
112. Ibid., pp. 613–4. Roberts corrects Schubert, Gindely, and Rushworth on this point and all those who have repeated the view that Gustavus Adolphus wanted to make Frederick V literally a vassal of Sweden. See notes 2 and 3.
113. 'Le traité avec [le Roi de Suède] sera traîné à l'infini'. Bromley, *A Collection*, p. 34.
114. Aretin, 'Sammlung', pp. 268–9.
115. 'Je serois bien plus heureux d'être auprès de vous, mais il faut voir ce qu'il plaira à Dieu d'en disposer, auquel je me remets et mes affaires'. Ibid., pp. 269–70.
116. Parker, *The Thirty Years' War*, pp. 115–16.
117. PRO, SP 81/38, fol. 111: 13/23 March 1632, 'Advices from Germany'. Roberts, *Gustavus Adolphus*, ii, p. 697.
118. Roberts, *Gustavus Adolphus*, ii, pp. 699–701.
119. Parker, *The Thirty Years' War*, pp. 116–17.
120. Weiß, *Die Unterstützung*, pp. 114–15.

121. PRO, SP 81/38, fol. 119: 26 March/5 April 1632.
122. PRO, SP 81/38, fol. 204: 21/31 May 1632, Report from Vane.
123. 'un brave prince; on ne s'ennuie pas près de lui: Dieu nous le veuille conserver!'. Bromley, *A Collection*, p. 36.
124. 'mais personne tant que moi'. Ibid., pp. 54, 34, 39, 50, passim.
125. Ibid., p. 48.
126. 'Je confesse que je m'ennuie bien ici; principalement parce que je ne puis si souvent avoir de vos nouvelles'. Ibid., p. 49.
127. 'Le tems me dure fort ici, car il ne se passe rien'. Ibid., p. 54.
128. 'je ne trouve rien si fâcheux ici que d'avoir si peu de nouvelles'. Ibid., p. 54.
129. 'cela n'importeroit guère'. Ibid., p. 33.
130. PRO, SP 81/38, fols 253–57: 13/23 June 1632, Vane to the Secretary of State. Michael Roberts asserts that regard for Saxony's preferences may have hardened the Swedish attitude towards Frederick's restoration to Bohemia. Roberts, *Gustavus Adolphus*, ii, p. 753.
131. Weiß, 'Die Unterstützung', p. 114.
132. PRO, SP 81/38, fol. 293: 1/10 July 1632, Report from Vane.
133. PRO, SP 81/38, fol. 294: 1/10 July 1632, Report from Vane. Weiß, *Die Unterstützung*, p. 115.
134. PRO, SP 81/39, fol. 12: 1/10 August 1632, Report from Vane.
135. Aretin, 'Sammlung', p. 274.
136. Roberts, *Gustavus Adolphus*, ii, pp. 615–16.
137. Aretin, 'Sammlung', p. 275.
138. 'ce sera une vraye penitence que je feray icy'. Aretin, 'Sammlung', p. 276.
139. Aretin, 'Sammlung', p. 277.
140. Roberts, *Gustavus Adolphus*, ii, p. 625.
141. 'S'il ne veut ni l'un ni l'autre, je ne sais ce que je dois faire'. Bromley, *A Collection*, p. 54.
142. Aretin, 'Sammlung', p. 276. PRO, SP 81/39, fol. 108: 24 September/4 October 1632, Frederick V to Charles I.
143. Bromley, *A Collection*, p. 59.
144. Ibid., p. 28.
145. Ibid., pp. 58, 61. 'Alsen' is the place name that appears in this letter, but Sir Henry Vane said that Frederick traveled to 'Altzeim'. PRO, SP, 81/39, fol. 148: 11/21 October 1632, Vane to Coke.
146. Weiß, *Die Unterstützung*, p. 116.
147. PRO, SP 81/39, fol. 188: 8/18 November 1632, John Durie to Roe. Bromley, *A Collection*, p. 29.
148. 'aussi bas qu'il pourra ... mais il ne pourra que ce que Dieu lui permettra'. Bromley, *A Collection*, p. 29.
149. Georg Irmer, *Die Verhandlungen Schwedens und seiner Verbündeten mit Wallenstein und dem Kaiser von 1631 bis 1634* (3 vols, Leipzig, 1888–91), vol. i, p. 280.
150. PRO, SP 81/39, fol. 148: 11/21 October 1632, Vane to Coke. Bromley, *A Collection*, pp. 29–30.
151. PRO, SP 81/39, fol. 148: 11/21 October 1632, Vane to Coke.
152. Bromley, *A Collection*, pp. 64–5.
153. 'il ne demeureroit huit jours en Mayence, en étant extrêmement las', Bromley, *A Collection*, p. 63. The 'il' refers to himself. Aretin, 'Sammlung', p. 277.

154. Bromley, *A Collection*, p. 60.
155. PRO, SP 81/39, fols 189–90: 20/30 November 1632, Petrus de Spina's report. The brain appeared normal, although the smaller veins were engorged with blood, but the lungs and heart were filled with puss and blood. One lung was so decayed that it could scarcely be removed from the chest.
156. Baker, *Letters of Elizabeth*, p. 86: 24 December 1624, Elizabeth to Charles I.
157. Ibid., p. 87.
158. Ibid.
159. For a detailed account, see Bilhöfer, 'Nicht gegen Ehre und Gewissen', pp. 228–46.
160. Pierre Congar, Jean Lecaillon, Jacques Rousseau, *Sedan et le Pays Sedanais: Vingt Siècles d'Histoire* (Marseille, 1978), p. 295.
161. Mout, 'Der Winterkönig', p. 270, n. 54.
162. For examples, see PRO, SP, 81/39.
163. Roberts, *Gustavus Adolphus* (1973), p. 160.

Chapter 10

Closure

To Westphalia

Even without Frederick V, the Palatine crisis remained an intractable problem. There was a chance for resolution three years after his death, in the Peace of Prague, 1635. By that time the war found a kind of stasis. Chancellor Oxenstierna had taken over management of the Swedish military forces, which had survived on a diet of plunder and rapine in numerous unfortunate Imperial bishopics and other estates. The war had dragged on inconclusively and somewhat chaotically, Wallenstein having been murdered in 1634 by his own officers for allegedly conspiring with the Swedes and the Saxons against the Emperor. Ferdinand's son, Ferdinand III, had then taken supreme command of the Imperial army, which, with the help of a Spanish army, had dealt the Swedes and their allies a crippling blow at Nördlingen in September 1635. The coalition around the Swedes collapsed, and Ferdinand II offered terms.

Most parties had compelling reasons to make peace, but few found the settlement very satisfactory. Overall it was advantageous for Ferdinand and many Catholic estates, though his Jesuit confessors and the pope said that it did not go far enough. It guaranteed Protestant possession of formerly Catholic estates and institutions in the Upper and Lower Saxon Circles, but the same provisions were not granted to princes and estates in western and southern Germany. While pardons were offered to many Protestant Imperial princes who had supported the Swedes against the Emperor, one was not extended to the new Count Palatine. Karl Ludwig, Frederick's eldest surviving son, had taken his father's title after his death and had inherited little else besides the well known, unfulfilled claims. In the Peace of Prague Ferdinand confirmed that the Palatine electoral title and all its lands east of the Rhine lay in the rightful possession of Duke Maximilian of Bavaria. This might have been the end of the matter if France had not declared war against Spain on 19 May 1635, a move that quickly began to tear the Peace of Prague to ribbons. The ensuing show-down between France and Spain had had many long-term and immediate causes, and it was to dominate the Thirty Years' War until its bitter end.

The war ravaged Germany until it became obvious to the major parties involved that armed forces could not solve the conflicts over the Imperial constitution; only a definitive clarification of the constitution's ambiguities would bring an end to the war. The Peace of Westphalia in 1648 finally resolved the Palatine crisis by restoring Karl Ludwig as Elector Palatine, but his restitution was not total.[1] His lands consisted of the Lower Palatinate alone, which had been utterly devastated, the population having been reduced by 75 percent or more.[2] And his electorate had to be newly created, the eighth in rank. Duke Maximilian had taken the Upper Palatinate and the foremost secular electoral dignity for Bavaria. In the end, King James I's old suggestion was the backbone of the compromise. Both branches of the Wittelsbach dynasty received an Imperial electoral title. The Peace also resolved other constitutional issues that had provided broad battlegrounds for the duration of the war. The Edict of Restitution was abrogated, and church lands were restored to their owners according to the normative date of 1 January 1624. Members of Protestant confessions enjoyed official toleration wherever they had privately worshipped as of the same date. Calvinists received the same rights as Lutherans, and the principle of *cuius regio eius religio* vanished from the Imperial constitution.

The Peace of Westphalia was not revolutionary. It did not transform the Imperial constitution into a loose federation of fully sovereign potentates; as far as possible, the German delegates had remained committed to establishing the Imperial constitution and the rights and privileges of its members. Innovations such as the eighth electorate for the Elector Palatine or the recognition of sovereignty for the United Provinces and the Swiss Confederation had been made out of necessity, without altering the structure of the Empire as a whole. The relationship between the Emperor and the Imperial princes and estates remained much as it had been. All estates of the Empire had been accepted as valid members at the peace negotiations, but they were not equal to the actual signatories of the treaty, the Emperor and the foreign potentates involved. And though the Peace of Westphalia confirmed the right of all Imperial princes and estates to conduct diplomacy and to make allegiances with foreign powers – they had done so long before 1618 – they were not to compromise their loyalty to the Emperor nor disrupt the peace in the Empire. The Emperor's powers were restricted only to the extent that the Habsburgs had no chance of establishing an absolutist monarchy in central Europe. His most important political decisions had to be ratified by the Imperial diet, but he maintained his supremacy as the highest judge of all legal conflicts and his traditional prerogatives as *Reichslehnsherr*, the feudal overlord of the Empire. With these resolutions, the Holy Roman Empire would never suffer another war between princes and estates over competing fundamental interpretations of the Imperial constitution.[3] The Empire's thirty years of civil war had not been fought entirely in vain.

The Problem of Religious War

More often than not, the Thirty Years' War is categorized as a 'war of religion' in school textbooks of various levels, if it is mentioned at all. I can think of more than a few instructors at colleges and universities who routinely describe the war as a purely religious conflict of appalling dimensions, in which Catholics and Protestants in Germany sought to wipe each other out. Despite such exaggerations, there is much justice in the classification. But few if any great historical events have a single, sufficient motive, and even those that seem to us to dominate the arena of inquiry often change their color and shape upon closer inspection.

It has been an argument of this book that the Thirty Years' War from Frederick's standpoint was a constitutional conflict of colossal dimensions and importance which entailed both religious and political interests. There was simply more to it than the strife between blocs determined by confession alone. Frederick did not fight on behalf of only Calvinists and Calvinism, but to uphold his whole vision of the Imperial constitution. He believed that the Habsburgs wanted to pervert the electoral structure of the Empire and transform it into an absolutist monarchy, which would annul the constitutional guarantees for Protestants in the Empire and their right to worship according to their chosen confession. His own restoration to his prior place in the Imperial constitution as Elector Palatine was the first and most necessary step in his struggle against the Emperor.

Frederick was not alone in his constitutional understanding of the crisis. Indeed all parties claimed to be fighting legitimately for a conservative restoration of the *status quo ante bellum* in the Empire. All could claim that they sought justice alone and desired to rid the Empire of recent constitutional innovations and corruptions. The agenda of various contenders could entail really any combination of constitutional interests: tenure of ecclesiastical and secular lands, possession of various privileges and dignities, and the legal right to practice a given Christian confession. For the Holy Roman Empire, the constitution encompassed the interests of religion and state together, and for most contemporaries the two were inseparably intertwined, though distinguishable nonetheless. There were no truly secular states in early modern Europe. To insist on an absolute dichotomy of church and state is to commit an anachronism.

This book suggests than an alteration in the historiographical landscape of early modern Germany may be in order. Examining the career of Frederick V, a long neglected figure of central importance to the development of the Thirty Years' War, demands that one abandon the metaphor of the exploding teapot for describing the events that began in 1618. There was no great, sudden effusion of violence between confessional groups in central Europe. This civil war began as a local crisis in Habsburg lands, and Palatine constitutionalism spread it throughout the Empire. Frederick V sustained and perpetuated the conflict until the intervention of other powers and the subsequent creation of new crises removed him and his causes from the central stage. It did not take long for the war to take on a life of its own, quite independent from the conditions of the Empire from 1600 to 1618.

Furthermore, the example of Frederick V may point to a limit in the historical effects of the process of confessionalization. The late sixteenth and early seventeenth centuries were undeniably times when secular and ecclesiastical authorities sought to indoctrinate their subjects in a given confession, but the degree to which these efforts determined the course of politics among the princes and estates of the Holy Roman Empire is questionable. There was certainly an expectation among Calvinists, Lutherans, and Catholics that they should help each other in times of need, but they neglected to do so more often than not. Frederick V, the Empire's premier Calvinist prince, did not pursue an exclusively or even primarily Calvinist policy. He wanted Protestants to overlook their differences instead of intensify them. He tried repeatedly to forge alliances with Lutheran, Roman Catholic, and Islamic powers. He detested Habsburgs not so much for their Catholicism as for their preferential support for the Jesuit order and their apparent desire to suppress Protestants and Protestantism in the Empire. Confessional interests were, for Frederick, not determinative in the formation of his political policy.

Religious and confessional interests, nevertheless, cannot and should not be denied. An absolutely necessary precondition for this conflict was the existence of at least three rival confessions in the Empire, which bred a large amount of mistrust and antagonism where tolerance, above all, was necessary for peace. Religious motivations certainly contributed to the formation of political policy, military alliances, and the course of events in general, but they alone do not satisfactorily account for the complex and confusing combinations of belligerents that populated the battlefields of the Thirty Years' War. The question of motivation is highly precarious, because the constellation of factors was subtly different for every participant. There can be as many explanations for the causes of the Thirty Years' War as there were individuals involved, whether they furthered the fighting or made every effort to stop it. But even if the historian looks at the broad sweep instead of the isolated instance, the number of inconsistencies makes it difficult to attribute the greatest force of causality to the interest of a given faith.

While it is certainly true that confession was a compelling determinant of a prince's or an estate's constitutional position, there were also considerations of dynasty, loyalty, finances, rivalry, and, above all, local security. Changing groups of warring princes determined the course of the war according to their desires, ambitions, and ability to fight. Often princes would argue that they were not pursuing a 'war of religion' and would accuse their opponents of doing so. Many officers and soldiers repeatedly switched sides with the changing winds of fortune on the battlefield, irrespective of nationality and religion.[4] Many Protestant princes supported Emperor Ferdinand II, and there were many Protestants in Wallenstein's armies. The French openly subsidized Gustavus Adolphus's campaign and, of course, declared war on Spain. In 1635 the Spanish invaded and occupied the lands of the Catholic Archbishop-Elector of Trier, and later Saxony and Sweden turned against each other. Still later Denmark declared war on Sweden.

In most cases, grand confessional coalitions of princes and potentates failed to achieve their objectives or even to get off the ground. At the beginning of the crisis, the Protestant Union and the Catholic League had managed never to engage in serious combat. Frederick's many calls for a grand military alliance of all Protestants in the Empire were normally met with a deafening silence. Sometimes Catholics and Protestants fought each other to further their confessional interests, but the exception seems to have been as binding as the rule.

What is certain is that until 1648 the war was responsible for its own perpetuation. War caused more war; battles demanded reprisals; losses had to be recovered and gains maximized. In many cases, the close proximity of hungry armies would secure or swing the allegiances of Imperial princes and estates more effectively than any number of more abstract arguments. Fortuitous circumstances were also paramount in determining the shape of the war. The deaths of potentates such as Emperor Matthias and James I were as influential as the persistent survival of the main belligerents. Many battles, skirmishes, assaults, and sieges could have gone either way. The fortunes of warring sides fluctuated with alarming irregularity. And no one should underrate the vast importance of decisions by individuals and small groups. Frederick's accepting the Bohemian crown, Ferdinand's secretly offering the Palatine electorate to Maximilian, the Spanish monarchy's decision to intervene militarily, and James I's adamant refusal to do so are just some of the innumerable determining factors in the direction the war took. It suffices to say that as long as there were men, resources, and enough will to fight, the conflict was as unpredictable as it was unstoppable.

The example of Frederick V supports these arguments. This prince was a more than willing belligerent. He readily took to arms in defense of his constitutional interpretation and only abandoned them when there were no alternatives available to him, and then only temporarily. He joined the Bohemian rebellion out of a firm conviction of the legitimacy of their cause and their constitutional right to elect him. A strong suspicion of Habsburg designs to corrupt the Bohemian and Imperial constitutions also contributed to the decision. Next to these considerations, confession appears to have been of lesser importance. Frederick's Calvinism was actually the basis of some arguments against the move, considering the marginal status of the Calvinist minority in Bohemia. One should not forget that the Catholic Duke of Savoy made every indication that he would take the crown if it were offered him. As king, Frederick did all he could to establish a regime that would be tolerant of religious differences and yet could maintain its own security. But time and circumstance were not on his side.

Frederick's acceptance of the Bohemian crown escalated the war; it transformed the uprising, a local struggle, into a crisis that concerned the whole of the Empire. His protestation that the quarrel was only between himself and the Archduke of Styria, not the Holy Roman Emperor, did not prevent Ferdinand Habsburg from using every legal and military means available to him to regain his usurped crown. Because the Dutch Republic, the Protestant Union, and England would not fight on Frederick's behalf, and because the rebel estates of Bohemia and the incorporated lands would not institute extreme measures to finance the war effort, it was almost impossible for the Emperor, supported by the Duke of Bavaria, the Catholic League, Spain, and the Elector of Saxony, not to secure an eventual victory on the field of battle. Frederick's ensuing flight across Europe and his proclamation of the Protestant cause shows how little Protestant potentates wanted to engage in a war of religion in the Empire.

Once Frederick lost the Palatinate as well as Bohemia, his restitution was fundamentally a constitutional issue between the Emperor and himself. He tried to attach his struggle for restitution with issues much larger than his own. For Frederick, his individual prosecution was a symptom of impending universal persecution in central Europe; the condition of the Empire, he believed, was as insufferable as his own. For years he contributed to the war's perpetuation by refusing to compromise on his position and by enlisting supporters when they were available and interested. The longer the war lasted, the more Frederick became certain that Ferdinand was determined to subject the Empire to his absolute will.

Frederick enjoyed temporary periods of vindication when England and then Denmark took up his battle standards for him, but when these projects ended in failure, he had nothing left but his sense of injured righteousness. The Palatine crisis soon lost its immediacy as a constitutional issue for the Empire, and when Ferdinand promulgated the Edict of Restitution, he presented the Imperial princes and estates with a new constitutional issue of wider application and greater consequence. It is no surprise that the Edict quickly subsumed the Palatine crisis in significance. The ensuing uproar in the Empire drowned out the Palatine's steady drone of protest.

The cause of Frederick's failure stems from repeated instances of fundamental miscalculation. He thrust himself into the middle of the arena of great power politics in Europe without the financial and military means to defend his position on his own. He incorrectly estimated his allies' willingness to fulfill their obligations, and luck was not on his side. Whenever he tried to foment a war of religion, it was primarily for the sake of his own restitution, and it failed miserably. For years the Kings of Denmark and England shunned Frederick's call for a general war of religion. The Dutch Republic granted hospitality to the exiled King of Bohemia and from time to time gave some money for the troops fighting in his service, but they were not the least bit interested in trying to topple the Catholic dominance over the Empire. The Dutch were rather pleased, however, to see a great portion of the Spanish Army of the Netherlands tied down in the war in the Palatinate. Gustavus Adolphus was glad to have the dispossessed King of Bohemia's company during his campaigns, because it bestowed an extra ornament of legitimacy on his actions, but when it came to restoring the Palatinate, the security of Swedish forces was the more important consideration.

Those who did fight for Frederick were primarily driven by interests other than the confessional. His most famous and notorious supporters, Mansfeld and Halberstadt, were *condottiere*, the former a Calvinist, the latter a Lutheran, or, according to others, both atheists. Both subscribed formally to Frederick's Protestant and common causes, but Mansfeld had served the Catholic Duke of Savoy earlier and constantly considered switching sides to serve the Emperor, the Duke of Bavaria, or the King of France. Halberstadt attributed his actions several times in his life to chivalric duty, imposed on him by virtue of his passionate love for Frederick's wife. Other supporters of the Palatine pair participated in the war only as far as it concerned their local interests. The Margrave of Jägerndorf, also a soldier of fortune, operated militarily only in the vicinity of his own lands, in Moravia and Silesia. The Transylvanian prince, Bethlen Gábor, a Calvinist vassal of the Turkish Sultan, switched sides and made deals with the Emperor, Frederick V, and the Turks so often in the early 1620s that even contemporary observers concluded that he was using religion to cloak his worldly, political ambitions in Hungary.

More Calvinists actually hampered Frederick's war effort than helped him. The most aggressive Calvinist in the Palatine regime, Prince Christian of Anhalt, gave up the whole cause within one year after the defeat at White Mountain, and at the same time Ludwig Camerarius recommended that Frederick give up his claim to the Bohemian crown and make peace with the Emperor. King James I accused his son-in-law of waging a war of religion and utterly refused to send aid except when domestic pressures in England forced him to do otherwise. The Elector of Brandenburg and the Landgrave of Hessen-Kassel, both prominent Calvinists in the Empire, withheld their support for Frederick's cause until the proximity of Imperial armies threatened their own estates and forced them to take defensive measures.

Lutheran princes and estates were almost wholly against Frederick's actions. Lutheran members of the Protestant Union refused to partake in his Bohemian adventure. The Landgrave of Hessen-Darmstadt and the Elector of Saxony criticized the Palatine's almost every move. The Duke of Württemberg and the King of Denmark expressed some sympathy for Frederick's state after the invasion of the Palatinate, the Battle of White Mountain, and the imposition of the Imperial ban, but they merely urged him to renounce his claim to the Bohemian crown and make amends with the Emperor. Still, there were a couple of Lutherans who adamantly supported Frederick, despite all apparent obstacles. Besides Halberstadt there was the Duke of Saxe-Weimar, Johann Ernst, who fought for the Protestant cause in Bohemian, Palatine, and Danish military forces until his death in 1626.

This approach to the history of Frederick V is easy to assault. One might say that the sources are unreliable, because he simply changed the tune of his correspondence according to the time, manner, and place of the writing, always suiting his words to the recipient's needs. While this is certainly true to some extent, it does not account for the consistency of his point of view regardless of the ebb and flow of political fortune. Some historians have simply dismissed Frederick as a narrow-minded man who was so blinded by his religion that he could not have handled himself or his affairs otherwise. Stubborn and narrow-minded he no doubt was, he was not blind to the complexities and ramifications of his situation, though his preferred path of action stayed more or less straight throughout. It makes little sense to attribute his personal characteristics to his religion or particular confession. Humanity has a way of maintaining its tremendous diversity of qualities and characters against the conforming pressures of race, class, gender, philosophy, or religion.

Frederick the Man

Frederick was a deeply religious man, but he did not always act in accordance with confessional interest. Religious feeling suffuses his extant correspondence. Successes and failures were always for him God's rewards and trials. Turning to God in all hours of need kept Frederick from despair and strengthened him against the bitter vicissitudes of fortune. His faith gave him patience and hope. His own confession was Calvinist, and it provided a framework for his personal faith. His policy, however, was not. He certainly believed that the Imperial constitution, despite its ambiguities, provided protection for Calvinist worship, but there his confessional politics came to an end. He gladly received assistance for his restitution from Calvinists, Lutherans, members of the English church, Catholics, and Muslims. He found Catholicism and Lutheranism to be flawed forms of Christian belief, but Catholicism and especially the Jesuit order revealed more traces of evil. He had always tried to bring Protestants together to increase their own security in the Empire, and their persistent lack of unity must have been one of his greatest recurring disappointments. Though it is tempting stereotypically to attribute his unrelenting obstinacy and his unwavering conviction of his own righteousness to the Calvinist tenet of predestination, one must remember that Emperor Ferdinand II and Duke Maximilian I, both Catholics educated by Jesuits, showed the same character trait. From the Battle of White Mountain till November 1632, Frederick neither wavered in his faith nor showed any recognition that he might have made a mistake in judgment regarding God's will. He knew what was right, acted on it, took the consequences, and refused to backtrack. His faith cemented his constitutional convictions.

For Frederick the question of his restitution was one of justice, and, in his opinion, the innocence of his actions and the illegality of the Emperor's were incontestable. The whole crisis stemmed from the Imperial ban declared against him in December 1621, from which derived the transfer of the Palatine lands and electorate. The constitutional transgressions, Frederick argued, were unprecedented:

> of such a form that in the ancient and recent events and histories of the German Empire there is no example to be found which may ever be surpassed in the like animosity, severity, and spite of a Roman Emperor against an Elector of the Empire.[5]

He was certain that without a favorable resolution, the war would continue unabated in the Empire. The Electors were supposed to be the guarantors of peace, the protectors of the constitution, and the checks on the

Emperor's power, and as long as Frederick was not recognized as the rightful Elector Palatine, he predicted that there would be no peace in the Empire. He did his utmost to fulfill the prophecy.

Frederick's greatest strength, for better for worse, was his persistence. At times this quality, combined with an extreme punctiliousness, reached eccentric levels. Pursuing a single rabbit for three to six hours on a hunt was not beyond him.[6] His doctor once noted the vehemence with which he strove to obtain the object of his desire.[7] While watching Frederick direct the remodeling projects at Rhenen, an observer noted 'how curious and exact he is'.[8] For Frederick, persistence was almost a matter of honor. Though he often bewailed his fate in the political arena and wished that he could retire to a private life with his dearly beloved wife and children, he said that his honor would not permit it. He was born an Imperial prince and elector and was elected and crowned a king. Retirement was an impossibility. He clung to his honor as he did to life itself. It above all is probably the main reason for his relentless belligerence. A dictum of Cardinal Richelieu provides the best explanation:

> A good reputation is especially necessary to a prince, for if we hold him in high regard he can accomplish more with his name alone than a less well esteemed ruler can with great armies at his command. It is imperative that he guard it above life itself, and it is better to risk fortune and grandeur than to allow the slightest blemish to fall upon it, since it is certain that the first lessening of his reputation, no matter how slight, is a step in the most dangerous of directions and can lead to his ruin.[9]

The irony in Frederick's case is that his every attempt to defend the honor of his name and the integrity of his cause actually contributed to his utter failure as a prince. He risked fortune and grandeur and was then unable to ward off the waves of blemishes that followed.

The Winter King was one of the most mocked figures in early modern Europe, and he knew it.[10] Bad luck and fatal miscalculation led him to lose all the trappings that made him a prince, except for his personal sense of honor and birthright. His unwillingness to acknowledge that he had committed any transgression against the Imperial constitution had disastrous consequences for the general population of the Holy Roman Empire, and arguably for much of western Europe, but he was not alone in his obstinacy. The war did not stop as long as the primary belligerents would not adjust their vision of the Imperial constitution or their status in relation to it. Frederick V, Ferdinand II, Maximilian I, and many, many others all share the responsibility for the perpetuation of the Thirty Years' War.

Notes

1. For a concise analysis of this process, see Dieter Albrecht, 'Bayern und die pfälzische Frage auf dem Westfälischen Friedenskongress', in Heinz Duchhardt, ed., *Der Westfälische Friede, Historische Zeitschrift*, Supplement 26 (1998), pp. 461–8.
2. Alexander Schweickert, ed., *Kurpfalz* (Stuttgart, 1997), p. 39. This estimate may be high. See John Theibault, 'The Demography of the Thirty Years War Re-Visited: Günther Franz and his Critics', *German History*, 15, 1 (1997), pp. 1–21.
3. Asch, *The Thirty Years War*, pp. 141–6.
4. Geoffrey Parker, 'The Soldiers of the Thirty Years' War', in Repgen, *Krieg und Politik*, pp. 303–15.
5. 'dergestalt daß in den alten undt newen geschichten undt historien des Teutschen Reichs kein exempel zu finden daß wieder einen Churfürsten des Reichs mit dergleichen animositet, rigor, undt bitterkeit, von einem Römischen Keiser were iemals præcedirt worden'. BHStA, KB, 121/3d, fol. 107: 8/18 April 1629, Frederick V to Christian IV.
6. Fiedler, 'Correspondenz', pp. 381, 407.
7. 'quod appetit, ... vehementer appetit' PRO, SP, 81/35, fol. 263: 3/13 November 1629, Nethersole to Dorchester.
8. PRO, SP, 81/35, fol. 256: 24 October 1629, SV, Dorchester to Elizabeth.
9. Henry Bertram Hill, trans., *The Political Testament of Cardinal Richelieu* (Madison, 1961), p. 119.
10. For a collection of the songs and fly-sheets produced at his expense, see E.A. Beller, *Caricatures of the 'Winter King' of Bohemia* (Oxford, 1928). Petr Voigt, 'Dosud Neznámá Verze Satiry na Útěk Fridricha Falckého', *Sborník Národního Muzea v Praze. Rada C: Literární Historie*, 31, 3–4 (1986), pp. 267–98. R. Wolkan, *Deutsche Lieder auf den Winterkönig* (Prague, 1898).

Bibliography

This study is primarily based on unpublished archival manuscripts. The greatest and most varied body of material generated by Frederick V and his regime is to be found in the *Bayerisches Hauptstaatsarchiv* in Munich, in the *Kasten Blau* and *Kasten Schwarz* collections especially. They contain documents from the Palatine government based in Heidelberg, the brief reign in Prague, and the extended exile in The Hague. Notes, drafts, and copies of political correspondence abound, as do letters that Frederick received from his connections throughout most of Europe. Only some of these items have been published, and most do not appear to have been consulted in the historical literature on the subject. I did not need to work through Camerarius' papers, the *Collectio Camerariana*, in the *Bayerische Staatsbibliothek*, relying instead on Friedrich Hermann Schubert's exhaustive publications, which make use of this material. Also in the *Staatsbibliothek* are the original letters from Frederick to Elizabeth that were published by Johann Christoph Freiherr von Aretin in 1806.

Another important collection of papers relating to the Palatine crisis in general is the State Papers Foreign Germany (Empire and States) in the Public Record Office, London, the vast majority of which I examined on microfilm. The original letters from Frederick to James confirmed the reliability of the copies that were kept in The Hague and are now stored in Munich. Another historian who worked through this material, though with quite a different topic in mind, is Arthur White, whose dissertation proved to be very useful in filling out my narrative. Some documents from the British Library in the Harleian, Tanner, and other manuscript collections were likewise consulted on microfilm at Widener Library, Harvard University.

The *Archivo General de Simancas* is a treasure chest of documentary material for establishing the Spanish monarchy's contribution and reaction to the Palatine crisis, especially *Estados Inglaterra* and *Alemania*. Published works by Peter Brightwell and Eberhard Straub were of central importance in developing the Spanish side of this project. Additional manuscripts in the *Biblioteca Nacional* and *Biblioteca Real* in Madrid helped particularly to enrich the analysis of Anglo-Spanish relations during the period in question.

Other archives supplied helpful material. The *Algemeen Rijksarchief* in The Hague yielded a few letters from Frederick's regime-in-exile. The *Státní Ústřední Archiv* in Prague has some of the documents from Frederick's one year reign as King of Bohemia, though not having Czech, I was only able to read those in German and Latin. The *Státní Oblastní Archiv* in Český Krumlov, also known as the *Státní Archív Třeboň*, has a collection of papers from Count Georg Ludwig von Schwarzenberg, including his correspondence with Emperor Ferdinand II during the embassy to England in 1622. The *Staatenabteilungen* in the *Haus-, Hof-, Staatsarchiv* in Vienna is replete with sources on the Imperial reaction to the Palatine crisis, but because this was not the central focus of this work, only some of these papers were used. At the *Rigsarkivet* in Copenhagen, there is a complete series of original and duplicate letters exchanged between Frederick V and King Christian IV, in *Tyske Kancelli, Udenrigske Afdeling, Speciel Del, Pfalz:* AI, *Brevveksling mellem Fyrstehusene.* In the *Generallandesarchiv* in Karlsruhe, there are the original letters that George Bromley published in 1787 and a typescript of an unpublished biography of Frederick V completed by John Gustav Weiß in 1942, which mainly concerns the Palatine's early years until 1619 and does not make extensive use of archival sources.

Below is a list of the printed works that I consulted, including primary sources, secondary literature, and unpublished theses. The works in Czech supplied an abstract, usually in German, that I could read.

Abelin, Johannes Philipp. *Theatrum Europaeum.* 21 vols. Vol. 1. Frankfurt am Main, 1643–1738.

Adams, Simon. 'Foreign Policy and the Parliaments of 1621 and 1624'. In *Faction and Parliament*, ed. Kevin Sharpe. Oxford: Clarendon Press, 1978.

Adams, Simon. 'Spain or the Netherlands? The Dilemmas of Early Stuart Foreign Policy'. In *Before the English Civil War*, ed. Howard Tomlinson. London: MacMillan Press, 1983.

Adams, Simon. 'The Protestant Cause: Religious Alliance with the West European Calvinist Communities as a Political Issue in England, 1585–1630'. Ph.D. Thesis, Oxford University, 1973.

Akrigg, G.P.V. *Letters of King James VI & I.* Berkeley: University of California Press, 1984.

Albrecht, Dieter. 'Bayern und die pfälzische Frage auf dem Westfälischen Friedenskongress'. In *Der Westfälische Friede*, ed. Heinz Duchhardt. *Historische Zeitschrift*, Supplement 26 (1998): 461–468.

Albrecht, Dieter. *Die auswärtige Politik Maximilians von Bayern, 1618–1635.* Vol. 6, *Schriftenreihe der historischen Kommission bei der bayerischen Akademie der Wissenschaften.* Göttingen: Vandenhoeck & Ruprecht, 1962.

Albrecht, Dieter. *Die deutsche Politik Papst Gregors XV: die Einwirkung der päpstlichen Diplomatie auf die Politik der Häuser Habsburg und Wittelsbach 1621–1623.* Vol. 53, *Schriftenreihe zur bayerischen Landesgeschichte.* München: C.H. Beck'sche

Verlagsbuchhandlung, 1956.

Albrecht, Dieter. *Maximilian I. von Bayern, 1573–1651*. München: R. Oldenbourg Verlag, 1998.

Albrecht, Dieter, Hans Günter Hockerts, Paul Mikat, Rudolf Morsey, ed. *Politik und Konfession: Festschrift für Konrad Repgen zum 60. Geburtstag*. Berlin: Duncker & Humblot, 1983.

Albrecht, Dieter. 'Zur Finanzierung des Dreißigjährigen Krieges: die Subsidien der Kurie für Kaiser und Liga, 1618–1635'. *Zeitschrift für bayerische Landesgeschichte*, 19, 3 (1956): 534–566.

Alcalá-Zamora, José. 'En Torno a los Planteamientos Hegemonicos de la Monarquía Hispana de los Felipes'. *Revista de la Universidad de Madrid*, XIX, 73 (1970): 57–106.

Alcalá-Zamora, José, and Queipo de Llano. *España, Flandes y el Mar del Norte (1618–1639)*. Barcelona: Editorial Planeta, 1975.

Allen, Paul C. *Philip III and the Pax Hispanica, 1598–1621: the Failure of Grand Strategy*. New Haven: Yale University Press, 2000.

Allgemeine Deutsche Biographie (ADB). 56 vols. Berlin: Duncker & Humblot, 1875–, 1967–71.

Almansa y Mendoza, Andres. *Cartas de Andres de Almansa y Mendoza, Novedades de Esta Corte y Avisos Recibidos de Otras Partes, 1621–1626*. Madrid: Miguel Ginesta, 1886.

Anderson, Alison D. 'The Jülich-Kleve Succession Crisis (1609–1620): a Study in International Relations'. PhD Thesis, University of Illinois at Urbana-Champaign, 1992.

Angual, David. 'Gabriel Bethlen', *Revue Historique*, clvii, 1 (1928), 19, 22, 26.

Aretin, Johann Christoph Freiherr von, ed. 'Sammlung noch ungedruckter Briefe des Churfürsten Friderich V. von der Pfalz, nachherigen Königs von Böhmen; von den Jahren 1612–1632'. In *Beyträge zur Geschichte und Literatur*. 9 vols. Vol. 7. München, 1806.

Asch, Ronald G. *The Thirty Years War: the Holy Roman Empire and Europe, 1618–1648*. London: Macmillan Press Ltd, 1997.

Babel, Rainer. *Frankreich im europäischen Staatensystem der Fruhen Neuzeit*. Vol. 35, *Beihefte der Francia*. Sigmaringen: Jan Thorbecke Verlag, 1995.

Babel, Rainer. *Zwischen Habsburg und Bourbon: Außenpolitik und europäische Stellung Herzog Karls IV. von Lothringen und Bar vom Regierungsantritt bis zum Exil (1624–1634)*. Sigmaringen: Jan Thorbecke Verlag, 1989.

Bacigalupe, Miguel Angel Echevarria. *La Diplomacia Secreta en Flandes, 1598–1643*. Leioa-Vizcaya: Universidad del País Vasco, 1984.

Bahlcke, Joachim. '"Falcko – české království" (Motivy a působení zahraničněpolitické orientace Falce od české královské volby po ulmskou smlouvu 1619–1620)'. *Časopis Matice Moravské*, 111, 2 (1992): 227–251.

Baker, L.M. *The Letters of Elizabeth, Queen of Bohemia*. London: The Bodley Head, 1953.

Ballesteros Beretta, Antonio, ed. *Correspondencia Oficial de Don Diego Sarmiento de Acuña, Conde de Gondomar*. 4 vols, *Documentos Inéditos para la Historia de España*. Madrid, 1936–45.

Barnes, Robin Bruce. *Prophecy and Gnosis: Apocalypticism in the Wake of the Lutheran Reformation*. Stanford: Stanford University Press, 1988.

Barteček, Ivo. 'Saská politika a české stavovské povstáni (květen 1618 – spren 1619)'. *Sborník historický*, 30 (1984): 5–47.

Barudio, Günter. *Der Teutsche Krieg*. Frankfurt am Main: Fischer Taschenbuch Verlag, 1988.

Bayer, Karl. 'Churfürst Friedrich V'. *Programm der Königlichen Studienanstalt zu*

Schweinfurt, (1873): 2–21.

Becker, Winfried. 'Ständestaat und Konfessionsbildung am Beispiel der böhmischen Konföderationsakte von 1619'. In *Politik und Konfession: Festschrift für Konrad Repgen zum 60. Geburtstag*, ed. Dieter Albrecht. Berlin: Duncker & Humblot, 1983.

Beladiez, Emilio. *España y el Sacro Imperio Romano Germanico*. Madrid: Editorial Prensa Española, 1967.

Beller, E.A. 'The Thirty Years War'. In *The New Cambridge Modern History*, ed. J.P. Cooper, Cambridge: Cambridge University Press, 1970, pp. 306–58.

Beller, E.A. *Caricatures of the 'Winter King' of Bohemia*. Oxford: Oxford University Press, 1928.

Beller, E.A. 'Contemporary English Printed Sources for the History of the Thirty Years' War'. *American Historical Review*, 32, 2 (1927): 276–82.

Beller, E.A. 'The Military Expedition of Sir Charles Morgan to Germany, 1627–9'. *English Historical Review*, 43, 172 (1928): 528–39.

Beller, E.A. 'Recent Studies on the Thirty Years' War'. *Journal of Modern History*, 3, 1 (1931): 72–83.

Benecke, G. *Germany in the Thirty Years War*. New York: St. Martin's Press, 1979.

Benecke, G. *Society and Politics in Germany, 1500–1750*. London: Routledge & Kegan Paul, 1974.

Benrath, Gustav Adolf. 'Abraham Scultetus (1566–1624)'. In *Pfälzer Lebensbilder*, ed. Kurt Baumann, Speyer: Verlag der pfälzischen Gesellschaft zur Förderung der Wissenschaften in Speyer, 1970, pp. 97–116.

Benrath, Gustav Adolf. *Die Selbstbiographie des Heidelberger Theologen und Hofpredigers Abraham Scultetus (1566–1624)*. Karlsruhe: Evang. Presseverband Karlsruhe, 1966.

Bérenger, Jean. *Histoire de l'Empire des Habsbourg, 1273–1918*. Paris, 1990.

Bezzel, Irmgard. 'Kurfürst Maximilian I. von Bayern als Reichsfürst in den Jahren 1623–1627'. Inaugural-Dissertation zur Erlangung des Doktorgrades, Ludwig-Maximilians-Universität zu München, 1957.

Bilhöfer, Peter. 'Nicht gegen Ehre und Gewissen: Friedrich V., Kurfürst von der Pfalz – der "Winterkönig" von Böhmen (1596–1632)'. Inauguraldissertation zur Erlangung des akademischen Grades eines Doktors der Philosophie der Universität Mannheim, 2000.

Birch, Thomas. *The Court and Times of James the First*. 2 vols. London: Henry Colburn, 1849.

Bireley, R.L. 'Maximilian of Bavaria, Adam Contzen, S. J., and the Catholic Restoration in Germany, 1624–1635'. Ph.D. Thesis, Harvard University, 1971.

Bireley, Robert, S.J. *Religion and Politics in the Age of the Counterreformation: Emperor Ferdinand II, William Lamoraini, S.J., and the Formation of Imperial Policy*. Chapel Hill: University of North Carolina Press, 1981.

Bireley, Robert, S.J. *The Counter-Reformation Prince: Anti-Machiavellianism or Catholic Statecraft in Early Modern Europe*. Chapel Hill: University of North Carolina Press, 1990.

Bonner, Robert E. 'Administration and Public Service under the Early Stuarts: Edward Viscount Conway as Secretary of State, 1623–1628'. PhD, University of Minnesota, 1968.

Bosbach, Franz. *Monarchia universalis: ein politischer Leitbegriff der frühen Neuzeit*. Vol. 32, *Schriftenreihe der Historischen Kommission bey der Bayerischen Akademie der Wissenschaften*. Göttingen: Vandenhoeck & Ruprecht, 1988.

Braudel, Fernand. 'En Espagne au Temps de Richelieu et d'Olivarès'. *Annales, E.S.C.*, 3,

July–September (1947).

Brightwell, Peter. 'Spain and Bohemia: The Decision to Intervene, 1619'. *European Studies Review*, 12, 2 (1982): 117–137.

Brightwell, Peter. 'Spain, Bohemia and Europe, 1619–1621'. *European Studies Review*, 12 (1982): 371–99.

Brightwell, Peter. 'The Spanish Origins of the Thirty Years' War'. *European Studies Review*, 9, 4 (1979): 409–31.

Brightwell, Peter. 'The Spanish System and the Twelve years' Truce'. *English Historical Review*, 89 (1974): 270–92.

Brinkmann, Günter. *Die Irenik des David Pareus: Frieden und Einheit in ihrer Relevanz zur Wahrheitsfrage*. Ed. Wolfgang Philipp and Axel Hilmar Swinne, *Studia Irenica*. Hildesheim: Verlag Dr. H.A. Gerstenberg, 1972.

Bromley, George. *A Collection of Original Royal Letters*. London, 1787.

Bruchmann, Karl. *Die Huldigungsfahrt König Friedrichs I. von Böhmen nach Mähren und Schlesien*. Vol. 9, *Darstellungen und Quellen zur schlesischen Geschichte*. Breslau: Ferdinand Hirt, 1909.

Brünink, W. *Der Graf von Mansfeld in Ostfriesland (1622–1624)*. Vol. XXXIV, *Abhandlungen und Vorträge zur Geschichte Ostfrieslands*. Aurich: Verlag Ostfriesische Landschaft, 1957.

Bryce, James. *The Holy Roman Empire*. London: Macmillan, 1866; New York: Schocken Books, 1961.

Buckisch und Löwenfels, Gottfried Ferdinand von. *Observationes Historico-Politicæ in Instrumentum Pacis Osnabrugo-Westphaliscum*. Frankfurt and Leipzig, 1722.

Burckhardt, Carl J. *Richelieu and His Age* . New York: Harcourt, Brace & World, Inc., 1940.

Burkhardt, Johannes. *Der Dreißigjährige Krieg*. Vol. 542, NF, *edition suhrkamp*. Frankfurt am Main: Suhrkamp Verlag, 1992.

Buschmann, Arno. *Kaiser und Reich*. München: Deutscher Taschenbuch Verlag, 1984.

Calendar of State Papers and Manuscripts Relating to English Affairs Existing in the Archives and Collections of Venice and in Other Libraries of Northern Italy. 38 vols. Nendeln/Liechtenstein: Kraus Reprint, 1970.

Carter, Charles H. 'Gondomar: Ambassador to James I'. *The Historical Journal*, VII, 2 (1964).

Carter, Charles Howard. *The Secret Diplomacy of the Habsburgs, 1598–1625*. New York: Columbia University Press, 1964.

Castroviejo, José María. *El Conde de Gondomar: un Azor entre Ocasos*. Madrid, 1967.

Chaline, Olivier. *La Bataille de la Montagne Blanche (8 November 1620)*. Paris: Éditions Noesis, 1999.

Christiansen, Theodor. *Die Stellung König Christians IV. von Dänemark zu den Kriegsereignissen im Deutschen Reich und zu den Plänen einer evangelischen Allianz, 1618–1625*. Kiel, 1937.

Chudoba, Bohdan. *Spain and the Empire 1519–1643*. Chicago: University of Chicago Press, 1953.

Chudoba, Bohdan. *Spanelé Na Bílé Hore*. Prague, 1945.

Church, William F. *Richelieu and Reason of State*. Princeton, New Jersey: Princeton University Press, 1972.

Clasen, Claus-Peter. *The Palatinate in European History*. Oxford: Basil Blackwell, 1963.

Clasen, Claus-Peter, 'The Empire before 1618', in *The Golden Age of Eurpoe*, ed. Hugh Trevor-Roper. London, 1987.

Cogswell, Thomas. *The Blessed Revolution*. Cambridge: Cambridge University Press, 1989.

Cogswell, Thomas. 'England and the Spanish Match'. In *Conflict in Early Stuart England,* ed. Richard Cust and Ann Hughes, London, 1989, pp. 107–33.

Cogswell, Thomas. 'Phaeton's chariot: The Parliament-men and the continental crisis in 1621'. In *The Political World of Thomas Wentworth, Earl of Strafford, 1621–1641,* ed. J.F. Merritt, Cambridge: Cambridge University Press, 1996, pp. 24–46.

Cohn, Henry J. *The Government of the Rhine Palatinate in the Fifteenth Century.* Oxford: Oxford University Press, 1965.

Cohn, Henry J. 'The Territorial Princes in Germany's Second Reformation, 1559–1622'. In *International Calvinism, 1541–1715,* ed. Menna Prestwich, Oxford: Oxford University Press, 1985, pp. 135–165.

Collinson, Patrick. 'England and International Calvinism, 1558–1640'. In *International Calvinism, 1541–1715,* ed. Menna Prestwich, 197–223. Oxford: Oxford University Press, 1985.

Congar, Pierre, Jean Lecaillon, Jacques Rousseau. *Sedan et le Pays Sedanais: Vingt Siècles d'Histoire.* Marseille: Laffitte Reprints, 1978.

Coryat, Thomas. *Coryat's Crudities.* 2 vols. Glasgow: James MacLehose and Sons, 1905.

Deleito y Piñuela, José. *El Rey Se Divierte (Recuerdos de Hace Tres Siglos).* Madrid: Espasa-Calpe, S. A., 1955.

Devèze, Michel. *L'Espagne de Philippe IV (1621–1665), ed. Victor-L. Tapié. 2 vols, Regards sur l'Histoire.* Paris: Société d'Édition d'Enseignement Supérieur, 1970.

Dollacker, Generalmajor z. D. *Das Ende der kurpfälzischen Herrschaft in der oberen Pfalz, 1618–1621.* Amberg: Josef Fenzl, 1918.

Dominguez Ortiz, Antonio. *Crisis y Decadencia de la España de los Austrias.* Barcelona: Ediciones Ariel, 1969.

Domínguez Ortiz, Antonio. *The Golden Age of Spain, 1516–1659.* Translated by James Casey. London: Weidenfeld and Nicolson, 1971.

Dotzauer, Winfried. *Der historische Raum des Bundeslandes Rheinland-Pfalz von 1500– 1815: der fürstliche Politik für Reich und Land, ihre Krisen und Zusammenbruche.* Frankfurt am Main; New York: P. Lang, 1993.

Dotzauer, Winfried. *Die deutschen Reichskreise in der Verfassung des Alten Reiches und ihr Eigenleben (1500–1806).* Darmstadt, 1989.

Du Boulay, F.R.H. *Germany in the Later Middle Ages.* London: Athlone Press, 1983.

Duchhardt, Heinz. *Deutsche Verfassungsgeschichte 1495–1806.* Stuttgart: Kohlhammer, 1991.

Duchhardt, Heinz. *Protestantisches Kaisertum und Altes Reich.* Vol. 87, Veröffentlichungen des Instituts für Europäische Geschichte Mainz, Abteilung Universalgeschichte. Wiesbaden: Franz Steiner Verlag, 1977.

Dunn, Richard S. *The Age of Religious Wars, 1559–1715.* New York: W. W. Norton & Co., 1979, 1970.

Dust, P.C. *The Carmen Gratulans Adventu Serenissimi Principis Frederici Comitis Palatini Ad Academiam Cantabrigiensem,* ed. J. Hogg. 2 vols, *Elizabethan & Renaissance Studies.* Salzburg: Institut für Englische Sprache und Literatur, 1975.

Egler, Anna. *Die Spanier in der Linkrheinischen Pfalz, 1620–1632.* Vol. 13, *Quellen und Abhandlungen zur Mittlerheinischen Kirchengeschichte.* Mainz: Anton Philip Brück, 1971.

Eickels, Christine van. *Schlesien im böhmischen Ständestaat, Neue Forschungen zur Schlesischen Geschichte.* Köln: Böhlau Verlag, 1994.

Elliott, J.H. *The Count-Duke of Olivares*. New Haven: Yale University Press, 1986.

Elliott, J.H. *El Conde-Duque de Olivares y la Herencia de Felipe II, Coleccion 'Sintesis'*. Valladolid: Universidad de Valladolid, 1977.

Elliott, J.H. 'A Europe of Composite Monarchies'. *Past & Present*, 137 (1992): 48–71.

Elliott, J.H. *Imperial Spain, 1469–1716*. New York: Penguin Group, 1963.

Elliott, J.H. and José F. de la Peña, eds. *Memoriales y Cartas del Conde Duque de Olivares*. Vol. I, *Tesis Alfaguara*. Madrid: Ediciones Alfaguara, 1978.

Elliott, J.H. 'A Question of Reputation? Spanish Foreign Policy in the Seventeenth Century'. *Journal of Modern History*, 55, 3 (1983): 475–83.

Elliott, J.H. *Richelieu and Olivares*. Cambridge: Cambridge University Press, 1991.

Elliott, J.H. *Spain and its World, 1500–1700*. New Haven: Yale University Press, 1989.

Elliott, J.H. 'The Statecraft of Olivares'. In *The Diversity of History*, ed. J.H. Elliott and H.G. Koenigsberger. London: Routledge & Kegan Paul, 1970.

Ernst, Hildegard. *Madrid und Wien, 1632–1637*. Vol. 18, *Schriftenreihe der Vereinigung zur Erforschung der Neueren Geschichte*. Münster: Aschendorff Münster, 1991.

Essen, Alfred van der. 'Le Rôle du Cardinal-Infant dans la Politique Espagnole du XVIIe Siecle'. *Revista de la Universidad de Madrid*, III, II (1954): 357–83.

Evans, R.J.W. 'Calvinism in East Central Europe: Hungary and Her Neighbours'. In *International Calvinism, 1541–1715*, ed. Menna Prestwich, 167–196. Oxford: Oxford University Press, 1985, pp. 167–196.

Evans, R.J.W., and T.V. Thomas, eds. *Crown, Church and Estates: Central European Politics in the Sixteenth and Seventeenth Centuries*. London: Macmillan, 1991.

Evans, R.J.W. *The Making of the Habsburg Monarchy, 1550–1700*. Oxford: Oxford University Press, 1979.

Evans, R.J.W. *Rudolf II and his World*. Oxford: Oxford University Press, 1973.

Febvre, Lucien. *The Problem of Unbelief in the Sixteenth Century: the Religion of Rabelais*, trans. Beatrice Gottlieb. Cambridge, 1982.

Fiedler, Joseph, ed. 'Correspondenz des Pfalzgrafen Friedrich V. und seiner Gemahlin Elisabeth mit Heinrich Mathias von Thurn'. *Archiv für Kunde österreichischer Geschichts-Quellen*, 31 (1864): 377–414.

Forst, H. 'Der türkische Gesandte in Prag 1620 und der Briefwechsel des Winterkönigs mit Sultan Osman II'. *Mittheilungen des Instituts für Österreichische Geschichtsforschung*, 16 (1895): 566–81.

Forster, Marc R. *The Counter-Reformation in the Villages: Religion and Reform in the Bishopric of Speyer, 1560–1720*. Ithaca: Cornell University Press, 1992.

Frank, Michael. 'Ehre und Gewalt im Dorf der Frühen Neuzeit: Das Beispiel Heiden (Grafschaft Lippe) im 17. und 18. Jahrhundert'. In *Verletzte Ehre: Ehrkonflike in Gesellschaften des Mittelalters und der Fruhen Neuzeit*, ed. Klaus Schreiner and Gerd Schwerhoff, 320–338. Köln: Bohlau, 1995, pp. 320–38.

Franz, Georg, ed. *Die Politik Maximilians I. von Bayern und seiner Verbündeten, 1618–1651*. Part I, vol. i, *Briefe und Akten zur Geschichte des Dreissigjährigen Krieges*. München: R. Oldenbourg Verlag, 1966.

Franz, Günther. 'Glaube und Recht im politischen Denken Kaiser Ferdinands II'. *Archiv für Reformationsgeschichte*, 49, 1/2 (1958): 258–69.

Franzl, Johann. *Ferdinand II. Kaiser im Zwiespalt der Zeit*. Graz: Verlag Styria, 1978.

Freytag, Gustav. *Aus dem Jahrhundert des großen Krieges, 1600–1700*. Vol. 4, *Bilder aus der deutschen Vergangenheit*. Leipzig: Paul List Verlag, 1925.

Freytag, Gustav. *Reformationszeit und Dreißigjähriger Krieg*. Vol. 2, *Bilder aus der deutschen Vergangenheit*. München: Orbis Verlag, 1987.

Frisch, Michael. *Das Restitutionsedikt Kaiser Ferdinands II vom 6. März 1629: eine rechtsgeschichtliche Untersuchung.* Tübingen, 1993.

Gade, John A. *Christian IV, King of Denmark and Norway.* Boston: Houghton Mifflin Co., 1928.

Gagliardo, John G. *Germany Under the Old Regime, 1600–1790.* London: Longman, 1991.

Gardiner, S.R., ed. *The Earl of Bristol's Defence of his Negotiations in Spain.* Vol. 104, *Camden Society.* London, 1871.

Gardiner, S.R., ed. *The Fortescue Papers, Camden Society.* London: Camden Society, 1871.

Gardiner, S.R. *History of England from the Accession of James I to the Outbreak of the Civil War, 1603–1642.* 10 vols. London: Longmans, Green, and Co., 1883.

Gardiner, S.R., ed. *Letters and Other Documents Illustrating the Relations Between England and Germany at the Commencement of the Thirty Years' War.* 2 vols. *Camden Society.* London, 1865, 1868.

Gardiner, S.R., ed. *Narrative of the Spanish Marriage Treaty, Camden Society.* London, 1869.

Gardiner, S.R. *Prince Charles and the Spanish Marriage, 1617–1623.* 2 vols. London: Hurst and Blackett, 1869.

Gardiner, S.R. *The Thirty Years' War, 1618–1648.* London: Longmans, Green, and Co., 1912.

Gerteis, Klaus. *Monarchie oder Ständestaat. Der Böhmische Aufstand von 1618. Quellen und wissenschaftliche Diskussion.* Vol. 2, *Wissenschaftlich-didaktische Arbeitshefte zur Geschichte des Mittelalters und der Neuzeit.* Trier: auenthal Verlag, 1983.

Gindely, Anton. *Friedrich V von der Pfalz, der ehemalige Winterkönig von Böhmen seit dem Regensburger Deputationstag vom Jahre 1622 bis zu seinem Tode.* Vol. 12, *Abhandlungen der königlichen böhmischen Gesellschaft der Wissenschaften – VI. Folge.* Prague, 1885.

Gindely, Anton. *Geschichte des dreissigjährigen Krieges.* 3 vols. Prague: F. Tempsky, 1882.

Glaser, Hubert. *Um Glauben und Reich: Kurfürst Maximilian I., Wittelsbach und Bayern.* München: Hirmer Verlag, 1980.

Goll, Jaroslav, *Der Convent von Segeberg (1621).* Prague: E. Gregr, 1875.

Goodman, Godfrey. *The Court of King James the First.* 2 vols. London: Richard Bentley, 1839.

Gotthard, Axel. *Konfession und Staatsräson: Die Außenpolitik Württembergs unter Herzog Johann Friedrich (1608–1628).* Vol. 126, *Veröffentlichungen der Kommission für Geschichtliche Landeskunde in Baden-Württemberg, Reihe B, Forschungen.* Stuttgart: W. Kohlhammer Verlag, 1992.

Gotthard, Axel. '"Politice seint wir bäpstisch." Kursachsen und der deutsche Protestantismus im frühen 17. Jahrhundert'. *Zeitschrift für Historische Forschung*, 20, 3 (1993): 275–319.

Gotthard, Axel. 'Protestantische "Union" und Katholische "Liga" – Subsidiäre Strukturelemente oder Alternativentwürfe?' In *Alternativen zur Reichsverfassung in der Frühen Neuzeit?*, ed. Volker Press, München: R. Oldenbourg Verlag, 1995, pp. 81–112.

Götz, J. B. *Die religiösen Wirren in der Oberpfalz von 1576 bis 1620.* Vol. 66, *Reformationsgeschichtliche Studien und Texte.* Münster: Aschendorffschen Verlagsbuchhandlung, 1937.

Green, M. A. E. *Elizabeth: Electress Palatine and Queen of Bohemia.* London: Methuen, 1909.

Gutmann, Myron P. 'The Origins of the Thirty Years' War'. *Journal of Interdisciplinary History*, xviii, 4 (1988): 749–70.

Hacket, John. *Scrinia Reserata*. London, 1692.

Hardwicke, Philip Yorke, Earl of, ed. *Miscellaneous state papers. From 1501–1726*. 2 vols. London: Printed for W. Strahan & T. Cadell, 1778.

Harrison, John. *A short relation of the departure of the high and mightie Prince Frederick King Elect of Bohemia*. Dort, 1619.

Haselbach, Karl. 'Die Politik der "Union" gegenüber dem Hause Habsburg'. *Jahres Bericht des kaiserli. königl. Gymnasiums in Krems*, (1862).

Häusser, Ludwig. *Geschichte der rheinischen Pfalz nach ihren politischen, kirchlichen und literarischen Verhältnissen*. 2 vols. Pirmasens, 1856, 1970.

Havran, Martin J. *Caroline Courtier: the Life of Lord Cottington*. London: Macmillan, 1973.

Havran, Martin J. *The Catholics in Caroline England*. Stanford: Stanford University Press, 1962.

Hecht, G. 'Schlesisch-kurpfälzische Beziehungen im 16. und 17. Jahrhundert'. *Zeitschrift für die Geschichte des Oberrheins*, 42, 1 (1928): 176–222.

Heinisch, Reinhard Rudolf. 'Habsburg, die Pforte und der Böhmische Aufstand (1618–1620)'. *Südostforschungen*, 33 (1974): 125–165.

Heinisch, Reinhard Rudolf. 'Habsburg, die Pforte und der Böhmische Aufstand (1618–1620), II. Teil'. *Südostforschungen*, 34 (1975): 79–124.

Hermkes, Wolfgang. *Das Reichsvikariat in Deutschland*, ed. Hermann Conrad and Ulrich Scheuner. Vol. 2, *Studien und Quellen zur Geschichte des deustchen Verfassungsrechts*. Karlsruhe: Verlag C.F. Müller, 1968.

Herold, Hans-Jörg. *Markgraf Joachim Ernst von Brandenburg-Ansbach als Reichsfürst*. Vol. 10, *Schriftenreihe der historischen Kommission bei der Bayerischen Akademie der Wissenschaften*. Göttingen: Vandenhoeck & Ruprecht, 1973.

Herrero García, Miguel. *Ideas de los Españoles del Siglo XVII*. Madrid: Biblioteca Románic Hispánica, 1966.

Hervey, Mary F. S. *The Life, Correspondence & Collections of Thomas Howard, Earl of Arundel*. Cambridge: Cambridge University Press, 1921.

Hill, Henry Bertram, trans. *The Political Testament of Cardinal Richelieu*. Madison: University of Wisconsin Press, 1961.

Howell, James. *Epistolæ Ho-Elianæ: Familiar Letters*. London, 1645.

Hsia, R. Po-Chia. *Social Discipline in the Reformation: Central Europe 1550–1750*. London: Routledge, 1989.

Hsia, R. Po-Chia. *The World of Catholic Renewal, 1540–1770*. Cambridge: Cambridge University Press, 1998.

Hughes, Michael. *Early Modern Germany, 1477–1806*. Philadelphia: University of Pennsylvania Press, 1992.

Hume, Martin. *The Court of Philip IV*. London: Eveleigh Nash, 1907.

Irmer, Georg. *Die Verhandlungen Schwedens und seiner Verbündeten mit Wallenstein und dem Kaiser von 1631 bis 1634*. 3 vols. Leipzig, 1888–91.

Iserloh, Erwin, Joseph Glazik, and Hubert Jedin. 'Reformation and Counter Reformation'. In *History of the Church*, ed. Hubert Jedin and John Dolan. New York: The Seabury Press, 1980.

Israel, Jonathan I. *Dutch Primacy in World Trade, 1585–1740*. Oxford: Oxford University Press, 1989.

Israel, Jonathan I. *The Dutch Republic and the Hispanic World, 1606–1661*. Oxford: Clarendon Press, 1982.

Israel, Jonathan I. *The Dutch Republic: its Rise, Greatness, and Fall, 1477–1806*. Oxford: Oxford University Press, 1995.

James, Mervyn. *English Politics and the Concept of Honour, 1485–1642. Past and Present*, Supplement 3, 1978.

Kagan, Donald. *On the Origins of War and the Preservation of Peace*. New York: Doubleday, 1995.

Kampmann, Christoph. *Reichsrebellion und kaiserliche Acht*. Vol. 21, *Schriftenreihe der Vereinigung zur Erforschung der Neueren Geschichte*. Münster: Aschendorff, 1993.

Kelly, J. N. D. *The Oxford Dictionary of Popes*. Oxford, 1986.

Kelly, James. '*That Damn'd Thing Called Honour', Duelling in Ireland, 1570–1860*. Cork: Cork University Press, 1995.

Kessel, Jürgen. *Spanien und die geistlichen Kurstaaten am Rhein während der Regierungszeit der Infantin Isabella (1621–1633)*. Vol. 113, *Europäische Hochschulschriften*. Frankfurt am Main: Peter Lang, 1979.

Khevenhiller, Franz Christoph von. *Annales Ferdinandei*. 12 vols. Leipzig, 1716–1726.

Kindleberger, Charles P. 'The Economic Crisis of 1619 to 1623'. *The Journal of Economic History*, 51, 1 (1991): 149–75.

Kirby, David. *Northern Europe in the Early Modern Period: The Baltic World, 1492–1772*. London: Longman Group, 1990.

Kishlansky, Mark A. *The Rise of the New Model Army*. Cambridge: Cambridge University Press, 1979.

Kleinman, Ruth. 'Charles-Emmanuel I of Savoy and the Bohemian Election of 1619'. *European Studies Review*, 5, 1 (1975): 3–29.

Koenigsberger, H.G. *The Habsburgs and Europe, 1516–1660*. Ithaca: Cornell University Press, 1971.

Koser, Reinhold. *Der Kanzleienstreit*. Halle: Hermann Gesenius, 1874.

Kraus, Andreas. *Maximilian I. Bayerns Großer Kurfürst*. Graz: Verlag Styria, 1990.

Krebs, Julius. *Christian von Anhalt und die Kurpfälzische Politik am Beginn des Dreissigjährigen Krieges*. Leipzig: Duncker & Humblot, 1872.

Krebs, Julius. 'Die Politik der evangelischen Union im Jahre 1618'. *Jahresbericht des Realgymnasiums am Zwinger zu Breslau*, (1890).

Krebs, Julius. *Die Schlacht am Weissen Berge bei Prag*. Breslau: Verlag von Wilhelm Koebner, 1879.

Krebs, Julius. 'Zur Geschichte der kurpfälzischen Politik am Beginn des dreißigjährigen Krieges, 1618–1619'. *Städtisches Gymnasium zu Ohlau*, (1875).

Kretzer, Harmut. *Calvinismus und französische Monarchie im 17. Jahrhundert: die politische Lehre der Akademien Sedan und Saumur, mit besonderer Berücksichtigung von Pierre Du Moulin, Moyse Amyraut und Pierre Jurieu*. Berlin: Duncker & Humbolt, 1975.

Laursen, John Christian, and Cary J. Nederman, eds. *Beyond the Persecuting Society: Religious Toleration Before the Enlightenment*. Philadelphia: University of Pennsylvania Press, 1998.

Lee, Jr., Maurice. 'The Jacobean Diplomatic Service'. *American Historical Review*, 72, 4 (1967): 1264–82.

Lipowsky, F. J. *Friderich V.* München: C. A. Fleischmann, 1824.

Lockhart, Paul Douglas. *Denmark in the Thirty Years' War, 1618–1648: King Christian IV and the Decline of the Oldenburg State*. Selinsgrove: Susquehanna University Press, 1996.

Lockyer, Roger. *Buckingham: the Life and Political Career of George Villiers, First Duke of Buckingham, 1592–1628*. London: Longman, 1981.

Lockyer, Roger. *The Early Stuarts: a Political History of England, 1603–1642.* 2nd edn. London: Longman, 1999.

Lonchay, Henri and Joseph Cuvelier. *Correspondance de la Cour d'Espagne sur les Affaires des Pays-Bas au XVIIe Siècle.* Vol. I (Précis de la Correspondance de Philippe III, 1598–1621) and IV (Supplément, 1598–1700), *Chroniques Belges.* Brussels, 1923.

Londorp, Michael Caspar. *Acta Publica.* 17 vols. Frankfurt am Main, 1668–1719.

Loomie, A.J., S.J. 'The *Conducteur des Ambassadeurs* of Seventeenth Century France and Spain'. *Revue Belge de Philologie et d'Histoire*, 53, 2 (1975): 333–54.

Loomie, A.J., S.J. *Spain and the Jacobean Catholics, Catholic Record Society.* Thetford, 1978.

Lorenz, Gottfried. *Quellen zur Vorgeschichte und zu den Anfängen des Dreißigjährigen Krieges.* Vol. 19, *Ausgewählte Quellen zur deutschen Geschichte der Neuzeit.* Darmstadt: Wissenschaftliche Buchgesellschaft, 1991.

Lorenz, Karl. *Die kirchlich-politische Parteibildung in Deutschland vor Beginn des dreißigjährigen Krieges im Spiegel der konfessionellen Polemik.* München: C.H. Beck'sche Verlagsbuchhandlung, 1903.

Löwenfels, Gottfried Ferdinand von Buckisch und. *Observationes Historico-Politicæ in Instrumentum Pacis Osnabrugo-Westphalicum.* Frankfurt and Leipzig, 1722.

Luttenberger, Albrecht Pius. *Glaubenseinheit und Reichsfriede: Konzeptionen und Wege Konfessionsneutraler Reichspolitik (1530–1552) (Kurpfalz, Jülich, Kurbrandenburg).* Vol. 20, *Schriftenreihe der historischen Kommission bei der Bayerischen Akademie der Wissenschaften.* Göttingen: Vandenhoeck & Ruprecht, 1982.

Lutz, H., F.H. Schubert, H. Weber. *Frankreich und das Reich im 16. und 17. Jahrhundert.* Göttingen: Vandenhoeck & Ruprecht, 1968.

Magen, Ferdinand. *Reichsgräfliche Politik in Franken.* Schwäbisch Hall: Selbstverlag des Historischen Vereins für Württembergisch Franken, 1975.

Maier, Franz. *Die bayerische Unterpfalz im Dreißigjährigen Krieg.* Vol. 428, *Europäische Hochschulschriften, Reihe III, Geschichte und ihre Hilfswissenschaften.* Frankfurt am Main: Peter Lang, 1990.

Mattingly, Garrett. *Renaissance Diplomacy.* Boston: Houghton Mifflin Co., 1955.

McCabe, Edward. 'England's Foreign Policy in 1619: Lord Doncaster's Embassy to the Princes of Germany'. *Mitteilungen des Instituts für Österreichische Geschichtsforschung*, 58 (1950): 457–477.

Morgan, Hiram. 'Festive Irishmen: an 'Irish' Procession in Stuttgart 1617'. *History Ireland*, 5 (1997): 14–20.

Mout, Nicolette. 'Der Winterkönig im Exil: Friedrich V. von der Pfalz und die niederländischen Generalstaaten 1621–1632'. *Zeitschrift für Historische Forschung*, 15, 3 (1988): 257–72.

Müller, Frank. *Kursachsen und der Böhmische Aufstand, 1618–1622, Schriftenreihe der Vereinigung zur Erforschung der Neueren Geschichte.* Münster: Aschendorff Verlag, 1997.

Müller, Johannes. 'Reichsstädtische Politik in den letzten Zeiten der Union'. *Mitteilungen des Instituts für Österreichische Geschichtsforschung*, 33 (1912): 483–514.

Müller, Konrad, ed. *Die Goldene Bülle Kaiser Karls IV. 1356.* Vol. 25, *Quellen zur Neueren Geschichte.* Bern: Verlag Herbert Lang & CIE, 1957.

Munck, Thomas. *Seventeenth Century Europe: State, Conflict and the Social Order in Europe, 1598–1700.* New York: St. Martin's Press, 1990.

Murdoch, Steve, ed. *Scotland and the Thirty Years' War, 1618–1648.* Leiden: Brill, 2001.

Nederman, Cary J. and John Christian Laursen, eds. *Difference and Dissent: Theories of*

Toleration in Medieval and Early Modern Europe. Lanham: Rowman & Littlefield, 1996.

Neuer-Landfried, Franziska. *Die Katholische Liga: Gründung, Neugründung und Organisation eines Sonderbundes 1608–1620.* Vol. 9, *Münchener Historische Studien Abteilung Bayerische Geschichte.* München: Verlag Michael Lassleben Kallmünz Opf., 1968.

Neuhaus, Helmut. *Das Reich in der Frühen Neuzeit.* Edited by Lothar Gall. Vol. 42, *Enzyklopädie Deutscher Geschichte.* München: R. Oldenbourg Verlag, 1997.

Nichols, John. *The Progresses of King James the First.* 4 vols. Vol. 2. London, 1828.

Nischan, Bodo. *Prince, People, and Confession: the Second Reformation in Brandenburg.* Philadelphia: University of Pennsylvania Press, 1994.

Nolden, Karl. 'Die Reichspolitik Kaiser Ferdinands II. in der Publizistik bis zum Lübecker Frieden 1629'. Inaugural-Dissertation zur Erlangung der Doktorwürde der philosophischen Fakultät der Universität zu Köln, 1957.

Notestein, Wallace, Frances Helen Relf, Hartley Simpson, eds. *Commons Debates, 1621.* 7 vols. New Haven: Yale University Press, 1935.

Obser, Karl. 'Markgraf Georg Friedrich von Baden-Durlach und das Projekt einer Diversion am Oberrhein in den Jahren 1623–1627'. *Zeitschrift für die Geschichte des Oberrheins*, 44 (1890): 320–399.

Ogilvie, Sheilagh C. 'Germany and the Seventeenth-Century Crisis'. *Historical Journal*, 35, 2 (1992): 417–41.

Oman, Carola. *Elizabeth of Bohemia.* London: Hodder and Stoughton Limited, 1938.

Osborne, Toby. 'Abbot Scaglia, the Duke of Buckingham and Anglo-Savoyard Relations During the 1620s'. *European History Quarterly*, 30, 1 (2000): 5–32.

Pagès, Georges. *The Thirty Years War 1618–1648.* English translation ed. New York: Harper & Row, 1970.

Parker, Geoffrey. *The Army of Flanders and the Spanish Road, 1567–1659.* Cambridge: Cambridge University Press, 1972.

Parker, Geoffrey. *The Dutch Revolt.* 2nd edn. London: Penguin Books, 1990.

Parker, Geoffrey. *Spain and the Netherlands.* 2nd edn. London: Fontana Press, 1990.

Parker, Geoffrey, ed. *The Thirty Years' War.* 2nd edn. London: Routledge & Kegan Paul, 1997.

Parker, Geoffrey and Lesley Smith, eds. *The General Crisis of the Seventeenth Century.* 2nd edn. London: Routledge & Kegan Paul, 1997.

Patterson, William B. *King James VI and I and the Reunion of Christendom, Cambridge Studies in Early Modern British History.* Cambridge: Cambridge University Press, 1997.

Pérez Bustamente, Ciriaco. *Felipe III, Semblanza de un Monarca y Perfiles de una Privanza*, Madrid, 1950.

Pettegree, Andrew, Alastair Duke, and Gillian Lewis, eds. *Calvinism in Europe, 1540–1610: a collection of documents.* Manchester: Manchester University Press, 1992.

Pettegree, Andrew, Alastair Duke, and Gillian Lewis, eds. *Calvinism in Europe, 1540–1620.* Cambridge: Cambridge University Press, 1994.

Pfister, Kurt. *Kurfürst Maximillian I von Bayern.* München, 1988.

Pithon, Rémy. 'La Suisse, théâtre de la guerre froide entre la France et l'Espagne pendant la crise de Valteline (1621–1626)'. *Schweizerische Zeitschrift für Geschichte*, 13 (1963): 33–53.

Pithon, Rémy. 'Les débuts difficiles du ministère de Richelieu et la crise de Valteline (1621–1627)'. *Revue d'Histoire Diplomatique*, (1960): 298–322.

Polišenský, J.V. *Anglie a Bílá Hora: The Bohemian War and British Policy, 1618–1620*. Prague, 1949.

Polišenský, J.V. 'Denmark-Norway and the Bohemian Cause in the Early Part of the Thirty Years War'. In *Festgabe für L. L. Hammerich*, Kopenhagen: Naturmetodens Sproginstitut, 1962, pp. 215–227.

Polišenský, J.V. *The Thirty Years War*. Berkeley: University of California Press, 1971.

Polišenský, J.V. *Tragic Triangle*. Prague: Charles University, 1991.

Polišenský, J.V. *War and Society in Europe, 1618–1648*. Cambridge: Cambridge University Press, 1978.

Press, Volker. *Alternativen zur Reichsverfassung in der Frühen Neuzeit?* München: R. Oldenbourg Verlag, 1995.

Press, Volker. *Calvinismus und Territorialstaat: Regierung und Zentralbehörden der Kurpfalz, 1559–1619*. Stuttgart: Ernst Klett Verlag, 1970.

Press, Volker. 'The Imperial Court of the Habsburgs from Maximilian I to Ferdinand III, 1493–1657'. In *Princes, Patronage, and the Nobility: the Court at the Beginning of the Modern Age c. 1450–1650*, ed. Ronald G. Asch and Adolf M. Birke, Oxford: The German Historical Institute London, 1991, pp. 289–312.

Prestwich, Menna. *Cranfield: Politics and Profits under the Early Stuarts*. Oxford: Oxford University Press, 1966.

Prestwich, Menna, ed. *International Calvinism, 1541–1715*. Oxford, 1985.

Pursell, Brennan C. 'Elector Palatine Friedrich V and the Question of Influence Revisited'. *The Court Historian*, 6, 2 (2001): 123–39.

Puyuelo y Salinas, Carlos. *Carlos de Inglaterra en España*. Madrid: Escelicer, S. A., 1962.

Rabb, Theodore K. *The Struggle for Stability in Early Modern Europe*. New York, 1975.

Rabb, T.K. *The Thirty Years' War: Problems of Motive, Extent, and Effect*. Boston: D.C. Heath and Co., 1964.

Redworth, Glyn. 'Of pimps and princes: three unpublished letters from James I and the Prince of Wales relating to the Spanish match'. *Historical Journal*, 37, (1994): 401–9.

Reeve, L. J. *Charles I and the Road to Personal Rule*. Cambridge: Cambridge University Press, 1989.

Reeve, L. J. 'Quiroga's Paper of 1631: a missing link in Anglo-Spanish diplomacy during the Thirty Years War'. *The English Historical Review*, 101, 401 (1986): 913–25.

Regel, M. *Christians des Zweiten von Anhalt Gesandtschaftsreise nach Savoyen, 1617*. Bernburg: A. Meyers, 1892.

Repgen, Konrad. *Dreißigjähriger Krieg und Westfälischer Friede: Studien und Quellen*. Paderborn: Ferdinand Schöningh, 1998.

Repgen, Konrad. *Krieg und Politik 1618–1648*. München: R. Oldenbourg Verlag, 1988.

Repgen, Konrad. *Von der Reformation zur Gegenwart*, Padernborn, 1988.

Riklin, Alois. 'Gemischte oder monströse Verfassung?' *Beiträge und Berichte*, Institut für Politikwissenschaft Hochschule St. Gallen, 190 (1992): 1–36.

Ritter, Moriz. *Deutsche Geschichte im Zeitalter der Gegenreformation und des Dreissigjährigen Krieges (1555–1648)*. 3 vols. Stuttgart, 1889; reprinted Darmstadt: Wissenschaftliche Buchgesellschaft, 1974.

Ritter, Moriz. 'Die pfälzische Politik und die böhmische Königswahl 1619'. *Historische Zeitschrift*, 79 (1897): 239–83.

Ritter, Moriz. 'Friedrich V., Kurfürst von der Pfalz'. *Allgemeine Deutsche Biographie*, 7 (1968): 621–27.

Ritter, Moriz. 'Untersuchungen über die pfälzische Politik am Ende des Jahres 1622 und zu Anfang des Jahres 1623'. *Historische Zeitschrift*, 38, NF (1895): 407–41.

Roberts, Michael. *Gustavus Adolphus.* Edited by Keith Robbins, *Profiles in Power.* London: Longman, 1992.

Roberts, Michael. *Gustavus Adolphus and the Rise of Sweden.* London: English Universities Press, 1973.

Roberts, Michael. *Gustavus Adolphus: A History of Sweden, 1611–1632.* 2 vols. London: Longmans, Green and Co Ltd, 1953–8.

Rodenas Vilar, Rafael. *La Politica Europea de España durante la Guerra de Treinta Años, 1624–1630.* Madrid, 1967.

Rowan, Steven W. and Vann, James A., eds. *The Old Reich: Essays on German Political Institutions, 1495–1806.* Vol. xlviii, *Studies Presented to the International Commission for the History of Representative and Parliamentary Institutions.* Bruxelles: Les Editions de la Librairie Encyclopédique, 1974.

Ruigh, Robert E. *The Parliament of 1624.* Cambridge: Harvard University Press, 1971.

Rusdorf, Johann Joachim. *Memoires et Negociations Secretes.* 2 vols. Leipzig, 1789.

Rusdorf, Johann Joachim von. *Consilia et negotia politica, ubi diversi tractatus et consilia, diverso tempore, [prout res in deliberationem cadebant, aut proponebantur, scripta & rerumpublicarum in Europa statum concernentia], continentur. Accedit Epistolarum familiarium ipsius autoris ad viros illustres & amicos scriptarum, collectio ex Bibliotheca Loeniana.* Frankfurt am Main, 1725.

Rushworth, John. *Historical Collections.* 8 vols. London, 1659–1701.

Russell, Conrad. 'The Foreign Policy Debate in the House of Commons in 1621'. *The Historical Journal*, 20, 2 (1977): 289–309.

Russell, Conrad. *Parliaments and English Politics, 1621–1629* (Oxford, 1979).

Russell, Conrad. 'Sir Thomas Wentworth and anti-Spanish sentiment, 1621–1624'. In *The Political World of Thomas Wentworth, Earl of Strafford, 1621–1641*, ed. J.F. Merritt, 47–62. Cambridge: Cambridge University Press, 1996.

Russell, C.S.R. 'Monarchies, Wars, and Estates in England, France, and Spain, c. 1580–c.1640'. *Legislative Studies Quarterly*, VII, no. 2 (1982).

Sanchez-Canton, Francisco Javier. *Don Diego Sarmiento de Acuña, Conde de Gondomar, 1567–1626.* Madrid, 1935.

Schaab, Meinrad. *Geschichte der Kurpfalz.* 2 vols. Stuttgart: Verlag W. Kohlhammer, 1988.

Schelven, Aart A. van. 'Der Generalstab des politischen Calvinismus in Zentraleuropa zu Beginn des Dreißigjährigen Krieges'. *Archiv für Reformationsgeschichte*, 36 (1939): 117–41.

Schiller, Friedrich von. *Geschichte des dreißigjährigen Kriegs.* Stuttgart und Tübingen, 1850.

Schilling, Heinz. *Aufbruch und Krise: Deutschland, 1517–1648, Das Reich und die Deutschen.* Berlin: Siedler Verlag, 1988.

Schilling, Heinz. 'Die Konfessionalisierung im Reich. Religiöser und gesellschaftlicher Wandel in Deutschland zwischen 1555 und 1620'. *Historische Zeitschrift*, 246 (1988): 1–45.

Schilling, Heinz. *Die reformierte Konfessionalisierung in Deutschland – Das Problem der 'Zweiten Reformation'.* Vol. 195, *Schriften des Vereins für Reformationsgeschichte.* Gütersloh: Gütersloher Verlagshaus Gerd Mohn, 1986.

Schindling, Anton, and Walter Ziegler, eds. *Die Kaiser der Neuzeit, 1519–1918.* München: C.H. Beck, 1990.

Schläfer, Helmut. *Die bayerisch-französischen Beziehungen von 1622–1625.* Kirchheimbolanden, 1938.

Schreiber, Roy E. *The Political Career of Sir Robert Naunton 1589–1635*. Vol. 24, *Royal Historical Society Studies in History*. London, 1981.

Schubert, F.H. 'Die Niederlande zur Zeit des Dreißigjährigen Krieges im Urteil des Diplomatischen Korps im Haag'. *Historisches Jahrbuch*, (1955): 252–64.

Schubert, F.H. 'Die pfälzische Exilregierung im Dreißigjährigen Krieg'. *Zeitschrift für die Geschichte des Oberrheins*, 102 (1954).

Schubert, F.H. *Ludwig Camerarius*. Vol. I, *Münchener Historische Studien Abteilung Neuere Geschichte*. München: Verlag Michael Lassleben Kallmünz, 1955.

Schwarz, Marc L. 'Lord Saye and Sele's Objections to the Palatinate Benevolence of 1622: Some New Evidence and its Significance'. *Albion*, 4, (1972): 12–22.

Schweickert, Alexander, ed. *Kurpfalz*. Stuttgart: W. Kohlhammer, 1997.

Schwerhoff, Klaus Schreiner and Gerd. *Verletzte Ehre: Ehrkonflickte in Gesellschaften des Mittelalters und der Frühen Neuzeit*. Edited by Gert Melville. Vol. 5, *Norm und Struktur: Studien zum sozialen Wandel in Mittelalter und früher Neuzeit*. Köln: Böhlau, 1995.

Schybergson, M. G. *Underhandlingarna om en Evangelisk Allians åren 1624–1625*. Helsingfors: J. C. Frenckell & Son, 1880.

Sellin, Paul R. 'John Donne: The Poet as Diplomat and Divine'. *The Huntingdon Library Quarterly*, XXXIX (1975–6): 267–75.

Serrano Sanz, Manuel. 'Libros, manuscritos ó de mano de la Biblioteca del Conde de Gondomar'. *Revista de Archivos, Bibliotecas y Museos*, Año VII, nos 1, 3, 4 (1903): 65ff., 222ff., 295ff.

Smend, Rudolf. *Das Reichskammergericht*, ed. Karl Zeumer. Vol. 4, Heft 3, *Quellen und Studien zur Verfassungsgeschichte des Deutschen Reiches in Mittelalter und Neuzeit*. Weimar: Hermann Böhlaus Nachfolger, 1911.

Smith, Logan Pearsall. *The Life and Letters of Sir Henry Wotton*. 2 vols. Oxford: Clarendon Press, 1907.

Smuts, Malcolm. 'Concepts of Peace and War in Stuart Court Culture'. In *Frieden und Krieg in der Frühen Neuzeit: Die europäische Staatenordnung und die außereuropäische Welt*, ed. Ronald G. Asch, Wulf Eckart Voß, and Martin Wrede, München: Wilhelm Fink, 2001, pp. 215–38.

Söltl, Johann Michael. *Der Religionskrieg in Deutschland*. 3 vols. Hamburg: Johann August Meißner, 1840–2.

Söltl, J.M. *Die Wittelsbacher mit ihren Zeitgenossen im Königreich Bayern*. Sulzbach, 1850.

Spanheim, Friedrich. *Mémoires sur la vie et la mort de Loyse Julian, Électrice Palatine*. Leiden, 1645.

Stanka, Rudolf. *Die böhmischen Conföderationsakte von 1619*. Vol. 213, *Historische Studien*. Berlin: Verlag Dr. Emil Ebering, 1932.

Steinberg, S.H. *The Thirty Years War and the Conflict for European Hegemony 1600–1660*. New York: W. W. Norton & Co., 1966.

Steiner, Jürgen. *Die pfälzische Kurwürde während des Dreißigjährigen Krieges (1618–1648)*. Vol. 76, *Veröffentlichung der Pfälzischen Gesellschaft zur Förderung der Wissenschaften in Speyer*. Speyer, 1985.

Sticht, Ernst. *Markgraf Christian von Brandenburg-Kulmbach und der 30jährige Krieg in Ostfranken, 1618–1635*. Vol. 23, *Schriften für Heimatforschung und Kulturpflege in Ostfranken*. Kulmbach: Freunde der Plassenburg, 1965.

Stoye, John W. *English Travellers Abroad, 1604–1667*. London: Jonathan Cape, 1952.

Stradling, R.A. *Europe and the Decline of Spain*. London: George Allen & Unwin, 1981.

Stradling, R.A. *Philip IV and the Government of Spain, 1621–1665*. Cambridge: Cambridge University Press, 1988.

Stradling, R.A. *Spain's Struggle for Europe, 1598–1668*. London: Hambledon Press, 1994.

Straub, Eberhard. *Pax et Imperium: Spaniens Kampf um seine Friedensordnung in Europa zwischen 1617 und 1635*. Vol. 31, NF, *Rechts- und Staatswissenschaftliche Veröffentlichungen der Görres-Gesellschaft*. Paderborn: Ferdinand Schöningh, 1980.

Straub, Eberhard. *Spanien: Eine Schwarze Legende?* Heidelberg: Manutius Verlag Frank Würker GmbH, 1991.

Sturmberger, Hans. *Aufstand in Böhmen: Der Beginn des Dreißigjährigen Krieges*. München: R. Oldenbourg Verlag, 1959.

Sturmberger, Hans. *Georg Erasmus Tschernembl: Religion, Libertät und Widerstand. Ein Beitrag zur Geschichte der Gegenreformation und des Landes ob der Enns*. Linz: Hermann Böhlaus Nachf., 1953.

Sturmberger, Hans. *Kaiser Ferdinand II. und das Problem des Absolutismus*. München: Verlag R. Oldenbourg, 1957.

Sturmberger, Hans. *Land ob der Enns und Österreich: Aufsätze und Vorträge*. Vol. 3, *Ergänzungsband zu den Mitteilungen des Oberösterreichischen Landesarchivs*. Linz: Oberösterreichisches Landesarchiv, 1979.

Sutherland, N. M. 'The Origins of the Thirty Years War and the Structure of European Politics'. *English Historical Journal*, July (1992): 587–625.

Tapié, Victor-L. *France in the Age of Louis XIII and Richelieu*. Cambridge: Cambridge University Press, 1984.

Tapié, Victor-L. *La Politique Étrangère de la France et le Début de la Guerre de Trente Ans (1616–1621)*. Paris: Les Presses Universitaires de France, 1934.

Tecke, Annelise. 'Die kurpfälzische Politik und der Ausbruch des dreißigjährigen Krieges'. Dissertation zur Erlangung der Doktorwürde der Philosophischen Fakultät der Hamburgischen Universität, 1931.

Theibault, John. 'The Demography of the Thirty Years War Re-Visited: Günther Franz and his Critics'. *German History*, 15, 1 (1997): 1–21.

Thompson, I.A.A. *War and Society in Habsburg Spain*. Aldershot: Variorum, 1992.

Thomson, Elizabeth McClure. *The Chamberlain Letters*. New York: G. P. Putnam's Sons, 1965.

Toegel, Miroslav, ed. *Der Beginn des Dreißigjährigen Krieges: Der Kampf um Böhmen. Quellen zur Geschichte des Böhmischen Krieges (1618–1621)*. Vol. 2, *Documenta Bohemica Bellum Tricennale Illustrantia*. Praha, 1972.

Townshend, Dorothea. *Life and Letters of Mr. Endymion Porter*. London: T. Fisher Unwin, 1897.

Trevor-Roper, Hugh, ed. *The Golden Age of Europe: from Elizabeth I to the Sun King*. New York: Bonanza Books, 1968, 1987.

Trevor-Roper, Hugh. *Religion, the Reformation, and Social Change*. London: Secker & Warburg, 1984.

Trevor-Roper, Hugh. 'Why do Great Wars Begin?' *Horizon: A Magazine of the Arts*, V, 2, November, (1962): 32–41.

Tumbült, Georg. 'Die kaiserliche Sendung des Grafen Jakob Ludwig zu Fürstenberg an den Kurfürsten Friedrich V. von der Pfalz i. J. 1619'. *Zeitschrift für die Geschichte des Oberrheins*, XIX, NF (1904): 8–18.

Uflacker, Hans Georg. 'Christian I. von Anhalt und Peter Wok von Rosenberg: eine Untersuchung zur Vorgeschichte des pfälzischen Königtums in Böhmen'. Inaugural Dissertation zur Erlangung der Doktorwürde der Hohen Philosophischen Fakultät

Sektion I, Ludwig-Maximilians-Universität München, 1926.

Vogler, Bernard. 'Le rôle des Électeurs palatins dans les guerres de religion en France (1559–1592)'. *Cahiers d'Histoire*, x, 1 (1965): 51–85.

Vogler, Bernard. 'Die Entstehung der Protestantischen Volksfrömmigkeit in der Rheinischen Pfalz zwischen 1555 und 1619'. *Archiv für Reformationsgeschichte*, 72 (1981): 158–96.

Voigt, Petr. 'Dosud Neznámá Verze Satiry na Útěk Fridricha Falckého'. *Sborník Národního Muzea v Praze. Rada C: Literární Historie*, 31, 3–4 (1986): 267–98.

Walzer, Michael. *The Revolution of the Saints: a study in the origins of radical politics.* Cambridge, MA, 1965.

Watanabe-O'Kelley, Helen. *Triumphal Shews: Tournaments at German-speaking Courts in their European Context, 1560–1730.* Berlin, 1992.

Weber, Hermann. 'Empereur, Électeurs et Diète de 1500 à 1650'. *Revue d'Histoire Diplomatique*, 89 Année, Numéro Double (1975): 281–97.

Wedgwood, C.V. *The Thirty Years' War.* London: Jonathan Cape Ltd, 1938; New York: Double Day, 1961.

Weigel, Helmut. *Franken, Kurpfalz und der Böhmische Aufstand, 1618–1620. Erster Teil: Die Politik der Kurpfalz und der evangelischen Stände Frankens, Mai 1618 bis März 1619.* Erlangen: Verlag von Palm & Enke, 1932.

Weiß, Elmar. *Die Unterstützung Friedrichs V. von der Pfalz durch Jacob I. und Karl I. von England im Dreißigjährigen Krieg (1618–1632).* Vol. 37, Reihe B, *Veröffentlichungen der Kommission für Geschichtliche Landeskunde in Baden-Württemberg.* Stuttgart: W. Kohlhammer, 1966.

Weiß, John Gustav. 'Beiträge zur Beurteilung des Kurfürsten Friedrich V. von der Pfalz'. *Zeitschrift für die Geschichte des Oberrheins*, 46, NF (1933): 385–422.

Weiß, John Gustav. 'Die Vorgeschichte des böhmischen Abenteuers Friedrichs V. von der Pfalz'. *Zeitschrift für die Geschichte des Oberrheins*, 53, NF (1940): 383–492.

Wertheim, Hans. *Der tolle Halberstädter: Herzog Christian von Braunschweig im pfälzischen Kriege, 1621–1622.* 2 vols. Berlin, 1929.

White, Arthur W. 'Suspension of Arms: Anglo-Spanish Mediation in the Thirty Years' War, 1621–1625'. PhD Thesis, Tulane University, 1978.

Wild, Adolf. *Les Papiers de Richelieu: Section Politique Extérieure Correspondance et Papiers d'État, Empire Allemand, Tome I, 1616–1629, Monumenta Europae Historica.* Paris: Editions A. Pedone, 1982.

Williams, Patrick. 'Philip III and the restoration of Spanish government, 1598–1603'. *The English Historical Review*, 88, 349 (1973): 751–69.

Willson, D.H. *King James VI and I.* London: Jonathan Cape, 1956.

Willson, D.H. *The Privy Councillors in the House of Commons, 1604–1629.* Minneapolis: University of Minnesota Press, 1940.

Wilson, Peter H. *The Holy Roman Empire, 1495–1806.* New York: St. Martin's, 1999.

Wittich, Karl. 'Christian der Halberstädter und die Pfalzgräfin Elisabeth'. *Zeitschrift für Preußische Geschichte und Landeskunde*, August (1869): 1–20.

Wolkan, R. *Deutsche Lieder auf den Winterkönig.* Vol. 8, *Bibliothek deutscher Schriftsteller aus Böhmen.* Prague: T. G. Calve'sche, 1898.

Wolkan, R. 'Politische Karikaturen aus der Zeit des dreissigjährigen Krieges'. *Zeitschrift für Bücherfreunde*, Heft II (1899): 457–67.

Würdig, L. *Königskrone und Bettelstab: Die Schicksale Kurfürst Friedrichs V. von der Pfalz.* Sechstes Bändchen, *Geschichtsbilder für Jugend und Volk.* Düsseldorf: Verlag von Selix Bagel, 1877.

Yapp, M.E. 'Europe in the Turkish Mirror'. *Past & Present*, 137 (1992): 134–55.

Yates, F.A. *The Rosicrucian Enlightenment*. London: Routledge & Kegan Paul, 1972.

Zaller, Robert. 'Interest of State: James I and the Palatinate'. *Albion*, 6, 2 (1974): 144–75.

Zaller, Robert. *The Parliament of 1621*. Berkeley, 1971.

Zeeden, Ernst Walter. *Das Zeitalter der Glaubenskämpfe*. Vol. 2, *Handbuchs der Deutschen Geschichte*. München: Deutscher Taschenbuch Verlag, 1973.

Zwiedineck-Südenhorst, Hans von. *Die Politik der Republik Venedig Während des Dreissigjährigen Krieges*. 2 vols. Stuttgart, 1882–5.

Zwiedineck-Südenhorst, Hans von. *Fürst Christian der Andere von Anhalt und seine Beziehungen zu Innerösterreich*. Graz: Leuschner & Lubensky, 1874.

Zwiedineck-Südenhorst, Hans von. *Hans Ulrich, Fürst von Eggenberg: Freund und Erster Minister Kaiser Ferdinand II*. Wien, 1880.

Index